THE AURA OF TORAH

University of Nebraska Press | Lincoln

The Aura of Torah

A Kabbalistic-Hasidic Commentary to the Weekly Readings

RABBI LARRY TABICK

The Jewish Publication Society | Philadelphia

© 2014 by Larry Tabick

All rights reserved. Published by the University of
Nebraska Press as a Jewish Publication Society book.
Manufactured in the United States of America.

♾

Library of Congress Cataloging-in-Publication Data

Tabick, Larry.
The aura of Torah: a Kabbalistic-Hasidic commentary
to the weekly readings / Rabbi Larry Tabick.

p.   cm.
Includes Hebrew and Aramaic texts.
ISBN 978-0-8276-0948-8 (pbk.: alk. paper)
1. Bible. Pentateuch—Criticism, interpretation
etc. 2. Cabala. I. Title.
BS1225.52.T33 2014   222'.106—dc23
2014007112

Set in Charis by Renni Johnson.
Designed by A. Shahan.

Contents

GENESIS

B'reishit

Noaḥ

Lekh Lekha

Va-yera'

Ḥayyei Sarah

Toledot

Va-yetse'

Va-yishlaḥ

Shemot

Va-'era'

Bo'

Be-shallah

Yitro

Va-yak'hel

Pekudei

LEVITICUS

Va-yikra'

Tsav

Shemini

'Emor

Be-har

Be-ḥukkotai

NUMBERS

Be-midbar

Naso'

Balak

Pinḥas

Mattot

Mase'ei

DEUTERONOMY

Devarim

Ki Tetse'

Ki Tavo'

Nitsavim

Va-yelekh

Ha'azinu

Illustration

Introduction

The Aura of Torah

The Torah really has two auras: one visible and one invisible. The visible aura can be seen in the many printed editions where the original Hebrew text of the Five Books of Moses is surrounded by a halo of commentaries and translations whose origins stretch over a thousand years or more.

But the Torah has a second aura, less visible than the first, but no less real. It is the aura of holiness and spirituality, and its effects can be seen wherever the Torah is read and studied around the world.

Sometimes these two auras intersect, when commentary points to deep spiritual truth and to hidden realms—the world of the divine and the world of the soul.

Sadly, that spiritual light is not always clearly visible in the text of the Torah itself. Spiritual seekers studying Judaism through its most ancient sacred Scripture are often disappointed that the enlightenment they desire is not immediately obvious amid the welter of stories and laws. Of course, all these have a strong communal purpose, giving shared faith, history, and practice to a vibrant religious community, but for many that purpose only makes sense within a spiritual framework, a framework that the Torah itself seems not to provide, at least not at first sight.

On the face of it, the Torah presents, for example, an image of a transcendent God, easily given to anger and punishment, who loves, but jealously. Where is the God who dwells within the human soul? Rituals are described in great detail, but many of those details, like the collection and sprinkling of sacrificial blood, are often disturbing to modern readers. Where is the inwardness so many seek? A detailed and challenging history of a people is given with a verbal map of their journeys, but where is a map and history of the soul?

The great kabbalists and mystics of our tradition were aware of this gap between their deeply held beliefs and their sacred texts. The Zohar, the classical text of Kabbalah, famously (and daringly) proclaimed that if the Torah dealt only with simple stories and ordinary matters we could have written a better one! Instead, we need to look "beneath its garments" to see its true beauty (Zohar III, 152a). The unavoidable fact is, simply, that the surface of the Torah frequently does not inspire us.

We moderns tend to approach the Torah from one side only, the side known traditionally as the *peshat*, the plain meaning or the surface of the text. The *peshat* is important, even vital, but not sufficient in itself. We need more. And in Judaism, there is more—much more. We need to learn to look beyond the *peshat*; we need to look "under the garments."

Jewish tradition has produced numerous metaphors to suggest that Scripture may be read in many differing ways. The Torah, our sages tell us, has seventy faces (*Be-midbar Rabbah* 13:15/16). Perhaps they thought of it as a jewel with seventy facets, each with its own beauty, each reflecting light in a unique way. Later tradition teaches that there are four levels of interpretation, which came to be known under the rubric of "PaRDeS" (meaning, "an orchard") where P stands for *peshat*, R for *remez* (allegorical interpretation), D for *derash* (homiletical interpretation), and S for *sod* (mystical interpretation) (e.g., see Zohar III, 110a). In the Ethics of the Fathers, Ben Bag Bag suggests that we "turn it, turn it, for everything is in it" (*Pirkei Avot* 5:22), while another Rabbinic source informs us that the Torah is, in fact, infinite: "Everything has a limit. Heaven and earth have limits. But there is one thing that has no limits. What is it? The Torah!" (*Bereshit Rabbah* 10:1).

Or as the early Hasidic writer Ze'ev Wolf of Zhitomir put it: "In truth the Torah is eternal and exists in all times" (*Or HaMe'ir* [Warsaw, 1883], pt. 2, p. 34).

Judaism's most sacred book, therefore, is meant to contain within itself an inexhaustible wealth of wisdom about all aspects of our lives. And as the product of the Infinite God, the Torah must be open to an infinite number of interpretations, to fit the exigencies of any time, place, or person. To many people, this may seem a fanciful, even dangerous, notion, but it has been the very essence of Jewish biblical interpretation since the dawn of Rabbinic Judaism more than two millennia ago. Without such freedom of interpretation, at least in matters of *aggadah* (nonlegal material), the wealth of Jewish Bible commentary and sermonic literature would never have been created. Nor would Jewish thought be able, again and again, to assimilate the best the outside world has to offer and use its own creative endeavors to ensure that Judaism remains relevant. This flexibility guarantees Jewish survival and renewal.

Yet all but the most basic levels of interpretation are closed to the majority of our people today, partly because works that explore these more esoteric levels are often highly complex, if not untranslatable, and partly because modern students of the Bible find it hard to divorce themselves, even temporarily, from the plain meaning of the stories and laws at their simplest level of *peshat*.

The Aura of Torah is my modest attempt to provide a wide variety of interpretations of texts from the Five Books of Moses, interpretations rooted in the mystical side of Jewish tradition. Authors quoted span many centuries and speak from within many schools of thought. There are kabbalists, who write from within the tradition of the Zohar and other works of a similar, gnostic type, making use of images of the ten *sefirot* (aspects of the divine). There are Hasidic teachers from the modern movement founded by the Ba'al Shem Tov in the eighteenth century in Ukraine. And other groups are represented as well: notably, the German pietists, or Hasidei Ashkenaz, of the twelfth and thirteenth centuries. If the Ukrainian and Polish Hasidim dominate the selections, it is because their books are the most numerous and accessible and because they often address issues of concern to anyone who takes their own spiritual development seriously.

Though their methods of interpretation are often far removed from the *peshat*, I believe that these texts build on the fundamental underlying principles of the Torah itself: the supremacy of God, the integration and interconnectedness of nature and morality, and the unique (though not exclusive) role of the Jewish people in the divine plan for all humanity.

The choice of texts has been a personal one. It arose out of a wish to present Jewish mystical teachings to the communities that I have had the honor of serving; thus, each selection originally functioned as the jumping-off point for an extemporized sermon explaining and applying the text to contemporary circumstances. No claim is made that the texts chosen are representative of their authors, of the movements from which they stem, or of Jewish mystical Bible commentary in general. Instead, I have chosen texts that have spoken to me and addressed what I consider to be important spiritual and moral issues (though admittedly I have sometimes gone beyond the apparent intention of the authors in my interpretations). My heartfelt thanks go, therefore, to the members of my communities for their patience and forbearance.

The more esoteric levels of interpretation often require by their nature the use of abstruse concepts, wordplays, numerical values (*gematriot*), and other methods of extracting meaning from (or reading meaning into) the Torah text. Where possible I have attempted to explain difficult concepts succinctly, and to present wordplays and other "unusual" exegetical methods as simply as possible, without, I hope, distortion.

Many texts comment on earlier expositions and midrashim at least as much as on the biblical text itself. In these cases, I have had to offer some insight into the earlier texts as well to make the authors' reinterpretations more explicit. Complex and convoluted though many texts undoubtedly are, I believe that they are well worth close study.

Most of our authors wrote for (or spoke to) Jewishly well-educated readers and therefore assume that we will recognize incomplete biblical or Rabbinic quotations. Wherever possible, I have completed the quotations and given references, even where our authors (or their publishers) have not done so.

The translations are rendered in language that is not gender specific so that everyone may find something in them without feeling excluded by the choice of wording. My personal theology makes it impossible for me to ascribe gender to God; hence I do not translate the four-letter divine name YHVH as Lord, preferring the more neutral Eternal. I have avoided using masculine pronouns for God, except in kabbalistic settings where the differentiation between masculine and feminine aspects is crucial to understanding the text.

Many of the texts speak in the third person: "A man should . . . ," "One ought to . . . ." To have translated in this way would have resulted in rather awkward formulations in English, and so I transpose such texts into the second person: "You should . . . ," "You ought to . . . ."

The texts are presented in the following format: first, a translation of the relevant Torah passage, followed by a twofold context: the first sets the passage in the context of the Torah itself, and the second offers some background on the kabbalistic or Hasidic comment on that Torah selection. Then come my own two levels of commentary: first, notes on the text (providing sources in earlier, nonbiblical literature as well as explications of unexplained concepts or historical details); and second, my application of the teachings of the text to our contemporary situation. Finally, one appendix provides the original Hebrew/Aramaic/

Yiddish texts, and a second, brief biography of the teachers or books mentioned.

I have often thought that this is, at heart, a very traditional work, and indeed that is the case, up to a point. My original idea was for an anthology modeled after the great compendia of the late medieval period: *Yalkut Shimoni*, a vast collection of midrashim on the entire Hebrew Bible compiled by Simon of Frankfurt-am-Main (sixteenth century), and *Yalkut Re'uveni* by Reuven Hoeschke (seventeenth century), who brought together midrashim and kabbalistic interpretations of the Torah. It was soon apparent that unlike these great anthologies, this work would have to be provided with introductions and comments to make the text accessible to a modern audience.

Critics might suggest that I would like readers to think like the Hasidim. This is also true, but only up to a point. I am not presenting texts prescribing the adulation of the *tzadikim* (the "righteous," referring to Hasidic rabbis), or attributing miraculous powers to them; and on those few occasions where I have chosen passages that emphasize the *tzadik*, I have also deliberately, consciously, and explicitly reinterpreted them because I do not believe in the worship of other human beings, however enlightened we may think they are, and because I do believe in the huge spiritual potential of every human being to become his or her own *tzadik*. I have also rejected passages that deprecate women or non-Jews, or that deny any validity to modern thinking. However, I do admire Hasidic antimaterialism, spiritual psychology, and God-centered living, and would encourage such thinking in others, as I do in myself.

I have kept transliterations to a minimum, and as simple as possible. The letters *ayin* and *alef*, for example, are not represented at the beginning and end of words by the symbols ' and ', unless they are relevant to the exegesis. *Kaf* and *kof* are both indicated by "k," and *chaf* and *chet* by "ch," apart from "Hasid," "Hasidism," "Hochmah," "Hesed," and "Hayyim." Names of biblical characters follow the spelling in the JPS Bible translation, and the titles of the weekly Torah readings likewise conform to those of the JPS TANAKH.

A note on references to Hasidic rabbis: most are known by the names of the towns where they lived, rather than by their family names. Rabbi Pinchas of Koretz, for example, had the surname Shapiro, but Hasidic texts almost never use it, preferring instead to state that he was "from/of Koretz," or simply to call him "the Koretzer." I have used both forms in order to vary the language, and have also employed the Ashkenazi transliteration "rebbe," instead of "rabbi," on occasion to refer to a given Hasidic teacher. An "R." before someone's name, as in R. Shlomo ben Akiva, is the abbreviation for "Rabbi" or "Rebbe." Alternatively, each may also be called a *tzadik* (righteous man).

I fervently hope and pray that this work will help to bring the profound spiritual and mystical insights of our tradition as they relate to our Torah to a wider audience.

Many of the extracts, often with accompanying comments, appeared on my website (www.tabick.abel.co.uk) or in *divrei Torah* distributed by the Leo Baeck College and the Movement for Reform Judaism in the United Kingdom, but they have been totally rewritten for this work.

I would like to acknowledge the help of numerous individuals who have encouraged and assisted me in the work of producing this anthology. In fact, there are just too many to mention, but I would like to single out the late Rabbi Dr. Louis Jacobs of blessed memory, my teacher at the Leo Baeck College who taught me the basic skills of how to read and decipher kabbalistic and Hasidic texts; Dr. Ada Rapoport-Albert, who introduced me to the academic study of Hasidism; and Rabbi Lionel Blue, whose lectures and writings, and personal chats, have inspired me and helped me to keep the important spiritual goals before me. In addition, I owe an unpayable debt to the late Rabbi Gunther Plaut of blessed memory, formerly of Holy Blossom Temple in Toronto, who gave me invaluable career assistance that allowed me to study at the Leo Baeck College in London, and to his then-assistant Stephen D. Franklin, now rabbi emeritus of Riverdale Temple in the Bronx, who helped guide me toward my chosen path.

I have many congregants to thank, most especially those of the Leicester Progressive Jewish Congregation and Shir Hayim, the Hampstead Reform Jewish Community, who have had the kindness not to complain about the constant diet of mysticism I invariably serve up each Shabbat. And at the risk of offending many others, I would like to mention Lois George of Shir Hayim, who, along with my wife, Jackie, first gave me the idea of making a book of these study passages. Thanks are also due to those faithful members of the class I taught at the West London Synagogue over two years during which we explored in some detail many of the texts included here. Elizabeth Arbuthnot was particularly instrumental in checking biblical quotations as well as helping me to refine my thinking and translations. Gratitude is also due to all members of the De'ah study group—Linda and Ray Kann, Stephanie and

Imre Szilagy, and Warren Bernhaut—and the Monday evening Kabbalah study group—Margot Garcia, Leon and Vivienne Ellenport, Cynthia Lewis, and my colleague Rabbi Michael Hilton—who helped me clarify many of the spiritual issues that figure in the text. My friend Simone Lakmaker provided great encouragement, while Simon Rozas was instrumental in helping fill in the historical and geographical background to some of the extracts.

Thanks also to Rabbi Barry Schwartz of The Jewish Publication Society (JPS) for his enthusiasm and support for this project and to Carol Hupping of JPS for her patience. Not forgetting Ann Baker, my dedicated project editor, and Michele Alperin, who copyedited this difficult text with great enthusiasm and skill.

And I must not forget the encouragement and background support offered so freely by our good friends Lauretta and Martin Dives. They also generously provided the picture for the cover of this work.

Thanks are also due to my long-standing friend Robert (Bob) Ross, formerly of New Hampshire, now of Ottawa, Ontario. Neither of us knew it then, but my subsequent career path and this book began with intense conversations we had as undergraduates at the George Washington University.

Thanks also to my mother, Deborah Silverman, of blessed memory, whose deep spirituality was to lead me to follow paths she (and I) never dreamed of.

Despite all the many people to whom I owe a debt of gratitude for having made this book possible, it remains the case that all errors within it are to be laid at my door.

Patience has been the hallmark of the person to whom I owe the most: my wife, Rabbi Jacqueline Tabick, without whose encouragement this book would never have been written. Many thanks also go to my children, Mikki, Roni, and Jeremy, for their understanding.

But above all, thanks and praise are due to the One, who has given me the strength and the wit to proceed as far as I have.

L.T.

15 July 2012
25 Tammuz 5772

The World's Aura

An Introduction to Jewish Mysticism and Kabbalah

Like the Torah, the world too has an aura, an aura of mystery and holiness, an aura that only the mystics among us perceive. And mystics of all ages, of all traditions and none, have been pointing to and exploring this aura throughout human history. This aura cannot be penetrated by science. It goes to the root of our existence, and examining it means considering the deepest questions: Why is there a universe? What is the meaning of the universe and of our lives within it? What is the relationship between the spirituality that we experience inside ourselves and the physicality we experience beyond the confines of our minds?

THE MERKAVAH MYSTICS

Over the three millennia of Jewish history, questions such as these have been posed and answered in a variety of ways, but most modern scholars believe that the history of Jewish mysticism began in the late Rabbinic period (second or third century CE) with the Merkavah (chariot) mystics. Their number is said by tradition to have included some of the leading lights of mishnaic Judaism, like Rabbi Akiva and Rabbi Ishmael.

The few manuscripts that describe the teachings of the Merkavah mystics reveal that they were primarily concerned with experiencing the divine chariot as graphically depicted by the prophet Ezekiel, especially in chapters 1–3 of his biblical book. In a similar vein, they sought to penetrate into the deepest recesses of God's heavenly palaces (*heichalot*), past fearsome angels, into the immediate presence of the divine sovereign. Because their concern was not with the Torah text itself, they are not directly represented in this work. They did, however, influence later mystical tradition, and I will reference Metatron, a key figure in the Merkavah literature. This supreme angelic being is mentioned in the Talmud, but is said to be a transfiguration of Enoch, the mysterious biblical character who "walked with God, and then he was not, because God took him" (Genesis 5:24).

THE HASIDEI ASHKENAZ

The teachings of the Merkavah mystics are known to us primarily because they were preserved in the circles of the Hasidei Ashkenaz, the German pietists of the twelfth and thirteenth centuries. Two of their leaders, Yehudah HeHasid and Elazar of Worms, are both quoted in this work, the first in Kedoshim and the second in Devarim. Although not systematic theologians, they apparently held a view that God's presence in the universe is essentially twofold: the universal Presence of God, the Shechinah, and what they called the Kavod, the "Glory of God." The first is undifferentiated, that is, everywhere and always the same; and the second, they believed, manifests itself in unusual occurrences, such as the appearance of angels or demons, or in miracles. They promoted extra strict observances in the moral as well as the ritual sphere, but only for their own limited circles. They also took a keen interest in the precise details of the texts of the Bible and the Jewish prayer book, searching for hidden patterns that would confirm talmudic teaching or point to some deeper spiritual lesson, or sometimes just to revel in the discovery of the pattern itself.

KABBALAH

The word "kabbalah" means something that is received, tradition. The term appears in the Mishnah (ca. 200 CE), but there it refers to the Prophets and the Writings, the second and third parts of the Hebrew Bible. Only much later was it applied to the mystical tradition, when the visible history of the Kabbalah proper begins with the appearance of the *Sefer HaBahir*, the Book of Brightness, in the late twelfth century in Provence, France. This deeply enigmatic work probably had its origins in a much earlier period, but its history before publication is difficult to trace. The *Bahir* may have triggered a great outpouring of kabbalistic speculation and writing—in Provence, and later in Catalonia, and in Castile in Spain—that culminated about a century later in the Zohar. Central to this literature is the concept of the ten *sefirot*.

The difficult-to-define concept of *sefirot* first appears in the opening chapter of the mysterious *Sefer Yetzirah*, a book of uncertain origins. In that work, the term *sefirot* seems to indicate the primordial numbers, that is, the idea of the numbers embedded in the universe from the beginning along with the letters of the Hebrew alphabet. By the time the *Bahir* emerges, the *sefirot* have taken on the meanings that they retain throughout the later history of Kabbalah. Each *sefirah* represents an aspect of God's personality (as it were), and is as well part of a great chain of being that stretches from the unknowable aspect of divinity, the Ein Sof (the Infinite), down to this world. But the *sefirot* are also said to exist within everything that is and, most crucially, within human beings.

There are always ten *sefirot*, never more, never less, and they can be presented in a number of configurations. The most common of these is a tree.

The depiction of the *sefirotic* tree on the next page comes from Moshe Cordovero's *Pardes Rimmonim* (Orchard of Pomegranates). Ein Sof is not shown, for how can you draw the Infinite?

At the top is the *sefirah* of Keter (Crown). It is considered so mysterious, so close to the Ein Sof, and so far removed from our plane of existence that it is sometimes called Ayin (Nothingness). Below and to the right of it is the *sefirah* of Hochmah (Wisdom). It represents inspiration, the thought that seems to emerge from nothingness into consciousness. Opposite it on the left is the *sefirah* of Binah (Understanding), where the thought that emerged in Hochmah may be examined, considered, and its implications realized. This first triad of *sefirot* represents the mental and intellectual aspects of both God and human beings.

Many charts depicting the *sefirot* as a tree also show a *sefirah* known as Da'at (Knowledge) below and between Hochmah and Binah on the central pillar. There it plays the same role in this triad as Tiferet and Yesod do below, reconciling opposites. However, there can only be ten *sefirot*, not eleven; therefore, it is best to treat Da'at as Cordovero does, as the "external," conciliatory aspect of Keter.

The second triad, of Hesed (Lovingkindness), Gevurah (Might), and Tiferet (Beauty), represents the emotional side. Hesed is unlimited, unrestrained, unconditional love; Gevurah is absolute strict judgment; and these opposites are reconciled in Tiferet, balanced justice.

Beneath them is the third triad, that of Netzach and Hod (Victory and Majesty), which are nearly always treated as a pair, plus Yesod (Foundation), where all the energies of the previous eight *sefirot* are concentrated.

Below the third triad, on its own, is the *sefirah* of Malchut (Sovereignty), also known as the Shechinah (Presence of God). Malchut is the

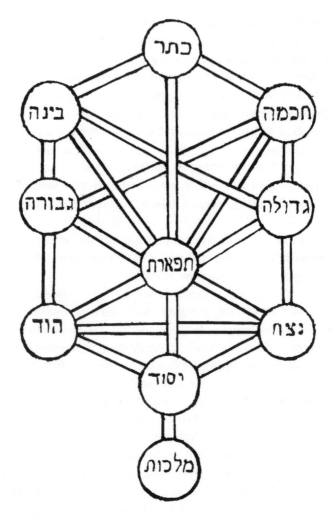

Figure 1. The ten *sefirot* as a tree, from Moshe Cordovero's *Pardes Rimmonim*.

channel between this universe and the world of the *sefirot*. Indeed some say that it is identical with this world.

It is also possible to think of the *sefirot* in the tree configuration in vertical groups. Thus we have the right branch characterized by Hesed, the left by Gevurah, and the central one by Tiferet.

Much of kabbalistic literature, and its offshoots like modern Hasidism, tends to focus on the second triad of Hesed, Gevurah, and Tiferet, which we have already outlined, or on the male-female pair of Tiferet and Malchut.

In fact, Kabbalah deals heavily in symbolism. Each of the *sefirot* has its unique, but sometimes overlapping, groups of symbols, often in contrast or conjunction with one or more of the other *sefirot*. Thus, for example, there are several gender pairs: Hochmah is frequently known as Abba (Father) and Binah as Imma (Mother), and Binah in turn gives birth to the seven lower *sefirot*. Tiferet is the son and Malchut the daughter, but these two unite, first to produce, and then to sustain, the physical universe that we inhabit.

The *sefirot* can also be mapped out against the human body, with Keter manifesting as the skull or the will, and Hochmah and Binah as the right and left hemispheres of the brain, or the brain and the heart, respectively. Hesed is the right arm, Gevurah the left, while Tiferet is the torso. Netzach and Hod are the two legs, and Yesod the genitals (traditionally male). Malchut is this masculine figure's feminine consort. When discussed in this way, the ten *sefirot* are often referred to as Adam Kadmon (the Primordial Man), not to be confused with Adam Rishon, the first human being, whose creation is depicted in Genesis 2.

It would be a mistake to imagine that the *sefirot* are static. We are meant to think of them as dynamic, with divine energies flowing in channels between them, and from them into this world, via Malchut. And, going the other way, our actions (good or bad), our thoughts, prayers, and meditations—all produce effects in the realm of the *sefirot*, which in turn filter back down to the created world. Thus, our sins may provoke Gevurah above, and therefore negative consequences here. Conversely, our good deeds stimulate Hesed, with positive results below.

Much ink was expended among kabbalists considering the age-old problem of the origin of evil. One answer, among many, was the concept of the Sitra Achara (the "Other Side"). In the Zohar and elsewhere this is a set of ten *sefirot* of evil, parallel to the ten *sefirot* of holiness. The "Other Side" is, however, not totally autonomous, since all things must come from Ein Sof. Instead, it draws its power from the Side of Holiness, through the *sefirah* of Gevurah.

Another doctrine, not found in the Zohar proper, also comes from this period. It is the notion of the four worlds, which later, in its Lurianic guise, would become much more important. The idea is that there are four worlds or realms of existence between the Ein Sof and this universe. Sometimes they are identified with groups of *sefirot*, at other times with interlocking sets of the ten *sefirot*. The highest world, and nearest to the Ein Sof, is that of Atzilut (Emanation); next is the world of Beri'ah (Creation), followed by Yetzirah (Formation), and finally Asiyah (Making). Asiyah includes the material universe, while the various types of angels inhabit Beri'ah and Yetzirah. The world of Atzilut is the most spiritual, and least material, of the worlds.

Kabbalistic Torah commentaries are primarily concerned with "finding" confirmation for their doctrines in Scripture, using Scripture to "explain" processes within the divine, or employing their theories to cast light on the Torah's choice of words.

PROPHETIC KABBALAH

During the late thirteenth century, when the Zohar came to light, we find an active mystical teacher who started with a different, nonkabbalistic, set of premises. Avraham Abulafia built his system on the twin pillars of the *Guide for the Perplexed* by Maimonides (1135–1204) and the anonymous *Sefer Yetzirah*. Following Maimonides, Abulafia believed that it was possible to train oneself to become a prophet, first, by a thorough study of philosophy and science, and second, through meditational techniques derived from the *Yetzirah*. Abulafia himself wrote numerous books of prophecy, as well as many others describing his methods, plus a full Torah commentary of which only four of its five volumes are extant. (Leviticus is missing.)

KABBALAH IN SAFED

The publication of the Zohar represents the end of a truly creative phase in the development of Kabbalah. Afterward, most (though not all) kabbalistic writers would concentrate on expounding the Zohar rather than on creating new approaches. In the late sixteenth century there was another great period of creativity, centered around Safed, a city in the northern Galilee. In the middle of that century, it became home to an entire galaxy of stars of the Kabbalah, most famously Moshe Cordovero, the Ari Yitzchak Luria, and Shlomo Alkabetz, the author of the hymn for Erev Shabbat, *Lechah Dodi*. This group was to have a profound affect on the wider Jewish world, well beyond the cloistered realm of the kabbalists. Their ideology would become dominant in Jewish communities wherever they existed up to the end of the eighteenth century and, in some cases, to this day.

Moshe Cordovero might be considered the philosopher of Kabbalah; his works are dedicated to providing a rational and systematic exposition of its teachings, and of the Zohar in particular. His influence was considerable, but the hero of Safed was Yitzchak Luria, the Ari (Lion). Though Luria lived in the town for only a brief period before his untimely death, he was the most creative kabbalist since the Zohar. Through the works of his students, especially Hayyim Vital, his dramatic and mythic teachings entered the Jewish consciousness.

The Ari based his teachings firmly on the Zohar, but he gave its thought and imagery a radical new twist, emphasizing its messianic elements and turning what were originally alternative ways of describing the *sefirot* into separate stages of a complex process. Luria's dramatic doctrine can be summarized in three terms: *tzimtzum* (contraction), *shevirat ha-kelim* (the breaking of the vessels), and *tikkun olam* (repairing of the world). Before time and space existed, Luria says, there was only the Ein Sof, the Infinite God; and because God filled any space that would come into existence, there was no room for Creation. So what did God do? God concentrated the divine essence on a single point and then removed divinity from a sphere surrounding that central point. This process, known as *tzimtzum*, would give space for the universe that was yet to emerge; but how could it come forth without some elements of divinity in the sphere? Without the presence of God, the sphere would just be empty nothingness incapable of producing anything.

According to the Ari, God then proceeded to inject the ten *sefirot* in the form of a circle, with Keter on the outside and Malchut in the center, into the sphere, followed by the ten *sefirot* in a line, as in figure 1. This second set of *sefirot* he called Adam Kadmon, the primordial man. From the various limbs of Adam Kadmon were meant to proceed the lights that were to be captured by vessels prepared for them in the next lower world, the world of Atzilut (Emanation). Whether by "accident" or by design, the vessels intended for the lights of Adam Kadmon's lower seven *sefirot* were not strong enough for them. The vessels broke, and the broken pieces fell down into the space where this universe would be created later. There, these became known as *kelipot* (shells). The lights descending from above mostly returned to their source in Ein Sof, but some descended as sparks and were captured by the *kelipot*. This process is known as *shevirat ha-kelim*, the Breaking of the Vessels.

The process of the emanation of divine energies continued, and eventually the universe we know came into existence, with humanity placed within it. Human beings in general, but Jews in particular, have been given a crucial role in the spiritual economy of the universe. It is now our task to repair the world (*tikkun olam*) by liberating the sparks trapped here in the *kelipot* with our good deeds, prayers, and meditations. When all the sparks have been set free, and restored to Ein Sof, the world (and God) will be redeemed.

This Lurianic myth of the God who requires our help was almost universally accepted throughout the worldwide Jewish community and was one of the factors that contributed to the rise of the failed messiah Shabbetai Zevi in the mid-seventeenth century. And that failure was itself a factor in the opposition that greeted the nascent Hasidic movement in Ukraine in the late eighteenth century. Spiritual innovators were often suspected, rightly or wrongly, of being followers of Shabbetai Zevi and therefore persecuted by Jewish religious authorities. One exception seems to have been the community of Izmir (Smyrna) in the Ottoman Empire, Shabbetai Zevi's hometown, where known Shabbateans included some of the town's rabbis, like Meir Bikayam. Shabbateans elsewhere were forced to keep their views to themselves or to disguise their allegiance in otherwise Orthodox works.

HASIDISM

Rabbi Yisra'el ben Eliezer, the Ba'al Shem Tov (the good master of the Name), inaugurated the modern Hasidic movement in Ukraine. He believed that it would one day spread throughout the Jewish world, and that then the Messiah would come. Progress at first was slow. The Ba'al Shem Tov would travel about the countryside helping people, and soon miraculous stories about him circulated. He revered the Zohar and the Lurianic teachings, but gave them a new and popular emphasis. No longer would feeling a strong attachment to God (*devekut*) be the province only of scholars capable of undertaking complex Lurianic meditations. In the Ba'al Shem's view, *devekut* was, in theory, attainable by everyone, though in practice only a few would achieve it. Those few could then help the many by including them in their attachment to God, and the many could assist the few by attaching themselves to them as their followers. These few came to be called *tzadikim*, "the righteous," and the many, *hasidim*, "the pious."

The Hasidic movement added little that was new to kabbalistic thought, but it did shift the focus from spiritual activity in the upper worlds to human psychology. A clear example of this concerns the concepts of *katnut* (smallness) and *gadlut* (greatness). In the Lurianic scheme, these terms, though drawn from human personal development (i.e., "immaturity" and "maturity"), were related primarily to Tiferet and Malchut;

Tiferet, also known as Ze'eir Anpin (the Impatient One), has to attain *gadlut* before it can unite with Malchut, or Nukva (the Feminine). When Ze'eir Anpin is in the state of *katnut*, such union is not possible, and blessings are withheld from the world. In the hands of the Hasidic masters from the Ba'al Shem Tov onward, *gadlut* usually refers to a higher state of consciousness in which one feels spiritually aware and attached to God, while *katnut* indicates a lower, ordinary level of consciousness. (But see Avraham Yissachar ber HaCohen of Radomsk's comment on *parashat Be-midbar* below.)

Hasidism gleaned its understanding of the broad outlines of human psychology from Kabbalah, which in turn had borrowed from medieval Jewish philosophy the notion of the threefold nature of the soul. Although details vary, there are said to be three souls, or aspects of the soul: *nefesh*, *ruach*, and *neshamah*. Of these, the first is the most primitive. All living things have a *nefesh* (soul); it is what distinguishes them from inanimate objects. The *ruach* (spirit), which we share with animals, is our emotional drive, while the *neshamah* (soul), unique to humans, is the rational mind, where thought takes place and inspiration may occur.

From the late eighteenth to the early twentieth century, the Hasidic movement grew in Eastern and Central Europe. From its roots in Ukraine, it spread into Poland, Hungary, Lithuania, and beyond. The Ba'al Shem Tov was succeeded by Dov Ber, the Maggid of Mezritch. He in turn taught many of the great *tzadikim* of the next generation, including Elimelech of Lyzhansk, who brought Hasidism to Poland; Shlomo of Karlin, who took the Hasidic message into Lithuania; the much-loved Levi Yitzchak of Berditchev; and Shneur Zalman of Liady, the founder of the movement we know as Chabad Lubavitch Hasidism; among many others.

Elimelech of Lyzhansk served as mentor to another impressive list of students, including Menachem Mendel of Rymanov; Ya'akov Yitzchak, the Seer of Lublin; Yisra'el ben Shabbetai, the Maggid of Koznitz; Avraham Yehoshua Heschel of Apt/Apta; and a host of others.

The Seer of Lublin broke away from his master against the latter's wishes and then found that his favorite disciple, Ya'akov Yitzchak, the Holy Jew of Pshische, did the same to him. With the Holy Jew a new school came into being, led after his death by Simchah Bunam of Pshische and then Menachem Mendel of Kotzk. This new grouping placed much greater emphasis on individual spiritual development than had previously been the case in Hasidic circles.

Unlike the Ba'al Shem Tov, most of the later *tzadikim* established dynasties so that on their deaths authority would pass to their son or son-in-law, or to a favorite disciple. As teachers proliferated, groups would often split and splinter, though large communities still remain.

Every Hasid is a follower of a specific *tzadik* and his teachings. They are either Lubavitchers, Kotzkers, Karliners, Gerers, or whatever. Each school has its own emphases and nuances within the Hasidic fold, and sometimes that leads to competition and conflict between groups.

Hasidic sermons and commentaries are often characterized by a concern for what might be called mystical psychology: What should be the relationship between God and the individual? How do we experience the divine? How can mystical teachers, the *tzadikim*, help their followers, the *hasidim*, and vice versa?

MITNAGDIM

The Hasidic movement did not grow and spread unopposed. On the contrary, it aroused a great deal of opposition throughout all the areas to which it spread. Later opposition would come from Westernized "enlightened" Jews; but in the early generations, it came from the traditional Orthodox community, a group that came to be called *mitnagdim* (*misnagdim*, in Yiddish, meaning, "opponents"). Chief among the early *mitnagdim* was the Vilna Ga'on, Eliyahu ben Shlomo, a truly outstanding scholar in his generation. He was also a major kabbalist, but his hostility to Hasidism was probably because he feared that the movement was another manifestation of Shabbateanism. (The Ga'on is not represented in this work, but his student Zevi Hirsh Minkovitz of Semyatitch is.)

IN MODERN TIMES

The modern study of Kabbalah and Jewish mysticism in all its phases really began with Gershom Scholem (1898–1982), but he believed that the history of Kabbalah was over, apart from the (then apparently) dwindling Hasidic movement. In the 1960s and 1970s this began to change, and a new generation of Jews began exploring this area of Jewish spirituality with the aim of finding lessons for living in the late twentieth and twenty-first centuries. Before long, Hasidic communities like Lubavitch and Breslov (Bratslav) had begun outreach programs, and the Kabbalah Center and other groups were established, and latterly publicized by celebrities. Now the word "Kabbalah" is well known, if not always well understood. The history of Kabbalah is far from over. It lives on in the hearts of all those who seek a deeper, more spiritual understanding of the Jewish heritage.

Suggestions for Further Reading

Blumenthal, David R. *Understanding Jewish Mysticism*. 2 vols. New York: Ktav, 1978 & 1982.

Dan, Joseph. *Kabbalah: A Very Short Introduction*. Oxford: Oxford University Press, 2006.

Kushner, Lawrence. *The Way into the Jewish Mystical Tradition*. Woodstock, VT: Jewish Lights, 2001.

Matt, Daniel C. *The Essential Kabbalah: The Heart of Jewish Mysticism*. San Francisco: Harper, 1995.

Rabinowicz, Harry M. *The World of Hasidism*. London: Vallentine Mitchell, 1970.

Scholem, Gershom. *Kabbalah*. Jerusalem: Keter, 1974.

Steinsaltz, Adin. *The Thirteen Petalled Rose*. New York: Basic Books, 1980.

Unterman, Alan J. *The Kabbalistic Tradition*. London: Penguin, 2008.

———. *Wisdom of the Jewish Mystics*. London: Sheldon Press, 1996.

Weiner, Herbert. *9 1/2 Mystics: The Kabbala Today*. New York: Collier, 1969.

Wiesel, Elie. *Somewhere a Master*. London: Penguin, 1982.

———. *Souls on Fire*. London: Penguin, 1972.

THE AURA OF TORAH

GENESIS

B'reishit

---

[1] Unfinished Business

"In the beginning, God created heaven and earth."
Genesis 1:1

CONTEXT

The Torah opens with the story of Creation. Why? One reason is to teach us that the universe has divine origins. A second might be to affirm the unity of the world, since it all originates with the one God. But might there also be other lessons here that we need to learn?

Rabbi Menachem Mendel of Kotzk was both a hard master and a strong believer in accepting personal responsibility, berating his followers when he felt they were not doing so.

> When R. Leibl Eger returned from Kotzk, his father, R. Shlomo, asked him: What did you learn in Kotzk?
>
> He replied, I learned three things:
>
> 1. That a human being is a human being and an angel is an angel.
> 2. That if one wishes, a human being can become more than an angel.
> 3. "In the beginning, God created" [Genesis 1:1]—the Holy One created only the beginning, and the rest God left to human beings.
>
> Menachem Mendel of Kotzk (1787–1859), *Sefer Amud HaEmet* [The book of the pillar of truth] (Bnei Brak, 2000), p. 11

NOTES

Leibl Eger. Yehudah Leib Eger (1815–88). He came from a long line of Orthodox, non-Hasidic rabbis, and his association with the rebbe of Kotzk would not have pleased his father. Later he led his own Hasidic community centered in Lublin.

R. Shlomo. R. Shlomo ben Akiva Eger (1786–1852) is Yehudah Leib's father. A communal rabbi and head of a yeshivah, he was a signatory to an 1834 memorandum from the rabbis of Warsaw attacking the Hasidic movement.

COMMENTS

Humans are not angels, but we have a potential that even angels do not have: we can freely choose the good. The Kotzker emphasizes, reinforces, and extends the ancient Rabbinic notion that we are "partners with God in the work of creation" (Talmud, *Shabbat* 10a and 119b). God set things up, but it is up to us to make of the world what we will, for good or for evil. "Don't call on God," he is saying, "to do the things that we can control." We have the potential to improve things or make them worse all by ourselves.

If there is one lesson that the history of the modern world teaches, it is the law of unintended consequences. Many well-meaning efforts to make the world better have simply produced greater problems. To choose just one example: adding lead to gasoline to avoid knocking in automobile engines has put lead in the air and produced psychological and mental problems in children. Indeed, the entire process of industrialization, though it has produced much good, has brought pollution, exploitation, and environmental destruction in its wake. Our efforts to improve the world must be undertaken with the humility implied by our being partners with God in Creation.

---

[2] The Soul's Mate

"Therefore, a man should leave his father and his mother
and cling to his wife, and they become one flesh."

Genesis 2:24

CONTEXT

The story of woman's creation from the rib of man is a teleological tale, that is, one intended to explain why things are as they are—in this case, why men seek women as mates. Could there be a deeper, more spiritual meaning to this story?

Menachem Mendel of Rymanov was a disciple of Rabbi Elimelech of Lyzhansk, and therefore a fourth-generation Hasidic teacher. *Ilana deChayyei* (the title is Aramaic), edited by Yitzchak Podvah, is a collection of Menachem Mendel's teachings, as well as those of other Hasidic masters.

This should be understood along the lines of the statement of [the rabbis]: "There are three partners in a human being: the Holy One, the father, and the mother." In regard to this, Scripture says: "A man [person] should leave his father and his mother" [Genesis 2:24] — [meaning,] they should leave the bodily soul "and cling to his wife" — cling only to the Shechinah [the Presence of God]. "Wife" [*'eSHeT*] is made up of the opening letters of the words *'Adonai sefatai tiftach* ["O God, open my lips" — Psalm 51:17], which refers to the Shechinah.

Yitzchak Mordechai ben Yisra'el Aharon Podvah (1884–1942), ed., *Ilana deChayyei* [The tree of life] (Jerusalem, 1986), pt. 1, p. 10

NOTES

"There are three partners." Talmud, *Kiddushin* 30b and *Niddah* 31a.

Bodily soul. In Hebrew, *nefesh*. In medieval Jewish thought, the *nefesh* is that soul or aspect of the soul whose presence or absence determines whether we are alive or dead. It is also the seat of the bodily desires and is instrumental in our feelings of hunger, thirst, etc.

Shechinah. Often treated in Kabbalah and Hasidism as distinctly feminine.

'Adonai sefatai tiftach. . . refers to the Shechinah. This verse from Psalms is used to introduce the *Amidah* (standing prayer) in all statutory prayer services. *'Adonai* in this verse is not substituting for the unpronounceable four-letter name of God (YHVH), but is the word that actually appears in the Psalm. YHVH in kabbalistic symbolism indicates the *sefirah* of Tiferet, while *'Adonai* indicates Malchut (Shechinah).

COMMENT

This interpretation by Menachem Mendel of Rymanov shifts the focus of the verse from sociology and psychology to spirituality. Now it serves to emphasize the soul's mate, namely the Shechinah (the Presence of God). We use the expression "soul mate" most frequently to refer to our spouses, lovers, partners, but at the deepest spiritual level our souls are partnered with the divine in all things.

[3] The Enoch Enigma

"And Enoch walked with God."

Genesis 5:22,24

CONTEXT

Chapter 5 of Genesis comprises primarily a rather dry genealogical list that gives the very broad outlines of the lives of various individuals from Adam to Noah, usually concluding in each case with an explicit mention of their deaths. But Enoch stands out as an exception. Of him it is said, laconically, mysteriously: "And Enoch walked with God and then he was not, because God had taken him" (Genesis 5:24). We are left with the feeling that much more might have been said about Enoch that we are not being told.

The teaching offered here is from the writings of Rabbi Ya'akov Yosef of Polonnoye, a primary disciple of the Ba'al Shem Tov and author of the first Hasidic work to be published. In this text, he draws on an ancient legend of uncertain origin, before quoting his teacher directly.

> Our rabbis say that Enoch was a shoemaker, and that with each and every stitch he would unify the Holy One, blessed be He, and His Shechinah. . . . I heard in the name of my teacher the explanation of the verse: "Whatever your hand finds to do, do with all your strength, for there is no work or thought or knowledge in the nether-world [to which you are going]" (Ecclesiastes 9[:10]). For, the subject of Metatron, how he united the Holy One, blessed be He, and His Shechinah with every stitch, etc., [is explained by the fact that] thought is called infinite, [symbolized by the four-letter name] YHVH while action is [symbolized by the divine name] *Adonai*. When you join together action and thought, as you perform an action, it is called the union of the Holy One, blessed be He, and His Shechinah. Hence [the text] says: "Whatever your hand finds to do, do with all your strength"—that is to say, thought is [identical with] wisdom [*HoCHMaH*], "the power of what" [*KoaCH MaH*]. So, do the action with all your strength, that is, your thought, by joining

together the two things, which [represent] the Holy One, blessed be He, and His Shechinah.

Yisra'el ben Eliezer, Ba'al Shem Tov (1700–1760), *Sefer Ba'al Shem Tov* [The book of the good master of the Name] (Jerusalem, n.d., v. 1, pp. 107–9

NOTES

Enoch was a shoemaker. See Reuven Hoeschke (seventeenth century), ed., *Yalkut Re'uveni* [Reuven's collection] (Warsaw, 1883), pt. 1, p. 120, which in turn is based on Menachem Azariah da Fano (1548–1620), *Asarah Ma'amarot* [Ten sayings] (Venice, 1597), p. 63c, (Amsterdam, 1649), p. 152b. The notion of Enoch as shoemaker is a late development of the ancient legend of Enoch's transformation into the archangel Metatron.

Unify the Holy One, blessed be He, and His Shechinah. A kabbalistic formula. The Holy One, blessed be He, refers to the *sefirah* of Tiferet, while the Shechinah is Malchut. Bringing together these two *sefirot* in the mind is a common basic kabbalistic meditation, whose effect is to produce their unification above in the world of the *sefirot*. When they come together, in a conjugal union, God's blessings are said to flow unimpeded into this world.

In the name of my teacher. The Ba'al Shem Tov.

Metatron. According to Rabbinic texts, God's supreme angel, second only to the divine being. Some ancient noncanonical texts, exploring the meaning of our Genesis verse, suggest that Enoch was transformed into Metatron as a reward for his piety and mystical attainments. Texts concerned with Enoch may be found in the Apocrypha and Pseudepigrapha as well as the Heichalot (Palaces) or Merkavah (Chariot) literature.

YHVH. Because this divine name is never pronounced, it may be considered as indicating the infinite. A fixed pronunciation would limit it, making it finite. Thus it represents thought, which is potentially infinite.

Adonai. The name we say whenever we come across YHVH in Hebrew texts. Since it is actually pronounced, it represents action. The reading of YHVH as *Adonai* itself constitutes a unification of the *sefirot* of Tiferet (represented by YHVH) and Malchut (*Adonai*).

When you join together action and thought. This teaching actually turns the original kabbalistic meditation on its head. It is no longer about keeping the *sefirot* in mind; it is now about concentrating solely on whatever you are doing.

Thought is [identical with] wisdom [*HoCHMaH*], "the power of what" [*KoaCH MaH*]. The letters of *Hochmah* are "analyzed" into two words.

The meaning is that thought may be translated into physical action, as represented by "what," and all action originates in thought.

COMMENT

Ultimately, the Ba'al Shem Tov's interpretation of the legend of Enoch's meditational technique is that spiritual benefit can be obtained from even the most mundane task, if your thoughts are totally given over to what you are doing.

Every act is a spiritual act. For convenience we divide the world and our lives into religious and secular segments, but for the believer everything is religious. Even our mundane jobs, our everyday little tasks, can be infused with spirituality. We can all be like Enoch the shoemaker.

Noaḥ

---

[4] Wisdom or Cleverness?

"Then God said to Noah, 'I have decided to make an end of all
flesh, because the earth is full of violence because of them; now
I am going to destroy them along with all the earth.'"

Genesis 6:13

CONTEXT

God announces to Noah the intention to send a flood to destroy humanity.

Krasna is a town in southeastern Poland. Very little is known of Hayyim of Krasna, except that he was a disciple of R. Yisra'el ben Eliezer, the Ba'al Shem Tov. The book from which this teaching comes is a late compilation.

With his holy tongue [R. Hayyim of Krasna] said: In the past, the letters of *HoCHMaH* [wisdom] stood for *CHilu Millefanav Kol Ha-aretz* ["Tremble before God all the earth"—1 Chronicles 16:30]. But nowadays, due to our many sins, the letters of *HoCHMaH* stand for *Ki Mal'ah Ha-aretz CHamas* ["because the earth is full of violence"— Genesis 6:13].

Hayyim of Krasna (eighteenth century), quoted in Pinchas ben MaHaRaM of Koretz, ed., *Beit Pinchas* [Pinchas's house] (Bilgoraj, 1926), p. 19

NOTE

The letters of *HoCHMaH* stand for. Reb Hayyim indulges in a bit of *no-tarikon*, the system whereby the letters of a given word are taken to be the initial letters of the words of a phrase or sentence. He finds two biblical phrases that have words beginning with the four Hebrew letters that spell *Hochmah* (Wisdom), though he is not bothered about the order in which they come.

Hayyim of Krasna's point is that Wisdom can mean respect for God and God's world, or it can mean violence. Can he be right about that? Surely violence cannot be called "wisdom"! Apart from self-defense, violence is more likely to be foolishness of a very serious kind. *Hochmah* does mean Wisdom, but it can also mean mere cleverness, and cleverness is not always the virtue that Wisdom is. Sometimes, by trying to take advantage of a situation, we may think we are being wise, but we may only be clever. And that cleverness may well bring destruction and violence. Instead, we have to have respect for all God's creatures by beginning with respect for God.

---

[5] Misplaced Anger

"Then God said to Noah: 'Leave the ark. . . .' Then he took some of the clean animals, and some of the clean birds, and offered sacrifices on the altar."

Genesis 8:15,20

CONTEXT

How did Noah feel when he emerged from the ark after the Flood? And why does he offer sacrifices immediately afterward? Is he giving thanks that he has been saved, or is there some other motive at work?

Sitrei Torah [Secrets of Torah] is a text within the broad scope of Zoharic literature.

"Then God said to Noah: 'Leave the ark.'" How did the Holy One respond to Noah when he had left the ark, saw the world destroyed, and began to cry? [Noah] said: "Ruler of the universe, You are called merciful; You should have been merciful to Your creatures . . . !"

The Holy One responded by saying: "Foolish shepherd! Now you say this! Why didn't you say this when I said to you: 'For I have seen that you are righteous before Me' [Genesis 7:1], or again [when I said]: 'Look here, I am bringing a flood of water' [Genesis 6:17], or again [when I said]: 'Make yourself an ark of gopher wood' [Genesis 6:14]? At any point, I could have delayed and said to you: '[I will refrain] because you asked for mercy for the entire world.' And as a result of this decision, it would have been saved by repentance. But it did not enter your mind to ask for mercy for the civilized world. Had you done so, it would have been saved. But now that the world is destroyed, you open your mouth to complain to Me with weeping and supplication!?"

When Noah perceived this, he brought sacrifices and burnt offerings, as it is written: "Then he took some of the clean animals, and some of the clean birds, [and offered sacrifices on the altar]" (Genesis 8[:20]).

Zohar, *Sitrei Torah*, I, 254b

COMMENT

In this passage, Noah's anger is once again directed toward God. How could God allow evil? The answer is clear: Why didn't Noah take the responsibility for his world that might have averted the catastrophe? Noah's anger is misplaced; it should have been directed against himself. The sacrifices he offers are intended to assuage the guilt he bears for his failure.

The task of the righteous is not merely to pray, or to address complaints to God when things go wrong. It is our responsibility to act as Noah should have, to speak out and take action that will put things right before it is too late. As we face an ecological catastrophe potentially every bit as dangerous as the flood Noah faces in the Torah, we would do well to bear this in mind.

[6] The Wine of Torah

"Noah began to be a farmer; he planted a vineyard, drank some of the wine and became drunk and lay uncovered in his tent."

Genesis 9:20–21

CONTEXT

Noah's first act after leaving the ark and offering sacrifices is to plant a vineyard, make wine with the produce, and get drunk. The Torah's narrative of this agricultural and industrial process is telescoped into a mere two verses, which in turn leads to the midrashic interpretation referred to in our text below.

Avraham ben Shmuel Abulafia was a controversial figure in his own lifetime. A self-proclaimed prophet and messiah, he created meditational techniques designed to make all who practice them into prophets. Among his many works are commentaries on each of the books of the Torah, though the one on Leviticus is lost. The text below, where he engages in allegorical interpretation, comes from his work on Genesis.

> Noah's planting of the vineyard: it has been suggested that the planting, the drinking of the wine, and the revealing of his nakedness all happened on the same day.
>
> But the wine is the wine of the Torah, and on the day that we plant its root [in our souls] we immediately drink and have our "nakedness" revealed through our [newly acquired] wisdom. This is the nakedness of existence and the nakedness of our being. For then we know that our true being derives from the sexual act, the beginning of our existence, that we are a [mere] putrid drop [begun] by an act of intercourse, that we are here for an instant and gone in an instant, and that if we were to live for a thousand years several times over, we would still have come from nothing, even though we had had real existence, and that we are going back to nothing, even though each of our limbs had existed, but not, in the end, of themselves.

Avraham ben Shmuel Abulafia (1240–after 1291), *Mafteach HaChochmot* [The key to the (spiritual) sciences], ed. Amnon Gross (Jerusalem, 2001), p. 59

NOTES

It has been suggested. In the midrash *Bereshit Rabbah* 36:4.

All happened on the same day. If the tale is taken literally, as the midrash has done, then, Abulafia says, this seems highly unlikely.

Of themselves. Their existence is temporary, and bound up with that of their (and our) physical nature.

COMMENT

Wine is a frequent symbol for Torah in Rabbinic literature (see, e.g., *Shir HaShirim Rabbah* 1:19). Like wine, Torah leaves its mark on people, changing their behavior. Like wine, Torah gladdens the heart. Abulafia applies this symbol to the story of Noah's drunkenness. In his view, this explains the midrash's insistence that the planting, harvesting, fermenting, drunkenness, and nakedness all occurred on the same day—Torah study can also lead to nakedness, although a metaphorical or spiritual nakedness, to be sure. Torah study, Abulafia holds, reveals to us our true situation in the world: that we are born as the result of a strikingly earthly act and live but a moment in the history of the universe. Study of the Torah's laws may uncover how far we stray from its ideals.

Though we moderns may differ about the details, Torah shows us the sweep of human and cosmic history. It reveals to us our place in it and the obligations that arise from that place. It shows us how vulnerable we are, subject to the whims of nature and history, subject to God's will. Our existence is fleeting. Though Abulafia doesn't mention it here, Torah also reveals how to make the most of our brief existence, by living for each other, not just for ourselves, and by dedicating our lives to God's service.

Lekh Lekha

---

[7] "Go for Yourself"

*"Go [for yourself] from your land and from your birthplace and
from your father's house, to the land that I will show you."*

Genesis 12:1

CONTEXT

The *sidrah* opens with God's first command to Abraham: "Go from your
land." The word in the Hebrew that means "for yourself" gives added
emphasis to the command "go," though it is superfluous in English. Even
in Hebrew it is not strictly necessary, so what is its purpose?

Rabbi Simchah Bunam of Pshische, in Poland, was one of a new breed
of Hasidic rabbis who were simultaneously trying to renew Hasidism
and engage with the newer, Westernizing trends that were beginning
to spread through Eastern European Jewry in the early nineteenth century. Simchah Bunam himself was trained as a pharmacist and scandal-
ized many Hasidim by wearing "German" (Western European) clothing.
Although I have assigned this teaching to Simchah Bunam of Pshische,
the context in Yo'etz Kayyam Kadish Rokotz's *Siach Sarfei Kodesh*, an
anthology of sayings by many teachers, is unclear, and it may originate
with his disciple, Hanoch of Alexander (1798–1870).

> He said: "Go for yourself" [which really means] "for yourself." The
> meaning is that each person should test themselves to see if their ways
> may be improved. Furthermore, there is another intention in this
> verse, which is well known to those with understanding: its meaning
> is that each person must sense for themselves what level they are on
> and [whether] they need to do anything.
>
> Yo'etz Kayyam Kadish Rokotz, ed., *Siach Sarfei Kodesh* [The conversation of
> the holy seraphim] (n.p., n.d.), pt. 1, p. 20

Those with understanding. An expression usually referring to kabbalists.

What level they are on. Which of the ten *sefirot* or the four "worlds" represents their state of mind.

COMMENT

Two interpretations of this verse are given here, one behavioral, the other psychological. The first, "Go for yourself," means you should consider the way you are going, that is, your behavior, and improve it where necessary. The second: Examine your spiritual state and do what is needful to elevate it.

These two interpretations go hand in hand. Improving our behavior may result in a higher spiritual awareness, and a higher spiritual awareness should result in better behavior. Much of traditional and modern Judaism is geared toward the behavioral side, but we ignore the spiritual at our peril. Conversely, spirituality without accompanying good deeds is self-indulgent and misses the point.

---

[8] Going About for Wisdom

*"Up, walk about [hit-halech] the land, through its
length and breadth, for I will give it to you."*
Genesis 13:17

CONTEXT

A conflict has arisen between Abram's men and those employed by his nephew Lot, and as a result the two men decide to separate from each other. God now speaks to Abram, offering him words of encouragement, perhaps to counteract any feeling of loss he may be experiencing at his nephew's departure. God promises that one day the land through which Abram is traveling will belong to his descendants, but note that the verbal form *hit-halech* (walk about) is rare in the Hebrew Bible.

Bachya ben Asher ben Chlava was a preacher and *dayyan* in Spain, usually called Rabbenu (our teacher) Bachya, perhaps as an indication of his popularity or to distinguish him from another famous Bachya, the moralist Bachya ibn Pakuda. "Our teacher" wrote his commentary on the Torah in 1291. Here I have drawn from two of the four levels of interpretation that he applies to the Torah: the plain meaning or *peshat*, and the allegorical or rational, the way of *sechel*.

According to the plain meaning [*peshat*], the Holy One wanted Abraham to take possession of the Holy Land, which God was to give him and his descendants from this point. God told him to go about through its length and breadth like a person who is giving a friend a gift of land and shows him its boundaries, saying that he should take possession of it.

But according to the rational approach, [you should note that] the phrase "walk about" is mentioned with respect to wisdom, as it is written: "When you walk about, it shall lead you" (Proverbs 6[:22]). . . . This refers to the mind, which is only mentioned in relation to singular righteous people from among those who seek wisdom, namely, Noah, Enoch, Abraham, and the like.

Because Abraham moved his consciousness from one level to the next in his search for wisdom, and allowed his mind to go back and forth in the attainment of that which the "south" contains, the blessed God said, "Up, walk about the land," as if to say, "Let your consciousness move about in seeking those things that exist in the land," for we do not find that Abraham [actually] went about the length and breadth of the land, but we do find that he "dwelt" and did not [literally] "go," [as] it is written: "Abram took down his tent, went and dwelt [in the plain of Mamre]" [Genesis 13:18]. Thus, this "going" was a movement of the intelligent soul, accompanied by the quietness of the body . . . for the seeking of wisdom requires movement of the intelligent soul and quietness of the body; this is the opposite of the needs of the body, which require movement of the body but quietness of the soul. So [God] said: "I will give it to you" [meaning] "I will give you knowledge and wisdom so that you may know the essence of [all] that exists. In a similar vein, it is written: "And the Eternal gave wisdom to Solomon" (1 Kings 5[:9]).

Rabbenu Bachya ben Asher ben Chlava (thirteenth century), *Perush Al HaTorah* [Commentary on the Torah] (Jerusalem: Blum, 1988), pt. 1, p. 78

NOTES

"It shall lead you." The subject of the verse is "wisdom."

This refers to the mind. In Hebrew, *ha-nefesh ha-sichlit*, literally, "the intelligent soul."

Noah, Enoch, Abraham, and the like. Abraham is one of a select band of individuals denoted by the unusual form of the verb, *hit-halach*. This form occurs only in relation to Noah, Enoch, and Abraham. Thus, of Enoch it says: "Enoch walked [about] with God" (Genesis 5:22). Of Noah it is written: "Noah walked [about] with God" (Genesis 6:9). In the case of Abraham, we read later in Genesis that God commanded him to "walk [about] in My presence and be perfect" (Genesis 17:1). (English translations, including the JPS, usually do not include the word "about," but the verbal forms are similar in all these verses.) In Rabbenu Bachya's view, these verbs indicate that these three men were characterized by their relentless search for wisdom.

Consciousness. *Sechel* in Hebrew.

Which the "south" contains. "South" symbolizes the *sefirah* of Hesed (Lovingkindness), associated with Abraham. Earlier, in Genesis 13:14, God tells Abraham to "look out from where you are, to the north and south, to the east and the west."

Those things that exist in the land. "Land" in kabbalistic symbolism often indicates Malchut (Shechinah). Is Rabbenu Bachya indicating that Abraham could enter into full mental communion with the immanent Presence of God? Or should "land" be taken more literally here?

COMMENT

The biblical Abraham is an active person. We see him moving from one country to another, herding his flocks, leading a nomadic life. Rabbenu Bachya's Abraham is a contemplative person, using the power of his mind to explore the land. But even the scriptural Abraham has spiritual experiences; God speaks to him on numerous occasions. Perhaps there is a lesson here for us. Everyone can experience the spiritual in their different ways. For Rabbenu Bachya, the intellectual approach is paramount. He offers us the way of contemplation. I am a great supporter of his view, but I am aware that it is not the only way. Indeed, action and contemplation both have their place in our spiritual lives. At different times one or the other may be more appropriate.

[9] God Fills and Surrounds All Things

"Walk in My presence and be perfect."

Genesis 17:1

CONTEXT

When Abram was ninety-nine years old, God appeared to him and promised once again that he would have numerous descendants. God changed his name to Abraham as a sign that this would happen, but God's speech commences with the words above.

Mordechai of Chernobyl was the son of Menachem Nachum, a traveling preacher from the same Ukrainian town. The father had visited the Ba'al Shem Tov and had been a prominent disciple of the Maggid of Mezritch; the son became the founder of the Hasidic dynasty of the Twersky family, which survives to this day.

> In order to understand the expression "[walk] in My presence," [we have to appreciate] that according to its plain meaning it refers to the aspect of [God as] enveloping, that is, that you should trust with complete faith that the light of the Infinite envelops and surrounds you on all sides, in the sense of "filling all worlds and surrounding all worlds," and as Scripture says, "Whoever trusts in the Eternal is surrounded by lovingkindness" (Psalm 32:10). And when that is so, then, as it were, you walk "in God's presence." Then, in this way, you can "be perfect." Occasionally, you may fall and be battered; nevertheless, when you constantly adhere to this trust, you may return and be made perfect and whole [once more].

Mordechai of Chernobyl (d. 1837), *Likkutei Torah* [Torah gleanings] (Jerusalem, 2001), p. 51

NOTES

"**[Walk] in My presence.**" Often translated "Walk before Me." JPS: "Walk in My ways."
"**Filling all worlds and surrounding all worlds.**" Zohar III, 225a.

Most of us live our lives surrounded by technology and the multifaceted artificiality of man-made culture. Nature doesn't impinge on us in the way that it did on our ancestors, as long as natural disaster doesn't strike. Perhaps our predecessors found it easier than we do to accept that they walked in God's presence, but now more than ever, despite, or even because of, our dependence on our technology, we need to rediscover that dependence on God and awareness of God's constant, loving presence. Then we can engage in true repentance and bring true healing to ourselves and the earth.

Va-yera'

[10] Lovingkindness in All That Happens

"The Eternal said, 'Shall I hide from Abraham what I am doing?'"

Genesis 18:17

CONTEXT

One day Abraham is visited by three men. Or are they angels? After they eat of Abraham's fare, one announces that Sarah and Abraham will indeed have a child. Then the two remaining angels proceed with Abraham toward Sodom. At some point they leave the Patriarch behind, while God allows him to engage in a spate of bargaining to try to save the lives of the wicked people of Sodom. This verse explains God's reasoning for opening that dialogue.

Yitzchak of Vorki was a well-known Hasidic teacher, founder of a dynasty of Polish Hasidim. (Vorki, or Warka, is a suburb of Warsaw.) A student of Simchah Bunam of Pshische and friend of Menachem Mendel of Kotzk, he was known as a "lover of Israel," a mark of his great compassion.

> There is no action of heavenly origins in the world that does not contain within it the element of Hesed [Lovingkindness], even in times of transgression and judgment—may God preserve us. Thus, when Sodom was overthrown, the element of Hesed was present in that Lot was rescued. Hence Scripture says, "Shall I hide from Abraham"— that is, the attribute of Abraham, the attribute of Hesed, "what I am doing"—there cannot possibly be any act that does not contain within it an element of Hesed.

Yitzchak of Vorki (1779–1848), *Beit Yitzchak* [The house of Isaac] (Jerusalem, 1992), p. 11

The attribute of Abraham. Abraham represents the *sefirah* of Hesed (Lovingkindness). The overthrow of Sodom and Gomorrah seems to be an act of Gevurah (Might), also known as Din (Strict Judgment), the *sefirah* opposite and opposed to Hesed.

COMMENT

Yitzchak of Vorki was no stranger to suffering. He worked tirelessly to alleviate the discriminatory laws aimed at Jews under the Tsarist regime in the mid-nineteenth century. Yet here he affirms, as a matter of faith, that everything that happens, no matter how bad it seems, contains some element of Hesed, of God's lovingkindness. In his view, it is as if God were asking, "Can I keep the attribute of Love out of the destruction of Sodom?" and the answer that is implied is no. Yes, God destroyed the wicked of Sodom and Gomorrah, a clear act of Din (divine judgment), but God also saved Lot and his daughters. The divine attribute of Hesed, symbolized by Abraham, is not absent even in that disaster.

Many people say that they cannot believe in God because of the disasters and tragedies of life. If God were a loving god, then surely these things would not happen; hence, God must not be loving. Alternatively, if God were indeed loving, God must be powerless to stop these things from occurring. In either event, there seems no point in believing in or worshiping such a God. Yitzchak of Vorki, like many religious people, avoids this apparent dichotomy, preferring instead to affirm God's goodness even in tragedy, whether natural or man made. God's love is always present, no matter what has occurred. It may be found in the courage, solidarity, and compassion that tragedy inspires.

---

[11] Fear of God

"Because I thought: 'Surely there is no fear of God at all
in this place, and they will kill me for my wife.'"

Genesis 20:11

CONTEXT

On two occasions Abraham passes his wife Sarah off as his sister, and Isaac does the same with Rebecca. This time, when Abimelech, king of

Gerar, discovers the deception, he demands to know why Abraham acted in this way that so nearly brought disaster. The verse above is his answer.

Rabbi Pinchas of Koretz was an early Hasidic teacher, possibly a disciple of the Ba'al Shem Tov. His sayings often display a folksy quality not always found in the teachings of other Hasidic masters.

> Thus did the Rav speak to a man who was afraid of a nobleman. He said: "Do not be afraid of him! I urge you not to be afraid, as it says in Jeremiah, 'Do not break down before them, lest I break you before them' [Jeremiah 1:17]. For when people are not afraid of a thing, they are above that thing. This is not so when they are afraid of something; then the thing is higher than they are. Then they truly have something to fear." Thus far [did he speak].
>
> In the name of the Rav: This is [the explanation of] the popular saying "I have a fear of fear." Understand!
>
> This is [also the explanation of what he said to Abimelech]: "Because I thought: Surely there is no fear [of God at all in this place]" [Genesis 20:11]. That is, since an improper fear had entered his heart, he [wrongly] deduced from this that there was no fear of God "in this place." The place may cause the mind to be confused by extraneous thoughts.

Pinchas of Koretz (1726–91), *Imrei Pinchas* [Pinchas's sayings] (Tel Aviv: Arnberg, 1974), §10, p. 20

NOTES

Thus did the Rav. In the collected sayings of Pinchas of Koretz and his circle, the title "Rav" always indicates Pinchas himself.

Afraid of a nobleman. In this period of Ukrainian history, Polish noblemen were largely absentee landlords, often employing Jews as their agents. This meant that Jews in this position were under pressure from both sides: the local Ukrainians saw them as representatives of the hated Poles, while the Poles could fire or extort their Jewish employees with impunity.

"I have a fear of fear." Cf. Franklin Roosevelt's famous dictum: "We have nothing to fear but fear itself."

An improper fear. Fear of Abimelech and the people of Gerar, rather than of God, who should be the only object of our fear or awe.

Extraneous thoughts. In Hebrew, *machshavot zarot*. In Hasidic literature, there is considerable interest in the question of how to deal with the extraneous thoughts that come to us at moments when we should be concentrating on our divine service, particularly during prayer and Torah study. Here, the Koretzer sees this issue in the wider context of maintaining one's mental focus on God in all circumstances—what is often called *devekut*, attachment to God. Arriving in an unfamiliar place may distract even the most dedicated meditators, as Abraham is supposed to be, from their mental and spiritual tasks.

COMMENT

The fear of God, that is, the awe of being in God's presence that keeps us from inappropriate behavior, is not achieved once and then possessed. It is a constant struggle. Our emotions get in the way, distract us; and we are sucked into fearing other things when we should be putting our trust in God. If even Abraham succumbed, we might ask, what hope do we have? But Abraham (and Sarah) came through it. The result of the story, if the Koretzer is correct, is that they were strengthened in their trust in God, because the end result demonstrated that they should have trusted all along.

---

[12] Silent Screaming

"Then God heard the voice of the child. . . ."

Genesis 21:17

CONTEXT

Ishmael and his mother, Hagar, have been expelled from Abraham and Sarah's camp. The provisions that Abraham had given them are exhausted, and in desperation Hagar casts Ishmael under a bush so she doesn't have to watch him die. An angel appears and declares that God has heard Ishmael's cry.

Menachem Mendel of Vorki was perhaps more famous for not speaking than for anything he said. He clearly believed that unnecessary talk should be curtailed; only talk of Torah should be encouraged. He was the son of Yitzchak of Vorki, founder of the dynasty.

I also heard [the following] on the verse "Then God heard the voice of the child" [Genesis 21:17] (for you will not find in the Torah that

Ishmael cried out or said anything at all). He [Menachem Mendel of Vorki] spoke as follows: "[It was] a still, silent scream." (And in fact, [this rabbi] was himself at this level, for he would always make a silent "hubbub" before the Blessed One, without cessation.)

Menachem Mendel of Vorki (d. 1868) in *Gedulat Mordechai uGedulat HaTzadikim* [The greatness of Mordechai and the greatness of the righteous] (Warsaw, 1934), pt. 2, p. 18, §45

NOTE

He would always make a silent "hubbub." For the rebbe of Vorki, true, heartfelt prayer does not have to be accompanied by shouts or other noises—in contrast to the practice of some Hasidic groups. For him, prayer is an internal process, and Ishmael's cry is an example.

COMMENT

The truest spiritual experiences, our deepest religious awakenings, are often beyond the power of words to express. The words, when they come, serve not only to explain, but also to confine our experience and reduce it to the routine. Thereafter, our conversation about that experience will tend to follow the initial lines we laid down when we first found words. Menachem Mendel of Vorki teaches us that silence is indeed golden, potentially bearing a wealth of meaning that words cannot carry.

Ḥayyei Sarah

[13] For All

"And the Eternal had blessed [et] Abraham with everything [bakol]."

Genesis 24:1

CONTEXT

With Sarah gone and laid to rest in the cave of Machpelah, Abraham now tries to make provision for the future by arranging Isaac's marriage. To this end, he delegates his servant to go back to Haran to find Isaac a wife from within his family. This verse sets the scene for Abraham's conversation with the servant.

Levi Yitzchak of Berditchev is one of the best-loved Hasidic teachers. A disciple of the Maggid of Mezritch, he became a leading light of the next generation. He established no dynasty, but his influence is still felt through his book and the many tales that circulate about him, often emphasizing his love for ordinary Jews.

There are righteous people whose whole desire is on behalf of the totality, and there are righteous people whose desire is for themselves. Abraham's desire was for the totality. Hence, [it says]: "And the Eternal had blessed [et] Abraham," that is to say, with Abraham "with everything [bakol]," for et, can mean "with." Our rabbis have alluded to this [when they taught] that Abraham our ancestor had a daughter [bat] and her name was Bakol, for bat can mean an "attribute" or a "measure," as in the verse "it contained two thousand bat" [1 Kings 7:26]. That is to say, his attribute is "her name was Bakol," for he bestowed goodness upon all things.

Levi Yitzchak of Berditchev (1740–1809), *Kedushat Levi* [The holiness of Levi] (Munkacs, 1829), p. 12c

On behalf of the totality . . . for themselves. A frequent theme of Hasidic sermons is the contrast between those people whose righteousness is directed outward, to the wider community and beyond, and to those whose focus is exclusively inward.

"And the Eternal had blessed [*et*] Abraham." The particle *et* is used in Hebrew most commonly to indicate the direct definite object of the verb. It has no equivalent in English and is therefore usually left untranslated (JPS: "And the Lord had blessed Abraham"). This is the case in the verse before us. However, sometimes *et* denotes "with," and Levi Yitzchak makes full use of this fact.

"With everything [*bakol*]." JPS: "in all things." The underlying question here is what does the Torah mean when it says that Abraham was blessed with everything? How can anyone be blessed with everything? The talmudic reply is referred to below. Levi Yitzchak's answer is more mystical. For him, as for all kabbalists, Abraham represents the *sefirah* of Hesed (Lovingkindness). "All" indicates Malchut (Shechinah). God blessed all things through Abraham, blessing him also in the process.

Our rabbis have alluded to this [when they taught] that Abraham our ancestor had a daughter [*bat*] and her name was Bakol. Talmud, *Bava Batra* 16b. In a kabbalistic context, "daughter" is a cipher for Malchut (Shechinah).

Bat can mean an "attribute" or a "measure." Levi Yitzchak says that the word *bat* can indicate a *middah*, either "attribute" or "measure."

"It contained two thousand *bat*." The reference is to the bowl of the washstand that stood in the Temple of Solomon. Here a *bat* is a unit of liquid measure.

His attribute is "her name was *Bakol*." In the lower world, Abraham embodied Hesed (Lovingkindness), which he bestowed generously on all. This is paralleled in the upper world, where the *sefirah* of Hesed bestows generously on Malchut (Shechinah).

COMMENT

Most people are good people, in my experience, but their goodness seems to be confined to their nearest and dearest friends and relatives. The truly good go beyond that, well beyond, and are concerned for their communities and for the world. By widening the circle of their concern, they not only benefit the world, they benefit the Shechinah, adding to the store of goodness upon which the continuation of civilization depends. Abraham is our guide in this work.

[14] Kindness and Compassion

"And if she says to me, 'You drink, and I will also draw for your camels'—let her be the woman whom the Eternal has singled out for my master's son."

Genesis 24:44

CONTEXT

Abraham's servant retells the tale of how he met Rebecca and realized that she was destined to be the wife of his master's son.

Zevi Elimelech of Dinov was a Hasidic teacher and leader in Galicia, Poland. His magnum opus, *Benei Yissachar*, deals with kabbalistic ramifications of the yearly events of the Jewish calendar. The text below comes from his discussion of *Shabbat HaGadol* (the "Great" Sabbath), which falls just before Passover.

There is a difference between the quality of Hesed [Lovingkindness] and that of Rachamim [compassion]. Rachamim is when people ask others for something they lack, and they [in turn] have compassion on them and give them what they want. This is not the case with the quality of Hesed, where people show kindness to each other even with regard to something they have not asked for. . . . [An example of this is] in the story of the servant and Rebecca. He set himself a sign of the young woman who gave him what he had not asked for, that is, when he said, "'and I will also draw for your camels'—let her be the woman whom the Eternal has singled out for my master's son." She would be appropriate to bring into the house of Abraham, the man of Hesed.

Zevi Elimelech of Dinov (1785–1841), *Benei Yissachar* [The sons of Issachar] (Jerusalem, 1983), v. 1, p. 51b

NOTE

Abraham, the man of Hesed. Abraham is associated with lovingkindness partly because of his attempt to save Sodom and Gomorrah from God's wrath, partly because he was said to be very hospitable (cf. Genesis 18:1), and also because there is a verse that links him to this attribute: "You will give truth to Jacob, lovingkindness [*hesed*] to Abraham" (Micah 7:20). In kabbalistic symbolism, Abraham is identified with the *sefirah* of the same name, Hesed. (*Rachamim*, on the other hand, represents Tiferet, where the energies of Hesed are mixed with their opposites from Gevurah or Din [Might or Strict Justice].)

COMMENT

The difference between these two positive qualities, as defined by the Dinover, is awareness of a need. If you have to be asked, it is because you are unaware of the need. If you give freely without being asked, it is because you have become aware of a need without it being put into words. Most of us, I suspect, would give generously if approached; how many of us could go one step further and give without being approached?

---

[15] God Sees Me

"Isaac comes from the way of the well of Lachai Ro'i."

Genesis 24:62

CONTEXT

Abraham's servant is returning to his master with Rebecca. On the way, they see Isaac from a distance. The Torah tells us where he was coming from when they saw him.

Moshe Hayyim Efraim of Sudylkov was a grandson of the Ba'al Shem Tov, one of two sons of his daughter Odel. He was a retiring man and never had a following, but his book remains a classic Hasidic source.

You might say that this alludes to what is written at the beginning of the *Shulchan Aruch*. . . : "'I have set the Eternal before me always' [Psalm 16:8] is the greatest principle of the Torah . . . , and that a person should imagine standing before a sovereign, for the 'whole earth is full of God's glory' [Isaiah 6:3], and the Blessed One sees all our deeds . . . and in this way, we may be filled with awe." See there.

You might say that this is alluded to here in this verse:

"Isaac"—meaning "awe," symbolized by Isaac;

"Comes"—to a person;

"From the well"—from that Source;

"*Lachai Ro'i*" [literally, "of the Living One who sees me"]—for you should always consider that you stand before the Living One of the Worlds, who sees and examines all your movements and deeds and actions. [It is from] this Source that your awe and submission spring, as mentioned above. Understand.

Moshe Hayyim Efraim of Sudylkov (d. 1800), *Degel Machaneh Efraim* [The flag of the camp of Ephraim (Numbers 2:18)] (Jerusalem, 1963), p. 33

NOTES

"Isaac comes." JPS: "Isaac had just come back." The present tense is required for the Sudylkover's interpretation.

Shulchan Aruch. "The Set Table." The preeminent medieval code of Jewish law by R. Yosef Karo (1488–1575), it is divided into four sections, the first of which is *Orach Hayyim* (The path of life), which presents the laws of everyday religious practice, *Shabbat*, and the festivals. Embedded in Karo's text is a running commentary, known as the *Mappah* (Tablecloth), by Moshe Isserles (ca. 1530–72). The passage quoted above comes from Isserles's comment on the very first paragraph of *Orach Hayyim* (1:1).

"I have set the Eternal before me always" (Psalm 16:8). In the literature of Jewish meditation, this verse is frequently quoted and held up as an ideal.

"Isaac"—meaning "awe." Isaac symbolizes the *sefirah* of Gevurah (Might), also known as Pachad or Yir'ah (Awe, Fear).

"From the well"—from that Source. I.e., God.

COMMENT

Keeping God's presence in mind always is where theology and morality meet. If we assimilate this notion into our lives, if we can live it rather than just pay lip service to it, it will help us avoid sin and selfishness.

Toledot

[16] Falsehood and Truth

*"The first one emerged red, like a hairy mantle all over; so
they called his name Esau. Then his brother emerged, holding
on to the heel of Esau, so they named him Jacob."*

Genesis 25:25–26

CONTEXT

Isaac's wife Rebecca has become pregnant after some initial problems
and then has a difficult pregnancy and labor. She is bearing twins who
struggle within her womb, and continue their struggle even during their
birth, and indeed throughout their lives. They are Esau and Jacob, and
from the start the Torah describes them as two very different people.

Moshe Hayyim Efraim of Sudylkov was the eldest of two sons of Odel,
the daughter of the Ba'al Shem Tov. His book, usually called simply the
Degel, is a Hasidic classic.

You ought to understand this difference: Regarding Esau, Scripture
says, "they called his name" [*vayikr'u*], but with regard to Jacob, it
says, "he called his name" [*vayikra'*], in the singular. Now, the exposition of the sages is well known, and there are some who say, by way
of a hint based on the midrash mentioned above, that Esau [*esav*] represents vanity [*shav*] and lies, and that this is hinted at in the verse
[in the word] *vayikr'u*, an expression of pulling and gathering, that
is, that the crowd is drawn after lies and vanity. But regarding Jacob,
who represents the attribute of truth, based on the verse "You will
give truth to Jacob" (Micah 7:20), *vayikra'* in the singular is written
because this one represents a small minority, or even one in a city,
who approaches the truth.

Moreover, you may say that falsehood [results] in separation, based
on the verse "a whisperer separates a close friend [*aluf*]" [Proverbs

16:28], that is, one. Thus, "and they called his name," which represents the separation [brought about by a] lie, which is called Esau, as mentioned above, for he causes separation. But truth is the opposite, for it binds and unites in perfect unity. Therefore, of Jacob it is written that he is truth, and "he called" is in the singular.

On the other hand, you may say that "he called his name Jacob" hints that he [Isaac] called upon the name of the Holy One. [Which raises the question]: Who is able to call the name of the blessed God? "Jacob," that is, one who is on the level of truth, as it is written, "The Eternal is close . . . to all who call God in truth" (Psalm 145:18). Understand.

Moshe Hayyim Efraim of Sudylkov (d. 1800), *Degel Machane Efraim* [The flag of the camp of Ephraim (Numbers 2:18)], (Jerusalem: 1963), p. 36

NOTES

The exposition of the sages is well known. *Bereshit Rabbah* 63:12 (in some editions, 63:8).

Esau [*esav*] represents vanity [*shav*] . In Hebrew the letters *shin* and *sin* look the same. In texts with vowels, they are distinguished only by whether they have a dot above the upper left-hand corner, or the right. The text of the midrash referred to in the previous note makes the pun on Esau's name (*Esav*, in Hebrew) for the first time in Rabbinic literature: "[God says,] 'It is for vanity [*shav*] that I created him in My world.'"

"A close friend [*aluf*]" (Proverbs 16:28), that is, one. *Aluf* is connected to *alef*, the first letter of the Hebrew alphabet, whose numerical value is one.

It binds and unites in perfect unity. Truth brings people together and binds them in perfect unity, providing a parallel to God's perfect unity.

You may say that "he called his name Jacob" hints. Moshe Hayyim Efraim treats this phrase as if it were two: "and he called his name [i.e., God's name]" and "Jacob."

"To all who call God in truth." The person who lives truth has the right to call upon the God of Truth.

COMMENT

"Misery loves company," they say, but the Sudylkover says that liars need company. Those who tell the truth, on the other hand, can have the confidence to stand alone. Truth connects us to God and to others; falsehood disconnects us from both, from God when we tell it, from others when it is discovered. But is this the way things work? Jacob was not a truthful person, at least not in his early years. Remember how he disguises himself to steal his brother's blessing. But he learns truthfulness: witness his speech before Pharaoh in Genesis 47. On the other hand, many people recognize the truth but do not have the courage to stand up for it. Like Jacob, they too must learn, learn to speak up for what is true, even if it means standing alone. God is on the side of truth. Ultimately truth triumphs, and the lone truth sayer can become a leader and an inspiration to us.

[17] Digging Our Own Wells

"And all the wells that his father's servants had dug in the days
of Abraham his father were filled up by the Philistines. . . . Then
Isaac returned and dug. . . . And he called it Esek [discord],
because they contended with him. Then he called it Sitnah
[hatred]. . . . Then he called it Rechovot [open spaces]."

Genesis 26:15,18,20–22

CONTEXT

Chapter 26 of Genesis, the only one in which we see Isaac as an active protagonist, is the record of his encounters with the Philistines and, in particular, the dispute that arises between them over the ownership of certain wells. Apart from a possible historical interest, what is the significance of this story?

Simchah Bunam of Pshische placed great emphasis on individuals developing their own personal spiritual paths. As if to illustrate this point, he was a bit of a maverick in the Hasidic world, dressing in Western European clothing, for example.

It appears [that] the interpretation is [as follows]: Any path that people make toward God must have an internal life force within it, and if it does not, it will not ascend. Now the Philistines wanted to walk in the paths of our ancestor Abraham, so they would act like our ancestor Abraham did, only without the internal life force in those acts. And this resulted in the stopping up of the path. Understand!

Now Isaac, our ancestor, wanted to dig this well, even though he had other paths to God from his own side. Nevertheless, he was not prevented from [re]digging the wells of his father, as it says. Afterward he himself dug wells, for every Israelite who approaches the service of the blessed God must dig a well with their own essence by which they may cling to the blessed and exalted Creator.

At first, this well will not be perfect from your soul's [point of view], for it will still [contain] good mixed with bad, from [within] yourself, and this is called "discord [*esek*] because they contend with[in] him" [Genesis 26:20]. Later, when you move on from this level where you have no hindrance from within yourself, then you are on the level of Hatred ["Sitnah," verse 21], where Satan opposes and confuses you. Later still, you are at the level of Spaciousness [*rechavah*], called Rechovot [verse 22], in accordance with the saying: "When the Eternal is pleased with a person's conduct, God turns even enemies into allies" (Proverbs 16[:7]). This is the secret of the wells.

Simchah Bunam of Pshische (d. 1827), *Kol Simchah* [The sound of joy (Jeremiah 7:33)] (Jerusalem: HaMesorah, 1986), p. 30

NOTES

"Then he called it Sitnah [hatred] ." Refers to a second well.

"Then he called it Rechovot [open spaces] ." A third well.

Internal life force. Human actions must be given a power from within if they are to "ascend," to have a spiritual impact in the "upper worlds." Merely imitating someone else's acts will not work.

From his own side. While Abraham represents the *sefirah* of Hesed, Isaac represents its opposite, the *sefirah* of Gevurah.

He was not prevented from [re] digging. It may be necessary to follow in someone else's footsteps (to change the metaphor) before setting out on one's own path.

At first, this well will not be perfect. The names given to the wells in the Torah text become signs of stages on one's spiritual journey. Each stage is part of the ongoing struggle toward real spiritual achievement. First we wrestle with our inner demons, and then with outward challenges, before finally reaching the stage of Spaciousness, when even our negative traits can be used for positive ends.

Hatred ["Sitnah," verse 21] , where Satan opposes. Sitnah and Satan share the same linguistic root.

COMMENT

Simchah Bunam has presented us with a road map to our own spiritual development. It may be a lonely journey, but certainly an important one. Each of us has our own path to walk, our own wells to dig, but we may begin by redigging those of others who went before us. First, you will encounter internal obstacles, for there is a part of ourselves that rebels against self-discipline and that craves self-indulgence; here we find inner conflict. Later, we may find that obstacles present themselves from outside. We find our way blocked by the needs and demands of others, or by their lack of understanding of our way. Finally, we may achieve spiritual spaciousness and freedom. If we neglect our spiritual journey, we will never become the people we could and should have become.

[18] Positive from Negative

"Then Esau went to Ishmael and took Machalat the daughter of Ishmael, sister of Nevayot, as his wife, in addition to his other wives."

Genesis 28:9

CONTEXT

After tricking his father into giving him the blessing meant for Esau, Jacob flees from his brother's wrath. He goes with Isaac's blessing and his command not to marry a Canaanite woman. Esau, learning of this command, decides likewise not to marry another Canaanite (he already has two Canaanite wives; Genesis 26:34) and instead marries his cousin Machalat, daughter of his uncle, Ishmael.

Mordechai Leiner was the founder of the Hasidic dynasty of Izbica-Radzyn. He was famous and controversial in his own time, partly because of his public break with his teacher, Menachem Mendel of Kotzk, and partly because of his challenging and novel ideas. The following passage is an example of those ideas.

It says in the midrash: "[She was called] Machalat because the Holy One had forgiven [*machal*] all his transgressions." The point here is that Esau's character was murderous and Ishmael's character was adulterous, but look here: all the deficient qualities that exist in the world have a good side. For example, the root of anger: even though it is evil, nevertheless it has its good side, because you might also become angry against those who transgress the will of the Blessed God. And the root of adultery, although it is also evil, nevertheless it has its good side, for the flaw with adultery is that you are doing good in a place where it is not the will of the Blessed God [that you do so]. Therefore, it has a good side, because the good have permission to do good.

Mordechai Yosef Leiner of Izbica (1800–54), *Mei HaShiloach* [The waters of the Siloam (Isaiah 8:6)] (Bnei Brak, 1995), v. 1, pp. 37–38

NOTES

It says in the midrash. *Bereshit Rabbah* 67:13.

Esau's character was murderous. This view of Esau is typical of traditional Jewish literature. See, e.g., *Bereshit Rabbah* 63:12.

Ishmael's character was adulterous. Also a typical opinion in Rabbinic texts. See *Bereshit Rabbah* 53:11.

The good have permission to do good. It is a matter of the right act in the right time. (In the continuation of these comments, R. Mordechai argues that the forgiveness Esau achieves is so that he can remove the good aspects of himself to concentrate on the evil.)

COMMENT

I find this one of the most extraordinary teachings of an extraordinary Hasidic teacher. From passages like this it is easy to see why copies of the first edition of this work were burnt by other Hasidim. Here we see the Izbicer Rebbe apparently rehabilitating the reputations of two of the most hated characters of the Genesis narrative, at least as seen through Rabbinic tradition, but even more astonishingly, he also points out the positive uses or origins of anger, and, stranger still, adultery. If all things originate with God, it is hard to maintain an alternative position; if one is to be consistent, then anger and adultery must have their positive place.

Most people are not deliberately wicked. When we go astray, it often has less to do with a desire to do evil than with a wish to do good that has become distorted. Sins need to be atoned for, despite our original good intentions. But the recognition of those good intentions may help us to forgive ourselves.

Va-yetse'

[19] You Are a Ladder

"And look, there was a ladder standing upon the earth with its head reaching up to heaven, and the angels of God were ascending and descending on it."

Genesis 28:12

CONTEXT

Fleeing his twin brother's anger, Jacob heads for his maternal uncle's home in Haran, toward an uncertain future. One night on his journey he experiences a dream of a ladder reaching to heaven.

This passage comes from Yishayah Horowitz's *Shnei Luchot HaBrit*. He was a rabbi, teacher, and popular author from Prague. In the section titled *"Bayit HaGadol"* (The great house), he addresses the issue of human psychology in the light of Rabbinic and kabbalistic teaching.

> Look here, a human being [*adam*] is a ladder "standing upon the earth with its head reaching up to heaven," that is, the Holy One took the human body from the earth [*adamah*], from the site of the altar of earth, that it might be sanctified. But the head, that is, the soul, is from the highest heights.

Yishayah HaLevi Horowitz (ca. 1570–1626), *Shnei Luchot HaBrit* [The two tablets of the covenant (Deuteronomy 9:9,11)] (1863; repr., Jerusalem: 1975), *"Bayit HaGadol,"* v. 1, p. 27b

NOTES

A human being [*adam*] ... from the earth [*adamah*]. This wordplay is found in the Torah itself: in Genesis 2:7, Adam, the first human, is made from *adamah*, "earth."

The altar of earth. An altar of earth for sacrifices to God is prescribed in Exodus 20:21. According to a number of Rabbinic sources, God took the earth to make Adam from the site where the altar of earth would later stand in the Temple. See Jerusalem Talmud, *Nazir* 35b; Midrash Tanchuma (Warsaw), *Tsav* §14.

The soul, is from the highest heights. Horowitz follows this universalistic sentiment by asserting, in clear contradiction to the Adam and Eve story, that the term "human being" (*adam*) applies only to Jews. Sadly, such views are not unknown in Jewish mystical literature.

COMMENT

Human beings are composed of body and soul. The body has its origins in the physical aspects of the earth, the soul has its origins in heaven. Each of us is therefore like Jacob's ladder, with our feet on earth and our heads in heaven.

We are physical as well as spiritual beings. So much of our time and effort is devoted to our physical aspect, and that is fair enough. We need physical well-being as a prerequisite for life and creativity. But we also have a spiritual aspect, and we often neglect it. Horowitz's metaphor challenges us to pay more attention to our spiritual needs, to understand our dual nature.

---

[20] "The Young Woman with No Eyes"

"Leah had weak eyes, but Rachel was shapely and beautiful."
Genesis 29:17

CONTEXT

Jacob approaches Haran where his mother's brother, Laban, lives. At a well, he asks some shepherds if they know him. They do, and as they answer, Laban's daughter Rachel arrives. For Jacob, it is love at first sight. He rolls a massive stone away from the wellhead—a job that would normally require the combined strength of all the shepherds—just to impress her. Laban invites Jacob to work for him, and just before Jacob asks to be allowed to work for Rachel's hand in marriage, the Torah pauses to tell us of the relative beauty of Laban's two daughters, Leah and Rachel.

Naftali Hertz Bacharach was born in Frankfort, but spent many years in Poland. He was a great kabbalist, with a special interest in the mystical and magical aspects of Kabbalah. The text that I have chosen is embedded in a discussion about the mystical significance of the tzitzit, the fringe worn at each corner of the tallit (prayer shawl). The worshiper is meant to look at them each morning while reciting the Torah passage that commands their use, Numbers 15:37–51.

This is the mystical meaning of the verse: "Leah had weak eyes, but Rachel was shapely and beautiful" [Genesis 29:17], yet [Rachel's] eyes are not mentioned! Therefore, she is called "the beautiful young woman with no eyes." We, her servants, have to make her eyes with our intentions. This riddle is mentioned at the beginning of *Sava deMishpatim*, where Rabbi Yose is amazed at the riddle. He thinks that this [refers to] ordinary matters and is almost punished. But it is in fact a mystical secret.

Naftali Hertz ben Ya'akov Elchanan Bacharach (seventeenth century),
Emek HaMelech [The valley of the sovereign] (Amsterdam, 1653), p. 154a

NOTES

"Leah had weak eyes, but Rachel was shapely and beautiful." These sisters symbolize the *sefirot* of Binah, also known as the "upper Shechinah," and Malchut, the "lower Shechinah," respectively. Rachel thus represents the Presence of God in this world.

"The beautiful young woman with no eyes." As Bacharach states, this image is found in the section of the Zohar titled *Sava deMishpatim* (see next note). No mention is made there of Leah and Rachel.

We, her servants, have to make her eyes with our intentions. This is Bacharach's interpretation of the image of the beautiful young woman, based on the Lurianic tradition. "Our intentions" refers to the *kavanot*, the mystical meditations to accompany the performance of rituals and the recital of prayers with the purpose of producing positive effects in the upper realm of the *sefirot*.

This riddle is mentioned at the beginning of *Sava deMishpatim*. This work, whose translation is "The Old Man of Mishpatim," is an extended mystical exposition of the laws found in *parashat* Mishpatim (Exodus 21ff.), presented in a narrative framework. In Zohar II, 94b, a mysterious old man asks a pair of rabbis a series of riddles, including: "Who is the beautiful young woman with no eyes?" Later on (II, 99a–b), the answer is given: the Torah is like a beautiful woman with no eyes, i.e., with no eyes upon her, because she is hidden away and only reveals herself to her lover, and then only fleetingly.

Like her, the Torah reveals her mystical secrets only to adepts who are dedicated to study and open to mystical insight. Most Zohar commentators, however, understand "the beautiful young woman with no eyes" as a symbol of the Shechinah in this world, and it is this sense that Bacharach has in mind. This is not such a great leap, as the Torah itself is a symbol of the Shechinah in that it too is a manifestation of the divine in the created universe.

Rabbi Yose. In *Sava deMishpatim*, Rabbi Yose meets Rabbi Chiyya and complains that the old man, a donkey driver, has been annoying him with stupid questions. Rabbi Chiyya is open to the possibility that the old man may be more than he seems, but Rabbi Yose is not, at least not until the old man begins his discourse.

COMMENT

The Shechinah (the Presence of God) may seem an elusive concept. On the one hand, she/it is everywhere and, therefore, undifferentiated. She is the same everywhere. Because of that, it is easy to ignore her, to be unaware of her. The Presence of God, as it were, dies. Only when we remember that we are in the presence of God, as we are always and everywhere, does she come alive. The Shechinah is everywhere, but our minds are often elsewhere. By thinking of ourselves as being in that Presence, we remind ourselves of our obligations to kindness, truth, justice, and so forth, and we may begin to act more righteously. We become her eyes, noticing need and wrongs, and trying to address them.

---

[21] Coming and Going in Thought

"By day, heat consumed me, and cold by night; sleep fled from my eyes."
Genesis 31:40

CONTEXT

In response to Laban's accusation that Jacob has stolen his household goods, the Patriarch replies angrily with a list of the hardships he has endured while working for his father-in-law.

Uri of Strelisk was a disciple of Shlomo of Karlin as well as a Hasidic teacher in his own right. His fiery prayer style led to him being nicknamed "the Seraph."

[R. Uri of Strelisk] said: "People always have to be in a state of 'coming and going' [Ezekiel 1:14]."

Then he told a story: "Once a soldier went on guard duty at the entrance to a general's [quarters] on a winter's night, for it is the practice of kings and princes to have people constantly at the entrances [to] their [quarters]. The soldier said to himself, 'I have no luck at all! For, "by day, heat consumes me, and cold by night; sleep flees from my eyes" (Genesis 31:40). If I were appointed to some slightly higher rank, I would have altogether more rest from these things.' But then he reconsiders his words and realizes that there would be more drawbacks to such a slightly higher appointment, and so he moves from one level to another, higher level, yet never finds rest for his soul. If he were the king himself, then he would have complete rest! But then he reconsiders this, and finds more and more drawbacks and worries. In this way, he comes to appreciate that it is better for him to be a soldier, the lowest of the low. In exactly this way must a Jewish person be 'coming and going,' at each and every moment."

Uri of Strelisk (the Seraph) (d. 1826), *Sefer Imrei Kadosh* [The book of the sayings of a holy man] (Netanya, 2001), p. 59

NOTE

"Coming and going." This phrase comes from Ezekiel 1:14, part of the prophet's vision of the chariot of God, recounted in the opening chapters of his book. The original subject was the fantastic four-faced creatures that accompanied the chariot on its journeys. Hasidic texts regularly employ this phrase to indicate the constantly shifting focus of human consciousness and fluctuating nature of the human life force.

COMMENT

Uri of Stelisk is of the opinion that we cannot help complaining and imagining how things might be better for us. We are constantly doing this, he says. We imagine that a better job would give us more leisure, but it would only bring more responsibilities and more anxiety. In fact, he says we have to undergo this mental process. Why? So that we can appreciate where we are, the position that we have reached; however lowly it may seem, it has its advantages.

Each role, each station in life, brings its own responsibilities and anxieties. Our society encourages personal ambition, even selfishness. This teaching by Uri of Stelisk reminds us of the personal dangers inherent in ambition. He urges us to consider carefully before we seek to "improve" our standing in society, in our workplace, in our community. Perhaps the cost will be too high. And there is a wider message here, too, for capitalist societies. Achieving our industrial, commercial, and economic goals also brings greater responsibilities and anxieties. Concerns about the global economy and the environment multiply. We need to realize, in Rabbi Michael Lerner's words, that "we have, and are, enough."

Va-yishlaḥ

---

[22] Prayers Are Messengers

"Jacob sent messengers before him to Esau his brother toward the land of Seir, the country of Edom."

Genesis 32:4

CONTEXT

After all the years Jacob spent working for his uncle/father-in-law Laban, he now heads for home. But he is troubled by the memory of how he treated his twin brother, Esau. Will Esau remember how Jacob swindled him out of his birthright and stole his blessing? Is he still angry? Jacob sends messengers and gifts to try to placate Esau, just in case.

Aharon II of Karlin was the fourth leader of the Karliner Hasidim, the first Hasidic dynasty founded in Lithuania, by his grandfather, also called Aharon.

> Look here, since it is stated that Ahasuerus is called the Holy One, it is obvious that we can say that Esau [*'EiSav*] represents the Holy One, for God alone has done, does, and will do [*'aSaH ve'oSeH veya'aSeH*] all deeds. Hence, it says, "Jacob sent messengers before him to Esau his brother" [Genesis 32:4], for every day, a person must pray before the Holy One, and not say, "I already prayed yesterday." Rather, every day things should appear new to you.
>
> Prayers are called "messengers" (or, "angels"), because with each and every word that issues from the mouth of a righteous person an angel is formed, which is then dispatched to the Holy One.

Aharon (II) ben Asher of Karlin (d. 1872), *Beit Aharon* [Aaron's house] (Brody, 1875; repr., Jerusalem, 1990), p. 21

Ahasuerus is called the Holy One. Ahasuerus is the name given to the Persian king in the book of Esther. The midrash (*Esther Rabbah* 3:10) suggests that whenever the book mentions King Ahasuerus by name it refers only to him, but that when it simply says "the king" it may refer to Ahasuerus or to God. From this, it is just a short jump to the notion that Ahasuerus represents God.

It is obvious. It is extraordinary that the Karliner should say "it is obvious . . . that Esau represents the Holy Blessed One"! It is not obvious; usually in Rabbinic and medieval Jewish literature, Esau is a villain, representing the hated oppressor, Rome, and later, Christianity.

Esau [*EiSav*] represents the Holy One. The meaning of Esau's name is not known, but the Karliner connects it to the root *'aSaH* (to make, do), with which it shares two consonants, *'ayin* and *sin*. Hence he has free rein to identify Esau with God, who is the only true Maker or Doer in the universe.

COMMENT

If Esau represents God, then the messengers that Jacob sent to him must represent prayers. Our prayers should never be allowed to grow stale; every day is new, and our prayers should reflect that. Our prayers are like messengers or angels (the word is the same in Hebrew), because like the angels, they are a channel of communication between us and God — the angels come from God to us, and our prayers go from us to God.

Prayers should be new every day. If they are not, boredom soon sets in, and no spiritual progress is made. Does that mean that the words of prayer have to be new every day? No, but the thoughts we have around them must be new. We have to invigorate the prayers we recite precisely because they are angels, messengers to God, sent by us. They are our link to the world of the spirit.

[23] Houses for the Soul

"Then he built a house for himself, but for his cattle he made shelters."
Genesis 33:17

CONTEXT

Peace between Esau and Jacob has been established, and they go their separate ways, Esau to Seir and Jacob to Sukkot. There Jacob builds a house and shelters (*sukkot*) for his cattle, and gives the settlement the name Sukkot.

Shalom of Belz was the rabbi of that Galician town as well as the founder of the Hasidic dynasty centered on it. His was a popular and magnificent Hasidic court, but he was also known as a distinguished talmudist.

A human being's service [to God] is to repair the bit of soul that is within. Although a human being requires the things of this world, for without them that bit of soul could not exist, nevertheless, the essence of service is to see to the repair of the soul. Through the doing of commandments and good deeds, one builds "houses" and pleasant structures for the soul. This is alluded to in the verse, "then he built a house for himself," that is, he made a house for himself, which is the essential thing, "but for his cattle," that is, the things of this world, which are subordinate, "he made shelters."

Shalom Rokeach of Belz (d. 1855), *MaHaRaSH miBelza* [Our teacher, the rabbi, Shalom of Belz], ed. Yisra'el Klepholtz (Bnei Brak, 1987), pt. 1, p. 219

NOTES

"He built a house for himself . . . for his cattle he made shelters." Why does the Torah tell us that Jacob built a house for himself, but only shelters for the cattle? The mention of the shelters alone would have been sufficient to explain the name the Patriarch gave to the settlement.

He made a house for himself. I.e., for his soul.

COMMENT

Our society teaches us to be concerned with the things of this world, our standard of living, so called. It seems to measure our worth by how much money we have, how big our house or our car is, which famous or powerful people we know. The Belzer calls us to regard those things as transitory, as indeed they are. Instead, we need to concentrate on the things that really matter: the good deeds we do that make this world a better, less material, more spiritual place.

[24] How to Love God

"Because he [Shechem] took delight in Jacob's daughter."

Genesis 34:19

CONTEXT

One day, while Jacob and his family are camped near the town of Shechem, his daughter, Dinah, goes out to visit friends. A young man from the town, also called Shechem, son of the town's chief, sees her, wants her, and sleeps with her. Is it rape or consensual? Whatever the case, it is an affront to the honor of Jacob and his family. Shechem loves Dinah. He delegates his father, Hamor, to ask Jacob for her hand in marriage. Jacob agrees, on condition that all the men of the town of Shechem are circumcised. Hamor and Shechem agree to the condition, and persuade their fellow townsmen to agree too. However, two of Dinah's brothers, Simeon and Levi, are very unhappy. In revenge for their sister's defilement, they attack Shechem, killing all the men while they are recovering from their operations. Jacob is very angry, and he leads his family to Bethel in a successful effort to avoid any reprisals. What does this horrific story have to teach us?

Hayyim of Kosov followed in the footsteps of his father and grandfather to become rabbi of the town of Kosov and leader of the Hasidic community there.

It says in the Midrash Rabbah:

"The Holy One loves Israel with three expressions of love: attachment, desire, and delight. Attachment: 'But you are attached to the Eternal your God' [Deuteronomy 4:4]. Desire: 'the Eternal did not desire you . . . because you were more in number than any people' [Deuteronomy 7:7]. Delight: 'And all nations shall call you happy; for you shall be a delightful land' [Malachi 3:12]."

From this passage we may learn how to serve the Blessed One with attachment, desire, and delight, and to give our soul for the Blessed One, like that wicked man [Shechem] gave his soul for his lust.

Hayyim ben Menachem Mendel of Kosov (1795–1844), *Torat Hayyim* [The Torah of life] (Ordea, Rumania: 1927), pp. 9–10

In the Midrash Rabbah. *Bereshit Rabbah* 80:7. In the continuation not quoted here, the midrash goes on to demonstrate how the same qualities that characterize God's love for Israel are also present in Shechem's love for Dinah. Hayyim of Kosov, however, turns the midrash on its head. The distinguishing characteristics of God's love for Israel, he believes, are a recipe for the love we should have for God.

COMMENT

Under the name of ambition, Western society fosters lust: lust for power, lust for material goods, lust for sex without consequences. While ambition may be good if not turned into an idol, lust only destroys. It destroys the object of the lust and the one who lusts. And often others are destroyed in the process. But what would happen if we could apply that level of commitment and emotion that we use in support of our lust to the love God? The love of God should bring in its wake not fanaticism and intolerance, but humility and the acceptance of others. Ambition would then be directed toward real self-improvement and the benefit of all members of society and the earth itself.

Va-yeshev

---

[25] Renewed Each Day

"Joseph was seventeen years old . . . and he was a young man."

Genesis 37:2

CONTEXT

Joseph now moves to the fore. He is a seventeen-year-old with a strong sense of his own importance, but why does the Torah also tell us that he is a young man? Surely that is obvious! Perhaps it means that even though at seventeen he might have been considered an adult in those times, he still behaved as a youth. Or perhaps there is another explanation.

Rabbi Aharon II of Karlin, named after his grandfather who founded the dynasty, brought Karliner Hasidism to its greatest influence.

This was because every day he was like a young man [as in the verse] "I was a young man, though now I am old" [Psalm 37:25]. You must renew yourself at every moment, as Scripture says: "May your youth be renewed like an eagle's" [Psalm 103:5]. Therefore, Israel may be compared to the moon, as it is renewed at every moment. And so we say "it is crown of beauty in honor of those who were carried by God from the womb." And what is the meaning of this renewal? That its light is diminished in order that it may be renewed later more strongly.

Human service [of God] should be like this. After the day has passed, you think: What was it about and what service have I accomplished? You start your service on the next day anew and begin with new deeds and a renewed struggle against the inclination toward evil, as if you had done nothing before.

During this discourse, he told a story of our teacher Sa'adiah Ga'on, who was staying with a certain householder, etc., and how each day he would repent for the day that was before him.

"And this is the teaching for human beings" [2 Samuel 7:19] for each day until the end of time, and this is [the meaning of] "young man."

Aharon (II) ben Asher of Karlin (d. 1872), *Beit Aharon* [Aaron's house] (Brody, 1875; repr., Jerusalem, 1990), p. 76

NOTES

"May your youth be renewed like an eagle's." The biblical *nesher* may refer to the griffin vulture rather than the eagle, but in this verse it seems to have phoenixlike qualities.

Israel may be compared to the moon. This comparison is common in Rabbinic literature. See, e.g., *Shemot Rabbah* 15:22,27. In the Kabbalah, the Shechinah (the *sefirah* of Malchut) is symbolized by both the moon and the Community of Israel.

And so we say "it is crown of beauty." A quotation from *Kiddush Levanah* (the Sanctification of the New Moon), a traditional service usually performed before the tenth day of the Hebrew month, preferably on a Saturday evening.

It is crown of beauty. I.e., the moon.

Sa'adiah Ga'on. Egyptian born (892–942), he rose to fame as a head of yeshivah in Babylonia (Iraq). The first of the great medieval Jewish philosophers, he was also prominent in many other fields.

He would repent for the day that was before him. It is unclear whether this refers to Sa'adiah Ga'on or his host.

"And this is the teaching." This is the lesson we should learn.

COMMENT

Life can seem stale. We get into routines. They can be comfortable, but they can be traps, keeping our minds in check. Judaism, with its focus on daily ritual acts may be especially liable to foster such routines. Rabbi Aharon urges us to renew ourselves each day, to rededicate ourselves, to see each day as a new beginning and ourselves as new people.

[26] Rebound

"Then they [Joseph's brothers] sent the coat of many colors, and
it was taken to their father, and they said, 'We found this.'"
Genesis 37:32

CONTEXT

As Joseph comes to meet his brothers, they are plotting to do away with
him. When he comes into reach, they grab him, strip off the special
coat his father had given him, and put him into a pit with the intention
of killing or selling him. They dip the coat into the blood of a goat and
bring it to show Jacob, so that he can draw the inference that Joseph
has been attacked by a predator.

Reuven Hoeschke was an anthologist and descendant of the Torah
commentator Efraim of Luntshits. Here he has abbreviated a source in
the Zohar, the preeminent text of Kabbalah.

Said R. Yehudah: Because of the anxiety that Jacob had caused Isaac, his
father, Jacob was punished via the affair of Joseph, for at that moment
he [Jacob] suffered great anxiety. "They said to him, 'We found this.'"
[Genesis 37:32]. Isaac said: "Who? Where is [*efo*] [the one who hunted
game . . .]?" [Genesis 27:33]. Jacob was punished with *efoh*, for it is
written: "Where [*efoh*] are they pasturing their flocks?" [Genesis 37:16].
And there Joseph [unwittingly] brought about [Jacob's] punishment.

Reuven Hoeschke (seventeenth century), ed., *Yalkut Re'uveni* [Reuven's
collection] (Warsaw, 1883), pt. 1, pp. 310–11 (based on Zohar I, 144b)

NOTES

The anxiety that Jacob had caused Isaac. By pretending to be Esau and thus
deceiving Isaac into giving him the blessing intended for the firstborn son.

"We found this." "This" indicates Joseph's bloodstained coat.

Isaac said. He said this when Esau arrived at his bedside with food after Jacob's deception.

"Where is [*efo*]?" JPS: "Who was it then that hunted game and brought it to
me?" *Efo* (with an *alef* as the last letter) actually means "then," but the Zohar connects it with its homonym, *efoh* (last letter *heh*), meaning "where."

"Where [*efoh*] are they pasturing their flocks?" This is the question that
Joseph puts to an unnamed man when he is unable to find his brothers.
Without the directions the man gave him, Joseph would never have fallen
into their trap.

COMMENT

We often make decisions without being able, or even trying, to consider
the consequences, which are sometimes, even frequently, beyond our
capacity to fathom. Many decisions may not matter a great deal, but
others may have ramifications that go on for years or longer. In Jacob's
story we see how deceit and deception come back at him in later life.
We don't know if his sons were ever deceived by him, but they seem to
have learned the art of deception from a master, and who would that
be if not their father? Perhaps their uncle, Laban. But the deceptions
he perpetrated on Jacob may also have been part of the payback Jacob
was due for his ill treatment of Isaac and Esau. Psychological and ecological studies, at different ends of the continuum, have demonstrated
the importance of seemingly unimportant decisions. An untimely or
uncalled-for rebuke of a child might cause deep distress. The wrong
choice of food products might bring in its wake health or environmental issues. We cannot escape consequences. We can only do our best to
try to anticipate them, minimize the possible negative ones, and then
trust in God that we are doing the right thing. There is hope: Jacob the
trickster becomes Jacob the tricked and, finally, Israel the Patriarch.

---

[27] The Double Test

"The Eternal was with Joseph; he became a successful man,
and was in the house of his master the Egyptian."

Genesis 39:2

CONTEXT

Joseph is the archetypal self-made man, working his way up in Egyptian
society from slave to high official, second only to Pharaoh. As he begins
his ascent up the ladder, we read that God was with him, he was doing very well, but he was still in his master's house, that is, still a slave.

Simchah Bunam was a Hasidic leader in the generation of Eastern European Jews who were beginning to be influenced by the Western ideas of the Enlightenment. During that period, some Jews were becoming wealthier due to growth in trade with the West, but others were still poor.

That is to say, that he stood up to the two tests that the Eternal was with him, that is, [God was] in his heart, both at the time when he was "a successful man," at the heights, and at the time that he was "in the house of his master the Egyptian," at the lowest level.

Simchah Bunam of Pshische (1765–1827), *Midrash Simchah* [Simchah's interpretation] (Jerusalem: Mossad HaRYM Levin, 1988), v. 1, p. 66

NOTE

"The Eternal was with Joseph." If God was with Joseph, why does it say both that he was successful and that he was still a slave? God's presence "with" someone in biblical texts usually indicates material success. That works fine with the second phrase, but the third phrase ("was in the house of his master") seems to contradict this.

COMMENT

In Eastern Europe in the eighteenth and nineteenth centuries, most, though by no means all, of our ancestors were religious, and a great many of them were also very poor. Was this a coincidence? No doubt many other factors were at work, but perhaps one of them was that in their poverty they felt a strong dependence on God. Later, at the turn of the twentieth century, when they emigrated to the United States, Britain, and elsewhere, many of them gradually ceased to be religious, though again by no means all. Once again, there were many factors, but perhaps one of them was that they slowly became more prosperous. Today, when most Jews are more prosperous than they have ever been, much of the Jewish community is seriously lacking in spirituality. We Jews may have felt that God was with us "in the house of our master," but what about now when we are "successful"?

Mikkets

---

[28] The Light of Consciousness

*"At the end of two years, Pharaoh had a dream, and
look, he was standing by the Nile [ha-ye'or]."*

Genesis 41:1

CONTEXT

In prison Joseph has successfully interpreted two of his fellow inmates'
dreams. As predicted, the baker goes to his death and the butler goes
back to his old job at Pharaoh's side. Despite his promise to remember
Joseph, the butler completely forgets him—until Pharaoh has a dream
that needs interpreting. The dream begins with Pharaoh standing on
the bank of the Nile.

Simchah Bunam of Pshische felt that he was reviving the essence of
Hasidism after it had been in decline. Hence his call to repentance in
this text.

> On this, . . . Simchah Bunam of Pshische said the following: Every Jew
> should make an end to years of slumber, [and] instead, do everything
> in a revealed, wide-awake manner—this refers to repentance—and
> "stand by the light ['or]," "standing by the *ye'or*." "The commandment
> is a lamp and the Torah is light" [Proverbs 6:23]. Thus far his words.
> "Words from a wise person's mouth are gracious" [Ecclesiastes 10:12].
> The enlightened person will understand.

> Yo'etz Kayyam Kadish Rokotz, ed., *Siach Sarfei Kodesh* [The conversation of
> the holy seraphim] (n.p., n.d.), pt. 3, p. 128

NOTES

"Stand by the light ['or]," "standing by the *ye'or*." He is connecting *ye'or*
(the Nile) with *'or* (light).

"Words from a wise person's mouth are gracious." . . . The enlightened person will understand. These two expressions are regularly found at the end of Hasidic expositions. The first indicates that you should remember the holy person with whom this teaching originated, and therefore respect and follow it, and the second that you should go and meditate on it, if you wish to be enlightened. (Obviously, the editor added these last two sentences.)

COMMENT

Habits can be helpful, allowing us to perform regular and frequent tasks without having to give them too much thought. That may be fine with respect to putting out the garbage or making a cup of coffee, but when it comes to religious rituals, prayer for instance, habits may deaden the mind and deprive those rituals of their power. I believe strongly in the importance of daily prayer, but sometimes it can sink to the level of mechanically repeating words from a prayer book while I think of something else. That defeats the purpose of the exercise. Simchah Bunam challenges us to keep our minds from wandering and to give our thoughts over to what we are doing, whether it is prayer or some mundane task.

---

[29] Broken Torah

"Then Jacob saw that there was grain [shever] in Egypt,
and said to his sons, . . . 'Go down there and buy us
some from there, that we may live and not die.'"
Genesis 42:1–2

CONTEXT

Joseph, now second-in-command in Egypt, gathers together the surplus grain through the seven good years he has predicted, in preparation for the seven bad years still to come. Then the famine starts. In Canaan, the famine is severe too, so Jacob, on the strength of news of Egyptian plenty, dispatches his sons (minus Benjamin, the youngest) to purchase grain.

Menachem Mendel of Vitebsk was a prominent student of the Maggid of Mezritch. He was one of the main leaders of the Hasidic movement in Ukraine until his emigration to the Land of Israel with a group of Hasidim and others in 1777.

"In [or, 'with'] the beginning" (Genesis 1:1)—with the Torah, called the "beginning of God's way" (Proverbs 8:22), did the Holy One create the universe. Therefore, all the worlds were created through the Torah, and the power of the Actor is latent in that which has been acted upon. In that case, the power of the Torah exists in every world and in every thing, because it [represents] the power of the Actor, and hence it is written: "This is the Torah: a person" (Numbers 19:14), for a person is the Torah, as the Blessed One below. "The Torah and the Holy One are one;" therefore, the Holy One is in everything, as it is written: "And You give life to them all" (Nehemiah 9:6). God concentrated [the divine essence], as it were, down to the lowest level and placed "a portion of divinity from above" in the midst of the "tabernacle" of matter. Thus, every pleasure is, as it were, essentially a raising of lower levels upward, for "light is superior to darkness" (Ecclesiastes 2:13).

This is the meaning of the descent of Joseph into Egypt [*MiTZRaYiM*]—into the boundary of the sea [*MeTZeR YaM*], meaning, the lowest level. We have already said that everything was created through the Torah, and that the power of Actor is latent in that which has been acted upon, and that everything contains within it the letters of the Torah that give it existence and life, and that without that, they would be nothing and chaos. Truly did [the sages] say, "The unripe fruit of the supernal wisdom is Torah," for there is Torah that is "unripe fruit."

Hence, "Then Jacob saw that there was grain [*shever*] in Egypt"—he saw that there was broken Torah [*Torah shevurah*] in Egypt, the "unripe fruit," as it says, "So he said, . . . Go down there"—for they went down there in order to repair, elevate, and bring it back to its own life force. Hence, "that we may live."

Menachem Mendel of Vitebsk (1730–88), *Likkutei Amarim* [Collected sayings] (Jerusalem, 1969), p. 40b

NOTES

"In [or, 'with'] the beginning." The opening word of Genesis in Hebrew is *B'Reishit*, where *B'* is a preposition and *Reishit* a noun (meaning, "beginning"). *B'* can be translated as "in" or "with," indicating instrumentality.

With the Torah, called the "beginning of God's way" (Proverbs 8:22). The notion that *Reishit* in this text indicates the Torah goes back at least as far as Rabbinic times. See *Bereshit Rabbah* 1:1, where the same verse from Proverbs is employed as a prooftext.

"This is the Torah: a person." JPS: "This is the ritual: When a person dies in a tent." (The Hebrew of our text gives the biblical reference incorrectly as Numbers 17:14.)

For a person is the Torah, as the Blessed One below. Human beings may become manifestations of Torah, and therefore, of God.

"The Torah and the Holy One are one." Zohar II, 60b.

"A portion of divinity from above." A phrased recycled from Job 31:2.

Every pleasure. All the pleasures of life have the potential to elevate this world spiritually.

Everything contains within it the letters of the Torah. This concept is perhaps unique to Hasidism.

The unripe fruit. An alternative understanding might be "incomplete form." *Bereshit Rabbah* 44:17.

In Egypt, the "unripe fruit." Just as the Torah, the Five Books of Moses, is the "unripe fruit" of divine wisdom, so too Egyptian culture, with all its idolatry, contains the "unripe fruit" of Torah. (In Rabbinic literature, Egypt was considered the archetypal home of idolatry and magic.)

Back to its own life force. I.e., reconnect the "broken Torah" to its source in the supernal wisdom.

Hence, "that we may live." The passage continues with a discussion of Joseph's descent into Egypt, and his death and mummification, in the light of the doctrine of the Torah's presence in everything.

COMMENT

We know from archaeology that ancient Egypt was a great civilization. Menachem Mendel of Vitebsk lived just before some of the great discoveries that brought that civilization and its achievements to light. Nevertheless, his theology, his belief that everything is filled with God, and therefore with Torah, meant that he had to recognize divinity even in idolatry. Such divinity may be "broken" or "unripe," that is, it is distorted and pale in comparison with Judaism, but it is still divinity. Modern secular life, for all its undoubted benefits, is largely godless. Yet might there not be elements of divinity even in its materialist excesses? Perhaps modern science and technology, modern art and music, modern literature and entertainment, and modern business and enterprise are all manifestations of "broken Torah" and the "unripe fruits" of Torah. Our involvement with them must be like Jacob's descent into Egypt, undertaken with the intention of purifying and spiritualizing them.

[30] The Importance of Truth

"And you [ve'atem], go up in peace to your father."

Genesis 44:17

CONTEXT

As his brothers leave Egypt for the second time, Joseph gives orders for his silver goblet to be placed in Benjamin's sack. He is testing his brothers to see if they will support Benjamin in the way they had failed to support him. So, he sends his men after them to arrest the one in possession of the goblet. Of course, it is found and all the brothers are then brought back to Joseph's palace. The "Egyptian" says that Benjamin must remain as a captive, but the others may return home to their father.

Yitzchak Podvah was a Hasidic teacher and anthologist who perished in the Holocaust. The Shpole Zayde, R. Aryeh Leib, was known as a miracle worker in his own day, and was felt to have a close affinity with the common people. It is not clear to me who is meant by the phrase "the holy rabbi of Lublin"; perhaps it refers to R. Ya'akov Yitzchak, the Seer of Lublin.

> Now, *'aTeM*, [you] has the same letters as *'eMeT* [truth], [because] it is through truth that you get up and strive to do the will of your Parent in heaven. It is as our holy rabbi of Lublin said, namely that he valued the wicked who know they are wicked more than the righteous who know they are righteous. The wicked who know they are wicked are attached to truth, and are therefore attached to God, whose seal is truth, while the righteous who know they are righteous are not attached to truth, for it is written: "For there is not a righteous person upon earth who does good and does not sin" [Ecclesiastes 7:20]. Thus, they are attached to falsehood, which the Holy One hates, as it is written: "those who tell lies shall not be established in My sight" [Psalm 101:7] — since they are opposed to the One whose seal is truth. Truth is the best medicine of all, and there is no better quality. (In the name of the holy [rabbi] of Shpola.)

> Yitzchak Mordechai ben Yisra'el Aharon Podvah (1884–1942), ed., *Ilana deChayyei* [The tree of life] (Jerusalem, 1986), p. 1, pp. 29–30

"**And you.**" A literal rendering; JPS: "the rest of you." This phrase would seem to be superfluous; the text need only have said "Go up in peace." (In Hebrew, there are four personal pronouns that can be translated as "you" in English, depending on whether the subject is masculine or feminine, singular or plural. *'Atem* is the masculine plural form.)

Our holy rabbi of Lublin. Probably a reference to Ya'akov Yitzchak HaLevi Horowitz, the Seer of Lublin (1745–1815).

God, whose seal is truth. Talmud, *Shabbat* 55a, and frequently in Rabbinic literature.

The holy [rabbi] of Shpola. R. Aryeh Leib, the Shpole Zayde (Grandfather), 1725–1812.

COMMENT

The rabbi of Lublin's remark is rather curious. At least the wicked who know they are wicked are honest, he says, which is more than can be said of the righteous who know they are righteous—they are just hypocrites, since no one can truly be righteous. Of course, the rabbi of Lublin and the Grandfather of Shpola are not suggesting that we become wicked, only that we work harder to be honest about ourselves and recognize that however much we try we can never be totally righteous. Ultimately, truth is healing and brings us closer to God.

It is clear from experience that truth is not always healing. It can also be damaging. But I believe that the damage caused by truth is more often than not temporary, and that true healing can only take place after acknowledging the truth. Failing to do so because it might hurt only postpones the inevitable and delays the process of healing. This text deals primarily with the truth about ourselves. It challenges us to take greater risks to be honest about our behavior, feelings, and thoughts, for our righteousness is only as strong as our self-awareness permits.

Va-yiggash

---

[31] Ways of Coming Closer

*"Now Judah came closer to him [Joseph] and said, 'Please, my
lord, let your servant appeal to my lord, and do not be impatient
with your servant, you who are the equal of Pharaoh.'"*

Genesis 44:18

CONTEXT

Now—when Benjamin seems to be on his way to prison or worse, and
it looks like Joseph's brothers will be forced to return to Jacob without
his youngest son—Judah, who had solemnly promised their father that
he would look after the young one, approaches the still-unrevealed Joseph to put forward a heartfelt plea.

Simchah Bunam of Pshische, a student of the Seer of Lublin and a
maverick Hasidic teacher, frequently comments on midrashim rather
than directly on the Torah.

> In the midrash on the verse "Then Judah came closer to him [Joseph],"
> it says that coming closer can only be for battle, for conciliation, or for
> prayer. Commentators on the Torah pose the question: Surely Judah
> was [already] standing and talking with Joseph, and vice versa, so
> why [does the text use] the expression "came closer"? Now it appears
> that prayer is accepted only if you pray from the depths of the heart
> and the essence of your soul—such a prayer is received favorably.
> Similarly, in the case of war, you must arouse yourself with all your
> inner powers in order to fight with your opponent, and similarly with
> conciliation—consider this carefully. So this is the meaning of [the
> phrase] "Then Judah came closer to him"—that Judah "came closer
> to" his own essence, and on this basis we may explain the midrash.

Simchah Bunam of Pshische (d. 1827), *Kol Simchah* [The sound of joy
(Jeremiah 7:33)] (Jerusalem: HaMesorah, 1986), p. 51

"Now Judah came closer to him [Joseph] ." In the original context of Genesis, "came closer" means simply that Judah approached Joseph, whom he still did not recognize, with a view to making a private appeal, but the Rabbis in the midrash quoted above examine the motives that might lie behind such an approach. It offers the three alternatives mentioned above, battle, conciliation, and prayer, plus a combination of all three.

In the midrash. *Bereshit Rabbah* 93:6.

COMMENT

There is already a lesson here in the midrash about preparing for potential conflict: we need to face it with an open mind, ready to fight, make peace, and/or pray. But Simchah Bunam delves even more deeply, suggesting that whatever the motives for Judah's approach, the most important thing for him to do was gather and focus his inner strengths. Rabbi Bunam therefore posits the notion that the approach was an inner, psychological movement, rather than an external, physical one.

Any conflict, or indeed any problem, needs to faced with our full powers if we are to succeed and move forward. Focusing our mental energies through meditation may help us form a clearer picture of what is necessary as well as giving us greater inner resources upon which to draw.

---

[32] The Voice of Prayer

"And the voice [vehakol] was heard in Pharaoh's palace."

Genesis 45:16

CONTEXT

Joseph reveals his identity to his brothers. He is impressed by Judah's plea to take Benjamin's place rather than risk their father's death from shock if they were to return without him. The brothers can hardly believe that this "Egyptian" is their long-lost brother. Amid much weeping, they accept him, and the emotions released are so overwhelming that even Pharaoh gets to hear of this tearful reunion.

The Zohar, the classic text of Kabbalah, appeared at the end of the thirteenth century in Spain, but claims to originate in second-century

Israel. Much of it is couched in symbolic language that needs decipherment before its meaning can be discerned.

Anyone who says their prayer before their Ruler should not allow their voice to be heard, for the prayer of those who make their voice heard is not accepted. What is the reason? It is because the prayer is not identical with the audible voice, for the audible voice is not the prayer. So what is the prayer? It is another voice that depends on the audible voice. And what is the audible voice? It is the voice [*KOL*] that is written with a *vav*. And the voice that depends on it? It is the voice [*KoL*] that is written without a *vav*. Therefore, a person must not allow their voice to be heard in prayer, but should pray in a whisper, in an inaudible voice, for this prayer is always accepted. And the proof of this is [in the phrase] "And the voice [*vehaKoL*] was heard" [Genesis 45:16], [i.e.,] the *KoL*, the voice, without a *vav*, is heard. This refers to an inaudible prayer, like that of Hannah, of whom it is written, "but her voice could not be heard" (1 Samuel 1[:13]). This is a prayer that the Holy One accepts, when it is done willingly, with devotion, and with proper concentration on the unity of your Ruler every day, as is fitting.

Zohar I, 209b–210a

NOTES

"And the voice [*vehakol*] was heard." A literal rendering. JPS: "The news reached Pharaoh's palace."

Anyone who says their prayer. I.e., anyone who recites the *Amidah*. This sequence of prayers, recited three times daily, should be said in a whisper so that only the worshiper, and no one else, hears the words (see Talmud, *Berachot* 24b). (In the presence of a minyan, or quorum, the *Amidah* is then repeated aloud by the leader of the service in Morning and Afternoon services.)

The voice [*kol*] that is written with a *vav*. The word *kol* (voice, sound) is most commonly written with three letters: *kof-vav-lamed*, where the letter *vav* is employed as a vowel letter.

The voice [*KoL*] that is written without a *vav*. Unusually, the word *kol* in the verse under consideration is written without a *vav*.

This is a prayer that the Holy One accepts. The true prayer, and the only prayer that is acceptable to God, is the silent, inner prayer. The outer, vocalized prayer is only representative of the inner prayer, and it is in fact meaningless without the appropriate inner thoughts.

What are we doing when we pray? No doubt, a great many things, both social or psychological as well as spiritual. But what do we achieve if we recite words from a prayer book without paying attention to their meaning or their spiritual significance? The Zohar would answer: not much, maybe nothing. The real prayer is not in the words we say, but in the words we mean!

---

[33] The Level of Israel, the Level of Jacob

"Then God spoke to Israel in visions of the night, and said, 'Jacob, Jacob.'"

Genesis 46:2

CONTEXT

Joseph's brothers leave Egypt laden with wagons filled with gifts as well as other goods, and they return to Jacob, their father, with the good news that his favorite son is still alive and is the virtual ruler of Egypt. Jacob is finally convinced that they are telling the truth, and he accepts Joseph's invitation to come to Egypt. As he sets out on his journey, accompanied by his extended family, Jacob may be worried about emigrating from the land; after all, his father, Isaac, never set foot beyond its boundaries. God speaks words of reassurance: it is God's will that he go.

Aharon II of Karlin was fourth in the line of Karliner leaders in Lithuania.

Question: Why does [the first part of the verse] begin with "Israel," but end later with "Jacob." Yet, we can say that this is the meaning of the verse:

"And God spoke to Israel"—that is, if you ascend to the level of "Israel," which is a very high [spiritual level], do not let [thoughts of] "greatness" enter you as a result. Instead, remember that you are [still] "Jacob," [i.e.,] lower. Hence, "and said, 'Jacob.'"

But this can also be interpreted from the end to the beginning: When you are at the level of "Jacob," that is, "smallness," do not let this depress you. On the contrary, remember that you can ascend to the level of "Israel" through repentance and good deeds, and encourage yourself more and more. Take care to understand! And this is a necessary part of the service of God through the levels of piety.

Aharon (II) ben Asher of Karlin (d. 1872), *Beit Aharon* [Aaron's house] (Brody, 1875; repr. Jerusalem, 1990), p. 101

NOTES

Begin with "Israel," but end later with "Jacob." Unlike his father (who had only one name, Isaac) and his grandfather (Abram, who came to be called Abraham exclusively), the third Patriarch is known by two names used almost interchangeably: Jacob and Israel. Moreover, throughout the Torah and the Prophets, both names are used to designate the People of Israel.

If you ascend to the level of "Israel." Aharon II of Karlin is following a tradition that stretches back into kabbalistic symbolism in suggesting that the names Jacob and Israel refer to different spiritual levels.

"Greatness" . . . "smallness." In Hasidic literature, these terms refer to two different mental and spiritual states, "greatness" characterized by awareness of God and heightened understanding, and "smallness," our ordinary, day-to-day awareness.

From the end to the beginning. Aharon II follows a long Rabbinic tradition by suggesting that the phrase he is discussing can be read backward as well as forward.

COMMENT

Hasidic psychology says that we all go through periods of greater and lesser spiritual awareness. We never stay still spiritually: we are either ascending or descending. Sometimes we are "Israel," sometimes we are "Jacob." Recognizing where we are on the scale is an important part of our spiritual training. Knowing how to deal with where we are is a necessary skill. Being "Israel," being spiritually awakened and feeling near to God, may lead to unhealthy and dangerous feelings of superiority and invincibility. We need to remind ourselves that we will not stay at this level. That will make us realistic. Being "Jacob," feeling far from God and spiritually asleep, may make us depressed and even angry. Once again, we have to remind ourselves that we will not stay at this level. That will bring us relief.

Va-yeḥi

---

[34] Body and Soul

*"Jacob lived in the land of Egypt seventeen years; so the
whole age of Jacob was a hundred and forty-seven years.
And the time drew nearer that Israel must die. . . ."*

Genesis 47:28–29

CONTEXT

Genesis is drawing to a close. Its last remaining central characters, Jacob, and later Joseph, are dying. But why do these verses that begin the narrative of Jacob's last days call him "Jacob" twice, and then "Israel"?

In the introduction to Rabbenu Bachya's Torah commentary, he promises to discuss the biblical text from the perspective of the four levels of interpretation: the plain meaning, the midrashic or homiletic interpretation, the intellectual, and the mystical. Here, he fulfills at least part of that promise.

According to the plain meaning, why is Israel mentioned [in verse 29]? It does not say "the time drew nearer that Jacob must die," though it says earlier "Jacob lived," [and] "so the whole age of Jacob was." From the moment that the Holy One called him by the name of Israel and said to him, "Your name shall no longer be called Jacob, but Israel" (Genesis 25[:10]), the weekly Torah readings have followed the practice of calling him Jacob sometimes and Israel at other times. The fact that it says "Your name shall no longer be called Jacob, but Israel" is not an obstacle [to using the name "Jacob"], it is simply that the name "Israel" is the essence, and the name "Jacob" is secondary. . . .

According to the way of the intellect, the fact that the Scripture in this parashah sometimes calls him Jacob and sometimes Israel is all

[done] with care and with deliberate intent, for the name "Jacob" is used of the attributes of the body, physical matters of this world, because he is called Jacob [Ya'aKoV] due to [the verse] "and his hand was holding on to Esau's heel ['eKeV]" (Genesis 25[:26]). The name "Israel" [yiSRa'el] is used of the attributes of the soul, as it is written: "For you have wrestled [SaRita] with God" (Genesis 32[:29]).

It is well known that the essential thing is the attributes of the soul and not the attributes of the body. Nevertheless, it is impossible for a human being to completely uproot the attributes of the body and not make use of them, for you cannot live without them. However, the intention is that the soul should be the essential and the body secondary. . . . Whoever makes the attribute of the body the essential and the attributes of the soul—namely, the service of the Blessed One—secondary, is killing the soul.

Rabbenu Bachya ben Asher ben Chlava (thirteenth century), *Perush al HaTorah* [Commentary on the Torah] (Jerusalem: Blum, 1988), pt. 1, p. 218

NOTE

"Israel" is the essence, and the name "Jacob" is secondary. A similar view is put forward in the midrash *Bereshit Rabbah* 78:3.

COMMENT

All this begs the question: what is the soul? There is no easy answer to this; many researchers today deny that there is any such entity. I find Rabbenu Bachya's almost offhand suggestion at the end of this passage, that the soul's purpose is the service of God, a useful one. In that case, the soul is that part of us that strives for something beyond the needs and requirements of the body. It is the aspect of human nature that longs for beauty, truth, love, righteousness, and all those things that lift our lives above the "rat race." If we care only for the body, we kill off all that makes us truly human; we kill the soul.

[35] Being a Jew

"Judah [Yehudah], you ['atah], your brothers
shall acknowledge you [yoducha]."

Genesis 49:8

CONTEXT

Jacob's blessing of his sons has been the subject of much analysis and study over the generations, not least because he often uses puns and wordplays to make his points, points which are as a result sometimes obscure or even opaque to us. Here he blesses Judah with a preeminent role over his brothers.

Moshe Hayyim Efraim's analysis of this verse is based on his grandfather's remarks about the denial of idolatry as the hallmark of a Jew. The grandson's comment begins with the words "It seems to me."

One might say [the following], based on what I heard from my master and grandfather:

"Anyone who denies idolatry is called a Jew," while pride is called idolatry. So anyone who denies idolatry, meaning, the trait of pride, and holds fast to the trait of humility and lowliness, is called a "Jew."

It seems to me that melancholy and depression are also "idolatry," though they are not as severe as all [other] bad traits.

Now it is well known that even if a person has Torah and good deeds but no fear of heaven, it amounts to nothing. [The letter] *yod* is the smallest of the letters; nevertheless, you can make from it all the twenty-two letters that are in the Torah, for when you begin to write you begin [by making] a small point [like a *yod*]. Then, you can extend it into any letter you wish. Thus, it seems that from the tiny *yod* you could make all the twenty-two letters and the five books of the Torah. Hence anyone who denies idolatry is called a Jew and is worthy of all the twenty-two letters and the five books of the Torah. This is [the meaning of the verse] "Yehudah," that is, when you are called a Jew, then "you" ['*aTaH*] may be extended and made from this, that is, the twenty-two letters from '*alef* to *tav* and the five books of the Torah. . . . Understand this!

Moshe Hayyim Efraim of Sudylkov (d. 1800), *Degel Machaneh Efraim* [The flag of the camp of Ephraim (Numbers 2:18)] (Jerusalem, 1963), p. 76

"Judah [*Yehudah*] , . . . shall acknowledge you [*yoducha*] ." A play on words in the biblical text.

"**Anyone who denies idolatry is called a Jew.**" Talmud, *Megillah* 13a.

Even if a person has Torah and good deeds but no fear of heaven. See Talmud, *Yoma* 72b.

[The letter] *yod.* Also read as *yud,* and another clear pun on Jew and Yehudah. It is also the smallest letter of the Hebrew alphabet, sometimes consisting of little more than a point, but this little point can become any of the twenty-two letters, and these in their turn can become the words that make up the most sacred of Jewish texts, the Torah.

"**You**" **[***'aTaH***]** . Composed of three consonants: *'alef* and *tav,* the first and last letters of the alphabet, plus *heh,* the fifth letter, with a numerical value of five.

COMMENT

Just as the *yod* can become every letter of the Hebrew alphabet and the entire Torah, so too that which is most humble has the potential to become great in God's eyes. This is the challenge of being a Jew: being humble, so that you may be truly great.

Being Jewish is not a given nor a source of unalloyed ethnic pride; it is a challenge. We may be born into it, or we may choose it, but either way, it calls upon us to be humble before God and to be prepared to extend ourselves for the sake of greater understanding and for the sake of others.

---

[36] The General and the Particular

"And this [zot] did their father say to them, as he blessed them. Each according to his blessing did he bless them."

Genesis 49:28

CONTEXT

Jacob concludes his blessing of his sons with Joseph and Benjamin, the two youngest and the only children of his beloved wife Rachel. This verse brings the chapter to its conclusion.

Simchah Bunam of Pshische, a disciple of the Seer of Lublin, left the Seer with his friend the "Holy Jew" and eventually set up as a Hasidic leader in his own right after his friend's death. It is characteristic of Simchah Bunam that he lays great emphasis on the uniqueness of each individual.

For the source of worship is one point, known as "this [zot]," even though the form of the service may change according to the "quarry" from which the souls were "cut." Hence, "and this"—the generality of all levels "did their father say to them." ["Say"] is an expression [meaning] "guidance," and this is the general; but on [the level of] the particular [it is] "each one according to his blessing," meaning, he blessed [BeR-aCH] them [from] the pool [BeReiCHah] from which we are blessed.

Simchah Bunam of Pshische (1765–1827), *Kol Simchah* [The sound of joy (Jeremiah 7:33)] (Jerusalem: HaMesorah, 1986), p. 53

NOTES

"As he blessed them . . . did he bless them." In this verse, we are present-ed with two clauses that seem to be saying essentially the same thing, that Jacob blessed each of his sons. But following an ancient principle of bibli-cal interpretation, something different must be intended by each clause.

"This [zot]." This feminine singular demonstrative pronoun symbolizes the Shechinah (Malchut), in the kabbalistic scheme.

The "quarry" from which the souls were "cut." A phrase derived from Isa-iah 51:1: "Look to the rock from which you were hewn and the quarry from which you were cut; look to Abraham your father and to Sarah who gave you birth." Each person's service will be different in some respect, since our souls may originate in different places within the divine realm of the *sefirot*.

The generality of all levels. This also indicates Malchut (Shechinah), where all levels, the *sefirot* above and the universe below, meet.

The pool [BeReiCHah]. A symbol for the *sefirah* of Binah (Understanding). Malchut and Binah are frequently linked in the symbolism of the Kabbalah. Both are called "mothers," "the Shechinah," and "mouths," one the upper and the other the lower. Here Malchut is the general and Binah the particular.

COMMENT

We too, in our encounters with others, must recognize their generality, as fellow human beings and as members of certain social and ethnic groups, as well as their particularity. Indeed, recognizing and appreciating their individuality represents a higher understanding, when contrasted with seeing them only as members of groups. And, after all, that is the way most of us would like to be seen by others: as members of our groups, but also as individuals who may or may not conform to our group in all respects. We can be most effective in helping others only when we can recognize these two levels on which they exist, just as we do. A stranger's ethnic origins or group affiliations may be a reasonable place to begin to understand him or her, but we are not permitted to stay at that level, for real understanding only starts when we recognize and accept his or her individuality. Then we can truly bless them through our actions as well as our words.

EXODUS

Shemot

---

[37] Bodies of Holiness

"But the Israelites were fertile and prolific; they multiplied and
increased greatly, so that the land was filled [with] them."

Exodus 1:7

CONTEXT

The book of Genesis closes with the deaths of Joseph and his brothers in
Egypt. Now, at the start of the second book of the Torah, we find their
descendants, the People of Israel, still in Egypt and doing very nicely,
until political circumstances change with a new pharaoh. Soon, they
will be enslaved and, eventually, redeemed.

Meir Bikayam was a kabbalist in Smyrna (Izmir), Turkey, and a secret follower of the failed messiah Shabbetai Zevi, though this is never
explicitly stated in his works. He composed two kabbalistic commentaries on the Torah.

We have to consider why there are four terms here, "fertile and prolific; multiplied and increased," and also [why] it says "the land was
filled them," for it implies that the land [actually] filled them. It
should have said "the land was filled with them" or "they filled the
land". . . .

These four terms are intended to allude to the four worlds from
which souls had entered into the "shell." Hence it says "were fertile
and prolific . . . so that the land filled them"—meaning, the "land,"
that is, Malchut, completed them. That is to say, it completed them
by building for them bodies of holiness, which is perfection for souls.
For this reason, it does not say "the land was filled with them," because it would not have been appropriate for the land of Egypt to be
filled with them. Rather, the intention is that their souls should be

completed by having bodies built of holiness, as has been mentioned. Consider this matter well.

Meir ben Chalifa Bikayam (d. 1769), *Me'orei Or* [Giving light (Ezekiel 32:8)] (Salonika, 1752), p. 41b

NOTES

"The land was filled [with] them." The word "with" is not actually represented in the Hebrew, a fact that gives some space for Bikayam's interpretation.

The four worlds. These are the four realms between the unknowable God and this created universe, namely, the worlds of Atzilut (Emanation), Beri'ah (Creation), Yetzirah (Formation), and Asiyah (Action). Human souls of varying degrees of holiness are said to derive from each of these worlds.

The "shell." In the Lurianic scheme, the sparks of divine light that fell into this world have been kept from returning to their divine source by being imprisoned in the "shells." Here, the specific reference is to the soul being encased in the body.

The "land," that is, Malchut, completed them. "Land" or "earth" is a common symbol for the lowest of the *sefirot*. The Israelites were perfected by being filled with Malchut, also known as the Shechinah. This spiritual influx made their bodies holy, too.

Perfection for souls. When the soul is illuminated with the presence of the divine, that illumination is transferred to the body as well. The soul's perfection lies in making the body holy.

COMMENT

Some religious faiths and spiritual philosophies hold that the body is the seat of uncleanness and therefore must be subdued or ignored if there is to be spiritual progress. Some Jewish schools of thought seem to have taken this view as well, but I believe that the majority of Jewish spiritual teachers are of the opinion that, while the body must be tamed, it too can be a vehicle for spiritual growth. If my interpretation of his words is correct, then Meir Bikayam was one of those.

Spirituality is not confined to the mind or the soul or the spirit. It must spread from there to our entire bodies, otherwise such spirituality is not real, but just a mind game we play. Unless our behavior is transformed, spirituality remains dead.

[38] Habits Get in the Way

"Do not come any closer; take your shoes off your feet [raglecha], because the place where you are standing is holy ground."

Exodus 3:5

CONTEXT

Moses flees Egypt after it becomes clear that he is wanted for the killing of a taskmaster. He arrives in Midian where he is taken in by Jethro, marries one of his daughters, and goes to work for him as a shepherd. While out with his flock, he sees a strange sight: a bush is burning but not burning up. And a voice speaks to him from the fire, telling him not to come closer.

Yosef of Yampole was the son of Yechiel Michal, the Maggid of Zlotchov, a disciple of the Ba'al Shem Tov.

> [R. Yosef of Yampole] said, "Do not come any closer"—you should not say, "If I had such and such, it would certainly improve my service of God, but service is so very difficult." Do not say this, but "take your shoes off your feet [raglecha]"—that is, set aside the foolishness of your usual habits [regilut], and then you will see that "the place where you are standing is holy ground"—in that exact place, you can serve God, as the holy Ba'al Shem Tov said [on the verse] "And you should seek the Eternal your God from there, and you will find [God]" (Deuteronomy 4[:29])—"from there," precisely from the place where you are, at whatever level you are on. Even if you are not in an exalted place, nevertheless, "from there" you will find the Eternal your God, and you will be able to attach yourself to God.

> Yosef ben Yechiel Michal of Yampole (d. 1812), in *Tzeror HaHayyim* [The bundle of life (1 Samuel 25:29)], ed. Hayyim ben Yishayah Liebersohn of Berditchev (Bilgorai, 1913), p. 25

COMMENT

Why does God tell Moses to remove his shoes? What makes the ground upon which the burning bush stood holy? Surely it is God's presence. In that case, if God is everywhere—a given in Hasidism—then every place is holy. But why do we not notice the holiness if it is inherent in the world? Because, says R. Yosef, our mental habits get in the way. They blind us to the holiness, and make us see only the mundane. Like Moses, our rabbi tells us, we need to metaphorically take off our shoes.

Some people go in search of mystical, spiritual experiences, visiting famous teachers or reading mystical books. They imagine that if only conditions were perfect, they could be spiritual or religious. But Yosef of Yampole implies that this is a fantasy, or an excuse. Spiritual experience starts wherever we are. But our habits of thought get in the way and prevent us from seeing what is in front of our eyes: that God is present, here and now, and addressing us just the way God addressed Moses. No burning bush is necessary, no vision, only an inner realization of God's presence.

---

[39] Joining with the Pain of the Shechinah

"Then Moses returned to the Eternal and said: '. . . For since I went to Pharaoh to speak in Your name, he has treated this people worse, while You have not even rescued this people.'"

Exodus 5:22–23

CONTEXT

Moses complains that God has not only not rescued the people, but, by bringing matters to Pharaoh's attention and raising Israelite expectations, God has actually made things worse!

Elimelech of Lyzhansk was a key student of the Maggid of Mezritch, and in his turn trained a whole school of students of his own, many of whom went on to become *tzadikim* in their own right.

On the face of it, [the phrase] "while You have not even rescued [this people]!" is a duplicate expression; when [Moses] said, "he has treated this people worse," God had obviously not rescued them.

It seems that the meaning is that now, when we are in this bitter exile, in our affliction "[God too] is afflicted," and the Shechinah [the Presence of God] is in exile with us, it is our task to worry and complain only about the exile of the Shechinah; not to think at all about our own pain, but only about the pain and exile of the Shechinah. And if our orientation and our pain were only directed toward the pain of the Shechinah, rather than our own, we would be redeemed immediately.

But we are flesh, and it is not possible for us to bear afflictions and agony. Therefore our days in bitter exile are prolonged, because of our many transgressions, because our pains are coupled with that of the Shechinah, but we are anxious [only] about our own pains. If only there were a righteous person . . . who could save the entire world from exile!

This is what Moses our teacher [meant when] he said: "For since I went [to Pharaoh] to speak in Your name": all my words were only for the sake of Your great and holy name, which is in exile, and not on account of our exile.

Elimelech of Lyzhansk (1717–87), *No'am Elimelech* [The pleasantness of Elimelech], ed. Gedalyah Nigal (Jerusalem: Mossad HaRav Kook, 1978), v. 1, p. 175

NOTES

In our affliction "[God too] is afflicted." Based on Isaiah 63:9.

The Shechinah [the Presence of God] is in exile with us. A common notion in Rabbinic literature. See, e.g., *Shemot Rabbah* 23:5. It is characteristic of Hasidism, starting with the Ba'al Shem Tov, to say that the purpose of prayer is to pray on behalf of the Shechinah rather than ourselves.

If only there were a righteous person. Elimelech of Lyzhansk means the wonder-working Hasidic rebbe, and Moses as setting the pattern the rebbe follows.

Your great and holy name, which is in exile. I.e., the Shechinah.

COMMENT

If the ultimate purpose of religion, and that which all the great world religions have in common, is concern for others, then this must represent the greatest ideal of Judaism. Our concern should not simply be for others: family, friends, and ultimately all humanity and the environment. Even the divine Presence itself, as it were, needs our concern. For divinity is in exile in this world, trapped in a web of materialism, and only we, the universe made conscious, as the paleontologist and Jesuit Teilhard de Chardin put it, can redeem it from its exile.

Va-'era'

---

[40] Service for Positive Reasons

*"I have also heard the moaning of the Israelites because
the Egyptians have made them serve."*

Exodus 6:5

CONTEXT

Parashat Shemot concluded with Moses complaining to God that going before Pharaoh to demand Israelite emancipation had not only not
achieved the desired result, it had actually made things worse. At the
beginning of Va-'era', God responds with an assurance that things will
ultimately produce the promised Exodus from slavery.

Moshe of Kobrin was a modest teacher who strove to bring Hasidic and
Jewish values into the daily lives of his followers. Although the virtue
of joy does not normally play a large part in his teaching, this passage
seems to be an exception.

> All of the moaning of the Israelites was because of the service of God.
> Every one of Israel should serve God with joy and with a clear mind,
> [but] in the end, the Egyptians had to bring us to service. This was
> the essence of Israel's moaning.

Moshe ben Yisra'el Polier of Kobrin (1784–1858), *Amarot Tehorot* [Pure
sayings (Psalm 12:7)] (Warsaw, 1910), p. 8

NOTES

"Because the Egyptians have made them serve." JPS: "Because the Egyptians are holding them in bondage." *Ma'avidim otam* can mean "enslaved
them, held them in bondage," as the context of Exodus requires, but the Kobriner's interpretation demands "made them serve."

Because of the service of God. The word 'avodah, from the same root as
ma'avidim, can mean "service," "work," or "worship."

This was the essence of Israel's moaning. Israel's complaint, according to
the Kobriner, was that Egyptian persecution, rather than the joy of serving
God, led them to pray. Needless to relate, this is quite contrary to the *peshat*, the plain meaning of the biblical text.

COMMENT

Synagogues tend to fill up when a Jewish tragedy seems to loom, or in
its wake. Hence the large numbers of worshipers in the run-up to the
Six Day War in 1967 and other Arab-Israeli conflicts, or in the aftermath
of the Munich massacre at the Olympics in 1972 and similar dreadful
events. But Moshe of Kobrin reminds us that it is not tragedy that should
bring us to shul, but celebration, the celebration of being Jewish, the
celebration of life.

---

[41] Performing Signs

"For Pharaoh will say to you: 'Perform a sign for yourselves.'"

Exodus 7:9

CONTEXT

God now lays out a possible scenario for Moses and Aaron's approach to
Pharaoh. When Pharaoh asks for a sign to prove that they have indeed
been commissioned by God, they are to throw down Moses's staff, and
it will become a snake. And this is what occurs.

Shalom Rokeach, also known as Sar Shalom, was the founder of the
Hasidic dynasty of Belz, which continues to this day.

It would seem that [Scripture] should have said "Perform a sign for
Me." The fact is, though, that "a fool has no desire for understanding"
[Proverbs 18:2], as we find with [King] Ahaz, who said: "I will not
ask or test the Eternal" (Isaiah 7:12). Therefore, on his own behalf,
[Pharaoh] would not seek any sign at all. But, in his great wickedness,
he was saying, "You yourselves do not perfectly and truly believe, so
'perform a sign for yourselves.'"

One may add to this: It is written in books that there are righteous people [*tzadikim*] who do not perform saving acts and there are righteous people, though only a few, who facilitate saving acts. The explanation is that, because of the lowliness of their spirit, they do not have complete faith and trust that they have the power to facilitate good and saving acts. And therefore they are unable to act in that way. Hence Pharaoh says: "Perform a sign for yourselves," for you yourselves do not believe that you have the ability to perform a sign.

Shalom Rokeach of Belz (d. 1855), *MaHaRaSH miBelza* [Our teacher, the rabbi, Shalom of Belz], ed. Yisra'el Klepholtz (Bnei Brak, 1987), pt. 2, p. 4

NOTES

"Perform a sign for yourselves." A literal translation, as required by the Belzer's comment. JPS: "Produce your marvel."

[King] Ahaz, who said: "I will not ask or test the Eternal." Isaiah 7 relates how the kings of Aram and the Northern Kingdom of Israel formed an alliance to attack the capital of the Southern Kingdom of Judah at Jerusalem. God commands Isaiah to present himself to Ahaz, king of Judah, and offer him divine assurances that the attack will come to naught. He tells Ahaz to demand a sign of God, but the king piously refuses, only to be chastised by the prophet, who offers him the sign of a young woman bearing a son who will be called Immanuel (God is with us). Like Ahaz, Pharaoh is a fool, and would not be convinced by a miracle. According to the Belzer, his challenge is directed not at the ability of Moses or of Aaron, but at their faith.

Therefore, on his own behalf, [Pharaoh] would not seek any sign at all. Pharaoh is a "fool" who does not believe in the power of God.

Righteous people [*tzadikim*] who do not perform saving acts and . . . righteous people . . . who facilitate saving acts. The Belzer clearly has other Hasidic leaders in mind. Some, he says, lack trust in their own abilities.

COMMENT

Anyone can see that there are many good people in this world, and that a few bad people can make life a misery for thousands, even millions. If we take "*tzadikim*" in its original sense of "righteous people," then the analysis offered here would suggest that what distinguishes a few from the mass of good people is their understanding that they are, indeed, powerful, and not helpless. It is that understanding that distinguished

Moses and Aaron from their compatriots; it is that understanding that can inspire us still today.

---

[42] Sensitivity to Others

"Moses said: 'It is not proper to do so, that we should sacrifice to the Eternal our God what is an abomination for the Egyptians before their eyes, and will they not stone us?'"

Exodus 8:22

CONTEXT

Three plagues have passed, blood, frogs, and lice, and still Pharaoh is adamant. The fourth plague, of wild beasts, arrives, and Pharaoh, in frustration, offers to let the Israelites sacrifice to their God, but only in Egypt itself, not out in the wilderness as Moses had requested (Exodus 7:16). In the verse quoted, Moses explains why this will not work.

Mordechai of Neschiz was first rebbe of the Neschiz dynasty and famous for his miracles. He had been a disciple of Yechiel Michal of Zlotchov.

That is, [Moses intended] to say, "Clearly, it is true that they will not stone us"—because [Moses] trusted in God—"but, because of my sensitive nature, it is not proper in my view to do this thing that is so opposed to their view." These were not his actual words.

Mordechai of Neschiz (d. 1800), *Rishpei Esh* [Coals of fire (Song of Songs 8:6)] (Jerusalem, 1997), pp. 9–10

NOTES

"Will they not stone us?" This phrase is usually taken as a question. R. Mordechai prefers to see it as a statement; there are no indications in the Hebrew that it is a question, other than the original context. (It is, in fact, a rhetorical question: Moses assumes that the answer is "Yes, they will stone us.")

Because of my sensitive nature. R. Mordechai suggests that Moses's refusal to offer sacrifices to God in Egypt is due to his unwillingness to upset Egyptian sensibilities.

These were not his actual words. The editor of *Rishpei Esh* (R. Mordechai's grandson Eliezer Immanuel Horowitz) is informing us that this is a paraphrase, not a direct quotation.

COMMENT

According to the rebbe of Neschiz, Moses is not prepared to sacrifice in Egypt, out of respect for Egyptian beliefs. The ancient Egyptian god Khnum had the head of a ram. The sacrifice of sheep by the Israelites would have been seen as an affront. Like the Israelites of old, we too live among people of many religious faiths, all different from our own, or none at all. Even if we do not fear attack by those whom we might upset, we should be careful not to offend others, especially with regard to their religious beliefs, which are often dearly held, even if not always acted upon. Religious beliefs, by their nature, deal with that which is ultimately unknowable. Therefore, no one faith, no one group, can possess the whole Truth; each has at best only a portion. It is our duty to respect the faiths of others, for they too may have a portion of Truth.

Bo'

---

[43] Darkness between Us

"There was a thick darkness throughout all the land of
Egypt for three days. No one could see their fellows, nor
did anyone get up from their place for three days."
Exodus 10:22–23

CONTEXT

The plague of darkness, the ninth, strikes Egypt.

Yitzchak of Vorki was one of Menachem Mendel of Kotzk's disciples. He established his own dynasty, and his son, also called Menachem Mendel, succeeded him.

There is no darkness or gloom greater in the world than this: that people do not see, and do not want to see, their fellows, but each one worries only about themselves.

When no one sees their fellow, and worries only about themselves, then "no one gets up from their place," for there is no hope for revival or progress.

Yitzchak of Vorki (1779–1848) and Menachem Mendel of Vorki (d. 1868),
Beit Yitzchak [The house of Isaac] (Jerusalem, 1992), p. 44

NOTES

There is no darkness. In *Beit Yitzchak*, this paragraph is credited to R. Yitzchak of Vorki.

When no one sees their fellow. This teaching is by Menachem Mendel of Vorki.

COMMENT

The Torah speaks of a tangible darkness across Egypt, apart from the region of Goshen where the Israelites lived. The rabbis of Vorki, father and son, speak of a spiritual darkness, where selfishness rules and no one is concerned for others. In such a situation, what hope is there? Too often, modern global society looks spiritually dark. Where are the people who still care? Without them, we are doomed. With them, there is always hope.

[44] How to Eat

*"Speak to the whole congregation of Israel, and say that
on the tenth of this month, they shall each take a lamb
for each clan, a lamb for each household."*

Exodus 12:3

CONTEXT

In the course of describing the commandment of the Passover lamb, instructions are given on how to cook it and eat it. It had to be roasted and eaten with matzah and bitter herbs by people who were all dressed and ready to depart from Egypt.

Moshe Cordovero was one of the great kabbalists who gathered in Safed in the late sixteenth century. He is the author of many classic texts of Kabbalah; the following is taken from his commentary on the prayer book.

Our rabbis have said: If two people are eating the Passover lamb, and one eats it for the sake of [fulfilling the commandment of eating] the Passover lamb, and the other eats it for the sake of the physical act of eating, of the first it is said: "the righteous eats for the satisfaction of the soul" [Proverbs 13:25], while of the second it is said: "but the belly of the wicked shall be lacking" [Proverbs 13:25]. In this way, they teach us that although eating the Passover lamb is a physical act, everything follows from the intention. If a person, by good intentions, draws spirituality from a holy source, as for example when one eats for the sake of [fulfilling the commandment of] the Passover lamb, [and] since it has been commanded by the Creator, then that act, by virtue of this drawing down from on high, brings perfection to the soul.

Moshe Cordovero (1522–70), *Tefillah LeMoshe* [A prayer of Moses (Psalm 90:1)], (Jerusalem, 2004), Gate 1, §4, p. 4a

NOTE

Our rabbis have said. What follows, up to "of the first it is said," is a paraphrase of the Talmud, *Horayot* 10b. A different prooftext (Hosea 14:10) is
offered there.

COMMENT

Cordovero's point is based on the basic kabbalistic understanding of the
relationship between the spiritual and physical realms. These are not two
distinct realms of existence; they are intimately interconnected, with
the spiritual as the "root" and the physical as the "branch." Therefore,
each and every act we do, and most especially so-called religious acts
(i.e., rituals) should involve both our physical and spiritual selves. And in
the case of Jewish rituals, where a blessing normally precedes the ritual
action, the act of saying the blessing mediates between the two realms:
the spiritual, exemplified through our *kavanah*, our mental concentration on the ritual; and the physical, the actual act we are engaged in.

Turning to the ancient ritual of eating the paschal or Passover lamb, he
argues, based on a talmudic precedent, that one's mental intention is an
essential part of fulfilling the ritual. Indeed, it is a sine qua non. Without
it, the ritual is worse than meaningless. With it, we may rise to spiritual
heights and bring untold benefit to ourselves, and perhaps to the world.

---

[45] The Firstborn Thought

"Dedicate to Me all the firstborn. . . ."

Exodus 13:2

CONTEXT

The fact that the firstborn males of the Israelites and of their animals
were spared, when those of the Egyptians died in the tenth plague, means
that all firstborn in perpetuity are to be dedicated to God: the firstborn
of kosher cattle were to be given for sacrifice, firstborn donkeys were
to be killed and thus removed from normal use, while the firstborn of
the Israelites were to be redeemed.

Yisra'el of Ruzhyn, the great-grandson of the Maggid of Mezritch, inaugurated a dynasty of his own that continues to the present.

The firstborn is the first thought as you rise in the morning. You ought to dedicate it to the Eternal, whether it is a thought of love, as love of the Eternal, or of some other quality. And this corresponds to that: when a thought falls in with the qualities of the Other Side, it is called "the firstborn of Egypt."

But the essential thing is to connect the [first] thought with its root, so that it should be solely for the Eternal alone, when you wrap yourself in the fringes [tzitzit]. For there are a total of thirty-two threads, and [this is the numerical value] of the [divine] name by which [God] struck the firstborn of Egypt, as Scripture says, "And the Eternal [*VaYHVH*] struck down all the firstborn [in the land of Egypt]" (Exodus 12[:29]), that is, with the [divine] name of thirty-two. When you annihilate the firstborn [thought] of the "shells," you [automatically] connect yourself to the firstborn of holiness. Therefore, immediately after putting on the fringes, it is possible for you to put on the phylacteries [tefillin], which [include within them] the section [that begins with the words] "Dedicate [to Me all the firstborn]."

Yisra'el Friedman of Ruzhyn (1797–1850), *Irin Kadishin* [Holy angels] (n.p., 1885), pt. 1, p. 23

NOTES

And this corresponds to that. The positive virtues symbolized by the *sefirot* are paralleled by the negative forces of the universe, the so-called "ten *sefirot* of the Other Side."

The Other Side. The side of evil.

"The firstborn of Egypt." Egypt usually represents the forces of evil in Kabbalah, just as the ancient Rabbis thought of Egypt as the embodiment of magic and idolatry.

A total of thirty-two threads. There are eight threads at each of the four corners of the tallit.

"And the Eternal [*VaYHVH*] ." The Ruzhyner considers the *vav* (and) to be part of the divine name. The result has a numerical value of 32: (*vav* = 6) + (*yod* = 10) + (*heh* = 5) + (*vav* = 6) + (*heh* = 5) = 32. In Rabbinic literature, this combination is said to indicate God and the divine court. See, e.g., *Shemot Rabbah* 12:4.

The "shells." A metaphor for the forces of evil that hold divine sparks, preventing them from ascending to their Source.

The phylacteries [tefillin]. On weekday mornings, the tefillin are traditionally put on after the tallit (prayer shawl) and before the morning service.

Which [include within them] the section. The tefillin contain little strips
of parchment on which are written four passages from the Torah: Deuteronomy 6:4–9, 11:13–21; Exodus 13:1–10 (the passage under discussion); and
13:11–16.

COMMENT

I hate to get up in the morning. It's a fact. And I find that waking to a
blaring alarm clock is worse than waking up by myself, though that is
bad enough. Still, one has to get up. There are things that need doing,
people that need you. And God "needs" our service.

In the Ruzhyner's comments, he reminds us that our attitude toward
getting up in the morning is in our own hands. We have the power to
take whatever thought we have on waking and dedicate it to God, or
not. It is up to us to decide which way to go. Whatever the thought, it
can be turned to God.

They say that breakfast is the most important meal of the day. The
Ruzhyner implies that the first thought is the most important one of the
day. This is also the message of two of the great law codes of the Middle Ages, Ya'akov ben Asher's *Arba'ah Turim* and Yosef Karo's *Shulchan
Aruch*. Both begin with laws for rising in the morning with strength and
the readiness to do God's will. Our first thought may set the tone for the
day just beginning.

Be-shallaḥ

---

[46] Going Up

"The Israelites went up armed from the land of Egypt. . . ."

Exodus 13:18

CONTEXT

The Torah tells us that the Israelites "went up" from the land of Egypt. Is the use of this verb indicative of the terrain they had to cross, or is there a deeper significance to this term?

Simchah Bunam of Pshische was a key leader in a Hasidic school that included the Holy Jew of Pshische and Menachem Mendel of Kotzk; it placed new emphasis on the importance of each individual.

> Rabbi Simchah Bunam, the rebbe of Pshische, said: Jews need to go higher and higher. "Went up" [means] "went higher." "Words from a wise person's mouth are gracious" [Ecclesiastes 10:12]. The enlightened person will understand.

> Yo'etz Kayyam Kadish Rokotz, ed., *Siach Sarfei Kodesh* [The conversation of the holy seraphim] (n.p., n.d.), pt. 3, p. 130

NOTES

"Went up" [means] "went higher." The original Hebrew is translated into Yiddish in this text.

"Words from a wise person's mouth are gracious." . . . The enlightened person will understand. These two expressions are regularly found at the end of Hasidic expositions. The first indicates that you should remember the holy person with whom this teaching originated, and therefore respect and follow it, and the second that you should go and meditate on it, if you wish to be enlightened. (In fact, these last two sentences are an editorial addition.)

This rather terse statement from Rabbi Simchah Bunam suggests that the role of a Jew is always to reach ever higher in the spiritual quest. Perhaps he also has in mind the word translated above as "armed," *chamushim*. In fact this word is obscure, and the subject of much interest among the commentators, some of whom connect it with the word *chamesh* (five) and then with the Torah (*chumash*), because it is made up of five books. (See Ephraim of Luntshits's comment on this verse in *Keli Yakar*.) Hence Rabbi Bunam seems to be implying that study of the Torah is one of our primary means of spiritual ascent and the way we arm ourselves to face the challenges of life.

[47] Turn to Israel First

"Then the Eternal said to Moses: 'Why are you crying to Me?
Speak to the descendants of Israel and let them move on!'"

Exodus 14:15

CONTEXT

Egyptian chariots are waiting for an opportunity to strike at the Israelites, who have their back to the Reed Sea. What are the Israelites to do? They complain to Moses that they should have stayed in Egypt. Moses tells them not to be afraid and, in turn, calls on God. God replies: Why are you crying to Me?

The "holy rabbi of Lentshna" is probably R. Yitzchak (1767–1846) of that town. Like the Kotzker, he had been a disciple of the Seer of Lublin, but unlike the Kotzker, he had opposed the new, more individualistic approach taken by the Kotzker's friend and teacher, the Holy Jew of Pshische.

One of the disciples of the holy rabbi of Lentshna was once at our rabbi's. He [the Kotzker] inquired after the health of his rabbi, but added: I love him very much, but why does he cry out to the Holy One to send the Messiah? Why doesn't he cry out to the descendants of Israel that they should turn in repentance? This is the meaning of [the phrase]: "Why are you crying to Me? Speak to the descendants of Israel!"

Menachem Mendel of Kotzk (1787–1859), *Sefer Amud HaEmet* [The book of the pillar of truth] (Bnei Brak, 2000), p. 45

COMMENT

The responsibility for bringing the Messianic Age lies, in the first instance, with us. Prayer is only one means to that end. It is an important tool in that it can give us the space to purify our thoughts and motives, but in the end the Messianic Age will be achieved through carefully thought-out human action, informed by spirituality not materialism.

---

[48] The War against Amalek

"The Eternal is at war with Amalek in every generation."

Exodus 17:16

CONTEXT

Traveling through the wilderness, the Israelites come up against one challenge after another. They have to hold back from collecting the manna on *Shabbat* as they do on the six working days. At one place, they complain that there is no water, and Moses is told to strike a rock in order to obtain water for them to drink. And then they are attacked by the Amalekites. Joshua, Moses's second in command, leads the battle against them, but the Israelites only win as long as Moses's hands are held high. After the Amalekite defeat, a reminder is written down in a book and an altar built. God, it is declared, will always be at war with Amalek.

Natan of Nemirov was Nachman of Bratzlav's amanuensis. Nachman of Bratzlav was a powerful and controversial figure in the history of Hasidism, and a great-grandson of the Ba'al Shem Tov. Natan of Nemirov wrote down all that he heard from his teacher, and added what others told him of Nachman's teaching and behavior. But Natan too was an important Hasidic teacher of spirituality and morality, as the little book from which this extract comes demonstrates.

The war against Amalek, that is, the war against the inclination [toward evil] is an extremely long war. The essential method for subduing it is by means of self-encouragement, for whatever happens to a person throughout the days of their lives, they should be very strong not to allow themselves to fall into the state of "If I make my bed in Sheol, You are there" [Psalm 139:8]. But from there too you may call and cry out to the Eternal with soulful longing in the state of "From the belly of Sheol, I cried out . . ." [Jonah 2:3]. This is the essence of the way to repentance in which we are engaged continually during the holy Days of Awe: Rosh Hashanah, Yom Kippur, and the Ten Days of Repentance. And it is the essence of victory in the war in which we are engaged during those days, for whenever people do not allow themselves to be discouraged, but encourage themselves to begin anew each time, they can somehow be called "victors" in the war.

In truth, the war belongs to the Eternal, for it is impossible for a person to be victorious on their own, as our sages have said: "If it were not for the help of the Holy One, [one would not be able to prevail]"; and as it is said: "The Eternal is at war with Amalek [in every generation]" [Exodus 17:16]. But people are obliged to encourage themselves anew every time so that they do not retreat from this war, nor be discouraged in any way.

This is hinted at in the words of the holy Zohar when it says: "Who is the victor? Whoever holds weapons in their hands [at the end of the battle]." It is clear that we do not see with any certainty who is victorious because this is a very long war indeed; the exile is overpowering, and everyone commits whatever transgressions they commit. Nevertheless, as long as we still hold our weapons in our hands [we may be considered victors], and our main weapon is prayer, as has been explained in other places. As long as we do not discourage ourselves in this battle but still hold on to our weapons, we are certain to be victorious. As long as people encourage themselves with prayer and crying out to God, they are in the general category of those who are victorious in battle, for this is the essence of victory, as stated above.

Natan of (Nemirov) Breslov (1780–1844), *Meshivat Nafesh* [Restoring the soul (Psalm 19:8)] (Jerusalem, 1976), §40, pp. 56–57

The state of "If I make my bed in Sheol." Sheol is the shadowy under-world mentioned occasionally in the Bible, or, in the opinion of some biblical scholars, it is the grave. In our text, it is a metaphor for depression. We should not allow ourselves to get into such a state, but if it happens, then even in the depths of our depression we can still call on God for help.

The state of "From the belly of Sheol, I cried out." The opening words of Jonah's heartfelt prayer in the belly of the great fish.

"If it were not for the help." Talmud, *Bava Batra* 75a. The prooftext that follows does not occur on this page of the Talmud.

"Who is the victor? . . ." This quotation is not found in our standard Zohar text, but cf. Zohar I, 221a: "Whoever emerges [from the battle] with the standard of the king has been victorious."

COMMENT

A significant element in any great religion must be the encouragement to live a life of purity and holiness. Yet anyone who has embarked on such a course knows how difficult it is. There are so many temptations and pitfalls as well as internal, and even external, enemies lying in wait that it may indeed seem like a war, a never-ending war. And that thought can be depressing. To overcome that, we need to encourage ourselves and each other constantly. The war can only be won little by little; big battles are rare, small battles the norm. Fight the good fight! As long as we keep at it, we can win.

Yitro

---

[49] Reacting to Fear

"Jethro, the priest of Midian, the father-in-law of Moses,
heard all that God had done for Moses and for his people,
that the Eternal had brought Israel out of Egypt."

Exodus 18:1

CONTEXT

After the Israelites journey farther into the wilderness and defeat the Amalekites in battle, they camp at the foot of the Mountain of God, Sinai. Then, Moses's father-in-law, Jethro (Yitro), arrives in the camp with Moses's wife and two sons. News of the Exodus of the Israelite slaves has reached him, and he is eager to hear the story.

The Kotzker was a great believer in the value of truth, even if it was painful. To this end, he never ceased to challenge his followers to confront the truth within themselves.

> In the Midrash Tanchuma [it says]: "'Jethro . . . heard'—there are those who hear and suffer and those who hear and are rewarded . . . thus 'the nations shall hear, [and] be afraid' [Exodus 15:14]. But Jethro heard and was rewarded, for he had been an idolatrous priest, but he came, attached himself to Moses [and entered under the wings of the Shechinah (the Presence of God)]." Thus far the midrash.
>
> You have to understand why the midrash teaches us this. For in one "hearing" some hear and are rewarded and others hear and suffer. Jethro heard of the miracles of the splitting of the Reed Sea and experienced the fear of God; so he came and drew near. The nations also experienced fear, but they fled from God, because they wanted to get rid of the fear.

Menachem Mendel of Kotzk (1787–1859), *Ohel Torah* [The tent of Torah] (Lublin, 1909), p. 13b

In the Midrash Tanchuma. Yitro §2.

Thus, "the nations shall hear, [and] be afraid." I.e., suffer fear.

Thus far the midrash. This sentence marks the end of the quotation. The next represents the start of the Kotzker's comment.

For in one "hearing." According to the midrash, both Jethro and the nations of the world heard about the splitting of the Reed Sea.

COMMENT

The midrash quoted above suggests that there was a difference in attitude toward what Jethro and the nations heard, but doesn't suggest precisely what that difference was. The Kotzker attempts to reach behind the midrash to specify that difference. His view is that in both cases what they heard caused fear of God, but that only Jethro was courageous enough to stay with that fear. Sometimes people who have religious experiences of fear and awe retreat from those feelings, either by denying their reality or by escaping into cults where these emotions are artificially heightened and re-created in an environment separate from normal life. My reading of the Kotzker is that he is suggesting that we have to stay with those emotions, but integrate them into our lives, much as Jethro did through his conversion to Judaism, as the midrash intimates.

---

[50] The Greatest Treasure

"You shall belong to Me as a treasure."

Exodus 19:5

CONTEXT

Three months after their departure from Egypt, the Israelites arrive at the foot of Mount Sinai and prepare to receive the Ten Commandments. But first God instructs Moses on how they are to prepare and on the significance of what is about to happen: the divine revelation means that God and the People of Israel are now bound together in covenant forever.

Moshe of Kobrin was a popular and important figure in his time, known for his brief teachings and his kindness.

The meaning is: When you belong to Me, that would be the greatest treasure of all.

Moshe ben Yisra'el Polier of Kobrin (1784–1858), *Amarot Tehorot* [Pure sayings (Psalm 12:7)] (Warsaw, 1910), p. 10

COMMENT

The notion of the Jews as God's chosen people has been controversial since at least the Hellenistic period. Here, R. Moshe of Kobrin indicates that Jewish chosenness is not a license to accumulate wealth or power, but an invitation to draw near to God and to righteousness.

---

[51] Your Physical Being, Your Spiritual Being

"I am the Eternal, your God, who brought you out of the land of Egypt, out of the place of slavery. You shall have no other gods but Me."
Exodus 20:2–3

CONTEXT

The Ten Commandments open, not with a commandment, but with a summary declaration of God's saving acts toward the People of Israel. The prohibition of polytheism then follows.

Mordechai of Chernobyl succeeded his father, Menachem Nachum, a disciple of the Maggid of Mezritch, as leader of the Chernobyl Hasidim, but Mordechai was actually the real founder of that group, bringing it a new, higher standing in the Jewish community in the area. This text forms part of the opening essays in the work from which it is drawn.

First, a person must know and trust with perfect and robust trust that there exists a God who is One, singular and unique, and who brought about everything that exists out of nothing, faith derived both from tradition and from experience, as it is written: "Know the God of your father, and serve God" (1 Chronicles 28:9). In this verse, there are two types of faith.

On top of this faith in God, the person burning for divine service must give the soul for this, because this is the meaning [of the talmudic teaching that] "'I [am the Eternal your God]' [Exodus 20:2] and 'You shall have no [other gods]' [Exodus 20:3] were both heard [directly] from the mouth of the Mighty One."

A Jewish person must overcome the material side, subduing it and purifying it. Then you are illuminating your spiritual being through your physical being, and becoming a vehicle for God. [Thus,] "I [am the Eternal your God]" [Exodus 20:2] and "You shall have no [other gods]" [Exodus 20:3] encompass the entire Torah, and its fulfillment.

Mordechai of Chernobyl (d. 1837), *Likkutei Torah* [Torah gleanings] (Jerusalem, 2001), p. 12

NOTES

"Know the God of your father, and serve God." Apparently the first clause is taken to indicate faith based on tradition and the second, faith based on experience.

"Were both heard [directly] from the mouth of Mighty One." Talmud, *Makkot* 24a. Hearing the words of God directly implies a readiness to die.

A vehicle. In Hebrew, *merkavah* (chariot).

COMMENT

If, as is frequently suggested, the Ten Commandments represent the distilled essence of Judaism, then R. Mordechai has distilled that essence even further. For him, it all stands on our faith in God and our abandonment of idolatry. Idolatry is much more subtle than it used to be. I doubt if many Jews are tempted to worship statues or pictures, but many are drawn to the worship of ideologies, or Jewish nationalism, or their own bodies and personal images. Our Jewish calling is higher than that. We are called upon to abandon all worship of anything that is not God. That is the negative side. The positive aspect is that we are asked to give our very souls for God.

Mishpatim

---

[52] Whose Eye?

"An eye for an eye, a tooth for a tooth, a hand for a hand. . . ."
Exodus 21:24

CONTEXT

The discussion of the case of a pregnant woman injured in a conflict between two men leads to this general principle, the subject of much controversy, especially between Jews and Christians. As the passage below suggests, Rabbinic tradition is unanimous in understanding this to mean monetary compensation rather than mutilation.

Menachem Recanati was an Italian kabbalist, author of a Torah commentary and a book detailing the kabbalistic meaning of the commandments.

You already know concerning this verse [that] our Rabbis have taught that it is not [to be understood] in its plain sense, but as monetary payment. . . .

But perhaps you may ask: If the intention is not as it is written, why is it written like this, thereby giving space for heretics to rebel? The answer is [based on] what our Rabbis have taught: "There are seventy facets to the Torah." The explanation of the commandment according to its practical sense is given in the Oral Torah, and it is this we follow, but the language of the verse deals with another subject, so that other facets, which might not have been understood apart from that language, might be understood.

For instance, in the case of the phrase "An eye for an eye," the truth, according to the Kabbalah, is that one who injures another is liable on five counts, but it is written the way it is to [allude] to a very great mystery. . . . The human form, with its limbs and shape, in its entirety, is made on [the model] of the supernal human form. Thus, since human

limbs are intended by creation to be its limbs, that is, a throne for the
supernal limbs, they contain within themselves an extra potential and
continuity from the limits of Nothingness, and when you turn it and
turn it [over in your mind], this is the secret meaning of [the phrase]:
"When you give injury to another person"—as is well known, "so shall
it be given to you" [Leviticus 24:20]. Consider this well.

Menachem ben Binyamin Recanati (late thirteenth–early fourteenth
centuries), *Perush al HaTorah* [Commentary on the Torah] (Jerusalem,
2003), pt. 2, pp. 98–99

NOTES

It is not [to be understood] in its plain sense. This verse is not a license
for mutilation as a punishment. See Talmud, *Bava Kamma* 83b.

Thereby giving space for heretics to rebel. A literal interpretation of the
verse would invite ridicule and anti-Semitic attacks.

"There are seventy facets to the Torah." See the *Alphabet of Rabbi Akiva*
and *Be-midbar Rabbah* 13:15,16.

In the Oral Torah. In Rabbinic literature.

The language of the verse deals with another subject. If the literal meaning is not to be used for practical, legal purposes, it must be intended to be
understood as indicating something else, on another level of interpretation.

According to the Kabbalah. Actually, what follows immediately after this
phrase is a Rabbinic teaching, rather than Kabbalah in the strict mystical
sense.

Is liable on five counts. The Mishnah states that someone who accidentally
causes injury to another is liable to pay for injury, pain, healing, loss of
time, and loss of dignity (*Bava Kamma* 8:1).

**The human form . . . is made on [the model] of the supernal human
form** The human form is based on that of the configuration of the *sefirot*
often referred to in kabbalistic texts as Adam Kadmon (the "primordial human"). Historically, this was understood to be a masculine figure. Thus, the
top of the head corresponds to Keter, the hemispheres of the brain to Hochmah and Binah, the arms and hands to Hesed and Gevurah, the torso to
Tiferet, the legs to Netzach and Hod, the genitalia to Yesod, and the male's
feminine partner to Malchut.

A throne for the supernal limbs. The parts of the human body do not simply correspond to the *sefirot*; they are intended to make the *sefirot* manifest
in the world.

They contain within themselves an extra potential and continuity from the limits of Nothingness. Human limbs contain divine potencies from the *sefirot* and, although material, are ultimately one with them. They are at the "lower" end of a continuum that stretches back to Nothingness, the divine Nothing from which the *sefirot* emerge.

"When you give injury to another person"—as is well known, "so shall it be given to you." Recanati is telling us that our sins cause damage to the corresponding *sefirot,* and that this damage then rebounds back upon us. "Another person" in his view indicates the supernal human image in the *sefirot.*

COMMENT

The idea that humanity is made in the image of God is not simply a lovely metaphor, let alone the absurdity that some would have us believe. It is a profound spiritual truth. Recanati emphasizes the damage that the neglect or harm we perpetrate on others brings to the divine because each of us reflects God's image. But the concept can be stated positively: our hands are the expression of God's Hesed (Lovingkindness) when we act lovingly and kindly, when we use them to do good, give charity, shake hands in friendship, etc., and they are the expression of God's Gevurah (Might) when we act forcefully against wrongs. We are vehicles for the *sefirot,* for God's presence in the world. On the one hand, this implies that we must respect others, for they too are vehicles for the divine. And on the other hand, we must respect ourselves and avoid doing anything that might detract from the One whose image we bear.

---

[53] Soul on Loan

"When someone borrows [an animal] from his neighbor and it is
injured or dies, if the owner is not present, full payment shall be made.
If the owner is present with him, there shall be no payment. . . ."

Exodus 22:13–14

CONTEXT

Among the many and varied laws of Mishpatim is this one concerning the respective obligations of the borrower and the lender of an animal.

Simchah Bunam of Pshische had been a disciple of the Seer of Lublin before becoming a key figure in a more individualistic trend of Hasidism inaugurated by his friend Ya'akov Yitzchak, known as the Holy Jew of Pshische.

> Every person receives their soul and their life as a loan from heaven, on condition that they employ them for good, and hence you are a borrower and [as such] are responsible even for [sins that are performed] under compulsion. In that case, how can you [possibly] free yourself from transgressions committed under compulsion or by accident? Only when "the Owner is present with him," when you remember God continually, and take upon yourself the yoke of the kingdom of heaven, then "there shall be no payment."
>
> This is what King David says (Psalm 27[:4]): "One thing have I borrowed from the Eternal." This refers to the one and unique soul, but I have only borrowed it from the Eternal. In that case, the suspicion remains that I might be liable even for sins committed under compulsion. But "only this do I seek: to live in the House of the Eternal all the days of my life" [Psalm 27:4], for my ambition is always to draw nearer to God and to be with God. This, then, is "borrowing in the presence of the Owner."

Simchah Bunam of Pshische (1765–1827), *Midrash Simchah* [Simchah's interpretation] (Jerusalem: Mossad HaRYM Levin, 1988), v. 1, p. 113

NOTES

Only when "the Owner is present with him." For Simchah Bunam, the owner represents God, Owner of the soul.

"One thing have I borrowed from the Eternal." JPS: "One thing I ask of the Lord." The Hebrew root *sh-'-l* can mean "ask" or "borrow."

"Borrowing in the presence of the Owner." Simchah Bunam uses a talmudic phrase; see, e.g., *Bava Metzia* 96b.

COMMENT

We all commit sins. They are an unavoidable part of life, of being human and therefore fallible. Because of this, all the great religions are concerned with offering their adherents an understanding of the causes of sin, strategies for avoiding sin, and methods for overcoming the spiritual results of sin; and Judaism is no exception. Traditional Judaism recognized that much of our sinfulness originated within, when it adopted the notion of the inclination toward evil inside each of us. And it offered the process of repentance and atonement, culminating in Yom Kippur, as the means for overcoming the results of sin. R. Simchah Bunam stands in a long line of Jewish teachers when he posits the consciousness of the presence of God as a strategy for avoiding sin in the first place. If we could always bear in mind that God is with us, we would avoid bad behavior, and any sins that we had inadvertently committed would be forgiven. Like most spiritual goals, this one seems almost unattainable, but we can each make a start, and perhaps one day we will arrive.

---

[54] "Who Is This Life Force?"

"Then he [Moses] took the book of the covenant and read it in the hearing of the people, and they said: 'All that the Eternal has said we will do and we will listen.'"

Exodus 24:7

CONTEXT

Chapter 24 offers us a covenantal ceremony, a rite in which the People of Israel commit themselves to a covenant, a contract with God. Part of that ceremony included the reading of a Book of the Covenant by Moses.

Menachem Nachum of Chernobyl was a student of the Maggid of Mezritch and a traveling preacher.

"When Israel put 'we will do' before 'we will listen,' a heavenly voice went forth and said: 'Who revealed to My children this secret that the ministering angels use?'" . . .

We need to understand how it is possible to do before you have heard what to do, and the point of the praise that God confers because they put "we will do" before "we will listen."

Now the truth is that people cannot always remain at one level, because the life force ebbs and flows, comes and goes. That is, when you are attached to God, you feel a life force and pleasure, but afterward it goes and you fall from your level. Concerning this, there are secrets of the Torah in explanation of the matter of why it is necessary to fall from your level. One reason is in order to enter later into a higher level, for in everything there must be an absence prior to [something coming into] existence, so when people want to ascend to a higher level, there must be an absence beforehand. Therefore, you must fall from the level you are on now.

Look here, even when people fall, they may make an effort to ascend to the Eternal even at the level where they are, for you must believe that "the whole earth is full of God's glory" [Isaiah 6:3] and "that there is no place empty of God." Even at the level where you are, God is there, even though in a very contracted state. . . .

This is why we read "we will do" before "we will listen": Even though we may fall from our level, we should adhere to God at that very level, as mentioned above. Then, we can hear. For the essence of hearing is understanding, that is, that you enter a higher level, as mentioned above. This is the essence of the acceptance of the Torah that Israel received. Therefore, the Holy One praised them for this very much, for they had accepted the Torah with great truthfulness, and had attained the truth that they could always be attached to the Holy One and not be separated from God even when they fall from their level. This is the essence of Israelite practice, and we have to behave in this way.

But how may you come to God when the "mental forces" and knowledge have fallen away from you? Yet, God's "glory fills the earth" [Isaiah 6:3], that is, even in a place that is entirely earth, that is, entirely material, entirely coarse matter, even [that place] is filled with the glory of God. God is called the Life of Life, that is, all the life in the world, domestic or wild animals, birds, or the human eye—their life force is the Blessed One. Hence, God is the Life of Life, the life of [all] that lives. So, when you fall from your level, you should think: Am I not alive? And who is this life force of mine? Is it not the Creator? There you will find that God is also present, even though in a very contracted state.

Hence the Holy One said, "Who revealed to My children this secret?" That is to say, "Who?" meaning, when they thought "Who is this life force of ours?" this revealed to them this secret: to put "we will do" before "we will listen," as described above.

Menachem Nachum of Chernobyl (1730–97), *Me'or Einayim* [The light of the eyes] (n.p., 1952), pt. 1, pp. 68–69

"All that the Eternal has said we will do and we will listen." An overly literal translation, as required by the passage that follows. JPS has "we will faithfully do" in the body of the text, and "we will do and obey" as a literal translation in a footnote. Menachem Nachum follows the midrash in treating this phrase superliterally. The phrase has long been taken as "proof" of the willingness of the Jewish people to offer obedience to the Torah even before learning of its contents (see, e.g., *Mechilta*, Yitro §5).

"When Israel put 'we will do' before 'we will listen.'" Quoted from Talmud, *Shabbat* 88a. Here a divine voice queries how the Israelites came to be as spiritually advanced as the angels.

"Who revealed to My children." Menachem Nachum takes this positively, as a rhetorical question, as if to say, "No one revealed it! They worked it out by themselves!" He then goes on to consider what the secret might have been.

The life force ebbs and flows. This phrase comes from Ezekiel's vision of the chariot of God recounted in the opening chapters of his book, specifically Ezekiel 1:14. The original subject was the fantastic four-faced creatures that accompanied the chariot on its journeys. Hasidic texts frequently alter the vowels, reading *CHaYYuT* or *CHiYYuT* (life force) for *CHaYYoT* (living creatures).

One reason is in order to enter later into a higher level. Descending to a lower level of consciousness should be understood as an opportunity to prepare for ascent later.

"There is no place empty of God." *Tikkunei HaZohar* §70, p. 122b.

In a very contracted state. The Hebrew is *metzumtzam*, an adjective related to the Lurianic concept of *tzimtzum*, the divine contraction that was necessary to create an empty space in which the universe could exist.

Then, we can hear. Our author implies, but does not state, that we should adhere to God even when we are at low spiritual levels by continuing to perform spiritual acts, as suggested by the phrase "we will do." Then, when we reach a higher stage once more, "we will hear," i.e., understand, in ways we could not before.

And had attained the truth that they could always be attached to the Holy One. According to Menachem Nachum, this is the secret the Israelites had discovered, that you can be attached to God no matter what your psychological and spiritual state.

"Mental forces." The text has *mochin*, literally "brains." In the Zohar, this term refers to the three highest *sefirot*: Keter, Hochmah, and Binah. Here it alludes to the higher mental forces deriving from those supernal *sefirot*, or to the corresponding *sefirot* as they exist within us.

And knowledge. In Hebrew, *da'at*, a name sometimes applied to a *sefirah* between and below Hochmah and Binah. Moshe Cordovero suggests that it is the external aspect of Keter.

Am I not alive? . . . Is it not the Creator? These words in Hebrew, with a corresponding English version, have been set to a haunting melody by the late Rabbi David Zeller.

That is to say, "Who?" The pronoun "who" (*mi*) indicates the *sefirah* of Binah (Understanding), because it is hidden but a question may be asked of it. According to R. Menachem Nachum, the Israelites came to an understanding of the secret of God's presence everywhere and at all times.

COMMENT

Though this text is long and difficult, I believe it repays careful study. Its message of God's presence is in my opinion a crucial one in the materialistic environment in which we live. It teaches us that even when life's problems and challenges seem insuperable, God is with us, within us, and as long we can feel that, there is hope for us all.

Terumah

---

[55] Not Just Now

"Then the Eternal spoke to Moses, saying: 'Speak to the Israelites
that they may take an offering for Me. From everyone whose
heart encourages them shall you take My offering.'"

Exodus 25:1–2

CONTEXT

After the Ten Commandments, and the primarily civil and criminal case law of Mishpatim, the Torah turns to the subject of building the Tabernacle, the portable sanctuary used during the wilderness years. Terumah begins with a call for donations in kind.

Ze'ev Wolf of Zhitomir was a disciple of the Maggid of Mezritch.

This is a great principle of the Torah and of the service of God: that within everything in the universe there is a hint of wisdom, so that enlightened people can awaken their hearts within them to the service of their Creator, even when eating and drinking, and buying and selling. This is what the previous scriptural [verse] alludes to: "From everyone whose heart encourages them shall you take My offering"— that is, not just then, at the moment the command of the section of the *terumah* was given, or of the building of the Tabernacle, for in truth the Torah is eternal and exists in all times. Hence, "from everyone whose heart encourages them" toward the service of their Creator, from this time on, until the arrival of our Messiah, "shall you take My offering"—you are allowed to take the aspect of "My offering," for matters regarding the Israelites' service are ongoing.

Ze'ev Wolf of Zhitomir (d. 1800), *Or HaMe'ir* [The illuminating light] (Warsaw, 1883), pt. 2, p. 34

There is a hint of wisdom. All things derive ultimately from the *sefirah* of Hochmah (Wisdom), and therefore allude to divine wisdom.

You are allowed to take the aspect of "My offering." Anyone who is so moved may bring an offering to God.

COMMENT

We all have our obligations, to ourselves, to others, to God. But sometimes we feel we want to give more, above and beyond our obligations. If we are spiritually enlightened, we can be sensitive to need, and respond. When we do so, that is a religious act, just like the freewill donations made by the ancient Israelites to the Tabernacle. But instead of a physical building in which God was said to dwell, we are constructing a spiritual edifice for the divine Presence.

---

[56] Becoming a Menorah

"You shall make a candelabrum of pure gold; of beaten gold
[mikshah] shall the candelabrum be made. . . ."

Exodus 25:31

CONTEXT

The menorah of seven branches that was to stand in the Tabernacle had to be made of unalloyed beaten gold.

Mordechai of Neschiz was famous in his own day as a miracle worker.

The meaning is [that] the hardest service [*avodah haKaSHaH*] is "pure gold," namely, that a person's silver and gold should be pure, without [the violation of] any prohibition [and] without any impure thoughts. People like this, who purify their silver and gold to a great extent, are "made into a candelabrum," acting at a level where they are able to shed the light of their holiness on the world.

Mordechai of Neschiz (d. 1800), *Rishpei Esh* [Coals of fire (Song of Songs 8:6)] (Jerusalem, 1997), p. 15

The hardest service [*avodah haKaSHaH*] . *Avodah* can also mean "work."
The adjective *kashah* is obviously a pun on *mikshah*.

A person's silver and gold. Perhaps this is to be taken almost literally, as
a person's money or means of making a living. Alternatively, "silver and
gold" might mean our actions and our motives.

COMMENT

Purifying our thoughts is much more difficult than purifying our deeds,
and God knows how hard that can be! We all feel anger and lust, for example, but most of us act only rarely on those emotions. R. Mordechai
suggests that we may be able to purify our thoughts so that we do not
experience those feelings in the first place. We have learned to doubt this
possibility, as we have learned to doubt so much, but perhaps it is achiev-
able. To the extent that we do achieve it, we may help shed light for others, guiding them toward holiness. For holiness does not exist in a vacuum,
in isolated individuals; it survives and thrives only in community, where
the light of individuals can become visible so that others may see by it.

---

[57] Your Body Is an Altar

*"You shall make an altar of acacia wood, five cubits in
length, five cubits in width and three cubits in height."*

Exodus 27:1

CONTEXT

In Exodus 27 the Torah gives the dimensions, materials, and description
of the altar upon which sacrifices were to be offered.

Hayyim Yosef David Azulai, also known by his acronym as the CHI-
Da, was one of the great Sephardic rabbis of his age. He was a halachic
scholar as well as a kabbalist. Among his many works is the collection
of his sermons from which this extract was taken.

The altar is a hint that you should prepare your body as a great altar for the sacrifice of your inclination [toward evil]. Vain thoughts

should be burnt with the fire of the exalted Torah. It is a mitzvah to bring self-afflictions and fasts from ordinary people, and immediately an exalted fire is given by heaven, crouching like a lion in your heart. The heart is purified, and you can sacrifice upon it the inclination toward all evil thoughts, and they will be burnt up. Those who offer sacrifices [of this kind] love their fellow human beings, and draw them closer to Torah, righteousness, [and] deeds of lovingkindness. The dimensions of the altar are perfect: five [cubits] in length, five in width, and three in height, which add up to thirteen, the same as the numerical value of *'eCHaD* [one], for all your intention should be to unite the "lovers." Every day it is a mitzvah to "raise up the ashes," to remove the remnants of evil thoughts.

Hayyim Yosef David Azulai (the CHIDa) (1724–1806), *Chadrei Vaten* [Innermost parts] (Jerusalem, 1990), p. 147, §8

NOTES

It is a mitzvah to bring self-afflictions and fasts from ordinary people. The CHIDa, like most of his kabbalistic predecessors and contemporaries except for the Ba'al Shem Tov and his followers, had a positive view of ascetic practices. He believed that they purify the mind and energize the soul.

The same as the numerical value of *'eCHaD* [one]. The word *'eCHaD* is composed of three letters—*'alef* (= 1), *CHet* (= 8), and *Dalet* (= 4)—giving a total of 13. It is also the last letter of the first line of the *Shema*, which the CHIDa may have in mind.

To unite the "lovers." The "lovers" are Tiferet (Beauty) and Malchut (Sovereignty), the masculine and feminine respectively. Our self-affliction should be undertaken with the intention of uniting these disparate elements, thus allowing divine energies to flow. Perhaps our author also intends this as a *kavanah* (meditation) to be employed when reciting the *Shema*.

It is a mitzvah to "raise up the ashes." See Leviticus 6:4. The ashes of the sacrifices burnt on the altar were to be removed each day. Is the CHIDa suggesting that our evil thoughts should be raised to God, or simply discarded as best we can?

COMMENT

I am not as great a believer in asceticism as the Chida was, but I was attracted to his image of the body as an altar upon which we may sacrifice our bodily desires by controlling them. With our physical needs and wants under our control, we can apply our minds more effectively to spiritual issues, to prayer and meditation, to recognizing the essential oneness of all things implied in the *Shema*.

Tetsavveh

---

[58] The Ideal Jew

*"These are the garments that they shall make: a breastplate, an
ephod, a robe, a fringed tunic, a headdress, and a sash."*
Exodus 28:4

CONTEXT

The High Priest who will officiate in the Tabernacle when it is completed must also have special garments, appropriate to the importance of
his task. In chapter 28, the Torah presents us with broad instructions in
verses 1–5 and detailed instructions in the rest of the chapter.

Mordechai of Izbica was known for his controversial views acknowledging that even evil deeds have their role in God's plan. Here he sets
out his image of the ideal Jew.

> With these garments, God is showing Israel what [type of] person
> is divinely chosen, for from these garments the precious elements of
> Aaron the priest's soul may be recognized and understood.
>
> The headband alludes to him because he had to be attached to
> God, just as [God] had commanded that it should always be on his
> forehead. On the headband were engraved [the words] "Holy to the
> Eternal," that is, in the depths of his thought was always [the idea of]
> "Know the God of your father" (2 Chronicles 28:9).
>
> The breastplate alludes to him for in his heart was to be found no
> hatred of anyone in Israel, because the [names of] the tribes of Israel
> were engraved on his heart.
>
> The ephod with which he was girded alludes to his trust in God,
> upon whom he relied.
>
> The robe teaches [us] about the greatness of his awe [of God], be-
> cause it was of purple [*techelet*], which alludes to awe.

Mordechai Yosef Leiner of Izbica (1800–54), *Mei HaShiloach* [The waters of
the Siloam (Isaiah 8:6)] (Bnei Brak, 1995), v. 1, p. 88

The headband. See Exodus 28:36, "You shall make a headband of pure gold, and engrave upon the seal the inscription 'Holy to the Eternal.'" The point of the headband is to direct the mind to God.

The breastplate. According to Exodus 28:29, the breastplate was to bear the names of the tribes so Aaron would have them over his heart.

The ephod. Its exact nature is unclear, but it appears to have been some sort of overgarment.

Purple [*techelet*], which alludes to awe. The exact color indicated by the word *techelet* is the subject of some disagreement among scholars, but it is also the color of the one thread in the tzitzit that was not white; see Numbers 15:38. According to the Zohar III, 175a, the white symbolizes the right (i.e., the *sefirah* of Hesed [Lovingkindness]) while the *techelet* represents the left (Gevurah [Might], also known as Yir'ah [Awe]).

COMMENT

For Rabbi Mordechai of Izbica, the High Priest's garments provide us with clues for helping us come closer to God, as tradition maintains Aaron did. The requisite qualities, according to our rebbe, include constant attachment to God in thought (*devekut*), trust in and awe of God, plus not harboring any hatred against any other Jew. Though we may wish to extend the prohibition of hatred to all human beings, it is clear that the spiritual virtues espoused here would, if put into practice, make us wiser people and the world a happier place.

---

[59] Everyone Is a Priest

"And there shall be a hole in the top of the robe of the ephod, in the middle of it. It shall have a binding of woven work around its mouth, like the mouth of a suit of armor, so that it should not be torn."

Exodus 28:32

CONTEXT

Verses 31–35 of Exodus 28 give the instructions for making the ephod, a highly decorated overgarment of expensive materials that priests were to wear when officiating at sacrifices.

The following passage comes from one of the most popular Jewish books of its time, and specifically from the section in which the author discusses each parashah in turn. Here as elsewhere, Horowitz delineates the commands he believes are to be found in this Torah portion and draws moral conclusions from them.

[One of the commandments in Tetsavveh is] not to allow the robe to be torn. The rabbi mentioned above wrote that the reason for this mitzvah was so that the priest should put a "strong wall" around his mouth. Since he offers supplication for a holy people, no improper word should issue from his mouth. Since he is the one who "binds" and "sews" together, he should produce no separations or tears, as it is written: The mind's "drowsiness will clothe [a person] in torn clothing" (Proverbs 23:21). Since the body clothes the soul, and the robe clothes the body, and they are joined together, it is fitting that that which covers the soul, known as the "robe of our sages," should not be torn. Thus far his words.

Every person who serves God is like a priest, and their merit stands before the masses. Therefore, let everyone sanctify their mouth with extra holiness.

Yishayah HaLevi Horowitz (ca. 1570–1626), *Shnei Luchot HaBrit* [The two tablets of the covenant] (1863; repr., Jerusalem: 1975), v. 2, pt. 1, p. 50b

NOTES

"Its mouth, like the mouth." A literal translation, as required by Horowitz's comment. JPS has "opening" instead of "mouth."

The rabbi mentioned above. Menachem ben Moshe Bavli (d. 1571), quoted earlier in the discussion on the commandments in Tetsavveh. He lived in the sixteenth century in Safed, but little is known of his life.

Since he is the one who "binds" and "sews" together. As priest, it is his job to bring about reconciliation between God and humanity. Alternatively, this may be a reference to binding together the *sefirot* of Tiferet (Beauty) and Malchut (Sovereignty).

"Robe of our sages." According to Zohar I, 66a, the garment that clothes the righteous in the next world. Sins committed in this world may damage it.

Thus far his words. This phrase marks the end of the quote from Menachem Bavli. The next two sentences are by Horowitz.

Horowitz moves us from a consideration of the moral qualities required of the priests of old to a consideration of our own. As Jews we are meant to serve God. We are all priests, representatives of Judaism before the public. What we do and what we say will reflect back on Judaism and the Jewish community, for good or for ill. And those of us who consciously try to serve God also bear a responsibility to behave in ways that will reflect Judaism positively to our fellow Jews, as well as non-Jews. This is not about "what will the goyim say?"; it is about "what does God demand from us?" and "what does Judaism say?"

---

[60] God Is Still Our God

*"I will dwell in the midst of the descendants of Israel, and
I will be their God. They shall know that I am the Eternal
their God, who brought them out of the land of Egypt that I
might dwell among them; I am the Eternal their God."*
Exodus 29:46–47

CONTEXT

Chapter 29 of Exodus contains the instructions for the consecration of the priests and of the altar. It concludes with God's promise to be present among the Israelites.

Hayyim ibn Attar was a Moroccan rabbi and Bible commentator.

"I am the Eternal their God"—a reason why this is said twice [in these two verses]: Perhaps the intention was to include even the period when the Shechinah [the Presence of God] is not among us. The Eternal is [still] our God, and we [still] belong to God.

Or maybe it refers in this way to their knowledge and recognition of the fact [of God's presence], as it says before this: "They shall know. . . ." By this [recognition], they become fit to be called by My Name; thus it says: "the Eternal their God." But without this [recognition], they are throwing off the yoke and will belong to other gods than God.

Hayyim ben Moshe ibn Attar (1696–1743), *Or HaHayyim* [The light of life] (Jerusalem: A. Blum, 1994), pt. 2, p. 158

God's presence is always with us, whether we are conscious of it or not. If you believe in an omnipresent God, then that follows automatically. But that logic, the logic of Ibn Attar's first interpretation, is cold and irrelevant to the way we live our lives. It is his second interpretation that makes this a spiritual teaching rather than simply a theological point. We belong to other gods—we are idolators, in other words—whenever we fail to appreciate God's ever-constant presence. That is a tall order, but we have to learn to walk tall.

Ki Tissa'

---

[61] Ransoming Yourself

"Then each person shall give a ransom [for] themselves . . .
that there shall be no plague among them."

Exodus 30:12

CONTEXT

Ki Tissa' opens with a brief passage detailing the annual poll tax of one-half shekel that each Israelite male over twenty had to pay for the upkeep of the Tabernacle (and later the Temple in Jerusalem). But the passage also states that this payment was intended as a means of avoiding the plague that, it was believed, would occur as a result of taking a census.

Pinchas of Koretz was a younger contemporary, and possibly a disciple, of the Ba'al Shem Tov. His sayings are often reported in short passages like this one.

> When each person gives themselves as a ransom, then "there shall be no plague among them" (Exodus 30:12).

Pinchas of Koretz (1726–91), *Imrei Pinchas* [Pinchas's sayings] (Tel Aviv: Arnberg, 1974), §67, p. 30

NOTE

"A ransom [for] themselves." The word "for" is not represented in the Hebrew, but required in English. Hence, the Koretzer interprets the text as "Each person shall give a ransom: themselves."

COMMENT

The Koretzer rebbe seems to be suggesting that if we are to avoid "plague," that is, damage to our community and ourselves, we must give ourselves as a ransom, that is, make ourselves responsible for trying to put right what is wrong. Then the plague of indifference will not come among us.

Alternatively, on an even deeper, more spiritual level, we have to give ourselves totally to God as a ransom payment so that we may be redeemed of our sins and failings.

---

[62] Seeing the Face of God

"For no one can see My face and live."

Exodus 33:20

CONTEXT

Ki Tissa' continues with further instructions for items pertaining to the Tabernacle, the choice of builders, and a reminder of the importance of the Sabbath, before recounting the tale of the Golden Calf. After that debacle, Moses asks to see God's glory. God replies, "No one can see My face and live," but then allows the divine glory to pass before Moses while the divine attributes are proclaimed.

Mordechai of Chernobyl was the son and successor of Menachem Nachum of Chernobyl, who was a student of the Maggid of Mezritch. The passage below comes from the essays on leadership presented at the beginning of the book of R. Mordechai's collected sayings.

> The essential thing is to believe with perfect faith that the Creator "fills the entire world with divine glory" [Isaiah 6:3] and that "no place is empty of God," and that when you look at the world, you are looking at the Creator. When you speak to people, you are speaking to the soul within them, for if the soul were to depart from the body, you would not be able to speak with them, for they would be like a dumb stone. When they are alive, you can speak with the soul within them . . . , even though you cannot see the soul. How much the more so are you unable to see the Creator, for God is the Soul of Souls! . . . Therefore, you must believe that God is here, even though you cannot see God, as Scripture says: "For no one can see My face and live" (Exodus 33:20).

Mordechai of Chernobyl (d. 1837), *Likkutei Torah* [Torah gleanings] (Jerusalem, 2001), p. 14

"No place is empty of God." *Tikkunei HaZohar* §70, p. 122b. This is a favorite formula of many Hasidic teachers.

COMMENT

Even if you do not believe in the soul in a physical sense, we do speak to each other's minds—but what is a mind? Where in the body does it exist? It is clearly not identical with the brain, since it is possible to have a brain without a mind, when brain death occurs or when dementia takes hold. Yet we believe that we have minds, and that other people have minds too, even though they are invisible to us. We see only their effects, in people's behavior and speech. Can we believe in God in the same way, as Mordechai of Chernobyl suggests?

---

[63] The Danger of Generalizations

"Molten gods you shall not make for yourself."

Exodus 34:17

CONTEXT

Moses prostrates himself as he hears God proclaim the divine attributes, and then God renews the promise to look after Israel and bring them to the Promised Land, but with conditions. The observance of certain laws is reemphasized here; not the least of them is the prohibition of making idols out of molten metals—exactly the sin committed in the construction of the Golden Calf!

Mordechai of Izbica was a controversial figure, formerly a disciple of Simchah Bunam of Pshische and Menachem Mendel of Kotzk.

"Molten"—these are generalizations, and concerning this Scripture is saying that when you have the explicit understanding of the heart, you must not look to generalizations to determine your behavior, but with the understanding of the heart you will know how to behave in each specific case, as we find in the case of Elijah on Mount Carmel.

Mordechai Yosef Leiner of Izbica (1800–54), *Mei HaShiloach* [The waters of the Siloam (Isaiah 8:6)] (Bnei Brak, 1995), v. 1, p. 96

"Molten"—these are generalizations. General principles, however noble, are not to be made into gods.

When you have the explicit understanding of the heart. When your conscience moves you.

In the case of Elijah on Mount Carmel. 1 Kings 18 recounts the contest between Elijah, the last remaining prophet of the Eternal, and four hundred prophets of Ba'al, in which Elijah was spectacularly successful. But in Rabbinic literature, it is a controversial story, because Elijah offers a sacrifice to God outside of the Temple in Jerusalem after the Temple had been built. This was contrary to the law frequently expressed in Deuteronomy that all sacrifices were to be centralized in the "site where the Eternal your God will choose to establish the divine name" (Deuteronomy 12:11). (See Talmud, *Sanhedrin* 89b, 90a, and *Yevamot* 90b; and *Be-midbar Rabbah* 14:1.) 1 Kings 18 is the usual haftarah that accompanies *parashat* Ki Tissa'.

COMMENT

The rebbe of Izbica was, and is, famous for his teachings of individualism, and this passage is part of that approach. Enlightened people do not have their behavior determined by fixed general rules, as most people do. If they are truly spiritually enlightened, they are attuned to the needs of the moment and the ebb and flow of divine influx, and so are free to respond spontaneously to any situation that presents itself.

But notice that the rebbe's recommendation is not for everyone. Most of us need the fixed general rules to live by, but once they are internalized, once they become truly part of ourselves, rather than something imposed from the outside, we can become truly free. This is spiritual maturity: a small child needs to have limits set by adults; mature adults set their own.

Va-yak'hel

---

[64] Fiery Anger

"You shall not light a fire in any of your dwellings on the Shabbat day."

Exodus 35:3

CONTEXT

Moses assembles the people to give them their instructions for building the Tabernacle and its equipment. But he begins by reminding them of the importance of observing *Shabbat*, even while the crucial work of creating a sanctuary is being done. Lighting a fire is the only work specifically prohibited by the Torah.

Tikkunei HaZohar is a one-volume addition to the Zohar literature, probably produced within a few decades of the Zohar itself. It offers over seventy interpretations of the opening verse of Genesis, each one labeled a *tikkun* (repair).

> Worthy are those who guard the *"Shabbat* tent," that is, the heart, so that no grief from the spleen nor anger from the gallbladder, that is, the fire of Gehinnom, should approach it. Concerning this it is said: "You shall not light a fire in any of your dwellings on the *Shabbat* day" [Exodus 35:3], for it is certain that whoever indulges in anger has kindled the fire of Gehinnom.

Reuven Margoliot, ed., *Tikkunei HaZohar* [The repairs of the Zohar] (Jerusalem: Mossad HaRav Kook, 1948), *Tikkun* no. 48, p. 85a

NOTES

The *"Shabbat* tent." The refuge that *Shabbat* should be. In our author's view, the heart is where the rest that is characteristic of *Shabbat* should be most manifest.

No grief from the spleen nor anger from the gallbladder. In standard medieval medicine, these emotions were thought to be due to overactivity in these organs.

Gehinnom. Originally a valley in Jerusalem where garbage and the bodies of executed criminals were deposited. In Rabbinic literature, it came to mean the place where the wicked are punished after death, akin to Hell. In the Talmud. (*Berachot* 57b) it says, "Shabbat is one-sixtieth of the world-to-come" and "fire is one-sixtieth of Gehinnom."

"You shall not light a fire in any of your dwellings on the *Shabbat* day." In the hands of our author, this now means: "You shall not be angry in your heart on the *Shabbat* day."

COMMENT

Shabbat is more than just a day to abstain from work, or even a day of family togetherness. It is more than an opportunity to reconnect with your community by going to shul. It is a day of rest, not just externally by refraining from work, but internally. Worry and negative emotions should be set aside; their presence disturbs the peace that *Shabbat* is meant to bring.

But this text seems to go further, urging us to banish anger and grief from our hearts, so that we may experience the inner peace of which *Shabbat* is an outward manifestation.

---

[65] Stone or Wood?

"And Moses said to the Israelites: 'See, the Eternal has singled out by name Bezalel . . . and has endowed him with a divine spirit, ability and knowledge of every kind of craft: . . . in the carving of stone to "fill," and in the carving of wood, to "act" in any kind of skillful work.'"

Exodus 35:30,31,33

CONTEXT

The Israelites are given the task of assembling the materials for the Tabernacle and all its utensils. Moses now presents Bezalel as the skilled craftsman designated by God to undertake the work.

Yisra'el Taub of Modzhitz was the founder of Modzhitz Hasidism, a relatively recent Polish dynasty. He placed great emphasis on the importance of music and singing for spirituality.

> We need to understand this as an allegory:
> "Stone" indicates the inclination toward evil, as is well known.
> "Wood" represents the Torah, a "tree of life," as is well known.
> The propensity of the inclination toward evil is "to fill," that is, to let people imagine that they are already full to capacity and perfect at all levels. Hence, the text says "and in the carving of stone," that is, the propensity of the inclination toward evil is "to fill."
> The Torah's propensity is the opposite. After any Torah study or mitzvot or good deeds of any kind, it still seems to people that they have achieved nothing and have to act anew. Hence the text says, "and in the carving of wood," that is, the propensity of the Torah, the tree of life, is "to act" anew everyday; "in any kind of skillful work," that is, as is fitting and as perfectly [as possible].

Yisra'el ben Shmuel of Modzhitz (1849–1921), *Divrei Yisra'el* [Israel's words] (Tel Aviv, 1984), pt. 2, p. 91

NOTES

"To 'fill.'" JPS: "for setting." The Modzhitzer's comments require a superliteral translation.

"To 'act.'" JPS: "to work."

"Stone" indicates the inclination toward evil. See *Va-yikra Rabbah* 35:5.

"Wood" represents the Torah, a "tree of life." See *Be-midbar Rabbah* 12:4.

The propensity. The word literally means "a skill or craft."

COMMENT

Torah should make us question ourselves: our actions and, even more importantly, our motives. It is a weapon against complacency and self-satisfaction, both for ourselves and for our community. To the extent that we fail to question ourselves, we are in thrall to our inclination toward evil.

[66] Seeing Yourself in a Mirror

*"Then he made a basin of brass, and the base of it of brass, of the mirrors of
the serving women that did the service at the door of the Tent of Meeting."*

Exodus 38:8

CONTEXT

After Moses's speech to the people, the donations for the Tabernacle are
collected and the work begun. The Torah describes the manufacture of
each item in intricate detail.

Ya'akov Yosef of Polonnoye was a key disciple of the Ba'al Shem Tov,
and his books contain many quotations from his master.

> I heard in the name of my teacher an explanation of the [teaching
> in the] Mishnah, "Who is wise? One who learns from everyone," ac-
> cording to a parable. One who gazes into a mirror knows his own
> deficiency, etc. Similarly, one who looks at the deficiency of another
> knows that there is an element of that within him, etc. "Words from
> a wise person's mouth are gracious" [Ecclesiastes 10:12]. . . .
>
> In this way, you may understand the verse "he made the basin of
> brass"—that is, for washing. Is it possible that [a priest] would say
> that he had no need to wash? But the answer to this is that it was made
> "of the mirrors of the serving women," so that [a priest] would gaze
> at others in the mirror and see in what way they were deficient. Then
> he would feel that the way in which others were deficient is within
> himself as well, and he would know that he had to wash. Understand!
>
> Moreover, it is precisely the wise person who learns from every-
> one, just as someone looking in a mirror sees their own deficiency by
> seeing the deficiency of others. This is not the case with those who
> do not fall within the definition of "wise." They do not see their own
> deficiency in that of others.

Ya'akov Yosef of Polonnoye (died ca. 1782), *Toledot Ya'akov Yosef* [The
generations of Jacob Joseph (Genesis 37:2)] (Jerusalem, 1973), v. 1, p. 259

In the name of my teacher. The Ba'al Shem Tov, founder of the Hasidic movement in Ukraine.

The [teaching in the] Mishnah, "Who is wise?" *Pirkei Avot* 4:1.

"Words from a wise person's mouth are gracious" [Ecclesiastes 10:12]. An editorial comment frequently found in Hasidic texts at the conclusion of quotations from revered teachers.

COMMENT

The wise person is never self-satisfied, always self-critical; not self-centered, but an observer of others, learning from them both positive and negative lessons. The wise person never stops learning, and knows that others can be a mirror for self-reflection.

Pekudei

---

[67] Submitting an Account

"These are the accounts of the Tabernacle [mishkan]. . . ."
Exodus 38:21

CONTEXT

The Tabernacle has been completed; hence the Torah presents the final accounts, a list of all the materials that went into the construction of the portable sanctuary.

Mordechai was the real creator of the Chernobyl Hasidic group, although his father had also been a famous tzadik in his time.

The Holy One demands an account from humanity from day to day, ever since the day the Holy One created the universe. Thus, people must make an account and a reckoning with themselves before speaking words before the Holy One, whose divinity dwells within them.

Mordechai of Chernobyl (d. 1837), *Likkutei Torah* [Torah gleanings] (Jerusalem, 2001), pp. 103–4

NOTE

Whose divinity dwells. The Hebrew reads *SHoCHeiN*, from the same verbal root as *mishkan* (Tabernacle), and Shechinah (the Presence of God).

COMMENT

A group of Muslim students once asked me if I believed in the Day of Judgment, a concept found in all three Abrahamic faiths; and they clearly had in mind the notion of a Last Judgment. I told them I was an agnostic on the question of a final future reckoning for all humanity, although this idea is certainly found in Judaism. Instead, I said I preferred to think of every day as a day of judgment. Every day we act or fail to act, speak or fail to speak; and every day, what we have done contributes to the world in which we live. And the world reacts. The effect we have may be small or great, and the reaction too, but I believe that the world is an interactive system, and everything comes back to us, for good or for ill. And as Mordechai of Chernobyl says, before we pray, we have to try to account to God for how we have spent our time.

[68] Work or Service?

"Thus did the Israelites do the service [avodah]."

Exodus 39:42

CONTEXT

The priestly vestments have all been made, and now everything is ready for the erection of the Tabernacle. The people begin by bringing everything they have made to Moses for his approval. This he gives. It has all been done in accordance with God's plans.

Rabbenu Bachya is the author of the only major Torah commentary to try to explicitly offer comments on different levels. Though not labeled as such, the text below clearly falls into the category of *peshat*, the plain meaning.

> It should have said "the work [*melachah*]," but Scripture calls the work of the Tabernacle "service [*avodah*]" because they did it as a service to God, as it is written, "You should serve the Eternal your God" (Exodus 23[:25]), and it is written: "[God] shall you serve" (Deuteronomy 13[:5]).

> Rabbenu Bachya ben Asher ben Chlava (thirteenth century), *Perush al HaTorah* [Commentary on the Torah] (Jerusalem: Blum, 1988), pt. 2, p. 233

NOTE

"The work [*melachah*]," . . . "service [*avodah*]." The word *avodah* means both "work" and "service" or "worship," but as Rabbenu Bachya points out, there is another word that means "work," namely, *melachah*, the word used in particular regarding those activities that we should avoid on the Sabbath.

For the Israelites, building the Tabernacle wasn't just a job, says Rabbenu Bachya, it was the service of God. In modern times, when we often do not see the end product of our work because others finish the work we have begun, or we buy the finished product of other people's work, it is very easy to see the work we do as simply a way of earning money to be able to do the things we really want to do. And this means that the attitude we bring to our work can be negative at worst, or even just impersonal. Under either circumstance, however, we may take no pride in our work.

Rabbenu Bachya's comment suggests an alternative view of work. Perhaps we need to see the tasks we do, whatever they may be, as the service of God. In this way, we may find new meaning and significance in necessary jobs that might otherwise seem unfulfilling.

---

[69] Removing the Cloud

"Whenever the cloud was taken up from over the Tabernacle,
the People of Israel would travel on their journeys."

Exodus 40:36

CONTEXT

All the items produced for the Tabernacle have been assembled, and Moses now erects the structure and positions all the equipment. As a sign that all has been done according to divine will, a cloud, representing the presence of God, fills the Tabernacle, so that even Moses cannot enter. The lifting of the cloud would be the signal for the Israelites to resume their travels through the wilderness.

Avraham of Radomsk was a popular Hasidic leader in Poland, heading one of the largest groupings in the country.

It seems that there is an allusion in this, for you must see to it that nothing is interspersed between yourself and the wall when you pray, that is, between you and the holy Shechinah [the Presence of God], so that it may rest upon you. Hence, "whenever the cloud was taken up from over the Tabernacle"—that is, when the intervening "curtain" [was removed], then "the People of Israel would travel on their journeys"—that is, they would be able to walk the paths of the service of God. Consider this, and you will find that it is easy [to understand].

Avraham Yissachar Ber HaCohen of Radomsk (1843–92), *Hesed leAvraham* [Lovingkindness to Abraham (Micah 7:20)] (n.p., 1893–95), p. 258

NOTES

That nothing is interspersed between yourself and the wall when you pray. This principle is stated in the Talmud, *Berachot* 5b. Any such objects would distract you from your prayer.

Between you and the holy Shechinah. The Radomsker interprets "wall" in a spiritual sense. In this, he is following the Zohar II, 133a: "the Shechinah is called a 'wall,' as in the verse, 'And Hezekiah turned his face to the wall [and prayed to the Eternal]' (Isaiah 38:2)."

"Whenever the cloud was taken up from over the Tabernacle"—that is, when the intervening "curtain" [was removed]. In R. Avraham's hands, the cloud has become a barrier to the service of God, rather than a sign of the divine Presence.

COMMENT

Sometimes even the most spiritual people experience barriers between themselves and God. The service of God then becomes difficult, maybe even painful—indeed if you have devoted your life to God, how could this not be so! When the barrier is removed, prayer, observance, and spiritual study become easier. The truly spiritual person, as opposed to the spiritual tourist, will work through the barrier to try to reestablish the link, however hard it may be to do so, however long it takes. When they do so, they can resume their spiritual journeys once again.

LEVITICUS

Va-yikra'

[70] Going to Your Head?

"Then [God] called [vayikra'] to Moses. . . ."

Leviticus 1:1

CONTEXT

The third book of the Torah begins with the laws of different kinds of burnt offerings. The opening word of Leviticus is written with a small letter *'alef* in many Torah scrolls and printed Hebrew Bibles, and it is not at all clear why this should be so. Is there some lesson to be learned from it?

Simchah Bunam of Pshische was a student of the Seer of Lublin, until he left his teacher to become a follower of his friend and fellow student the Holy Jew, Ya'akov Yitzchak of Pshische.

> Vayikra' [is written with] a small [*'alef*]. A parable: A small bird came to rest on a particularly high roof. The roof was undoubtedly high, but the bird remained as it had been. The same applies to Moses our teacher. Even though the Holy One had called him, nevertheless he saw himself as the same as before.

> Simchah Bunam of Pshische (1765–1827), *Midrash Simchah* [Simchah's interpretation] (Jerusalem: Mossad HaRYM Levin, 1988), v. 1, p. 124

NOTE

A small [*'alef*]. Taken here as a symbol of Moses's humility. A similar point is made in the Torah commentary *Ba'al HaTurim* by Ya'akov ben Asher (1270–1340). The midrash *Va-yikra Rabbah* 1:5 says that just as Moses was humble at the burning bush, so he was here at the inauguration of the Tabernacle.

Humility is a crucial virtue in Judaism, and even more so in Hasidism. Pride is a trap, preventing us from really engaging with others, keeping us from realizing our true selves. How many of us can say that we are like Moses, as humble after we have achieved success as we were before?

---

[71] A Union of Opposites

"And every meal offering of yours you shall season with salt; neither shall you allow the salt of the covenant of your God to be lacking from your meal offering; with all your offerings you shall offer salt."

Leviticus 2:13

CONTEXT

Leviticus 2 is concerned with the laws of the meal offering.

Efraim of Luntshits was a renowned preacher in his day, as well as a popular commentator on the Torah. The *Keli Yakar* is frequently included in standard *chumashim*.

[This was said] in order to proclaim the Holy One ruler over the opposites that exist in the world and that cause many to leave [the faith] for atheism when they say that two opposites could not have arisen from one beginning. For salt, in its taste, is [simultaneously] one thing and its opposite, for it contains the power of fire and warmth but is the product of water, so that the sages of the Kabbalah say that it corresponds to [both] the attributes of judgment and of compassion. Therefore, it is called "the covenant of your God," for by this offering they make a covenant with the Eternal to proclaim divine rule over opposites.

Now, all the offerings, except for those of the priests, were [partially] eaten by the priests, and this is like charity, which is compared to salt that keeps and preserves flesh; so too salt [involves] the loss of money, while the charity [that accompanies] the sacrifice is greater than the sacrifice itself, as it says, "Doing justice and charity is more acceptable to the Eternal than sacrifice" [Proverbs 21:3]. On this it says, therefore, "And every meal offering of yours you shall season with salt," for salt is that which goes over every offering and is "more acceptable to the Eternal than sacrifice" [itself].

But the plain meaning of "with all your offerings" is that it acts also as a preservative of meat.

Efraim Shlomo ben Aharon of Luntshits (1550–1619), *Keli Yakar* [A precious vessel], loc. cit.

NOTES

To proclaim the Holy One ruler over the opposites. R. Efraim begins with a kabbalistic explanation.

Atheism. The Hebrew has *epikorsut* (Epicureanism), an ancient Greek school of philosophy. But in Rabbinic times this became the standard technical term for denial of God. (See the advice given in *Pirkei Avot* 2:14, "Know how to answer an Epicurean.") The existence of opposites in the world could be an excuse for denying the existence of God, since one might ask how one perfect Being could create two contradictory and apparently mutually exclusive qualities.

The power of fire and warmth but is the product of water. This derives from standard medieval physics, based on the ancient idea that all physical entities are made up of four "elements" (earth, air, fire, and water) and may be classified according to four criteria (wet or dry, hot or cold). Fire is hot and dry, water essentially wet and cold, while earth is considered dry and cold, and air wet and warm. Salt, however, seems to combine the properties of both fire and water, "elements" which normally cannot coexist in the same place.

The attributes of judgment and of compassion. Judgment is Din, identical with the *sefirah* of Gevurah. The Hebrew for compassion is Rachamim, an alternative name for Tiferet, but R. Efraim certainly has in mind Gevurah's opposite, Hesed (Lovingkindness), which is also occasionally known as Rachamim. Traditionally, fire represents Gevurah and water Hesed. In the divine world of the *sefirot* all opposites have their origins in, and in this case are reconciled by, Tiferet, which stands between them. Salt, in that event, represents Tiferet.

All the offerings . . . were [partially] eaten by the priests. When non-priests brought sacrifices, the priests received a share. This is the start of our author's interpretation, which is based on analogy. Salt was a very expensive commodity until modern times, so the analogy is not as far fetched as we might think. Just as salt was a necessary addition to the offering that made it acceptable, so too charity was a necessary addition that was more important than the offering itself. And like salt, which preserves meat, charity preserves the lives of those who need it as well as the social fabric of society.

COMMENT

We moderns have learned that too much salt causes all kinds of health issues, but our ancestors faced the problem of getting enough salt into their diets, not having too much. Hence the importance of salt, and its cost.

Salt as an accompaniment to sacrifice is, for the *Keli Yakar*, a statement of trust in the God who is the Source of Peace and will one day make it manifest in even the lowest levels of creation. It represents the task of everyone who would be righteous: the reconciliation of opposites. For example, we might try to bring together those in conflict; be open to new ideas, especially those with which we may disagree; or give charity to members of all communities, not just our own. But reconciling opposites may also mean striving to create peace among the conflicting forces within ourselves: between selfishness and generosity, the need for challenges versus the desire for comfort, and so on.

[72] Turning Good Deeds to Naught

"If a person sins and does one of the commandments of
the Eternal as it should not be done, but does not know,
then he is guilty and should bear his guilt."

Leviticus 5:17

CONTEXT

Chapters 4 and 5 of Leviticus deal with sin offerings of various kinds. This verse opens a brief passage detailing the rules for a sin offering in a case where the person concerned is not sure whether he or she has committed a sin or not.

Levi Yitzchak of Berditchev was a student of the Maggid of Mezritch, and rose to prominence in the succeeding generation. He strove to reconcile opposing factions in the Hasidic world. Here he follows in the

Hasidic tradition of emphasizing the examination of our motives for the performance of the commandments.

> For it is well known that the more people serve the Holy One the more they [should] consider themselves unimportant compared to the greatness of the Creator. But when people perform a commandment and suppose that they are [really] serving God, such a commandment is considered as nothing. This is the interpretation of the verse: "If a person sins"—that is to say, what is the sin?—"And does one of the commandments of the Eternal as it should not be done [...] then he is guilty"—that is to say, that this commandment would be turned to naught, while he thinks that he is serving God properly, "then he is guilty."

Levi Yitzchak of Berditchev (1740–1809), *Kedushat Levi* [The holiness of Levi] (Munkacs, 1829), p. 60b

NOTES

"One of the commandments of the Eternal as it should not be done." Or, "which should not be done." The plain meaning seems to be "the negative commandments," i.e., if anyone does things that are forbidden. JPS: "any of the Lord's commandments about things not to be done." Levi Yitzchak understands "as it should not be done."

What is the sin? No particular sin is specified. The Torah passage refers to any case where it is unclear if a sin has been committed.

COMMENT

Levi Yitzchak is making great demands of us. After we have performed a good deed, he wants us to feel inadequate, to understand that we have really only just begun to serve God, that we can never really do justice to God's commandments. I do not believe that this is good pedagogic technique for use with children, or even with many adults, but if we are really committed to our religion and our spirituality, then we need to be aware that our task is never ending. As long as we draw breath, there are mitzvot for us to do, to ever-higher standards. Even if we are just pleased with ourselves so far, we have substituted our own self-satisfaction for the true service of the divine. We need to be on our guard against this.

Tsav

---

[73] Harnessing Our Drives

"Command [tzav] Aaron and his sons. . . ."

Leviticus 6:2

CONTEXT

Leviticus 6 opens with the rules for the disposal of the ashes of the whole burnt offering.

The Seer of Lublin, in Poland, was so called because of his reputation for second sight. He was one of the leading lights in the fourth generation of the Hasidic movement, having studied with Elimelech of Lyzhansk. In turn, he inspired, and challenged, an important group of Hasidic leaders of the next generation.

> Look, *tzav* [command] is an expression denoting idolatry, as in [the phrase] "precept upon precept [*tzav latzav*]" [Isaiah 28:10,13]. Look here, we are explaining [the verse] "and in sin did my mother conceive me [*yechematni*]" [Psalm 51:7], for repentance is called a "mother" because through it a person becomes as if reborn as a new being. Now it is known you need great desire to serve heaven, and that desire comes from the side of the inclination toward evil. Hence, "and in sin did my mother conceive me [*yeCHeMatni*]"—giving me warmth [*CHiM-MuM*] for God, to serve God with enthusiasm. Hence, "Command [*tzav*] Aaron and his sons . . ."—an expression denoting the zeal and desire that come from the inclination toward evil indicated by *tzav*.

> Ya'akov Yitzchak HaLevi Horowitz, the Seer of Lublin (1745–1815), *Divrei Emet* [Words of truth (Ecclesiastes 12:10)] (Ashdod, 2004), p. 81b

"Precept upon precept [tzav latzav]" [Isaiah 28:10]. From an attack
upon the drunkenness of priests and prophets. JPS: "mutter upon mutter."

"And in sin did my mother conceive me [yeCHeMatni]." The Seer reinter-
prets this phrase to mean: "and through sin, repentance gives me enthusiasm to serve God."

Desire comes from the side of the inclination toward evil. See *Kohelet
Rabbah* 3:15: "If not for the inclination toward evil, no one would build a
house, marry, or have children." Idolatry stems from the inclination toward
evil, but, paradoxically, so does the desire to serve God.

"Command [tzav] Aaron and his sons." As if to say, "Use the enthusiasm
derived from the inclination toward evil to serve God as Aaron and his sons
did."

COMMENT

By juxtaposing virtually identical words from quite different contexts,
the Seer of Lublin arrives at the notion that our enthusiasm for God derives in fact from our less admirable attributes: our tendency toward
idolatry (materialism) and, he implies, lust.

These unsavory aspects of all of us, referred to by the Rabbinic term
yetzer ha-ra (inclination toward evil), must not be denied but harnessed
to the service of God, so that we can bring the same enthusiasm and
energy to serving God that we would certainly have brought to pursu-
ing those unworthy goals. A difficult task, but a necessary one, if our
service is not to be cold and devoid of passion.

---

[74] Torah Is What We Make of It

*"This is the Torah for the burnt offering [olah], for the meal offering
[minchah], for the sin [offering], and for the guilt [offering]. . . ."*

Leviticus 7:37

CONTEXT

The last verses of Leviticus 7 are the conclusion of the laws of sacrifices
begun in chapter 1.

Yisra'el Friedman of Ruzhyn was the great-grandson of Dov Ber, the Maggid of Mezritch, and a well-known Hasidic teacher in his own right. He was persecuted for many years by the Czarist authorities, eventually settling in Sadgora in the Austrian Empire. The dynasty he founded continues to this day.

For the truth is that concerning a person who studies the Torah for its own sake and in order to perform its commandments it is said, "[For the ways of the Eternal are upright;] the righteous walk on them" [Hosea 14:10], while if the opposite [is the case], it is said, "But the wicked stumble on them" [Hosea 14:10]. Hence, the explanation of [the verse] "this is the Torah"—sometimes [it is] "for ascent [*olah*]" and "for a gift [*minchah*]" and sometimes [it is] "for sin and for guilt." Consider this well!

Yisra'el Friedman of Ruzhyn (1797–1850), *Irin Kadishin* [Holy angels] (n.p., 1885), pt. 2, p. 8a

NOTES

"This is the Torah." The word "torah" in the original context of the verse simply indicates the teaching that follows. JPS: "Such are the rituals of the burnt offering." The Ruzhyner makes it refer to the whole of Judaism.

"The burnt offering [*olah*]." *Olah* usually means "burnt offering," but is related to the Hebrew root meaning "to ascend, go up," presumably because virtually the entire *olah* rose upward as smoke.

"The meal offering [*minchah*]." *Minchah* can mean a "meal offering" or a "gift" in biblical Hebrew. (Later on, it came to designate the afternoon service.)

"The sin [offering]." *Chatat* can mean both "sin" and "sin offering."

"The guilt [offering]." *Asham* means both "guilt" and "guilt offering."

COMMENT

For the Ruzhyner rebbe, the Torah can either be a vehicle for raising us to new spiritual heights and a gift we offer to God, or it can be a guide to counting up our sins and adding to our guilt. In other words, it can be a source of both positive and negative feelings. The choice is up to us.

[75] Sanctifying Sight

"Moses took the breast [chazeh] and raised it as an
elevated offering before the Eternal . . ."
Leviticus 8:29

CONTEXT

The ritual for the inauguration of the priests is described. After the
sacrifice of the animals is completed, the ritual involves lifting first
two cakes of unleavened bread (matzah) and then the breast of one of
the rams.

Yisra'el ben Shmuel Taub lived in Poland and founded the Hasidic dynasty of Modzhitz. He was more famous for his emphasis on music and
for the melodies he wrote than for his teachings. He died in Tel Aviv.

[The term *chazeh*] is an expression denoting "seeing" or "vision," as in
the phrase "[the vision (*chazon*) of Isaiah son of Amotz] which he saw
[*chazah*]" (Isaiah 1[:1]). That is to say, "[Moses] took the *chazeh*" —
seeing, "and raised it as an elevated offering before the Eternal" — this
[refers] to the sanctification of sight.

Yisra'el ben Shmuel of Modzhitz (1849–1921), *Divrei Yisra'el* [Israel's
words] (Tel Aviv, 1984), pt. 3, p. 45

NOTE

"Moses took the breast [chazeh]." The noun *chazeh* ("breast" or "chest")
is related to the verb *chazah* (to see) only by sound and appearance. There
seems to be no lexicographic connection. As the example from Isaiah illus-
trates, the verb is used primarily in a prophetic or poetic context.

COMMENT

How can we sanctify sight? Surely, we have little control over what
our eyes see. Actually, we have a great deal, especially nowadays when
electronic media are bringing photos and videos into very nearly every
part of our lives. Now, more than ever, we choose what to see. So how
do we sanctify what we see? I don't think the Modzhitzer is suggesting
we avert our eyes from bad events, whether in the news or in our physi-

cal vicinity. Those things cry out for our concern, and we must guard against complacency or indifference. I think he is saying that we need to try to see the good even in bad events if we can, to perceive God at work even in bad news. For even bad news can be a goad to our empathy and positive action.

Shemini

---

[76] It Depends on You

*"This is the thing that the Eternal has commanded you
to do that the glory of the Eternal may appear."*
Leviticus 9:6

CONTEXT

The previous parashah ends with a description of the seven-day inauguration ceremony for the priests. Shemini begins with the ritual undertaken on the eighth day.

The Seer of Lublin was an important link between his teacher, Elimelech of Lyzhansk, and the new Hasidic teachers of Poland in the following generation.

We have to say that this is a verse on its own, and that it is not especially intelligible. According to what is said in [the commentary by] R. Moshe Alsheich on the verse "Make Me a sanctuary that I may dwell among you" [Exodus 25:1], the Holy One desired to live among us in fact, and not just in the Tabernacle. Israel desired the Tabernacle, and they presumed and expected that, through the Tabernacle, the Shechinah [the Presence of God] would come to dwell [among them], "that the Glory of the Eternal may appear."

He told them: Do not trust in this, but only in the essential thing, which is [that] "this is the thing which the Eternal has commanded you to do"—it depends on the Torah; then "the Glory of the Eternal may appear." No Tabernacle is required, and it is obvious that it does not depend on a Tabernacle, but only what you do of "what the Eternal has commanded you."

Ya'akov Yitzchak HaLevi Horowitz, the Seer of Lublin (1745–1815), *Zikaron Zot* [A memorial of this] (Ashdod, 2004), p. 90

This is a verse on its own. In the previous verse, the entire community comes to the Tabernacle for the next part of the ceremony. In the subsequent verse, Moses speaks again, "then Moses said to Aaron," apparently a new speech. Hence, verse 6 seems to stand alone.

It is not especially intelligible. It is difficult to understand in its context.

R. Moshe Alsheich. A prominent member of the Safed community of kabbalists and author of a detailed Torah commentary, Alsheich died sometime after 1593. For this comment, see *Torat Moshe* [The Torah of Moses] (Warsaw, n.d.), v. 1, pt. 2, p. 177.

He told them. The subject seems to be the Seer of Lublin.

COMMENT

It has been said that in past generations Judaism flowed from the home into the synagogue, but that nowadays it flows from the synagogue into the home. This is an overstatement: synagogues always included opportunities for study as well as prayer, and the result of study often did flow into the home. But there was also a vast reservoir of Jewish observance in most homes, which in turn led to attendance at synagogue, and that is often lacking in today's communities. The Seer's discussion of the Tabernacle reminds us that the focus of our Jewish lives on synagogues is misplaced. Synagogues are important, for all kinds of social as well as religious reasons, but ultimately Judaism depends on us, on our thoughts and actions. Without our performance of the commandments, whether at home or in shul, synagogues are merely relics of a glorious past with a future only as museums. We cannot afford to confine our Judaism to synagogues.

[77] Refining Your Plans

"The sons of Aaron, Nadab and Abihu, each took their censers . . .
and fire burst forth from before the Eternal and consumed them."
Leviticus 10:1–2

CONTEXT

As the inauguration of the priests reaches its climax on the eighth day, Aaron's two eldest sons are tragically struck down for offering "strange" or "unauthorized" fire.

Copies of *Mei HaShiloach* were burned when it first appeared, and from the following example it is easy to see why. R. Mordechai suggests that people may step outside the boundaries of acceptable behavior, of Torah, if circumstances warrant. Here he adds the proviso that they must consider the case for doing so very, very carefully.

Look here, all the sins of Israel written in the Torah are intended to teach the whole of Israel words of Torah, as it states in the Talmud: "The Israelites made the [Golden] Calf only so that penitents could make a good case. . . . David was not the kind of man to commit that act. . . . [Thus,] if an individual has sinned, he or she could be referred to the individual [i.e., David], and if a community sins, they should be told: 'Go to the community' [i.e., those who made the Golden Calf]."

So too in the case of Nadab and Abihu: what is written in the Torah is there to teach the fear [of God] to the individual. They were innocent on account of their mother, who was the sister of Nahshon ben Amminadab, [and] from whom would come the dynasty of the house of David. Now, "a king may break boundaries" provided that he trusts that his will is the will of God. [Thus,] they had periods of relying on their own will—for security comes from God. Therefore, in this manner has God demonstrated that no one should undertake any act without refining it seventyfold.

Mordechai Yosef Leiner of Izbica (1800–54), *Mei HaShiloach* [The waters of the Siloam (Isaiah 8:6)] (Bnei Brak, 1995), v. 2, p. 76

As it states in the Talmud. *Avodah Zarah* 4b.

"David was not the kind of man to commit that act." I.e., adultery with Bathsheba. This story is found in 2 Samuel 11.

"He or she could be referred to the individual." If David was forgiven for his affair with Bathsheba, then other individual sinners should not despair of forgiveness.

"They should be told: 'Go to the community.'" The fact that the Israelites were forgiven after the Golden Calf affair can be held up as an example of how the community may be forgiven for other sins in the future.

Their mother, who was the sister of Nahshon ben Amminadab. This is stated in Exodus 6:23. Her name was Elisheba. Nahshon was fifth in the line of descent from Judah, patriarch of the tribe of the same name, and thus a prince of the tribe. His name appears in the genealogy that leads to King David in Ruth 4. Thus Nadab and Abihu are descendants of what was to become the royal line.

"A king may break boundaries." In its original context, this means that kings have the right to seize land for the building of roads. (See Talmud, *Bava Kamma* 60b, and Rashi's comment there.) For the rebbe of Izbica, this means a king like David has the moral and spiritual authority to act in an apparently immoral way for some higher good. In the case of his affair with Bathsheba, still married to Uriah the Hittite, this was so that the Davidic line would be continued through Solomon, their son, down to the Messiah.

They had periods of relying on their own will. With a background and a family future like theirs, Nadab and Abihu felt that they could escape punishment for bringing "strange fire" as an offering.

In this manner has God demonstrated. The tale of Nadab and Abihu is an object lesson in considering your actions very carefully. They clearly had not!

COMMENT

The lives of most Jewish people today are not bound up with the observance of *halachah*, Jewish law. The carefully observant are a minority in our overall numbers. *Halachah* fosters important values: community, reverence for God, and tradition are just examples. It provides a precise moral compass. But *halachah* can also feel like a straitjacket. The rebbe of Izbica lived in a strictly Orthodox environment, but he realized that sometimes we need to move outside its strict confines for the sake of a higher spiritual purpose, like some biblical figures did. He understood that sometimes we need to break a part of the law to uphold the whole of the law. The question for us as modern Jews is how far the process can go before the framework of the law is itself cast into doubt.

[78] Dedicated to God

"For I am the Eternal who brought you up out of the land of Egypt to be to you for God."

Leviticus 11:45

CONTEXT

Almost the last verse in a chapter devoted to the kosher food laws is this reminder of the Exodus from Egypt, reinforcing the idea that kashrut has a great deal to do with our self-identification as Jews.

Rabbi Yisra'el ben Eliezer is much better known as the Ba'al Shem Tov (nicknamed "the Besht"). The founder of the modern Hasidic movement, he brought a new, psychological understanding of Kabbalah to many ordinary people in Ukraine and beyond.

> In the name of Rabbi Yisra'el Ba'al Shem: The meaning is that you must see that even your "to you," that is, your permitted desires, should be "for God," only for the Eternal alone. Take care to understand this.

> Yisra'el ben Eliezer, Ba'al Shem Tov (1700–1760), *Sefer Ba'al Shem Tov* [The book of the good master of the Name], ed. Shimon Menachem Mendel of Govarchov (Jerusalem, n.d.), v. 2, p. 93

NOTE

"To be to you for God." The Besht's comment is based on a superliteral reading of the verse, including the actual word order employed in the Hebrew. JPS: "to be your God."

COMMENT

Chapter 11 of Leviticus is devoted to the laws delineating which animals may and may not be eaten according to the rules of kashrut. And although many types of animals are not permitted, others are, such as mammals that chew the cud and have cloven hooves, fish that have both fins and scales, and certain birds. Clearly, refraining from eating those that are not permitted is a religious act. But what about eating those that are allowed? Or to put it another way, is the observance of kashrut the sum total of our spiritual involvement with eating?

The traditional answer, of course, is no. There are blessings to be said before and after we eat, for example, which emphasize our dependence upon God.

It appears that for the Ba'al Shem Tov this does not quite go far enough. By reading this verse in a superliteral way, he comes to the teaching that all our permitted desires, that is, all the physical acts that we are permitted to engage in, not just eating and drinking, but also acquiring wealth, enjoying music, sex, and so forth, all these things must be dedicated to the service of God. The things permitted "to you" should also be "for God." The service of God is not confined to "religious" acts.

Tazria'

---

[79] We All Receive

"If a woman conceives and gives birth to a male. . . ."
Leviticus 12:2

CONTEXT

Leviticus 12, one of the shortest chapters of the Torah, is concerned with the ritual uncleanness incurred by women at childbirth. The mother remains in this state for thirty-three days after the birth of a son, and sixty-six days after the birth of a daughter, at the end of which she was to bring an offering and then become clean again. This opening section of Tazria' is troubling for many modern Jews. And it must be obvious that any mystical interpretations offered on it will probably be rooted in language that we would term "sexist" today.

Yisra'el of Ruzhyn was the great-grandson of Dov Ber, the Maggid of Mezritch, and founder of a dynasty of Hasidic teachers that continues to this day. His remarks here must be seen in the context of premodern notions of sexual inheritance. Before the development of modern genetic science, it was not understood that both parents contribute genetic material to the fetus. Instead, people's understanding was based on a limited idea of the sexual act itself, in which the male alone seems to be giving, and the female receiving, the seed.

It is written: "Who can precede Me that I should repay [him]?" [Job 41:3], for people should realize that all their actions, all, come from God—that is, that every mitzvah [commandment] that you do the Holy One has put into your hand. For [God] gives [you] a house, and you affix a mezuzah. [God] gives you a four-cornered garment, and you put fringes upon it. Similarly with any active commandment— the Holy One is the essence, that is, the internal aspect of anything. You should truly realize that everything is from God.

For example: If you are aroused to Torah or prayer or to reciting songs and praises, or if a penitent thought comes and you are able to bring about an "arousal from below," it must be with a broken heart and you should know that in truth you have only done what the Holy One has bestowed [on you]. However, if you have it in mind that you have [actually] achieved [something], it is vanity and very inferior. Even your Torah and prayer are from God. . . .

However, even though the human body is inferior to that of all [other] creatures, nevertheless it is written: "And the person became a living soul" [Genesis 2:7], which is translated as "became a speaking spirit." For it is in this [respect] that [human beings] are higher than all [other] creatures, for [by speaking] they are able to restore everything to God. Hence [the verse]: "If a woman conceives"—meaning, even when you have a penitent thought, or study, or pray, and bring about "arousal from below," you must nevertheless be in the state of the "feminine," that is, the state of receiving, and realize that all comes from God. Then "she gives birth to a male"—you may become one who bestows, a masculine state.

Yisra'el Friedman of Ruzhyn (1797–1850), *Irin Kadishin* [Holy angels] (n.p., 1885), pt. 3, p. 30

NOTES

A mezuzah. The compartment containing a parchment with two passages from the Torah (Deuteronomy 6:4–9 and 11:13–21) that is affixed to the doorpost.

Fringes upon it. According to Numbers 15:37–41, garments with four corners should have tassels or fringes at each corner. This is the origin of the tallit, or tallis (prayer shawl).

"Arousal from below." A term quoted from the Zohar, where it occurs frequently. Derived from the sexual act, it denotes human needs, desires, and spiritual longing that, in turn, stimulate "arousal above," a response from God.

Translated as. In the ancient Aramaic translation of the Torah attributed to Onkelos the proselyte.

"Feminine," that is, the state of receiving. In Kabbalah, the terms "masculine" and "feminine" are clearly derived from the sexual act, but also transcend it. In this view, "feminine" indicates a willingness to receive while "masculine" denotes a willingness to give.

Rabbi Yisra'el is telling us that when we can acknowledge our receipt of all good things from God, we can, in our turn, become givers to all. We can, as it were, act like God. This represents a very high spiritual level, and one that will seem foreign to many readers. Although human beings always seem to have had a sense that they control their own lives, at least to some extent, our Western society has fostered its own radical agenda—that of the autonomous individual. The existential truth probably lies somewhere in between; we do have some control over our own destiny, but there are a great many things over which we, as individuals, have little or no control: our health perhaps and our global economic and political circumstances. R. Yisra'el's idea of radical dependence, his apparent denial of free will (to phrase it differently), represents a paradox: we recognize our utter dependence, our "femininity," and this recognition frees us to act in generous, outgoing, "masculine" ways. When we truly, deeply accept our total reliance on God, we need no longer struggle to maintain our self-esteem or self-worth; we are free to act without self-seeking. We can focus on others, instead of ourselves.

---

[80] Spirituality: Moving or Stationary?

"But if the bright spot remains in one place and does not spread, it is the scar of the boil. . . ."

Leviticus 13:23

CONTEXT

This verse is part of the discourse on skin inflammations and boils that forms the majority of this chapter of Leviticus, down to verse 46. The rest of the chapter is concerned with discoloration on clothing.

Ya'akov Yolles was a talmudic scholar and communal rabbi, who was also a disciple of the Seer of Lublin. *Emet LeYa'akov* is a small collection of his sermons in Hasidic style, though he is perhaps best known today for the extensive kabbalistic dictionary that he compiled, titled *Kehillat Ya'akov*.

The fact is that there are two kinds of righteous people [tzadikim]. One might be called "moving," for each day they move to a higher level. [Those of] the second type are always stationary on one level. Every day they pray and study Torah, and yesterday is just like today and just like tomorrow. Now even though in truth the second type are very good, nevertheless there is still within them a handle for, and a bit of a residue of, the "Other Side." For if they were truly purified of everything, they would be adding a wondrous brightness every day the way the [other type of] tzadikim do. . . . Hence, "if the bright spot remains in one place," that is, if the brightness is stationary in one place, "and does not spread," that is, it is known that there is still a residue of the "Other Side"—thus, Onkelos translates ["the scar of the boil" as] "the residue of the boil"—[then] it appears that there is a bit of a residue of the "Other Side," referred to as a "boil."

Ya'akov Zevi Yolles (ca. 1778–1825), *Emet LeYa'akov* [Truth to Jacob (Micah 7:20)] (Lemberg, 1884), p. 10a

NOTES

Two kinds of righteous people *[tzadikim]*. In the Hasidic context, Yolles is referring primarily to the rabbis of the movement.

The "Other Side." An expression, frequently found in the Zohar, denoting the powers of evil. Righteous people who do not change are still slightly "stuck" in the thrall of the "Other Side," either by fear or indolence.

Onkelos. Said to be a convert to Judaism, Onkelos is credited with the ancient translation of the Torah into Aramaic.

COMMENT

All religious practice is prone to becoming habit. This is especially true for Judaism, which lays great stress on daily ritual and daily study. Yolles warns us of the dangers of getting stuck in a rut of habits, however worthy. When we do things by rote, our minds and souls stop growing.

[81] The Affliction of the Shechinah

"This [zot] is the teaching [torat] concerning a
leprous affliction in a woolen garment. . . ."
Leviticus 13:59

CONTEXT

This verse represents the conclusion of the subject of "leprous afflictions" (mildew, etc.) in cloth begun in verse 47.

Avraham Yissachar was the second leader of the Hasidic group based
at Radomsk. Before the Second World War, it was one of the largest in
Poland.

For the Shechinah [the Presence of God] is called "this [zot]," and so
Scripture is saying that "a leprous affliction," that is, the evil that the
descendants of Israel [do], is a blemish on the holy Shechinah and on
"the teaching concerning [*TORaT*]," that is, the two Torahs [*TORoT*],
the Written Torah and the Oral Torah, for the Torah and the Holy One
and Israel are one.

Avraham Yissachar Ber HaCohen of Radomsk (1843–92), *Hesed leAvraham*
[Lovingkindness to Abraham (Micah 7:20)] (n.p., 1893–95), pp. 283–84

NOTES

For the Shechinah [the Presence of God] is called "this [zot]." The feminine singular pronoun *zot* (this) has been associated with the Shechinah
(Malchut), one of the primary manifestations of the feminine in the *sefirot-*
ic system since the time of the Zohar.

"The teaching concerning [*TORaT*]," that is, the two Torahs [*TORoT*].
In a Hebrew text written without vowel points, *torat* could also be read
as *torot* (torahs). The notion of two Torahs, the Written and the Oral, is a
staple of Rabbinic literature.

The Written Torah. This comprises the Five Books of Moses plus the rest of
the Bible.

The Oral Torah. Texts found in Rabbinic literature, the Talmud, midrashim, etc.

The Torah and the Holy One and Israel are one. Though often attributed
to the Zohar, this equation in its fullest form appears only later, in Hasid-

ic literature, though it predates this text. The notion is that each of these three represents a unity. Despite there being two *torot*, different in form and presentation, they are really one in essence. Despite the doctrine of the ten *sefirot*, God is really one, as proclaimed in the *Shema* (Deuteronomy 6:4). Despite the divisions within the Jewish people, we are really one people. Moreover, Torah and Israel are manifestations of the one God.

COMMENT

In an age of profound individualism, we need to reestablish our sense of interrelatedness, of community, and of the cosmos. All reality is one fabric. Our Jewish life is not separate from that of our non-Jewish neighbors, nor is Torah somehow separate from life. They are all manifestations of the one God, but our failures and sins militate against that oneness. If we can reach an understanding of the underlying unity of all things, perhaps we can understand the bad we do, and learn how to avoid doing it and how to put it right when we cannot.

Metsora‘

---

[82] Humility at the Wrong Time

"Then the priest shall command the one who is to be cleansed
to take . . . cedarwood, and scarlet, and hyssop."
Leviticus 14:4

CONTEXT

Metsora‘ continues the subject of "leprosy" but moves from diagnosis
to treatment, of a ritual nature.

Rabbi Yitzchak Meir of Gur (or Ger), also known as the RIM, from his
initials, was the founder of the Gerer school of Hasidism, which continues into our own time. He had previously been a student of Menachem
Mendel of Kotzk.

In the name of the holy rabbi, the Rav Yitzchak Meir of Gur:
[Regarding people who are afflicted with skin complaints, their return to ritual] cleanliness is [brought about] by cedarwood and hyssop.
And Rashi explains [that this means] if they have prided themselves
like the cedar, they should humble themselves like the hyssop.
[The RIM] said: "One may understand this in the opposite way as
well. Those who humble themselves like the hyssop may pride themselves like the cedar. For sometimes [people] must seek atonement
for humility. For example, if people come to you and ask you to do
some kindness for them, and your reply is: 'Who am I that I should
do something good for you? Am I not lowly, without any honor at all
among people?' Despite the fact that if someone had insulted you,
you would persecute that person; nevertheless, when it comes to doing good for someone else, you are lowly in your own eyes! Humility

like this requires atonement." "The words of a wise person's mouth are graciousness" [Ecclesiastes 10:12].

Yitzchak Meir of Gur (1789–1866), in *Siach Sarfei Kodesh* [The conversation of the holy seraphim], ed. Yo'etz Kayyam Kadish Rokotz (n.p., n.d.), pt. 1, p. 29

NOTE

And Rashi explains. What follows is a paraphrase of Rashi's comment on the same verse, based on the Talmud, *Arachin* 16b.

COMMENT

Many people seem to "suffer" from too little humility, too high an opinion of themselves. Others seem not to have high enough self-esteem. Somewhere in between there must be a happy medium. Jewish tradition tends to be very strong on humility, perhaps because the arrogant can do a great deal of damage to society, destroying the ideals of communal solidarity, care for the weak and the poor, and so forth—violating key Jewish values. But a lack of self-esteem can prevent us from achieving anything. And sometimes we put on a false modesty because we would rather not get involved, because we do not want to take up our responsibilities. It is this that the RIM attacks. And it is this that we must all address.

---

[83] What Is Love?

"The owner of the house shall come [Uva 'asher Lo Habayit] and tell the priest, saying 'Something like a plague was seen by me in my house.'"
Leviticus 14:35

CONTEXT

The second half of Leviticus 14, beginning at verse 33, deals with the issue of "leprosy" in houses, probably referring to mildew, dry rot, and similar conditions. The homeowner would report the outbreak to the priest, who would then prescribe what should be done.

Little is known of the life of Zevi Hirsh Minkovitz other than that he was a student of Eliyahu ben Shlomo, better known as the Vilna Ga'on. Although the Ga'on was a fierce opponent of the nascent Hasidic movement, he was a great kabbalist as well as an outstanding halachic scholar. The text that follows is from Minkovitz's only known work, a kabbalistic commentary on the entire Hebrew Bible in which he "identifies" the divine names indicated by the initial letters of words in the text, connecting each name with its associated *sefirah*.

> The initial letters [of *Uva 'asher Lo Habayit* are the same as the letters of *'eLOaH* (God) which] is a name denoting Hesed (Lovingkindness). . . . This is mystically identified with light. . . . This is the mystical interpretation of the saying of our Rabbis, "'was seen by me' [Leviticus 14:35] — but not [by] the light of my [candle]," as well as [their dictum that] "the windows of a dark house may not be opened to examine its leprosy." And our Rabbis [also said,] "Always be humble and you will live" . . . and they employ this verse as a proof. Look here, this name is that of "lovingkindness *[hesed]* to Abraham" [Micah 7:20], and its associated quality is generosity, while, on the contrary, plagues in houses come as a result of selfishness, as our Rabbis have taught.

Zevi Hirsh ben Shmuel Zanvil Minkovitz of Semyatitch (d. 1819), *Margoliot HaTorah* [Pearls of Torah] (Poritzk, 1788), p. 96a

NOTES

The initial letters [of *Uva 'asher Lo Habayit*]. These letters are: *vav, 'alef, lamed, heh.*

[The same as the letters of *'eLOaH* (God)]. This divine name is spelled *'alef, lamed, vav, heh.*

A name denoting Hesed. All the divine names that occur in the Bible are associated with particular *sefirot.*

This is mystically identified with light. Light is a symbol of Hesed.

The saying of our Rabbis: "'was seen by me.'" In the Talmud, *Moed Katan* 8a, it is ruled that "leprosy" in houses must be seen in natural, as opposed to artificial, light.

"The windows of a dark house." According to the Talmud, *Hullin* 10b, the light used to illuminate the "leprosy" could not be increased by opening the shutters. The "leprosy" had to be viewed in its original circumstances. In *Sanhedrin* 92a, this teaching is used as an analogy to prove that the humble are saved by their humility, as expressed by the next quotation.

"Always be humble and you will live." Quoted from the Talmud, *Sanhedrin* 92a.

And they employ this verse as a proof. Talmud, *Hullin* 10b.

This name is that of "lovingkindness [hesed] to Abraham" [Micah 7:20]. This verse is the classic prooftext for the kabbalistic identification of Abraham with Hesed. This Patriarch is, of course, renowned in Rabbinic literature for his hospitality and generosity.

Generosity. Literally, "a good eye."

Selfishness. Literally, "a constrained eye."

As our Rabbis have taught. Talmud, *Arachin* 16a.

COMMENT

On a formal level, Minkovitz has used the divine name that he "discovered" in the biblical text, along with the twin symbols of light and sight, to forge a link between the Written and Oral Torah, between biblical and Rabbinic teaching on the subject of "leprosy" in houses. But perhaps there is a deeper level behind his comments, a level that says something about love, divine and human. Love is not blind, infatuation is. Love sees. It does not ignore blemishes, faults, and sins; but it neither shines a harsh light upon them nor does it view them in the warm glow of romantic candlelight. Love is humble, and truthful; generous, not stingy. And just as those terms describe God's love, so they should ours.

---

[84] Separation for the Sake of Cleansing

"Thus you shall separate [vehizartem] the People of Israel from
their uncleanness, so that they do not die in their uncleanness
by defiling My Tabernacle that is in their midst."

Leviticus 15:31

CONTEXT

This chapter of Leviticus deals with male and female bodily discharges. People who experienced such occurrences were, in one way or another, meant to avoid contact for a certain period with those who had not. Verses 31–33 bring the subject to its conclusion.

Menachem Mendel of Rymanov was a student of Elimelech of Lyzhansk.

VehiZaRtem [You shall separate] is derived from the word *neZeR* (a diadem or tiara), which is to say that when they repair themselves sufficiently, their sins become a diadem or a tiara, for our sages said that repentance out of love turns premeditated sins into merits.

"So that they do not die in their uncleanness" — "death" here refers to submission and humility, meaning that they should not remain in the midst of their transgressions.

"By defiling My Tabernacle that is in their midst" — that is to say, through transgressions, damage and "staining" are caused to the soul, to that "portion of divinity from above." Therefore, they should repent in this way so that the transgressions may be atoned for, and [the people] may be brought into the midst of holiness.

Amen. May this be God's will.

Yitzchak Mordechai ben Yisra'el Aharon Podvah (1884–1942), ed., *Ilana deChayyei* [The tree of life] (Jerusalem, 1986), pt. 1, p. 64

NOTES

"VehiZaRtem" [You shall separate] is derived from the word *neZeR*.
Both words derive from the same root: *n-z-r*.
Our sages said. What follows is a paraphrase of Talmud, *Yoma* 86b.
"Portion of divinity from above." A phrase from Job 31:2.

COMMENT

Sin has ramifications beyond the personal or social levels. Each sin we commit is a stain on our souls, a blemish on the divine that lives within us. Repentance, turning back to God, is our only method of cleansing ourselves. And true repentance does not just remove the sin from our soul, it turns it into something positive. It is a learning process with the power to remake us so that we may be truly in God's image.

'Aḥarei Mot

---

[85] Charity Begins at Home?

"The Eternal said to Moses, 'Speak to Aaron your brother,
and let him not enter the holy place at any time.'"

Leviticus 16:2

CONTEXT

Chapter 16 of Leviticus describes the ancient rituals for the Day of Atonement, including the rules for the scapegoat. In this verse, "at any time"
probably means "at will," as in the JPS TANAKH.

Uri of Strelisk, the Seraph, was a disciple of Shlomo of Karlin and a
key Hasidic leader in Lithuania.

> Jokingly, he discussed the saying of our sages "Who gives charity at
> any time? . . . One who supports sons and daughters when they are
> small." But here it says: "And let him not enter the holy place at any
> time." The meaning is, with this charity [given at] "any time" you do
> not enter into holiness.

> Uri of Strelisk (the Seraph) (d. 1826), *Sefer Imrei Kadosh* [The book of the
> sayings of a holy man] (Netanya, 2001), p. 11

NOTE

The saying of our sages. Talmud, *Ketubbot* 50a.

COMMENT

They say that "charity begins at home." True enough: we learn the
mitzvah of charity from our parents and immediate family. If they were
generous in giving to others, the chances are we will be too. And if we
are, probably our children will be also. But often charity seems to end
at home, and that is a shame, not only for those who might have re-

ceived but also for those who might have given. Of course we love our children, but providing for them isn't really charity; it's more like an investment in the future of our gene pool and our inheritance, and in our old age—it is an act in our own self-interest. Real charity goes beyond the home. It spreads its largesse as widely as possible. We often give to our children unconsciously, because it comes naturally to us. Real charity has to be given consciously and deliberately, if it is to carry us into holiness.

[86] Self-Cleansing

*"For on this day [God] shall put atonement upon you
to cleanse you [from all your sins]. . . ."*
Leviticus 16:30

CONTEXT

The essence of Yom Kippur is, of course, atonement, the restoration of our relationship with God that follows our repentance. With atonement comes the removal or cancellation of our sins.

Menachem Mendel of Kotzk was a fierce proponent of accepting personal responsibility.

That is, the obligation falls "upon you to cleanse" yourselves "from all your sins."

Menachem Mendel of Kotzk (1787–1859), *Ohel Torah* [The tent of Torah] (Lublin, 1909), p. 42

COMMENT

The plain meaning of the verse from Leviticus 16 suggests that it is God who cleanses us on Yom Kippur, and one might be tempted to think that this requires little or no effort on our part. But Menachem Mendel of Kotzk deconstructs the verse and arrives at the opposite conclusion. There is an obligation "upon" us to cleanse ourselves first. We must make the first move; otherwise we are not worthy of God's gift of atonement.

[87] Putting Life into the Commandments

"You shall therefore keep My statutes and My judgments,
which if people do, they shall live [veCHaI] by them."
Leviticus 18:5

CONTEXT

Leviticus 17 concerns rules for slaughtering animals for food and pro-
scriptions against eating the blood. Chapter 18 presents the list of forbidden sexual relationships. The verse quoted here forms part of the
introduction to this list, in verses 1–5.

The Kotzker rebbe was known for placing big moral demands on his
followers.

You should do the commandments with vitality [CHiYYut], and not
like "a human commandment learned by rote" [Isaiah 29:13].

Menachem Mendel of Kotzk (1787–1859), *Sefer Amud HaEmet* [The book of
the pillar of truth] (Bnei Brak, 2000), p. 71

NOTE

With vitality *[CHiYYut]*. *Chiyyut* and *chai* are both from the same three-
letter root, *ch-y-h*.

COMMENT

We are creatures of habit. We have our routines and, speaking person-
ally, the older I get, the more I find them helpful, even comforting. For
observant Jews, the commandments, especially the daily rituals, can
feel like that: they can become things we do because we have always
done them, or because that is what Jews do. But practices undertaken
out of habit are dead, devoid of life. The Kotzker is right: we need to
instill real life into them, even if we do them each day. They need to be
fresh. No, actually we need to be fresh!

Kedoshim

---

[88] Infinite Progression

"You shall be holy for I, the Eternal your God, am holy."

Leviticus 19:2

CONTEXT

Leviticus 17–26 is sometimes called the Holiness Code because its apparently random list of moral and ritual commands is given under the call to the People of Israel to be holy; that is, separated from other peoples for a higher, divine purpose. The start of chapter 19 is perhaps the climax of the code.

Hayyim ibn Attar was a Moroccan kabbalist and author of an important Torah commentary that was much appreciated by the Ba'al Shem Tov and others in the Hasidic movement in Ukraine.

[This] expression is in the future tense. The explanation is that there should be no pause in [the fulfillment of] this commandment, for whichever gate of holiness you enter, there still exists another gate beyond the boundary of the gate you are entering. For there is no limit to progress in the holiness that is appointed for anyone who wishes to take it on.

Go and learn this from the levels of the prophets, each higher than the other, with Moses above them all. But perhaps there is a level higher than [that of] Moses, and that would be the level of our holy king, our Messiah, who will be crowned with all manner of crowns. . . .

Therefore, it says, "you shall be," for this commandment has no pause and there is always [more to achieve] within the boundary of this commandment to be holy.

And it gives a reason for its teaching, "for I, the Eternal your God, am holy," for there is no limit to God's holiness, and the Eternal desires that the beloved children of the divine should imitate their Cre-

ator in the divisions of holiness. So now consider within your mind
the levels through which you may pass.

Hayyim ben Moshe ibn Attar (1696–1743), *Or HaHayyim* [The light of life]
(Jerusalem: A. Blum, 1994), pt. 3, pp. 99–100

NOTES

[This] expression. I.e., "You shall be holy."
In the future tense. Rather than the imperative: "Be holy!"
Moses above them all. See Deuteronomy 34:10: "Never again did there arise
in Israel a prophet like Moses."

COMMENT

Ibn Attar's thesis is a warning against religious and spiritual self-
satisfaction and complacency. Because God is infinite, our progress in
holiness can be infinite, limited only by our mortality and our will.
There are those who take the view that the Jewish people are spiritually superior to non-Jews, that Jews are inherently holy. This opinion,
expressed in the Middle Ages by the philosopher and poet Yehudah Ha-
Levi and by numerous kabbalists down to our own day, is at odds with
that expressed by Leviticus 19:2, as explained by Ibn Attar. Holiness is a
goal, not a starting point. And we Jews have no monopoly on holiness.
What we do have is a tradition that can guide us toward the goal—as
others have theirs.

---

[89] An Honest "Yes" and "No"

"An honest hin shall you have."

Leviticus 19:36

CONTEXT

Among a range of ethical, moral, and ritual commandments in Leviticus
19 are two verses (35 and 36) enjoining honest weights and measures
in business.

Rabbi Yehudah HeHasid (the Pious) was one of the primary leaders of
the German Hasidic movement of the late twelfth and early thirteenth

centuries. For him, true piety goes beyond the plain letter of the law. Piety is seeking to do more than is legally required.

> Even "your 'yes' [*hen*] and your 'no' shall be honest." And how do we know that even your gesticulations should be honest? Because it says, "[A scoundrel, an evil man lives by crooked speech,] winking his eyes, shuffling his feet, pointing his finger" (Proverbs 6[:12–]13), and it is written: "extend a finger and speak evil" (Isaiah 58:9). Even the movement of your head should be truthful, for if people want to say yes, they nod their head, and if they want to say no, they shake their head from side to side. And even all your other limbs should be truthful, as it is said: "the upright love you" (Song of Songs 1:4).

> Yehudah ben Shmuel HeHasid of Regensburg (d. 1217), *Sefer Hasidim* [The book of the pious], ed. Reuben Margoliot (Jerusalem: Mossad HaRav Kook, 1957), §1058, p. 546

NOTES

"An honest *hin*." A *hin* was a measure of volume, approximately three-and-a-half liters, or about six pints.

"Your 'yes' *[hen]* and your 'no' shall be honest." A quotation from Talmud, *Bava Metzia* 49a, based on this verse. In modern Hebrew "yes" is *ken*, but in ancient times it was *hen*. See, e.g., Genesis 30:34.

"The upright love you." To Yehudah HeHasid it appears that "upright" is to be understood literally as well as figuratively, while "you" indicates God.

COMMENT

Piety (*hasidut*) as understood by Yehudah HeHasid (and many others) meant going beyond what is required. Often this "beyond" is understood in ritualistic terms: more intensive praying or studying, for example. But this passage teaches us that the true meaning of piety is striving to be conscious of even actions we do unconsciously, in order to avoid committing any offense or hurt toward others or even giving the impression of wrongdoing. Under that definition, even those of us who might not be considered pious in the conventional, ritualistic sense might discover that we actually are!

[90] Always Be Prepared

"And you shall be holy. . . ."
Leviticus 20:7

CONTEXT

Leviticus 20 continues the theme of the Holiness Code, emphasizing family relationships. Contained within the chapter (at verses 7–8 and 26) are two reminders of the object of this legislation: holiness.

Menachem Mendel of Rymanov was a disciple of Elimelech of Lyzhansk, before becoming a popular rebbe in his own right.

> I heard [the following] from our revered master Rabbi Menachem Mendel: "Holiness" is a term denoting preparation, as it is written: "Make yourselves holy today and tomorrow" (Exodus 19:10). You should always be ready and prepared for holiness to dwell [upon you], like a wife who prepares herself in ritual cleanliness for her husband, lest he suddenly come home. Then he will find her in a state of ritual cleanliness. Understand well!

Menachem Mendel of Rymanov (d. 1815), *Yalkut Menachem* [Menachem's anthology] (Jerusalem, 1998), p. 170

NOTES

"Make yourselves holy today." This command is given to the people in preparation for receiving the Ten Commandments.

Like a wife who prepares herself. Traditionally, sexual relations are prohibited when a woman is menstruating and for a week afterward. Then, a visit to the *mikveh*, or "ritual bath," would render her ritually clean once again. If her husband is away at this point, she should prepare herself anyway, in case he should arrive unexpectedly.

COMMENT

Holiness is a goal, but the goal cannot be achieved without preparation. And we can get intimations of the goal when we least expect them. Therefore, the Rymanover tells us we must be prepared, as if we were anticipating the arrival of our partner—for God, the Author of Holiness, is our partner in the work of creation. We must work together to make creation holy.

'Emor

---

[91] Priests in Thought

*"Then the Eternal said to Moses: 'Speak to the priests, the sons of Aaron
and say to them: "He shall not become ritually unclean for a dead
person among his people except for his nearest relatives. . . .""'"*

Leviticus 21:1–2

CONTEXT

Leviticus 21 continues the theme of holiness, but narrows the focus from
the People of Israel to the priests, who are subject to greater restrictions
because of the greater degree of holiness required for their priestly tasks.
Specifically, a priest was not meant to be in close proximity to a corpse,
apart from those of first-degree relatives.

Ze'ev Wolf of Zhitomir was a prominent disciple of the Maggid of
Mezritch.

At first sight, we have to explain precisely that it would have been fitting if it had said "they shall not become ritually unclean," since [the
text] speaks of the totality of Aaron's sons. It begins with the plural,
but continues with the singular. "Speak to the priests" is [in] the plural, "the sons of Aaron" is also [in] the plural, "and say to them"—it
all refers to the totality of the priests. But it continues by using the
singular: "He shall not become ritually unclean for a dead person
among his people."

. . . For us, the totality of the People of Israel, the essence of our
holiness and the cleanliness of our souls depend solely on the internal
aspects of [each] individual's thoughts. In whatever direction you turn
your thoughts, to that extent does divinity dwell within and [to that
extent] do you become a vehicle for the side of holiness, etc.

Following on from this principle, the [true] teaching of how human beings should serve [God] is by purifying their thoughts, and

in particular, their senses, for the service of their Creator. Then they would be fit to be named and called by the name of "priests," a title [signifying] those who perform holy service.

Ze'ev Wolf of Zhitomir (d. 1800), *Or HaMe'ir* [The illuminating light] (Warsaw, 1883), pt. 3, p. 59

NOTE

We, the totality of the People of Israel. The focus has now shifted from the priests to the People of Israel, "a kingdom of priests" (Exodus 19:6), and, like the Torah text itself, from the communal to the individual.

COMMENT

Every individual Jew has a direct responsibility for the spiritual growth of the Jewish people. All the more reason to take your own spirituality seriously. And to do so is to be a true priest, regardless of whether or not you are a descendant of the *Kohanim* or you officiate in a priestly (or rabbinic) capacity. We can all become morally "unclean" by contact with those who are "dead" to morality and spirituality. We can all become a "kingdom of priests" when we each take up our role of performing holy service to the best of our abilities.

---

[92] Keeping Festivals Holy

"These are the appointed festivals of the Eternal that you shall proclaim [as] holy convocations. These are My appointed festivals."

Leviticus 23:2

CONTEXT

With Leviticus 23, the Torah turns to a consideration of the laws of the sacrifices to be offered on the Sabbath and other festivals.

The kabbalist, halachic scholar, and communal rabbi Yishayah Horowitz has embedded this comment in his discourse on the moral teachings found in *parashat* 'Emor.

This is to say that you should sanctify the appointed festivals by rejoicing in them for the sake of the Eternal, and by having meals that are like Isaac's savory dishes, [intended] to awaken [your] spiritual powers to attachment to God and to bring about the flourishing of [God's] holy Torah. Then they are "holy convocations" [and] God says: "These are My appointed festivals."

However, those who celebrate holidays and are glad and rejoice in order to fill their bellies, "[all their tables are full of] filthy vomit, with no place [left clean]" [Isaiah 28:8]—of them it is said: "Your appointed festivals does My soul hate" (Isaiah 1:14). . . . This is the reason why work is prohibited on the appointed festivals, so that you should not be troubled with your own work and so forget attachment to God. For the appointed festivals are sacred, and on them you may increase attachment to God. Then they [really will be] "the appointed festivals of the Eternal."

Yishayah HaLevi Horowitz (ca. 1570–1626), *Shnei Luchot HaBrit* [The two tablets of the covenant (Deuteronomy 9:9,11)] (Jerusalem: 1975), v. 2, p. 61d

NOTE

Isaac's savory dishes. See Genesis 27:4, part of Isaac's request to his elder son, Esau: "then prepare a dish for me such as I like." Horowitz implies that Isaac's desire for venison was for spiritual, not material, sustenance.

COMMENT

What is the purpose of the festivals? Rabbi Horowitz is asking—in specific: Why are they called "holy convocations"? Nowadays, we might be tempted to emphasize the historical or moral purpose behind each of the festivals of the Jewish year, but Horowitz stresses their spiritual aspect. The holy days are not just occasions for good food and drink and social contact. They are opportunities to commune with God. The eating and drinking we may do on these occasions must be seen in that light, and not as an end in themselves.

You might say that this teaching applies to all eating and drinking, and I do not think that Horowitz would have disagreed. But in many households the quality of food and drink is higher on festivals, and the quantity greater, than on ordinary weekdays or even on *Shabbat*; and thus the temptation to focus entirely on the sensual aspects, to the exclusion of the spiritual, is so much greater. Horowitz reminds us of where our priorities should lie. If we keep his teaching in mind, the festivals will indeed be "holy convocations"—opportunities to reconnect with the spiritual in our lives.

---

[93] It Will Come Back on You

"If anyone harms another of their people, whatever
they do shall be done to them."

Leviticus 24:19

CONTEXT

Leviticus 24 opens with rules for preparing and using the oil for the menorah as well as the twelve loaves of bread to be offered in the Tabernacle. From verse 10 on, it concerns the tragic case of the man with an Israelite mother and an Egyptian father who blasphemed against God and was put to death. Verses 17–20 reaffirm some of the basic rules of Israelite civil and criminal law.

Yisra'el of Modzhitz was famous for his melodies as well as his brief, but pithy, teachings.

> The meaning is [that] those who harm another of their people by disgracing colleagues or putting them to shame put themselves to shame. As they have done, so is it to be done to them. This follows the verse: "for those who honor Me I will honor" (1 Samuel 2[:30]). It is also a sign that this blemish is in them [too]. It may be found here, but exists there. This follows the teaching: "Do not taunt your colleague with a blemish that is within you."

Yisra'el ben Shmuel of Modzhitz (1849–1921), *Divrei Yisra'el* [Israel's words] (Tel Aviv, 1984), pt. 3, p. 123

NOTE

"Do not taunt your colleague." A quotation from Talmud, *Bava Metzia* 59b.

COMMENT

Encouraged by Western mores, we tend to believe that we are autonomous individuals. Of course, in many respects we are, but social responsibility is an essential element in civilized living. We inevitably interact with others in groups and singly all the time, whether in person or through social media. Most of us know that putting others to shame or submitting them to ridicule is wrong, because it hurts them. The rebbe of Modzhitz says it hurts us too! We are embedded in the social fabric; what happens to others happens to us. What we do to others rebounds on us.

Be-har

---

[94] Trust Only in God

"Speak to the Israelite people and say to them: When you enter the land that I assign to you, the land shall observe a Shabbat for the Eternal."
Leviticus 25:2

CONTEXT

Leviticus 25 details the laws of the sabbatical and jubilee years. In the seventh year, the land was to lie fallow. In the fiftieth year, all land was to revert to its original owners, or their heirs. All Israelite slaves were to go free, and all loans not yet repaid were to be forgiven and written off. Such loans were granted without interest. The intention of this legislation was to restore the social and economic equality of the original division of the land among the twelve tribes and their constituent clans.

Mordechai Leiner, rabbi of Izbica, was a student of the Kotzker rebbe, before their dramatic break.

> The point of the three portions presented here—the portion on the sabbatical year, the portion on freedom for slaves in the jubilee year, and the portion on interest—is that God is warning Israel not to put their trust in anything that seems to human eyes to be trustworthy.
>
> These three things—the sabbatical year, the jubilee year, and interest—are in "the world, the year, and the soul."
>
> The acquisition of fields and vineyards is the acquisition of things that a person has in this world, [things] in which a person may trust. But to counter this, God has issued the command of the sabbatical year, that is, that no one should put their trust in these things, but should recognize that they are the Eternal's. Thus, in the sabbatical year, no one recognizes his or her own possessions and everyone can see that the land is the Eternal's.

To counter the trust that people have in time—that is, they trust that wealth will increase [with the] hiring of time, that is, the taking of interest—the Torah teaches "do not take interest from them" [Leviticus 25:37] because the essence of interest is the hiring of time, as it says in the Gemara: "the general principle of interest is: All payment for waiting is forbidden."

To counter the trust that people have in other souls—the slaves whom they trust to perform all they require—to counter this, God has issued the command of freedom for slaves in the jubilee year, that is, so that you may see that no one can acquire the bodies of others [permanently], but must set them free. And even while they are slaves, God has commanded that we should not rule over them ruthlessly, that is, we must understand that [the slave's] body does not belong [to the owner].

And God has issued these three commandments so that we can realize that we cannot trust in the "world, year, and soul." A person can only trust in the Eternal.

Mordechai Yosef Leiner of Izbica (1800–54), *Mei HaShiloach* [The waters of the Siloam (Isaiah 8:6)] (Bnei Brak, 1995), v. 1, p. 131

NOTES

The portion on the sabbatical year. Leviticus 25:1–7.

The portion on freedom for slaves. Leviticus 25:39–55.

The portion on interest. Leviticus 25:35–38

"The world, the year, and the soul." A phrase quoted from the enigmatic *Sefer Yetzirah* (Book of formation) 6:1, a work of uncertain origin. There, these terms indicate the universe, time, and the human body. R. Mordechai takes "soul" to mean other people.

No one recognizes their own possessions. Because all land has been allowed to lie fallow.

As it says in the Gemara. Talmud, *Bava Metzia* 63b.

God has commanded that we should not rule over them ruthlessly. In Leviticus 25:43.

COMMENT

We live in society, we grow up, we age. We come to trust in others, and we come to believe that "time heals all things" and "everything will turn out all right." But we know that sometimes people let us down. Time is not always on our side. Things do not always turn out all right. The world we inhabit is constantly changing, and there are no certainties. But at its heart, as it were, and in our hearts, is the Unchanging One, the Only Reliable One.

---

[95] Only Passing Through

"You are resident aliens [gerim] and inhabitants [toshavim] with Me."

Leviticus 25:23

CONTEXT

Behind all the laws of Be-har that teach respect for the land lies this principle—that the earth belongs to God, not to us. We are, at best, temporary tenants.

Moshe of Sudylkov was one of the Ba'al Shem Tov's two grandsons. He lived modestly, without establishing himself as a rebbe, but his book bears testimony to his scholarship as well as his devotion to his grandfather's teachings.

You should understand this as an allegory, in accordance with what I heard from a certain sage on the verse "I am a resident alien on the earth; do not hide Your commandments from me" (Psalm 119[:19]). It is well known that, given the nature of the world, those who are resident aliens have no people to adhere to, to draw near to, or to tell all their news. And their hearts are united neither with Israel nor with non-Jews. But when they see another resident alien, then they tell each other their news.

Now it is well known that the Holy One is like a resident alien in this world, for God has no one upon whom to let the Divine Presence rest for "they are few." This is why King David prayed, "I am a resident alien on earth"—that is, I also want to be a foreigner in this world, and I am only a resident alien in this world. Therefore, "do not hide Your commandments from me": as resident aliens pour out their hearts to each other. And this is the allegorical interpretation of the verse "You are foreigners and resident aliens with Me." When you are in the category of a resident alien in this world and a foreigner in the world to come, then you are "with Me," for I am also a resident alien in this world, as mentioned above, and then I will obviously not hide My commandments from you, as implied above. Understand this well.

Moshe Hayyim Efraim of Sudylkov (d. 1800), *Degel Machaneh Efraim* [The flag of the camp of Ephraim (Numbers 2:18)] (Jerusalem, 1963), pp. 183–84

NOTE

From a certain sage. Who remains anonymous.

Resident aliens. *Gerim* in Hebrew. In Rabbinic Hebrew, "converts," but here it simply means "strangers living in the community."

For "they are few." These words are in Aramaic and probably refer to Zohar III, 68a: "Come and see, at the moment that holy souls come down below . . . they are few."

COMMENT

Whereas the Torah text seeks to emphasize that we are not the owners of the land, but only its temporary tenants, Moshe Hayyim Efraim of Sudylkov offers a deeper psychological and spiritual interpretation.

If we wish to experience the spiritual dimension of life, if we wish to come near to the divine, we must distance ourselves from the things of this world. We must recognize that we are only passing through—spiritual beings, not unlike God, sojourning through a physical universe.

---

[96] Taking No Personal Interest

"If others of you become poor, . . . [do] not take advance or accrued interest from them. . . ."
Leviticus 25:35,36

CONTEXT

As part of the legislation concerning the sabbatical and jubilee years designed to promote social equality, this chapter also prohibits the taking of interest. Lending was considered a form of charity rather than a necessary business practice; hence, this prohibition.

Elimelech of Lyzhansk, a student of the Maggid of Mezritch, trained a whole generation of Hasidic teachers who took the movement's message into the Jewish communities of Poland.

The meaning is [that] when you do anything good, do not desire to take any profit from God on account of your good deeds, for should any ulterior motive or pride occur to you—God forbid—you will be considered as if you were taking interest, as it were, from the Creator, who has great distress as a result, for "anyone who is proud of heart is an abomination to the Eternal" (Proverbs 16:5). On the contrary, let all your intentions be for the sake of heaven. Then you will be fully acceptable to our Creator, and by this means you may become worthy of redemption. Hence, "I am the Eternal your God [who brought you up out of the land of Egypt] to give you the land of Canaan, to be your God" (Leviticus 25:38).

Elimelech of Lyzhansk (1717–87), *No'am Elimelech* [The pleasantness of Elimelech], ed. Gedalyah Nigal (Jerusalem: Mossad HaRav Kook, 1978), v. 2, pp. 355–56

NOTE

Hence, "I am the Eternal your God." This is the last verse of the paragraph dealing with interest.

COMMENT

In traditional Judaism, hero status was usually achieved not through force of arms, but through good deeds and scholarship. But as Elimelech of Lyzhansk reminds us, disinterested behavior is our ideal too. The good deeds we do because we are hoping for recognition or praise, or just to make us feel better—these are somehow tarnished by our self-seeking.

Be-ḥukkotai

---

[97] Making God

"If you shall walk in My statutes, and shall keep
My commandments, and shall do them."
Leviticus 26:3

CONTEXT

Be-ḥukkotai opens with this verse, which introduces a short list of benefits that will accrue if we keep the Torah and a much longer list of negative consequences that failure to keep it will bring.

The Zohar, the classic work of Kabbalah, serves as a sacred text for future generations of Jewish mystics.

> What does "and shall do them" mean, since it [the verse] already says "you shall walk . . . and shall keep"? Why [does it say] "and shall do them" [as well]? Whoever does the commandments of the Torah and walks in God's ways is, as it were, as if they had made God above. Said the Holy One: "As if they had made Me."
>
> Zohar III, 113a

NOTE

It [the verse] already says "you shall walk . . . and shall keep." Surely "walking" and "keeping" are just alternative ways of saying "do them."

COMMENT

For the true believer, we cannot make God. God is the Power behind all that is; the Goal to which we aspire; the Home to which we will all one day return. We cannot make God. But we can make God a living force in our lives or allow God to die in our hearts. And we bring God to life in our world through our holy actions.

[98] "Two Structures"

"I am the Eternal your God who brought you out of the land of
the Egyptians to be their slaves no more, who broke the bars of
your yoke, and I made you walk upright [komemiyut]."
Leviticus 26:13

CONTEXT

The verse under consideration concludes the blessings that the Torah says will follow adherence to its laws.

Mordechai of Chernobyl succeeded his father as leader of the Hasidim in his city but did much more to increase the number of adherents.

The meaning is "two structures [*komot*]." For there is the "structure of holiness" and the "structure of the 'shell.'" When we build the structure of holiness through Torah and [performing] mitzvot [commandments], the power of the structure of the shell is annulled. Hence, "And I made you walk upright [*komemiyut*]" [means] "two structures," for when one rises, the other falls, as mentioned above.

Another [interpretation of] "two structures": the structure that exists below in the "lower" human being and the structure of the supernal Human Being. The meaning is [that] when a human being is in every respect a [complete spiritual] structure, without any blemish in any limb as a result of transgression or thought [of transgression], and in particular, through any act . . . then, you can bring about repair in the aspect of the supernal structure in general. You bring about "unifications" in the upper worlds and are also united with them in their generality. Hence, "upright [*komemiyut*]" [means] "two structures." That is sufficient for one of understanding.

Mordechai of Chernobyl (d. 1837), *Likkutei Torah* [Torah gleanings] (Jerusalem, 2001), p. 119

NOTES

"I made you walk upright." The plain meaning is that you were no longer bowed under the yoke.

The meaning is "two structures *[komot]*." This deconstruction of *kome-miyut* originates in the Talmud, *Bava Batra* 75a, where, however, it is explained quite differently.

The "structure of holiness" and the "structure of the 'shell.'" Meaning, the ten *sefirot* of holiness and their counterpart, the ten *sefirot* of the Other Side, the forces of evil.

The supernal Human Being. I.e., the ten *sefirot*.

The structure that exists below in the "lower" human being and the structure of the supernal Human Being. Human beings bear within themselves the structure of the heavenly *sefirot*, Adam Kadmon.

In particular, through any act . . . then, you can bring about repair in the aspect of the supernal structure in general. A particular good deed performed by a particular person can help to bring about beneficial effects in the realm of the *sefirot*.

You bring about "unifications" in the upper worlds. You promote positive interactions among the *sefirot*, in particular, between Tiferet and Malchut. As a result, positive energies flow into this world.

And are also united with them in their generality. Good deeds and Torah study unite you with the supernal *sefirot*.

COMMENT

Traditional religious texts, like this one, often assume that those who live in the world can be divided neatly into two categories: good and evil. We know that things are often not so clear cut. Good and evil exist, but most people and most actions are a mixture of both. It is a struggle not only to defeat evil and promote the good, but sometimes just to identify the evil and distinguish it from the good. Mordechai of Chernobyl does not address this modern challenge, but he does give us some clues as to how we might meet it. The study of Torah and the performance of mitzvot will help. His first comment suggests that merely engaging in study and ethical behavior will aid us in making the distinctions needed and in encouraging the good. His second comment reminds us that our ethical choices are not just matters for us, or even for society as a whole. They have cosmic spiritual ramifications: our good deeds increase the sum total of good in the world; our evil deeds decrease it.

[99] The Love of Inferior Things

"If a substitution is made, then shall both it and its replacement be holy."
Leviticus 27:33

CONTEXT

In the context of evaluating temple offerings, the Torah tells us that owners of flocks and herds had to count their animals and designate every
tenth one as sanctified. In practice, of course, farmers might be tempted
to substitute a sickly animal for a healthy one that happened to be the
tenth. Alternatively, an especially pious herdsman might be tempted to
replace a weaker animal with a particularly healthy one. The Torah declares that, in either case, the original animal and the one that was meant
to be its substitute are both holy and have to be given to the priests.

The Maggid (Preacher) of Mezritch, who succeeded the Ba'al Shem
Tov, trained most of the great leaders of the next generation of the Hasidic movement.

This refers to the love of inferior things that fell downward through
the mystery of the "breaking of the vessels" and that may rise upward.
Then you may take that love to serve God. And this is the meaning of
the verse "Then shall [*vehayah*]"—this is a term for happiness—"it
and its replacement shall be holy."

Dov Ber, Maggid of Mezritch (d. 1772), *Or Torah* [The light of Torah]
(Brooklyn: Kehot Publication Society, 1972), p. 88

NOTES

**The love of inferior things that fell downward through . . . the "break-
ing of the vessels."** Employing the language of the Lurianic Kabbalah, the
Maggid equates the love of "inferior things" with the divine sparks that are
said to have fallen into the space within which this world was to be created
as a result of the cosmic disaster known as the "breaking of the vessels."
The love we have for what he calls "inferior things" comes from the highest
sources, but is misdirected.

"Then shall [*vehayah*]"—this is a term for happiness. Rabbinic literature frequently interprets *vehayah* in the biblical narrative as a precursor of

happy events. "Vayehi [it came to pass]," the Rabbis say, introduces evil occurrences. For both interpretations, see e.g., *Be-midbar Rabbah* 13:5.

"It and its replacement shall be holy." I.e., both the love of inferior things and the love of God may be made holy.

COMMENT

There are many kinds of love, and it must be clear that some are more pure and worthy than others. After all, some of us love cars or computers, and others do not; and most of us are capable of loving other people, and even God. But what is the relationship between these different kinds of love? Some religious teachers might suggest that "lower" types of love, loves that focus on material things, should be rejected and set aside in the name of love of God. In the Middle Ages, some Jewish teachers took this approach.

But the approach of the Maggid of Mezritch is different. He suggests that all types of love have but one source, in God. (Specifically, he would have said, in the *sefirah* of Hesed, Lovingkindness.) In that case, why do these "lower" forms exist? The Maggid's reply is that this is a result of the cosmic catastrophe known as the "breaking of the vessels," envisioned by the great kabbalist Rabbi Yitzchak Luria. That event allowed "sparks" of higher divine energies to descend to this world, where they are held captive by lower powers.

When you realize that all love comes from God, the Maggid tells us, you will be able to apply all our "lower" forms of love to God; as a result, both our lower and our higher forms of love will be sanctified, just as in Torah both the original animal a shepherd had dedicated to the Temple and any animal he might have wished to substitute for it are holy. We may substitute love of material things for the love of God, but if we can turn our hearts to the love of God, that "lower" love will become holy too.

NUMBERS

Be-midbar

[100] The Spread of Torah

*"The Eternal spoke to Moses in the wilderness of
Sinai, in the Tent of Meeting. . . ."*

Numbers 1:1

CONTEXT

The fourth book of the Torah opens in the Sinai desert. God instructs
Moses to take a census of the people in order to ascertain the number
of men capable of bearing arms.
Naftali of Ropshitz was a student of Elimelech of Lyzhansk.

This teaches us about the holiness of the Torah, which comes from
an exalted place to a lowly place, for even the lowest of the low
is able to enter the service of God through the Holy Torah. And
in relation to this, Scripture comes to tell us that the word of God
was given in the wilderness, which is a very minimal place, a place
where the "shells" are strong, as it is said, "[the wilderness] where
there were venomous snakes, and scorpions, and drought, where
there was no water" (Deuteronomy 8:15), "not a place of seed, nor
of figs, nor of vines" (Numbers 20:5). Nevertheless, in this minimal,
inferior place, the word of God was given. And there, the Tabernacle of the Shechinah [the Presence of God] and the Tent of Meeting
[were erected]. For this represents the perfection of the Holy Torah,
that it can spread out to the lowest and most unsophisticated and
elevate every aspect. Even the most minimal may be raised by the
Holy Torah.

Naftali Zevi Horowitz of Ropshitz (1760–1827), *Zera Kodesh* [Seed of
holiness (Isaiah 6:12)] (Jerusalem, 1971), v. 1, p. 107a

A place where the "shells." In the theological worldview of Yitzchak Luria, the "shells" represent the forces of evil, which hold the "sparks" of divine light and prevent them from reascending to God.

The Tabernacle . . . and the Tent of Meeting. Although these terms are often used synonymously, the "Tabernacle" is the outer structure of the desert sanctuary, and the "Tent of Meeting" is the smaller edifice within it containing the Ark of the Covenant.

COMMENT

The Torah is the lifeblood of Judaism, and Judaism is Torah. If the Torah were to be confined to scholars, Judaism would die. Torah needs to be made accessible to all, whether scholars or laypeople. Synagogues and study centers, even small private study groups, are the Tabernacles of our day, from which Torah must radiate if it is to have any positive impact in our troubled world.

---

[101] Advice against Greatness

*"The Israelites shall camp each with his standard
[DiGLO], with the signs of their fathers' house."*

Numbers 2:2

CONTEXT

Numbers 2 presents the layout of the Israelite camp: three tribes on each of four sides of a square; at the center of the twelve tribes, the Levites; and at the center of the Levites, the Tabernacle.

Avraham of Radomsk was a very popular Hasidic teacher in his day, and his teachings often display considerable psychological insight.

DiGLO [his standard] has the same letters as *GaDOL* [big, great], alluding to "greatness" [*gadlut*]. Scripture is saying that if people want to truly be human, that is, to overcome "greatness," the advice is "with the signs of their fathers' houses," that is, [they must] bring a sign and reliable proof by considering "their fathers' houses," that is, by looking to the holy Patriarchs in whom the spirit of God dwelt. No one can reach their [level of] holiness, even though in their own eyes they seemed but dust and lowly, and in that case, how can someone who is full of desires wish to be "great"?

Alternatively, you may say that the advice against "greatness" is to consider "to their fathers' houses," meaning, [consider] if your thought and will are directed toward God alone. For although people might think that their fulfillment of the commandments and engagement with Torah are being done with all their ability, yet no one can escape from the power of thought. No one can say that they are innocent in thought, for the Torah and the commandments should be [done] with proper thought, with no ulterior motive.

Avraham Yissachar Ber HaCohen of Radomsk (1843–92), *Hesed leAvraham* [Lovingkindness to Abraham (Micah 7:20)] (n.p., 1893–95), p. 315

NOTES

Alluding to "greatness" [*gadlut*]. In Hasidic texts, *gadlut* frequently refers to heightened mental states, states of spiritual illumination. But the rebbe of Radomsk here uses the term as a synonym for pride or high self-esteem.

The holy Patriarchs. Abraham, Isaac, and Jacob.

In their own eyes they seemed but dust. See Genesis 18:27, where Abraham declares: "I am but dust and ashes."

How can someone who is full of desires. In contrast to the Patriarchs.

Alternatively, you may say. In this second approach to the verse, "fathers" is seen as an allusion to God rather than to the Patriarchs.

No one can say that they are innocent in thought. Although our actions may be blameless, our thoughts too need to be pure.

With no ulterior motive. It is not sufficient that we do right; we have to do right with the right motives, with no self-seeking.

COMMENT

Self-esteem is necessary for all of us. It is what normally protects us from the improper demands of others. But self-esteem can also be a trap. We may convince ourselves that we are right in a given situation and be unable to hear the voices of others with different opinions. This is the kind of "greatness" the Radomsker is talking about. He offers two solutions: The first is that we measure ourselves against the Patriarchs. The second is that we try to ensure that our motives are pure and directed toward God rather than serving our egos. Humility and pure motives in tandem may serve to keep us from thinking ourselves too "great" to learn and to compromise.

[102] Cheap Imitations

"But they shall not go in to see when the holy
thing is dismantled, lest they die."

Numbers 4:20

CONTEXT

This chapter details the number of Levite clans and specifies the tasks each clan was to undertake in the care and maintenance of the Tabernacle, particularly when it had to be taken apart and reassembled during the wilderness wanderings.

Moshe of Sudylkov was one of the grandsons of the Ba'al Shem Tov, whom he quotes at the start of this passage.

That is to say that there is a hint here along the lines of what I heard from my master, my grandfather, namely, that sometimes when [a Hasid] goes to a tzadik in order to learn from his acts, the tzadik may be in a state of "smallness," and [the Hasid] may receive some [inspiration] from him without realizing that there is [actually] a warning in it.

Something like this happened once when a man came to the famous master, Rabbi N. He saw him drinking coffee at that time with his tallit and tefillin on, so he went back to his own house and did the same too.

Hence the warning "they shall not go in to see," meaning, in order to see his acts and to receive [inspiration from] them, for immediately after this [the text says] "when they are dismantled"—that is, that there are times when [the tzadik] is in a period of "smallness," when the holiness that is within him is "dismantled," and thus "they die"—that is, [the people] fall from their level. [So,] they should not enter to receive [inspiration] unless they see that it is a time of "greatness"; then they should receive [inspiration] from him. Understand this, for when the knowledge of those who hear is limited, they do not understand..

Moshe Hayyim Efraim of Sudylkov (d. 1800), *Degel Machaneh Efraim* [The flag of the camp of Ephraim (Numbers 2:18)] (Jerusalem, 1963), p. 190

NOTES

My master, my grandfather. The Ba'al Shem Tov.

[A Hasid] goes to a tzadik. A tzadik (righteous man) in Hasidic parlance is an insightful mystical adept and communal leader. To this day, Hasidim attach themselves to a particular tzadik whom they regularly visit.

A state of "smallness." In Hebrew, *katnut*. In Hasidic texts, this usually indicates an ordinary mental state, without spiritual illumination or inspiration.

There is [actually] a warning in it. Rather than an act to be emulated. To the Hasid, the rebbe is not simply a teacher of Judaism; he is blessed with extra insight beyond that of ordinary people. Therefore, even his behavior in trivial matters might be liable to emulation by his followers, who would perceive in his actions deep mystical secrets.

The famous master, Rabbi N. This may be a reference to Nachman of Gorodenka (Horodenca), his sister Odel's father-in-law and a member of the Besht's circle, but there are other possible identifications.

Tallit and tefillin. Prayer shawl and phylacteries.

"They shall not go in to see." Ordinary people should not go to a tzadik to observe him, with a view to emulation.

COMMENT

Traditionally, leadership in the Hasidic community has been based on the tzadik or rebbe, who, by dint of his charisma and mystical insight, could command the unswerving loyalty of his Hasidim. And because rebbes were in touch with higher powers from supernal and spiritual realms, they were sometimes inspired (while in a state of "greatness") to create new modes of behavior that would then be liable to imitation by their followers. This, in turn, presents a problem, because the followers are not divinely inspired and might not understand the motives behind the rebbe's actions, and so be led into inappropriate activity. Or, alternatively, as Moshe Hayyim Efraim of Sudylkov points out here, the action that the Hasid seeks to emulate may not be divinely inspired at all, but something the rebbe did in a state of "smallness," in which case the potential spiritual damage caused by imitation may be greater still.

We, who are not Hasidim, may wonder what message there may be for us in the Sudylkover's analysis. Our leaders usually make no claim to divine inspiration, but they may still demand our loyalty and even our adherence to norms of behavior laid down by them. Hasidic teaching does demand unswerving trust in the rebbe, but modern free society does not. In our context, the Sudylkover's teaching suggests to me that, however good our leaders, we must never give them our adherence without question. Even those who truly inspire us can never claim our unquestioning allegiance. We all have our good and bad ideas, and our leaders are no exception. Each idea must be scrutinized for its own merits, each must be subjected to moral and spiritual questioning, so that we may distinguish between the good and the evil and achieve our own spiritual independence.

Naso'

---

[103] Joy Is Also a Mitzvah

"All the Levites . . . who came to do the service
of the service [avodat avodah]. . . ."

Numbers 4:46–47

CONTEXT

Parashat Naso' continues the theme of the end of Be-midbar, namely, the numbering of the members of the Levite clans and their assignments with regard to dismantling and transporting the Tabernacle.

Rabbenu Bachya, whose dates are unknown, is the author of a much-studied Torah commentary. He frequently begins his expositions of each parashah with quotations from the biblical book of Proverbs.

"Joy to the righteous is the doing of justice" (Proverbs 21[:15]). . . . [King] Solomon intends by this to teach us that a person should be happy when performing the commandments or when seeing others perform them. Hence, it says "the doing of justice" and not "when he does justice." It is known that the joy at the performance of a commandment is a commandment in its own right; and just as the commandment is service to God, so too is the joy at the command-ment called service. Thus it is written, "[All these curses will befall you . . .] because you did not serve the Eternal your God with joy" (Deuteronomy 28[:46–47]), and "Serve the Eternal with joy" (Psalm 100[:2]), meaning that joy is the perfection of service.

It was for this reason that there was song in the Temple and the Tabernacle. With singing and instruments, one conveys the human soul toward joy. And thus Scripture says of the Levites that they had "to do the service of the service," which our sages have interpreted [as follows]: "What is this 'service' for 'the service'? You must say that this is song." For the Levites were warned and commanded to sing and to stimulate joy at the [performance of] the commandment of sacrifice.

Rabbenu Bachya ben Asher ben Chlava (thirteenth century), *Perush al HaTorah* [Commentary on the Torah] (Jerusalem: Blum, 1988), pt. 4, p. 11

NOTES

"The service of the service [*avodat avodah*]. " A superliteral translation, as required by Bachya's comment. JPS: "duties of service."
King Solomon. The reputed author of the book of Proverbs.
Our sages have interpreted. In *Be-midbar Rabbah* 6:10.

COMMENT

Service can be given joyfully or grudgingly, and religious service is no exception. Judaism cannot have much of a future if people give it only lip service or undertake its tasks with a negative attitude. Our hypocrisy or our lack of joy in our Jewishness will communicate itself to others, especially to the young. But the absence of joy in the service of the divine has repercussions at the personal level as well as the social and educational. Judaism undertaken with a sense of acquiescence will become a burden to us, a burden that we may wish to discard when it no longer suits us.

On the other hand, our lives can be enriched, our souls revived, and depression avoided, if we can discover the joy and sheer pleasure that the service of God can entail. Judaism is not our fate; it should be our delight. We may choose to be chosen.

The late rabbi and philosopher Emil Fackenheim famously suggested that the Holocaust was a new revelation, revealing the commandment: "Thou shalt not grant Hitler a posthumous victory." I know a number of people for whom remembering the Holocaust seems to be the primary commandment of Judaism. Not for one moment am I suggesting that it be forgotten, even if that were possible, but an overemphasis on memorializing our dead drains the joy out of Jewishness, making us look back continually when we should be looking forward.

[104] A Gift from a King

"May the Eternal bestow divine favor upon you. . . ."
Numbers 6:26

CONTEXT

Numbers 6 concludes with what is perhaps the most famous passage in the book: the threefold Priestly Blessings (vv. 22–27).

Simchah Bunam trained as a pharmacist in the modern Western mode before becoming a Hasidic rebbe. Many of the comments attributed to him begin, as here, with lengthy quotations from the midrash.

In the Midrash Rabbah [it says]: "'May the Eternal bestow divine favor upon you'—but does the Holy One show favor? Hasn't [Scripture] already said: 'Who does not show favor' (Deuteronomy 10:17)? The Holy One says: If they show Me favor, I will show them favor. How? I have written in My Torah: 'And you shall eat and be satisfied and bless' [Deuteronomy 8:10]. If the Israelites sit down with their children and their household, but do not have enough to satisfy [their hunger], yet they show Me favor and recite the blessing, and they take care even with regard to an olive- or egg-sized [morsel], then 'May the Eternal bestow divine favor upon you.'"

This statement is wondrous to the understanding. Thus, it seems that its meaning is that if an ordinary person gives an insignificant gift to a friend, the one who receives it does not consider it important at all. This is not the case if the king gives him a gift, even though it might be an insignificant one. It will nevertheless be of great importance because it is the king who gave it. And so the one who receives it gets greater pleasure from it than if he had received a substantial gift from an ordinary person.

The image applies also to the "Grace after Meals," for even though it says in the Torah that we have to eat until we are satisfied [before saying the grace], this is from the side of those who receive. But when we realize that it is the Sovereign beyond all sovereigns who gives bread to all flesh and who prepares for each creature what it needs and what sustains it, then even if we have eaten only an olive-sized morsel, we consider it very important and gain very great pleasure from it since it comes from the Eternal, according to the analogy above.

And this is the meaning of the midrash: "How? [. . .] If the Israelites sit down with their children and their household, but do not have enough to satisfy [their hunger], yet they show Me favor and recite the blessing"—that is to say that they contemplate from whom the food has come and recite the blessing, and because of the greatness and importance of the One who gave it, they have pleasure from a small amount, and from this do they derive satisfaction and so recite the blessing. This is the meaning of the notion that they show God favor. Understand!

This is an attribute [of God] too, for the Holy One shows them favor and enjoys the insignificant service that they have performed before God, because God contemplates from whom this service comes, [appreciating] that we are [merely] human and of limited intellect, but serve God just the same. This is the explanation of "May the Eternal bestow divine favor upon you." Understand, because it is profound.

Simchah Bunam of Pshische (1765–1827), *Kol Simchah* [The sound of joy (Jeremiah 7:33)] (Jerusalem: HaMesorah, 1986), p. 87

NOTES

In the Midrash Rabbah [it says]. *Be-midbar Rabbah* 11:7.

Recite the blessing. I.e., the "Grace after Meals." Deuteronomy 8:10 is the Rabbis' prooftext for reciting "Grace after Meals."

We have to eat until we are satisfied [before saying the grace]. Based on the order of verbs in Deuteronomy 8:10. See the Talmud, *Berachot* 21a.

COMMENT

I particularly liked the dialectic aspect of this teaching and its suggestion that God and human beings are interdependent. Just as we depend upon God for the things that sustain our bodies, and our souls, so too God is dependent, as it were, on us to acknowledge God's divinity. To do so not only connects us with the One who is greater than we, but also brings that One into human life in concrete, even intimate, ways.

[105] Exertion Required

*"But to the descendants of Kohath, [Moses] did not give
anything, because the service of the holy belonged to
them; they were to carry it on the shoulders."*

Numbers 7:9

CONTEXT

The Tabernacle is complete, and each of the princes of the tribes brings
his offering for its inauguration. The identical offerings are then distributed among two of the three Levite clans, whose task it is to trans-
port them through the wilderness. But the clan of Kohath is not given
anything, because their special task is to carry the Ark of the Covenant.

Menachem Mendel of Kotzk was famous in his own day for having
very high moral and spiritual expectations of his followers.

"In the service of the holy," you must work hard.

"They were to carry it on the shoulders"—if someone says, "I have
not exerted myself, but I have found," do not believe them.

Menachem Mendel of Kotzk (1787–1859), *Sefer Amud HaEmet* [The book of
the pillar of truth] (Bnei Brak, 2000), p. 76

NOTE

"But I have found." I.e., found holiness, spirituality.

COMMENT

I believe that Judaism must be joyful if it is to survive in our hearts and
beyond our lifetime, but that does not mean that it cannot make demands
on us. A Judaism that makes no demands is just another form of entertainment, and one that may not be able to compete with the high-tech
forms so readily available in the twenty-first century.

So how do we square the circle, offering joy while making demands?
For me, the answer lies in a talmudic teaching based on the task given to
the clan of Kohath, that of carrying the Ark of the Covenant. It must have
been an arduous task indeed, walking for hundreds of miles carrying the
sacred chest with its contents, the stone tablets of the Ten Command-

ments. "The ark carried those who carried it," says the Talmud (*Sotah* 35a). If the Talmud is to be believed, the men of Kohath knew that they were engaged in singularly important work, and they were happy, fulfilled. They were so happy that the physical exertion required did not matter. They realized they were on a spiritual as well as a physical journey toward the Promised Land, and that thought filled them with joy.

People don't mind the demands made upon them if they understand and subscribe to the goals. We need to keep the goals of Judaism in mind at all times: nothing less than the repair of our world, the repair of our souls, the sanctification of the mundane, in a word: holiness.

Be-ha'alotekha

---

[106] Keeping It Fresh

*"Aaron did so; he mounted the lamps at the front of the
candelabrum, as the Eternal had commanded Moses."*

Numbers 8:3

CONTEXT

The Tabernacle has been dedicated, and Numbers 8 opens with the command to Aaron to position the seven-branched candelabrum so that it may illuminate the sacred area.

R. Mordechai of Izbica had been a loyal student of Menachem Mendel of Kotzk until their final dramatic break.

Rashi explains: "This is to praise Aaron because he did not change [*shinnah*]."

Shinnah [change, repeat] means that it was not something he felt he was just repeating, like someone acting out of habit. On the contrary, he always performed the commandment as something new that a person does with joy and enthusiasm. Hence it says in the Gemara: "People should purify themselves for a festival, as it is said, 'And their carcasses you shall not touch' [Leviticus 11:8]." "Carcass" refers to a thing from which life has departed, and thus, if anyone performs a commandment without joy and enthusiasm, simply as "a command learned from other people by rote" [Isaiah 29:13], it is as if it had no life in it. Therefore, [it says] "for a festival." Because God sends life to Israel, each person must receive that life with joy.

Mordechai Yosef Leiner of Izbica (1800–54), *Mei HaShiloach* [The waters of the Siloam (Isaiah 8:6)] (Bnei Brak, 1995), v. 1, p. 147

Rashi. The preeminent Bible commentator, Rabbi Shlomo Yitzchaki (1040–1105). His comment here is based on the midrash Sifre, Be-ha'alotekha §2.

"He did not change." I.e., he did not deviate from his instructions. But the verbal root *sh-n-h* can also mean "to repeat."

It says in the Gemara. Talmud, *Rosh Hashanah* 16b.

Therefore, [it says] "for a festival." Meaning, at a joyous time.

COMMENT

Aaron's job as High Priest involved a high degree of ritual that had to be repeated each day. Rashi, following the midrash, seems to praise him for never deviating from the prescribed rites. The Izbicer praises him for always treating them as if they were new.

The practice of Judaism involves a certain degree of repetition. The festivals come around each year, *Shabbat* each week, the prayers each day. Repetition can lead to boredom. The secret to avoiding boredom in repetition is carefully examining each instance to discern what has changed. No two moments are the same. Even if the words we are reciting are the same each time, we are different. We have a little more experience, perhaps a little more wisdom. Our emotional state is altered; we are elated, depressed, tired, energized. Each repetition must be greeted with new understanding, and new joy.

---

[107] Moving On with the Help of God

*"At the mouth of the Eternal they would move on and
at the mouth of the Eternal they would camp."*

Numbers 9:18

CONTEXT

Numbers 9 opens with rules that allow those who in ancient times might be ritually unclean at Passover, and therefore unable to eat the Passover lamb, to celebrate this crucial festival a month later. From verse 15 it records how the Israelites' movements through the wilderness were dependent on the cloud of God's presence covering the

Tabernacle. If the cloud moved, so would they. If it did not, neither would they.

Yishayah Horowitz was a communal rabbi and author of a work that was popular throughout the seventeenth century, the *Shnei Luchot HaBrit*, or *SHeLaH*. This passage comes from his comments on this parashah.

> Later on, it is written: "At the mouth of the Eternal they would camp, and at the mouth of the Eternal, they would move on" (Numbers 9:20). There is a hint of a [spiritual] discipline here: for every act or movement that you perform, you should say "God willing" or "with the help of God." For example, when going on a journey, you should say: "I am traveling with the help of God; it is my plan to camp at such and such a place, with God's help, if God wills it." And when you arrive at the intended place, you should give thanks and say: "With the help of God have I come here, and it is my plan to move on at such and such a time, with God's help, if God wills it." Thus, the name of heaven will regularly be on your lips whenever it arises in your thought or whenever you undertake any action.
>
> Yishayah HaLevi Horowitz (ca. 1570–1626), *Shnei Luchot HaBrit* [The two tablets of the covenant] (1863; repr., Jerusalem: 1975), Be-ha'alotekha, v. 2, p. 67c

NOTE

"At the mouth of." An overliteral translation of *al pi*, as demanded by Horowitz's comment. JPS: "at the command of." Horowitz inverts the meaning of the phrase, suggesting that "mouth" means "our mouths" rather than "God's mouth," as it were.

COMMENT

I believe that one of the aims of the commandments of Judaism is to remind us that we live in God's world and must behave accordingly, that is, with fully conscious respect for everything and everyone in God's world and for its Owner. But even the full panoply of the traditional mitzvot leaves space in our lives for other legitimate concerns. We all need, for example, to make a living; and provided we do so within an ethical, Torah-based framework, the exact manner of our earning that living does not matter. How can our nonhalachic activities be hallowed? Horowitz provides an answer: dedicate all our actions to God, whether they be "religious" or not. Pray for God's help when you strive to put plans into effect; thank God for successes when you have achieved them. This is a deep form of personal discipline, but one that I believe repays us handsomely in spiritual and ethical sensitivity. It reminds us of our ultimate dependence of God and teaches us true humility.

[108] Accepting Yourself

"Now the man Moses was very humble. . . ."
Numbers 12:3

CONTEXT

Chapters 11 and 12 both relate the stories of attacks on Moses. In Numbers 11, the people question his leadership and demand meat to eat. In the following chapter, Moses's brother and sister attack his personal life, alleging some unspecified problem regarding his wife. But, the Torah tells us, these attacks were unjustified: Moses was the most humble of people. Perhaps the greatest of the prophets might be forgiven for having a high opinion of himself, but the text asserts that power did not go to his head.

Simchah Bunam of Pshische was a disciple of the Seer of Lublin and a close friend of the Holy Jew of Pshische and Menachem Mendel of Kotzk; the Holy Jew preceded him as leader, and the Kotzker succeeded after Simchah Bunam's death. Here we present two versions of the same teaching. The editor of *Midrash Simchah* found these in two earlier compilations of Simchah Bunam's teachings. It is possible that these versions arose when two people were present when Simchah Bunam presented this teaching, but remembered it slightly differently, or perhaps the two versions were spoken on two separate occasions. Both versions are included here because each offers its own unique slant on the verse in question.

Rashi explains "humble" [as] "lowly and patient." Our holy teacher [Rabbi Simchah Bunam] used to speak about two [kinds of] people—those who, if they think that they are not fit at all, are unable to live, and the second who know their lowly state but nevertheless are patient with themselves—for the service of the latter is much superior, for they are lowly and accept their lowliness.

Rashi explains "humble" [as] "lowly and patient," meaning: even though Moses our teacher was lowly in his own eyes, that is, he knew the lowliness of his status, nevertheless he was patient with himself, as expressed in the verse: "His heart was lifted up through the ways of the Eternal" (2 Chronicles 17[:6]).

Simchah Bunam of Pshische (1765–1827), *Midrash Simchah* [Simchah's interpretation] (Jerusalem: Mossad HaRYM Levin, 1988), v. 1, pp. 135–36

NOTE

Rashi. The most popular of the medieval Bible commentators, Rabbi Shlomo Yitzchaki (1040–1105).

COMMENT

The first of Simchah Bunam's teachings here points out that the Torah is speaking about everyone, about us, in other words, not just about Moses. It teaches us that humility leading to a kind of moral paralysis in which we are unable to live in any meaningful sense is a trap. True humility means acceptance of ourselves, failings and all, but not allowing the awareness of our failings to interfere with our lives and prevent us from taking moral responsibility for our actions and our world.

The second version, although it speaks more directly of Moses, still has universal application. Our awareness of our lowly status does not mean that we cannot achieve anything worthwhile. On the contrary, if we pursue the ways of God, there is no limit to what we can achieve. In this way, we accept ourselves, but exalt our hearts in and through the service of the divine.

Shelaḥ-Lekha

---

[109] Beyond the Earthly

"A land consuming those who dwell in it."

Numbers 13:32

CONTEXT

Numbers 13 tells the story of the twelve spies sent into the land of Canaan. They come back with two reports. All of them agree that the land is wonderful, but only two believe that the Israelites can conquer it. The words quoted here from Numbers 13 are part of the majority report. The land, they suggest, is not worth conquering. Not only will it be difficult to defeat the Canaanites; the very influence of the land will be corrupting.

Ze'ev Wolf of Zhitomir was a prominent disciple of the Maggid of Mezritch, whom he quotes frequently.

> I heard concerning the Maggid that he gave an explanation of the verse "A land [*eReTZ*] consuming those who dwell in it." [Scripture] wants [to tell us that] the lower levels [of existence] known by the term "earthly" [*aRTZiyut*] "consume" and destroy those who "dwell" and remain there, for no one has permission to keep themselves in the [purely] earthly aspect, even for a single moment.

Ze'ev Wolf of Zhitomir (d. 1800), *Or HaMe'ir* [The illuminating light] (Warsaw, 1883), pt. 2, p. 33a

NOTE

The Maggid. Rabbi Dov Ber of Mezritch (d. 1772).

COMMENT

We have here a teaching from the Maggid of Mezritch, transmitted by one of his most original disciples, Ze'ev Wolf of Zhitomir. If our minds remain on the purely earthly, mundane, physical levels of existence, we deny our inner spirituality, the God-spark within us. And thus we deny our full humanity as well.

---

[110] Why God Can Forgive

"When the Egyptians hear the news . . . they will tell it to the inhabitants of that land. Now they have heard that You, O Eternal, are in the midst of this people; that You, O Eternal, are seen eye to eye. . . . If then You slay this people to a man, the nations who have heard of Your fame will say: 'It must be because the Eternal was not able to bring that people to the land God had promised them that God slaughtered them in the wilderness.'"

Numbers 14:13–16

CONTEXT

When they hear the report of the returning spies, the people panic. Moses and Aaron try to calm their nerves and renew their courage. God threatens to destroy them all and make a new people through Moses, but the prophet appeals for divine forgiveness, arguing, as in these verses, that God's reputation is at stake.

Moshe Leib of Sasov had studied with Dov Ber, the Maggid of Mezritch, and Elimelech of Lyzhansk, before becoming a rebbe in his own right.

"[It must be] because the Eternal was not able." In the midrash [it says]:
Moses said: "Master of the worlds! 'You are seen eye to eye [*ayin be'ayin*]' [Numbers 14:14]." What is the implication of *aYiN be'aYiN*? Resh Lakish explained: [Moses said:] "Look here, the scales are evenly balanced [*me'uYaN*]! You say, 'I will smite him with plague' [Numbers 14:12], and I say, 'Please forgive' [Numbers 14:19]. Let us see who will stand!" In fact it says: "And the Eternal said, 'I have forgiven as you have asked'" [Numbers 14:20]. Thus far the quotation from the midrash.

To understand this matter, we need to proceed by way of a parable. A king of flesh and blood must enforce the rules of the state in order that people do not swallow each other up, along the lines of the Mishnah in [*Pirkei*] *Avot* [3:2], "Pray for the welfare of the government, for without the fear of it, people would swallow each other alive." But on the surface, what does it matter to him, that he should intervene in a dispute that does not [directly] concern him? But the fear always hangs over him that the matter might extend to his authority. This does not apply to the Sovereign beyond all sovereigns, the Holy One. Because God possesses all power, God does not need [to impose] the rules of the state out of fear; God produced the rules for the good of humanity and gave them the Torah. This is the meaning of the midrash: "The scales are evenly balanced"—Moses our teacher said to the Holy One: "Why do you want to punish Israel? If they sin, what effect does that have on You? But if [You want to punish them] in order to clear them of sin, then I say, 'Please forgive,' then they will also be clear of sin! 'Let us see who will stand.'" Immediately, the Holy One said: "I have forgiven as you have asked."

Moshe Leib of Sasov (d. 1807) *Likkutei RaMaL* [Gleanings from Rabbi Moshe Leib] (n.p., n.d.), p. 25

NOTES

In the midrash. *Be-midbar Rabbah* 16:25.

"What is the implication of *aYiN be'aYiN*?" Moshe Leib is implying: Surely this phrase cannot be taken literally.

The matter might extend to his authority. Royal authority will be undermined.

COMMENT

The Talmud teaches us to see ourselves and the world as finely balanced between good and evil; our decisions may tip the balance one way or the other (*Kiddushin* 40a–b). The Kabbalah teaches us to seek the balance between the forces of Hesed (Lovingkindness) and those of Gevurah (Power). The midrash quoted by the Sasover suggests that this fine balance exists within God, between the desire to punish wrongdoing or forgive it. Moses tips the balance toward forgiveness by asking what good punishment would do when the same result could be achieved by forgiveness.

Perhaps Rabbi Moshe Leib would say that there is a lesson for us all here. When we feel ourselves aggrieved, it may be because we feel that our power has been challenged, that our authority is at stake, or even that our pride has been affronted. If we seek to punish those who have offended us, whom are we harming with our anger? Them or ourselves? Might we not achieve more positive results with those who have wronged us if we can find it in our hearts to forgive them? Wouldn't forgiveness bring us some measure of closure? Hatred has a way of eating at our hearts, at our spirits; forgiveness will restore them.

In my pastoral work, I have met many warring families, siblings or even parents and children who have not spoken in years. It seems to me that a little forgiveness in situations like that can bring benefits in terms of sanity and restored relationships.

---

[111] Not Even If You Have a Good Heart

"You will not turn astray after your heart and after your eyes. . . ."
Numbers 15:39

CONTEXT

After the debacle of the spies in Numbers 14, the Torah turns to a variety of matters in the next chapter: meal offerings, the challah or dough offering, sin offerings for idolatry, and the punishment meted out to the man found gathering sticks for firewood on *Shabbat*. Chapter 15 concludes with the instructions for wearing tassels or fringes at the corners of four-cornered garments, the origin of today's tallit, or tallis (prayer shawl).

In the following passage, we once more get insight into the strict demands that the Kotzker made upon his Hasidim.

Why doesn't [the text] say: "After your evil heart"? Because anyone who has a good heart is also forbidden from following their heart. This is to teach us that even the good must not be done [purely] out of the heart's inclination, but out of knowledge and effort. For the good that you do out of the heart's inclination is in the category of "though I walk in the stubbornness of my heart" (Deuteronomy 29[:18]). This is not true goodness. Hence, King Solomon said: "And walk in the ways of your heart, and in the sight of your eyes; but know" (Ecclesiastes 11[:9])—that is, when you walk in the ways of your heart, [do so] out of knowledge and seeking advice through your own effort.

Menachem Mendel of Kotzk (1787–1859), *Sefer Amud HaEmet* [The book of the pillar of truth] (Bnei Brak, 2000), p. 81

King Solomon said. Solomon is traditionally credited with the authorship of Ecclesiastes.

COMMENT

At first sight, the Kotzker's teaching here seems bizarre: why shouldn't we do good if we feel like it? Why does he condemn that? The answer is that anybody can be good when they feel like it. We can all be good if it makes us feel that we have achieved something or is likely to put us into the good books of someone we are trying to impress. But the true test of a person's goodness is whether they behave well even when they do not feel like it, even when it is to their detriment. The truly good person does good simply because it is the right thing to do, not because there is any gain to be had.

Koraḥ

---

[112] The Ongoing Struggle

"Now Korah son of Izhar son of Kohath son of Levi . . . took.

Numbers 16:1

CONTEXT

As its name suggests, the main subject of this *sidrah* is the rebellion of Korah, a descendant of Levi, against the leadership of his cousin Moses. Jewish tradition tends to see Korah as the archetypal self-seeking demagogue.

Ya'akov Yolles was a communal rabbi before he gained a reputation as a Hasidic tzadik. *Kehillat Ya'akov* is his encyclopedic dictionary of Kabbalah.

Korah is the reincarnation of Cain, and Moses is the reincarnation of Abel. Therefore, Korah opposed Moses and was jealous of him, thus awakening the ancient jealousy that Cain had for Abel. Moreover, the earth was cursed then, insofar as "it opened its mouth to accept your brother's blood" [Genesis 4:11], while here Moses brings about its repair, in that it opened its mouth to swallow Korah [Numbers 16:32]. One opening [compensating] for the other.

Ya'akov Zevi Yolles (ca. 1778–1825), *Kehillat Ya'akov* [The congregation of Jacob (Deuteronomy 33:4)] (Jerusalem, 1971), s.v. Korah, pt. 4., p. 7d

NOTE

Reincarnation. The doctrine that souls return to this world in new bodies after death is common in kabbalistic and Hasidic texts, though rarely found in Rabbinic sources or medieval Jewish philosophy.

In Genesis, Abel was defeated by his jealous brother's violence. Here, in Numbers, Abel/Moses is now victorious over Cain/Korah. There is violence—the earth opens and swallows Korah and his band—but this is not Abel's/Moses's doing, it is divine intervention. Perhaps Ya'akov Zevi Yolles is telling us that the struggle against evil is ongoing, indeed, never ending, but that we should never lose hope that ultimately, with divine help, good will emerge victorious and evil will be no more.

---

[113] The Spirit in Flesh

"They [Moses and Aaron] fell on their faces. They said, 'O God, God of the spirits of all flesh, if one man sins, shall You direct divine wrath at the entire community?'"

Numbers 16:22

CONTEXT

The rebellion of Korah and his band is gathering pace, and so are their attacks on Moses and Aaron. God intervenes with a threat to wipe out the entire people, but the two brothers appeal to God's sense of justice and fairness.

The popular Moroccan kabbalist and Torah commentator Hayyim ibn Attar puts forward a mystical interpretation of our verse.

"They said, 'O God [*el*], God of [*elohei*] the spirits of all flesh.'" [Moses] says the name *el* (God) because he perceived the increased arousal of the forces of judgment; so he mentioned God's lovingkindness in order to "sweeten" the forces of judgment.

And by saying "God of the spirits of all flesh," he puts forward a claim that will be heard by the Creator, for the Eternal desires that all souls should accept the divine essence upon themselves while they are still in the flesh in this world. And so [Moses] says "God of the spirits of all flesh." . . . Moses was being clever about this, appeasing God with something that God wanted, and said "God of the spirits of all flesh"; that is, "You desire that Your divine essence should belong to all souls while they are still in the flesh, but if You kill them,

You will lack [the means of fulfilling] this wish. And it is not right to increase the might of the forces of judgment that may damage the acceptance of Your divine essence by the spirits that are [still] in the flesh, which is Your greatest desire."

Hayyim ben Moshe ibn Attar (1696–1743), *Or HaHayyim* [The light of life] (Jerusalem: A. Blum, 1994), pt. 4, pp. 64–65

NOTES

The name *el*. Divine names are frequently associated with particular *sefirot*. El represents Hesed (Lovingkindness).

The increased arousal of the forces of judgment. This was brought on by Korah's rebellion.

To "sweeten" the forces of judgment. The judgmental forces (*dinim*) originate in the *sefirah* of Gevurah (Might). To sweeten their bitterness (counteract them), Moses mentions a name symbolizing Gevurah's opposite, Hesed.

COMMENT

We may not have the powers attributed to Moses and Aaron to directly affect the flow of divine energies, but we can strive to bring Hesed to situations that we encounter where Gevurah is prevalent.

The Jewish people have a crucial (though not exclusive) role in bringing spirituality to humanity. We have a uniquely Jewish approach to experiencing the divine presence, one characterized by concern for deeds and speech, and for bringing hidden thoughts to consciousness, that the good within may be separated from the evil. We must not allow this to be lost.

---

[114] Producing Blossoms and Almonds

"And it [Aaron's staff] produced buds, burst into bloom, and yielded almonds."

Numbers 17:23

CONTEXT

With Korah and his band removed from the scene, and after a plague in punishment for the rebellion, God moves to discourage any remaining opposition to the choice of Aaron and his descendants to the priesthood. Each tribe is instructed to place a staff in the Tent of Meeting overnight, and they do so. In the morning, the staff of Levi, with Aaron's name inscribed on it, has blossomed and produced fruit, thus confirming God's choice of Aaron's tribe and family.

Simchah Bunam of Pshische was a student of the Seer of Lublin before breaking away with his friend the Holy Jew of Pshische.

> There is a difficulty: why does the text say "produced buds, burst into bloom," when the whole point is to tell us that it "yielded almonds," as is clear. We may interpret [as follows]: The verse tells us, through hints, the way to serve the Creator—that even though you may feel within the limits of perfection, that is, in your old age, as [alluded to in the phrase] "yielded almonds," you must still be "producing buds and bursting into bloom," by always acting with enthusiasm and at a low level, as [you did] during your youth.

Simchah Bunam of Pshische (1765–1827), *Midrash Simchah* [Simchah's interpretation] (Jerusalem: Mossad HaRYM Levin, 1988), v. 1, p. 143

NOTES

There is a difficulty. Simchah Bunam asks why the Torah gives us apparently superfluous information about the buds and blossoms.

You may feel within the limits of perfection. You may feel that you are as perfect as you will get.

At a low level. I.e., with humility.

COMMENT

Buds, blossoms, and almonds are not static objects, but stages in the life of the almond tree. Our roles too will vary with age; that is, different stages of life will require different types of commitment from us. Simchah Bunam suggests that our middle and old age may be a time of self-confidence, something we may have lacked when we were young adults or children. Nevertheless, whatever life demands from us should be offered with all the enthusiasm and willingness to learn that are the finest attributes of youth.

We have our roles in life, the parts we have to play, which change as we grow older and hopefully wiser, but they all require those positive attributes we had when we were young.

Ḥukkat

---

[115] The Secret of the Red Heifer

"You shall take for yourself a red heifer. . . ."

Numbers 19:2

CONTEXT

While Numbers 18 deals with the responsibilities of the priest in relation to the sins of the people, tithes, and other issues, Ḥukkat opens
with the rite of the red heifer. A young cow of that color was to be
slaughtered and burned. Its ashes were then to be used in a purification ritual to render clean again those who had become ritually unclean through contact with a corpse. However, the priest who prepared
the ashes had to be clean to be allowed to do so, but became unclean
in the process.

This enigmatic passage by Menachem Mendel of Vorki, a student of
the Kotzker, is explained by the author's grandson.

The secret of the red heifer is: "And you shall love your neighbor as
yourself" [Leviticus 19:18].

(His grandson R. Mendel, the son of his son R. Simchah Bunam of
Otvotsk, offered this opinion: "Look here, the red heifer made the
[ritually] clean unclean and made the [ritually] unclean clean; that
is, the priest made himself unclean in order to cleanse [people] other
than himself.")

Menachem Mendel of Vorki (d. 1868), in *Beit Yitzchak* [The house of Isaac]
(Jerusalem, 1992), p. 80

NOTE

R. Mendel. He died in 1919. His father, Simchah Bunam, died twelve years
earlier.

The ritual of the red heifer was, and remains, a mystery. The rabbis designated it a *chukkah* or *chok*, a law for which they could find no clear reason. The Vorker's explanation seems only to deepen the mystery, but his grandson comes to save the day. For him at least, the rite of the red heifer is an example of selflessness on the priest's part. It was the priest's job to take on the uncleanness so that others might be clean.

I am sure that Menachem Mendel of Vorki, or at least the younger R. Mendel, intended the priest's self-sacrifice to be an example to us. Sometimes loving our neighbors as ourselves means getting dirty in order to help them.

---

[116] Brothers on the Inside

"Then Moses sent messengers from Kadesh to the king of Edom, 'Thus says your brother Israel.'"

Numbers 20:14

CONTEXT

The Israelites arrive at the desert oasis of Kadesh, and quarrels break out because there is no water. Moses reacts angrily, striking a rock to obtain water, despite being commanded simply to speak to it. After this incident, Moses sends an embassy to the Edomites asking for safe passage through their territory, but the request is denied, and Israel circumnavigates Edomite territory.

Ya'akov Yosef of Polonnoye was already a communal rabbi before he met the Ba'al Shem Tov, but the meeting changed his life. He went on to write the first Hasidic books to be published.

The dwelling place of the soul is in the brain, which is called Kadesh. The soul sends out agents to "matter," that is, the body, which [normally] pursues permitted desires, as Scripture [has Esau] saying, "Feed me, I beg you, [some of the red stuff (*adom*)]" (Genesis 25[:30]). For this [reason], he is called Edom.

Now, this is the king of Edom, who rules over the limbs of the body without being subject to "form," until you arouse your heart with holy thoughts, that is, thoughts of repentance, which come from Kadesh.

"Thus says your brother, Israel"—for you should pay attention to the purpose of your creation in matter and form in this world, [which is] in order to make your matter subject to form, so that they should exist in harmony and peace, and not be opponents.

Ya'akov Yosef of Polonnoye (died ca. 1782), *Toledot Ya'akov Yosef* [The generations of Jacob Joseph (Genesis 37:2)] (Jerusalem, 1973), v. 2, p. 558

NOTES

The soul. Ya'akov Yosef uses the word *neshamah*, which in medieval Jewish texts usually has the meaning of the intellect, the conscious mind.

Kadesh. From the root meaning "holy."

"Matter." The Polonnoyer frequently refers to the dichotomy of matter and form, familiar from ancient Greek and medieval philosophy as derived from Aristotle. All things are made up of matter, but it is their form that gives them their distinct shape and other characteristics. The soul is the form of the body; the body is the matter upon which the soul acts.

He is called Edom. Esau receives the name Edom as a result of the tale told in Genesis 25. Here, Edom represents the body. Esau's demand for food demonstrates his symbolic connection to the body.

This is the king of Edom. The *nefesh*, the animal soul, is sovereign over the body. The *nefesh* can be controlled by holy thoughts emanating from the *neshamah*, the mind.

"Thus says your brother, Israel." Edom is the nation descended from Esau; Israel's ancestor, of course, is his twin brother, Jacob.

They should exist in harmony and peace. Matter and form, body and soul, should work together harmoniously.

COMMENT

Medieval religiosity tended to see the body as the realm of evil that had to be tamed. According to legend, Ya'akov Yosef of Polonnoye had himself been an ascetic before he met the Ba'al Shem Tov. Here he has put forward an antiascetic agenda. The body is brother to the soul, and deserves respect, although it is still Esau to the soul's Israel.

Asceticism has largely disappeared from modern society, only to be replaced by an equally rampant hedonism that affects even the more spiritual among us. The Polonnoyer affirms the need for greater balance between body and soul, coupled with the recognition that, ultimately, it is the soul that is most important. The body is the imperfect vehicle that the soul requires to interact with this world.

---

[117] Prayer as Meditation

"Then Israel sang this song [ha-SHIRaH ha-zot]: 'Spring up, O well—sing to it—the well which the chieftains dug, which the nobles of the people started, with a mace, with their own staffs. . . .'"

Numbers 21:17–18

CONTEXT

Moses's brother Aaron dies on Mount Hor at the end of chapter 20. Chapter 21 describes a number of incidents on the journey through the wilderness, including the digging of a well with its accompanying work song.

Rabbenu Bachya offers a kabbalistic interpretation, in addition to his exposition of the plain meaning, which is not translated here.

According to the Kabbalah, [on the verse] "Then Israel sang this song": a song is like a prayer, drawing down the intention of your thought from above to below. Whether an individual or a group is singing a song, they are drawing down a blessing from above to below.

And you should realize that *SHIRaH* (song) has the same numerical value as *TeFiLaH* (prayer). . . . It says "*ha-shirah ha-zot*"—you already know what *ha-zot* (this) means . . .

"Spring up, O well—sing to it"—You should begin from below [and proceed] upward, so that the tenth attribute may be raised to the place from which she issued. Then draw down blessings from there, drawing down and proceeding from above to below. Hence it says "Spring up, O well—sing to it," as if to say, it is our duty to praise this attribute and to say to her: "Spring up, O well." This attribute is called a "well" because she receives energy from all of [the rest] and is emanated from them, for a well is a vessel for water. . . . The meaning of "Spring up, O well" is: "Raise yourself up to the place from which you were hewn."

"Which the chieftains dug"—[The chieftains are] Hochmah (Wisdom) and Binah (Understanding).

"The nobles of the people"—[The nobles are] Gedulah (Greatness), Gevurah (Might), and Tiferet (Beauty), identified with Abraham, Isaac, and Jacob. . . .

"With a mace"—[meaning,] "the righteous, the foundation (Yesod) of the world" [Proverbs 10:25].

"With their staffs"—[meaning,] Netzach (Victory) and Hod (Majesty).

Thus the entire structure is alluded to in the language of this song, as it is in the "Song of the Sea" [Exodus 15].

Rabbenu Bachya ben Asher ben Chlava (thirteenth century), *Perush Al HaTorah* [Commentary on the Torah] (Jerusalem: Blum, 1988), pt. 4, p. 97

NOTES

SHIRaH (song) has the same numerical value as *TeFiLaH* (prayer). Each letter of the Hebrew alphabet has a numerical value. The first ten letters represent the numbers 1 to 10, the next eight letters 20 to 90, and the remaining four 100 to 400. Thus, *SHIRaH* = 300 + 10 + 200 + 5 = 515; and *TeFiLaH* = 400 + 80 + 30 + 5 = 515.

What *ha-zot* (this) means. *Zot* in kabbalistic symbolism is indicative of Malchut (the Shechinah).

You should begin from below [and proceed] upward. Begin at Malchut, the bottom of the *sefirotic* tree and then proceed upward, eventually reaching Keter. Rabbenu Bachya is treating the "Song of the Well" as if it were a lesson in kabbalistic meditation.

The tenth attribute. Meaning, Malchut (Sovereignty).

To the place from which she issued. Malchut, in common with the other six lower *sefirot*, is said to emanate from Binah. However, as implied by the rest of Bachya's comment, all the *sefirot* derive ultimately from Keter (Crown), or beyond it, from Ein Sof (the Infinite).

Then draw down blessings from there. One ascends the ladder of the *sefirot* in order to benefit the world with blessings from their divine source.

It is our duty to praise this attribute. Malchut, as it were, needs our encouragement.

This attribute is called a "well." A common symbol for Malchut, which R. Bachya then explains.

A well is a vessel for water. "Water" in this case is a symbol for the divine energies flowing through the *sefirot* and collecting in Malchut.

"Which the chieftains dug." From this point onward, we proceed down the *sefirot* from Hochmah.

Gedulah. An alternative name for Hesed.

The entire structure. I.e., the structure of the *sefirot*.

COMMENT

There are many ways of thinking about prayer. For traditional kabbalists, prayer is an extended meditation on the realm of the *sefirot*, a mental exercise in which the worshiper attempts to draw divine energies into this mundane world. This is the approach adopted by Rabbenu Bachya, which he "finds" embedded in the "Song of the Well."

This offers an unconventional approach to prayer, when compared with popular notions today. It seems to me that most modern people view praying as talking to God. But they don't believe in that possibility, and so they don't pray. The kabbalistic view is different. It turns us from conversationalists into meditators, from supplicants into participants. Now, the response to prayer comes as much from ourselves as from God.

Balak

---

[118] The Soul Can See Everything

"When the donkey saw God's angel standing in the road. . . ."
Numbers 22:23

CONTEXT

When Balak, the Moabite king, realizes that the Israelites are due to pass through his land, and that military means for preventing them from doing so have not worked (as described in Numbers 21), he resorts to psychological and spiritual weapons. He calls upon the prophet Balaam to curse the Israelites. Balaam initially refuses, but later agrees, while stating explicitly that he can only say what God will allow him to say. Riding on his donkey, he sets off to do the job. On the journey, the donkey stops and refuses to proceed because it sees an angelic being blocking the way, but Balaam, the great prophet and seer, does not see this being.

Rabbi Uri of Strelisk was a disciple of Solomon of Karlin and a leader of Lithuanian Hasidism.

I also heard in his name that a man once spoke to him about his livelihood and his [worldly] success, and he replied in this fashion:

We find in the case of Balaam's donkey that it is written: "When the donkey saw God's angel standing in the road," but Balaam did not see it. This is surprising, given his great [spiritual] standing, for he was "falling, but with eyes opened" (Numbers 24:4,16) [yet] he did not see the angel, while his donkey did.

However, the truth is that the soul can see everything, so why do people not see? The reason is that a person's matter may be a curtain that divides, hinders, and covers the soul so that it cannot see. Therefore, [Balaam] was not able to see on his own. Only at the moment that the Eternal wanted to open his eyes did he fall down. His senses were shut down and [he experienced] the divestment of physicality. Then he had his eyes opened.

But animal matter is not a curtain that divides for the sake of the soul, neither does it hinder or cover it, but the soul rests in the midst of it, like [water] resting in a vase. Therefore, it sees all, and thus the donkey could see the angel.

Uri of Strelisk (the Seraph) (d. 1826), *Sefer Imrei Kadosh* [The book of the sayings of a holy man] (Netanya, 2001), pp. 16–17

NOTES

"Falling, but with eyes opened." A phrase indicating Balaam's prophetic talents. It occurs in verses 4 and 16, preceded by "the one who hears the word of God, who sees the vision of the Almighty."

Only at the moment . . . did he fall down. I.e., prostrate himself prior to delivering his prophecy.

The divestment of physicality. *Hitpashtut ha-gashmiyyut*, a state in which one loses all consciousness of the body.

The soul rests in the midst of it. The soul can only see when it is calm, like water standing in a vase.

COMMENT

The Strelisker does not deliver this message of the barrier to the soul's insight in a sermon to his followers and congregants. On the contrary, this is part of a conversation he is having with a businessman he knows, a man who seems intent upon telling his rabbi all about his financial dealings and successes. The Strelisker doesn't dismiss the man's concerns exactly, but he does suggest that these concerns may be interfering with the man's spiritual awareness, distracting him from his spiritual task in life.

We all allow our immediate material and emotional concerns to get in the way of our spirituality. We let our desire for money, status, and approval get in the way of doing what is right. We let our perceived wants and needs lead us away from prayer, meditation, and spiritual study. We put self-gratification before self-improvement and the repair of our world. Instead, we imagine that more goods, a bigger house, a better job, and more expensive vacations will bring us happiness. They don't. They only bring us more worries, more anxieties; as the great Jewish teacher Hillel taught, "the more property, the more anxiety" (*Pirkei Avot* 2:7). True happiness comes from learning who we really are: spiritual beings inhabiting a material world. Often we forget this fact, and even when extraordinary events occur to us, as they occur to Balaam, we fail to perceive them or to learn their spiritual lesson.

[119] Turning Things Around

"Look, a people that dwells alone and is not counted among the nations."

Numbers 23:9

CONTEXT

Balaam finally undertakes the task for which Balak has hired him. At the summit of Bamoth-Baal, the two offer sacrifices and Balaam begins to curse Israel. Or at least that is what he is supposed to be doing! In fact, his "curses" are blessings by any standard. Or are they?

Menachem Mendel of Rymanov was a disciple of the Polish Hasidic leader of the third generation, Elimelech of Lyzhansk.

Our sages have said: From the blessings of that wicked man we may learn what was in his heart to curse them [with], but his words became twisted and were overturned until he was forced to bless them from out of those same curses.

Apparently this is surprising: Weren't his blessings truly [meant]? [Clearly not! They were] only from his lips and exterior, but his heart was not in it. But if so, how could blessings such as these prevail and have force over the one who has been blessed? They have no life force! For we hold that anyone who blesses another must put life force and good understanding into their words, meaning that you must put in your knowledge, will, and complete desire, with a strong love. In this way the blessing will be established and will have force over the one who has been blessed. This is not the case with those who bless when their heart is not in it. Certainly such a person's silence is better than their words.

However, it is appropriate that when we read those blessings [that are found] in the Torah or when we study or occupy ourselves with them we must "sweeten" all those words and put into them good understanding and the life force of blessings, goodness, and loving-kindness. Through this life force, they may come to rest upon Israel.

Look here, in this verse too it was in the heart of that wicked man to curse them so that they should live totally alone, each individual on their own without community, and that they should not be counted and respected among the nations, as it says: "and is not counted among the nations."

But we must turn it around and intend this as a great blessing and interpret the word "alone" [*baDaD*] as a wondrous unity, that is, that we should all be one, as close friends [*DoDim*], united without division. This is the intention for good at the level of the plain meaning.

But there is another allusion [here], for *BaDaD* [alone] has a numerical value of ten, which is represented by the letter *yod*, a single point without any addition, and that is true unity.

Moreover, there is another allusion to good [here], for if you divide up the word *BaDaD* [alone] into its constituent letters, it alludes to the drawing down of all good influxes, [namely] "children, life, and sustenance," thus: *Ba DaD* [a breast is coming] — alluding to the suckling of good influxes from the holy supernal channels.

Menachem Mendel of Rymanov (d. 1815), *Divrei Menachem* [Menachem's words] (n.p., 1935?), p. 11a–b

NOTES

Our sages have said. What follows is a paraphrase of *Be-midbar Rabbah* 20:19.

We must "sweeten" all those words. Turn them to positive effect by instilling them with our love.

Through this life force, they may come to rest upon Israel. Balaam may not have put his life force into his blessings of Israel, but *we* can when we read or study them.

***BaDaD* [alone] has a numerical value of ten**. The letters of the Hebrew alphabet were also used as numerals. Thus, *BaDaD* = 2 + 4 + 4 = 10. The letter *yod*, the simplest letter of the Hebrew alphabet, little more than a point, also has a numerical value of ten.

***BaDaD* [alone] into its constituent letters . . . thus: Ba DaD**. The Rymanover is reading one word as if it were two.

"Children, life, and sustenance." A phrase recycled from the Talmud, *Mo'ed Katan* 28a.

The suckling of good influxes from the holy supernal channels. Our unity allows us to draw down positive influences from the realm of the *sefirot*.

COMMENT

The rabbi of Rymanov advises us that we have the power and the ability to turn whatever our enemies may say or plan against us to the advantage of the Jewish people. If they wish to isolate us and treat us differently from others, we must turn this into an opportunity to work together in harmony. Thus, it is we ourselves who may turn a curse into a blessing. Jewish separateness becomes an opportunity for Jewish unity and spirituality.

I believe that this principle can be applied to our personal lives as well. Whether our enemies are external or internal (i.e., our weaknesses or our "inclination toward evil"), we have the power to transform their attacks and curses into sources of strength and blessing. It all depends on what we make of them.

---

[120] The Internal Takes Precedence

"How good are your tents, O Jacob, your dwellings, O Israel."

Numbers 24:5

CONTEXT

Three times Balaam tries to curse Israel at Balak's behest, and three times he must bless them at God's command. This verse, which is traditionally said upon entering a synagogue or at the start of the morning service, occurs near the start of Balaam's third oracle.

Avraham Noach HaLevi Heller, the author of this teaching, was the brother of Meshullam Feibush of Zbarazh, who in his turn was a disciple of the Maggid of Mezritch and of the Maggid of Zlotchov.

The point of the awe [of God] is that it should be internalized rather than externalized, only in private and not as in the prayer text "One should be in awe of heaven in private as well as in public." Hence, "how good are your tents"—the reference is to the curtains that the tent of the Tabernacle had above it, and it is good that your tent above should be, as it were, "Jacob" in public, that is, on a "lower" level, but "your dwellings" refers to the internal, specified as "Israel," which is a higher level. This should be easy to understand.

After I had written these things, I actually heard these words spoken in the name of the pious R. Yisra'el Ba'al Shem Tov, and I was very happy about this.

Avraham Noach HaLevi Heller of Dolina, *Zerizuta de'Avraham* [The zeal of Abraham], (Lvov, 1900), p. 5a

"**One should be in awe of heaven.**" From the *Birchot HaShachar*, the morning blessings at the start of the daily morning service. It is interesting to note that Heller denies the validity of this approach.

The curtains that the tent of the Tabernacle had above it. They were therefore visible to the public.

COMMENT

I once attended a synagogue in Spain where a man had the habit of yelling out his prayers and amens from time to time. I don't wish to disparage his devotion. I didn't know the man and therefore have no idea why he did this, but it did trouble me, not just because he disturbed my concentration but also because he seemed to be showing off his piety. (I should point out that the other worshipers were not bothered by him; they were probably used to his praying style.) And yet, if Rabbi Avraham Heller is to be believed, the Ba'al Shem Tov himself opposed such outward displays of piety. Devotion to God should be a private affair between you and God. Public displays should be limited to what is necessary. I believe we have a duty to set an example to others who may be less pious than ourselves, but past a certain point our outward piety may just be self-serving. Piety should not be about the ego; it is about overcoming ego.

Pinḥas

---

[121] Inner Conflict

"Therefore, say: 'Look here, I am giving you My covenant of peace.'"

Numbers 25:12

CONTEXT

In all, Balaam tried to curse Israel four times, and each time he succeeded in blessing them instead. Israel seems to be winning the conflict
with Moab, but then a crisis ensues, as described in Numbers 25:1–9,
at the end of the previous *sidrah*. Israelite men are enticed to worship
Baal Peor, a local pagan deity, by young women from Moab. As a result, a plague, sent by God, erupts, and only the intervention of Phinehas, Aaron's grandson, saves the people from destruction. Phinehas is
overcome with anger when he sees an Israelite man slipping away with
a Midianite girl. He follows them and kills them both with his spear.
But this grisly tale is separated from its sequel, which begins *parashat*
Pinḥas. Here, Phinehas is apparently rewarded for his swift and dramatic action with the promise that the priests of the future will be his
descendants.

Ya'akov Yosef of Polonnoye was a key disciple of the Ba'al Shem Tov;
and his books, beginning with the *Toledot*, were central to the dissemi-
nation of the Ba'al Shem's teachings. Here he builds on the common
kabbalistic ideas of reincarnation.

> It is known that it is written in the Zohar . . . that Nadab and Abihu
> were two halves of the [same] body, and that therefore Phinehas
> saved both their souls because they were considered as one, as is
> written in the Zohar. See there. Hence it says, "Therefore say, 'Look
> here, I am giving you My covenant of peace,'" for it is known, in ac-
> cordance with what I heard from my teachers, that [when] you join
> together two things it is called peace, and that therefore [the *sefirah*

of] Yesod [Foundation] is called "peace" for this reason. . . . Similarly, when there is division between people, and someone comes who unites them, such a person is called "one who pursues peace." Now the cause of the sin of Nadab and Abihu was that they did not consult each other, as it is said, "And they each took his own censer" [Leviticus 9:1], [meaning] there was no peace between them. But it was Phinehas who repaired this, and was repaired by being given a "covenant of peace," by uniting the aspect[s] of the soul[s] of Nadab and Abihu into one body.

Ya'akov Yosef of Polonnoye (died ca. 1782), *Toledot Ya'akov Yosef* [The generations of Jacob Joseph (Genesis 37:2)] (Jerusalem, 1973), v. 1, p. 325

NOTES

Two halves of the [same] body. I.e., in kabbalistic terms, they represent the *sefirot* of Netzach (Victory) and Hod (Majesty), which are usually treated as a pair.

It is written in the Zohar. III, 57b.

Yesod [Foundation] is called "peace" for this reason. Because it unites the powers of all the *sefirot* that precede it, channeling them onto Malchut.

"And they each took his own censer." By putting it this way, instead of saying "they took their censers," the Torah is implying a conflict between them, in the Polonnoyer's view.

COMMENT

Why does Phinehas warrant a "covenant of peace"? By way of an answer, Ya'akov Yosef refers us to the Zohar, where we are taught that Phinehas had united in his person the souls of Nadab and Abihu, his uncles, who perished after offering "strange fire to the Eternal" (Leviticus 9). Why had they perished? According to Ya'akov Yosef, because, although priests, they were self-seeking and self-centered, each wishing to go his own way without regard to the other. Phinehas, on the other hand, could reconcile the conflicting demands that flowed within himself and act on behalf of the people he, as priest, was meant to serve.

Alternatively, perhaps the "covenant of peace" was less a reward and more of a rebuke, as if to say, "you did what might have been necessary then, but now you must learn to lead a life of peace." In which case, Ya'akov Yosef's point would be that Phinehas would have to learn to act peacefully by reconciling conflicts within himself.

We all have conflicting demands made upon us, apparently from out-side ourselves. Yet perhaps it is truer to say that these only feel like de-mands if they resonate with something inside us. We each carry within the recesses of our hearts and minds all sorts of desires and needs, some of which may be easily met, and others not so easily if at all. These are not constants within us, but fluctuate in and out of our consciousness. This movement can set up conflicts within, conflicts that can be exacerbated by demands from others around us. Rabbi Ya'akov Yosef offers us the prospect of making peace between opposing internal forces. Such inner peace may help to bring outer peace too.

[122] Leaders: Military and Spiritual

"Let the Eternal, the God of the spirits of all flesh, appoint a man over
the congregation who will go out before them and come in before them,
who will lead them out and lead them in, so that the congregation
of the Eternal may not be like a flock without a shepherd."
Numbers 27:16

CONTEXT

God has called Moses up to Mount Abarim to see the Promised Land and to tell him that he will not be entering the land at Israel's head because of his rebellion at the waters of Meribah (Numbers 20). Moses, for his part, asks God to appoint a new leader in his stead. The verse selected probably refers to the qualities required of a military leader. A man was needed who would "lead them out" to battle and "lead them in" after victory.

Of all the Ba'al Shem Tov's disciples, Ya'akov Yosef of Polonnoye was the most prolific in the literary sphere. The following comes from a volume of his sermons on the book of Genesis. Leadership is a key theme of all his works.

I write in the name of my teacher: The explanation of the verse "Let the Eternal [. . .] appoint a man over the congregation [. . .] who will lead them out and lead them in" (Numbers 27[:16]) is that the head of the generation should be able to raise the words and stories of the people of that generation, to combine the physical with the spiritual, like the two comedians. . . . "Words from a wise person's mouth are gracious" [Ecclesiastes 10:13].

Ya'akov Yosef of Polonnoye (died ca. 1782), *Ben Porat Yosef* [Joseph is a fruitful bough (Genesis 49:22)] (Brooklyn, 1991), p. 82a; (Piotrkov, 1884), p. 31a

NOTES

My teacher. I.e., the Ba'al Shem Tov.

Like the two comedians. In the Talmud, *Ta'anit* 22a, R. Beroka Hoza'ah asks the prophet Elijah to tell him which people in the marketplace are worthy of inheriting the world to come. Elijah points out two men, and when the rabbi inquires as to their occupation, they reveal that they are comedians, who cheer people up and make peace between them.

COMMENT

We may need to learn the value of spiritual teachers who can guide us in our inner search and help us connect what we have learned in that search with our lives "outside." And once we have embarked on that inner search, and found some inner truths, we may become leaders of others. We too may be able to "lead them out and lead them in." We need to lead ourselves and others to do battle against the evil within, so that we can do effective battle with the evil without.

---

[123] Feeding God

"My sacrifice, My bread for My fire offerings, a sweet aroma for Me."
Numbers 28:2

CONTEXT

Numbers 28 and 29 are the most frequently read chapters in the Torah, comprising, as they do, succinct procedures for the sacrifices to be offered on *Shabbat*, the New Moon, and all the major festivals. The appropriate selection from these chapters forms the traditional *maftir*, or concluding Torah reading, for those occasions.

Pinchas of Koretz was a younger contemporary, and possibly a disciple, of the Ba'al Shem Tov.

None can serve the Holy One without binding themselves to the Holy One, for Israel nourishes and feeds the Holy One. This is [the meaning of the verse] "My sacrifice [*KoRBani*]," that is, those who draw near [*meKaRVin*] God, are "My bread;" "for My fire offerings" refers to the angels; "a sweet aroma," to the Messiah.

Pinchas of Koretz (1726–91), *Midrash Pinchas* [Pinchas's interpretation] (Lemberg, 1874), §233, p. 24a; (Jerusalem, 1971), §35, p. 27a

NOTES

"My sacrifice [*KoRBani*]," that is, those who draw near [*meKaRVin*]. Both words share the same three-letter Hebrew root *k-r-b*, meaning, "to be near," or "to draw near."

"For My fire offerings" refers to the angels. R. Pinchas puns on the word *esh* (fire), and builds on the tradition stating that *ish* (normally, "man") indicates a type of angel.

"A sweet aroma," to the Messiah. The Talmud, *Sanhedrin* 93b, suggests that the Messiah will judge cases by his sense of smell.

COMMENT

Our service of God, our devotion to a divinely inspired morality alongside ritual observance, feeds the reality of God's presence in our lives. The God of the philosophers is abstract, cold. The Koretzer's God is alive and sustained in human consciousness solely by our devotion. And this devotion links us to spiritual realities beyond our ken and ultimately to the Messianic Age.

Mattot

[124] Moses Never Has Left Us

"Avenge the People of Israel on the Midianites; afterward you [Moses] shall be gathered to your people."

Numbers 31:2

CONTEXT

After giving us instructions for festival sacrifices (Numbers 29) and the laws of vows (chapter 30), the Torah resumes its narrative with the story of the Israelites' revenge on the people of Midian for their sexually charged enticement to idolatry (chapter 25). Why is Moses's imminent death mentioned in the same verse as retribution on the Midianites?

Pinchas of Koretz was a younger contemporary of the Ba'al Shem Tov, whom tradition suggests he met on only a few occasions. Nevertheless, he is sometimes listed as a disciple of the older man.

> Righteous people do not depart from the world until they have done a great mitzvah, and by this means they adhere to the Shechinah. Wicked people, on the contrary, do not die until they have committed a great transgression, and "their measure is full."
>
> In the name of the Rav, in accordance with the above: In the Zohar it says that Moses is spread throughout every generation and every sage, see there, and no sage can discover anything new unless the aspect of Moses is renewed within him. For whatever a keen student may innovate in the future has already been said by Moses. Therefore, it is impossible [to say anything really new]. Thus it follows that Moses exists in the world, among Israel. This [is the meaning of the phrase]: "you shall be gathered to your people"—it implies that you [Moses] will always be in the midst the People of Israel.

Pinchas of Koretz (1726–91), *Imrei Pinchas* [Pinchas's sayings] (Tel Aviv: Arnberg, 1974), §112, p. 38

"Their measure is full." See the Talmud, *Sotah* 9a, where Rav Hamnuna said: "The Holy One does not punish a person until the measure [of their guilt] has been filled."

In the name of the Rav. In the literature of this group, "the Rav" refers to Pinchas of Koretz.

In the Zohar it says. *Tikkunei HaZohar*, no.69, p. 112a.

For whatever a keen student. See the Jerusalem Talmud, *Pe'ah* 2:6.

"You shall be gathered to your people." Usually understood as a euphemism for "you will die."

COMMENT

Moses was both the great liberator, the implacable opponent of injustice and oppression, and the great lawgiver and builder of a stable society; he was both prophet and priest, conservative and radical. If the spirit of Moses dwells among us still, can we be any less?

Like Moses, we need to be radical for the poor and the oppressed, radical for justice and freedom of opportunity, but we need to be conservative about our traditions, laws, and moral codes. Our challenge is whether we can do both successfully.

---

[125] The War after War

"Eleazar the priest said to the soldiers who were coming to the war. . . ."

Numbers 31:21

CONTEXT

After the war with the Midianites described earlier in the chapter, Eleazar, Aaron's son and successor as High Priest, gives the returning soldiers instructions about ritually cleansing the spoils they have brought back.

The Kotzker rebbe was constantly pushing his followers to ever-greater heights of self-scrutiny.

[The text] should have said "coming *from* the war"! However, at this point they entered into a new war, spoken of now in this section on the cleansing of the Midianite [vessels and utensils]. It has been proven that thought is like deed, [so] they began to be concerned about thoughts of transgression also, and thus they were entering into a new war. Hence, "who were coming to the war."

Menachem Mendel of Kotzk (1787–1859), *Sefer Amud HaEmet* [The book of the pillar of truth] (Bnei Brak, 2000), pp. 88–89

NOTES

"Who were coming to the war." A literal rendering. Most Bible translations read "from the war," as demanded by the context. JPS: "who had taken part in the fighting."

Thought is like deed. Cleansing the newly acquired items made them think about cleansing their thoughts.

COMMENT

Usually we think of our enemies as being outside ourselves: other people, the weather, the "system," whatever. But sometimes we can be our own worst enemies, when habits of thought keep us from achieving what we might or even from imagining what we might achieve. This text addresses those internal enemies, traditionally amalgamated by the Rabbis under the title "the inclination toward evil." Thoughts of evil may not lead to evil acts, but they are still a distraction. They need to be analyzed and their sources within us exposed so that we can deal with the inclination toward evil at its roots within our own souls.

---

[126] Becoming Pure before God

"Then this land will be subdued before the Eternal; then after that you may return and you will be guiltless before the Eternal and before Israel, and this land shall be your possession before the Eternal. But if you do not do this, you have sinned against the Eternal."

Numbers 32:22–23

CONTEXT

Unexpectedly, the Israelites have conquered territory on the eastern bank of the Jordan. The tribes of Reuben and Gad, plus half the tribe of Manasseh, approach Moses with a view to remaining in this land.

They say that it is very good for cattle, which forms a large part of their wealth. Moses initially reacts with anger that they would therefore not support the rest of the tribes in their conquest of the land proper, on the western bank. But the petitioning tribes offer a compromise that is accepted: they will secure their cattle and families in the land they want but send their fighting men over the Jordan to help the others. Here, Moses lays out the agreement.

Menachem Mendel of Rymanov was a student of Elimelech of Lyzhansk. Yitzchak Podvah was the editor of *Ilana deChayyei*; most unattributed quotes in this work are to be credited to the Rymanover.

"Then the land will be subdued"—the interpretation is: How can you subdue desire and earthly qualities "before the Eternal"? By bringing to mind that you are standing before God, as stated in the verse "I keep the Eternal before me always" [Psalm 16:8], (as explained in *Orach Hayyim* §1). Then, since the inclination toward evil is called "other gods," "you will return," that is to say, you will repent and put [them] away from yourselves, "and be guiltless before the Eternal and before Israel." For in this way, by becoming worthy, you will cause no pain or distress to God and to Israel.

"And this land shall be"—"land" refers to the will, as our sages have said: "Why is it called 'land' [*eretz*]? Because it wants to do the will [*ratzon*] of its Creator."

"Your possession before the Eternal"—that is to say, even if you are unable to reach this stage, but have the desire and will for it—this too is precious in the sight of God. As a holy man once said on [the verse] "The heart of one who seeks the Eternal rejoices" [Psalm 105:3; 1 Chronicles 16:10]: "With regard to matters of this world, if you are looking for something you have lost, you are not happy until you find it. But with regard to the service of God, you are immediately happy that you are worthy of looking in the Sovereign's treasury." Hence [it says]: "But if you do not do this, you have sinned against the Eternal"—for through your sin you have caused a blemish in the soul, which is a part of the divine, and caused distress to the Shechinah [the Presence of God]. This follows [from the teaching] "My holiness is higher than your holiness," so that if a person sins, they cause distress to the Shechinah. "Let those who mourn feel the affliction."

Yitzchak Mordechai ben Yisra'el Aharon Podvah (1884–1942), ed., *Ilana deChayyei* [The tree of life] (Jerusalem, 1986), pt. 1, p. 90

How can you subdue desire and earthly qualities. Based on a wordplay between *eretz* (land, earth) and *artziyut* (earthliness).

As explained in Orach Hayyim §1. "The Path of Life" is the first of the four sections that form the *Shulchan Aruch* (Set table), the premier medieval code of Jewish law by Yosef Karo. In his opening paragraph, Karo quotes Psalm 16:8 as a kind of preamble and background to all Jewish law and practice, as described in the rest of this voluminous work.

"You will return," that is to say, you will repent. In Hebrew, "to return" and "to repent" are both indicated by the verbal root *sh-u-v*.

"Why is it called 'land' [eretz]?" A quotation from the midrash *Bereshit Rabbah* 5:8. Another wordplay.

"Your possession before the Eternal." The word *'aCHuZah* (possession) comes from the root *'-ch-z*, meaning, "to grasp, take hold of." To the Rymanover rebbe it means something that one tries to grasp, even if without total success.

As a holy man once said. His identity remains unknown.

"My holiness is higher than your holiness." *Bereshit Rabbah* 90:2 and *Va-yikra Rabbah* 24:9. For Menachem Mendel, this saying suggests that, although one is superior to the other, divine and human holiness are intertwined.

"Let those who mourn feel the affliction." Quoted from the Talmud, *Nazir* 23a, and *Kiddushin* 81b. If we have sinned, we should feel the Shechinah's pain as well as our own.

COMMENT

We moderns often fail to see what we do in its proper spiritual context. Our personal choices are not just personal; they impact many areas of life, often undreamed of by us. We have long understood, if not always appreciated, the economic, political, and social implications of our decisions, and in the last few decades we have begun to grasp their environmental ramifications—but when will we truly start to take on board their spiritual impact? God's purity is sullied when ours is; God's holiness is enhanced when we strive for holiness.

Mase'ei

---

[127] Journeys of Purification

"These are the journeys of the descendants of Israel as they came out of the land of Egypt, according to their troops, under the command of Moses and Aaron. Moses wrote down their departures to their arrival points at the command of the Eternal, and these are the arrival points of their journeys."

Numbers 33:1–2

CONTEXT

The final parashah of the book of Numbers opens with an overview of the Israelites' itinerary from Egypt, through the wilderness, to the plains of Moab.

Yisra'el of Koznitz was an itinerant preacher and, as the text itself states, a disciple of the Maggid of Mezritch. The following quotation from his teacher is set within a sermon whose main thrust is that people cannot serve God properly and achieve holiness until they have set aside the sins of their youth and joined themselves to the *tzadikim* (the Hasidic masters).

My master R. Dov Ber said that the essential reason for all the journeys that Israel made was to repair all the places and to elevate the holy sparks within them. Therefore, we find written in the Torah all the names of the stopping points and places where they brought about repair. Hence, "and Moses wrote down their departures [*mOTZa'eihem*] to their arrival points at the command of the Eternal" [Numbers 33:2]. Moses wrote of the holy sparks that he had liberated [*hOTZi*] at the arrival points to which they had traveled, and they had traveled at the command of the Eternal. They only went to the places that had to be repaired; hence [it says]: "and these are the arrival points of their journeys." "Words from a wise person's mouth are gracious" [Ecclesiastes 10:12].

Yisra'el ben Shabbetai Hapstein, Maggid of Koznitz (1733–1814), *Avodat Yisra'el* [Israel's service] (Jerusalem, 1998), p. 207

NOTES

My master, R. Dov Ber. The Maggid of Mezritch, d. 1772.

To elevate the holy sparks. According to the kabbalistic scheme of Yitzchak Luria, there are sparks of divine light scattered throughout the world, awaiting their liberation and return to the upper worlds from which they came. It is the duty of the pious to set them free.

"Their departures [*mOTZa'eihem*]." Literally, "the places of their bringing out."

He had liberated [*hOTZi*]. Literally, "brought out."

They only went to the places that had to be repaired. This is R. Dov Ber's answer to the unstated question of why both arrival and departure points are mentioned. Surely in a continuous journey they are the same and need only be listed once each.

COMMENT

No previous generations in human history have ever had the travel opportunities we have. In a matter of hours, we can be virtually anywhere in the world. This text suggests that no matter how long or short our journey, whether we are traveling for work or for pleasure, we should try to see the spirituality in the places through which we pass. The sparks of divine light are to be found wherever we choose to look, especially when we can see the beauty of our surroundings or the kindness of the people we meet.

On the other hand, our times have also seen unprecedented numbers of refugees fleeing war, persecution, and natural disaster. It would be arrogant and insensitive of us to preach to these refugees about the spiritual opportunities of their journeys. Instead, we should see the spiritual opportunities that their suffering presents to us and put our feelings of compassion into practical efforts on their behalf.

[128] Conquering Evil Within

"Command the Israelites and say to them: 'When you enter
the land of Canaan, this is the land that shall fall to you with
an inheritance: the land of Canaan to its borders. . . .'"

Numbers 34:2

CONTEXT

Numbers 33 provides a backward glance at the stages of the wilderness journey. Chapter 34 looks forward to the conquest of the Promised Land and the fixing of its borders. Later in chapter 34 (vv. 16–29), a committee of two priests and representatives of each of the twelve tribes is appointed to divide the land among the people.

Elimelech of Lyzhansk was a disciple of the Maggid of Mezritch and instrumental in bringing the Hasidic message to Polish Jews.

The explanation [is that] when you enter into submission [to God] and the breaking of the power of the "outside forces" and the "Other Side" that is known as the "land of Canaan," "this is the land that shall fall to you." Rashi explains: [The land shall fall to you] "by virtue of the fact that the Holy One makes the rulers of the nations [of Canaan] fall before you." Now, according to our interpretation, you may make the "Other Side" fall before you "with the inheritance," that is, with the Torah that is called an "inheritance."

"The land of Canaan to its borders," that is to say, you should see to break the borders of the "Other Side." . . .

May God make us worthy to serve the divine perfectly, so that the inclination toward evil should not rule over us; and may we soon be worthy of the coming of our Messiah, when the sin of the serpent will be repaired and the earth will be full of knowledge. Amen. May this be the [divine] will.

Elimelech of Lyzhansk (1717–87), *No'am Elimelech* [The pleasantness of Elimelech], ed. Gedalyah Nigal (Jerusalem: Mossad HaRav Kook, 1978), pp. 460–61

"**With an inheritance.**" JPS: "as your portion."

The "outside forces." In kabbalistic terminology, the forces of evil.

The "Other Side." A term in the Zohar that also indicates evil.

"Land of Canaan." Although the Promised Land, it was still the home of a civilization steeped in idolatry.

The Torah that is called an "inheritance." E.g., in the midrash *Shir HaShirim Zuta* 1:30.

The sin of the serpent. In misleading Adam and Eve in the Garden of Eden.

Will be repaired. In accordance with the kabbalistic doctrine of *tikkun*, repair.

The earth will be full of knowledge. See Isaiah 11:9: "For the earth will be full of the knowledge of God as the waters cover the sea."

COMMENT

For Elimelech of Lyzhansk, these instructions for implementation by the people when they enter the Promised Land are an allegory of our struggle against the forces of evil within us, represented by the land of Canaan. This "land" can be conquered with Torah, that is, with the aid of Jewish teaching throughout the ages.

Torah may be our inheritance from past generations of our people, but we have to make it our own, through study and practice. Only then can we purify ourselves, and the world. Only then will Elimelech's messianic prayer be fulfilled.

---

[129] Repairing What We Have Damaged

"And along with the six cities you shall give to the Levites, the
six cities of refuge that you have been given so that a murderer
may flee there, to them you shall add forty-two cities. . . ."

Numbers 35:6–7

CONTEXT

Numbers 35 tackles two problems and intertwines their solutions. On the one hand, there is the problem of the Levites. Unlike the other tribes, they will have no inheritance in the new land, because the focus of their lives will be the sacrificial system that will one day be centralized in the Temple in Jerusalem. Because this may not provide a livelihood for all members of the tribe of Levi if they are too numerous, this chapter specifies that they shall be given forty-eight towns to live in and that they will be able to pasture their flocks in the areas surrounding them. Among these towns will be six "cities of refuge." These are designed to deal with the second problem: the issue of vengeance in tribal societies. Virtually all tribal societies, where there is no central government, expect that revenge will be taken for the killing of community members. This is in order to discourage attacks by outsiders. But this can lead to injustices, for example, when the killing is accidental, or it can lead to the decimation of particular clans or even whole tribes in tit-for-tat retaliation. To avoid this, these six cities were designated as sites where those who killed accidentally could flee and live without fear of vengeance.

Avraham Yehoshua Heschel of Apt was a disciple of Elimelech of Lyzhansk and ancestor of the great twentieth-century Jewish thinker of the same name, Abraham Joshua Heschel.

In order to awaken the heart that you might understand and know, you must appreciate what is hinted at here, for this commandment applies to all time, since the Torah is eternal. In that case, [the law of the cities of refuge] even has relevance in our time, and it [provides a means of] reparation for "anyone who smites a soul unintentionally" [Numbers 35:11,15], that is, anyone who unintentionally commits sins and transgressions, and "anyone who damages the soul should do it" [Proverbs 6:32], that is, you should do this act of reparation: to accept the yoke of the kingdom of heaven with perfect love and great self-surrender, truly, with all your heart, before God, through the six words of the [first line of the] *Shema Yisra'el.* . . [Deuteronomy 6:4], which correspond to the six cities of refuge.

"To them, you shall add forty-two cities"—this refers to the first paragraph of the recitation of the *Shema*, namely *Ve'ahavta* ["And you shall love . . . ," Deuteronomy 6:5–9], which contains forty-two words and which constitutes the acceptance of [God's] love and [God's] Torah with all your heart and soul. Thus, through true self-surrender with all your heart, by accepting the yoke of the kingdom of heaven, and through the true acceptance of the love of God with all your soul, you may be forgiven for having smitten your soul unintentionally. . . .

And may God make us worthy to serve and love God, truly, perfectly, and knowingly. May this be the divine will. Amen. Consider this very well.

Avraham Yehoshua Heschel of Apta (d. 1825), *Ohev Yisra'el* [Lover of Israel] (Zhitomir, 1863), p. 158

NOTES

"And along with the six . . . you shall add forty-two cities." In the Talmud tractate *Makkot*, the legal distinctions between these two groups are drawn more clearly.

"Anyone who smites a soul unintentionally" [Numbers 35:11,15]. This is a literal rendering, as required by the Apter's interpretation. JPS: "anyone who has killed a person."

Accepting the yoke of the kingdom of heaven. Referring to Mishnah *Berachot* 2:2.

COMMENT

In life, with an unrelenting inevitability, we make mistakes. Things turn out very different from what we imagined or intended. Our plans go awry, our words come out wrong, our actions lead to unforeseen consequences. We may strive to be perfect, but we fail again and again, because we are human. So how can we pick ourselves up after we fall; how can we rededicate ourselves to the task of serving God? If the Torah is eternal, then it must contain the answer.

For Avraham Yehoshua Heschel of Apta, the first paragraph of the *Shema*, if spoken in truth and with selflessness, provides refuge for us today from the sins we inevitably commit without intending to do so, just as those two groups of cities provided refuge for someone who had killed unintentionally.

And in fact there is a deeper meaning here. For the lapses that harm our souls can only be overcome by rededication to the service of God, which is precisely what the *Shema* is about and precisely why tradition prescribes its daily recitation.

DEUTERONOMY

Devarim

---

[130] Overcoming Doubt

*"And the case that is too difficult from you, you shall
bring to me [elai] and I shall hear it."*

Deuteronomy 1:17

CONTEXT

"Deuteronomy" is Greek for "second law." The ancient Greek translators
noted that this fifth book of the Torah contains similar, and even identical, legislation to that found in the first four books. But Deuteronomy
also often presents alternative versions of some stories in Exodus and
Numbers, except that now Moses narrates. In this verse, he recounts how
God told him to delegate the authority to judge disputes, reserving the
difficult cases for himself. (In Exodus 18, the idea of delegating Moses's
judicial role comes from his father-in-law, Jethro.)

Ya'akov Yosef of Polonnoye here relates a teaching of his master, the
Ba'al Shem Tov, founder of the modern Hasidic movement.

This is what I heard from my teacher [the Ba'al Shem Tov], in the
name of the RaMBaN, who commanded his son [as follows]: If some
action seems uncertain to you, because there might be two paths of
action, or if it is uncertain whether it is a mitzvah or not, and whether
to do it or refrain from it—whatever gives pleasure will lead you to
try to find a reason to permit that which is forbidden. Therefore, before [you undertake] anything, remove from the doing of this action
any pleasure for yourself or your honor. After [you have done] this,
you will see which way to turn. Then God will let you know the truth,
and you can walk securely. "Words from a wise person's mouth are
gracious" [Ecclesiastes 10:12]. . . .

Hence, [the following] may be understood: "And the case that is too
difficult from you"—where you don't know what to do or to refrain

from doing, the uncertainty arises "from you," because [your choice] contains within it something that pleases you. Therefore, remove your honor and your pleasure from the action, "you shall bring [it] to me [*elai*]," where *elai* is more internal than *li*. The point is that [your action] should be for the sake of heaven, without any ulterior motive or pleasure. Then, "I shall hear" how to behave. This is easy to understand.

Ya'akov Yosef of Polonnoye (died ca. 1782), *Ben Porat Yosef* [Joseph is a fruitful bough (Genesis 49:22)] (Brooklyn, 1991), p. 56a–b; (Piotrkov, 1884), pp. 18b–19a

NOTE

"Too difficult from you." A literal translation as demanded by what follows. JPS: "too difficult for you."

In the name of the RaMBaN. Rabbi Moshe ben Nachman, Nachmanides (1195–1270), a kabbalist, communal leader, teacher of many rabbis, and author of a classic Torah commentary. Ramban did write a famous letter to one of his sons in which he offered moral guidance, but the teaching referred to here is not found in it.

"You shall bring [it] to me." In the biblical context, "me" refers to Moses; in the Polonnoye's interpretation, it means your inner self.

Where *elai* is more internal than *li*. Both of these words mean "to me," but Ya'akov Yosef differentiates between them.

Then, "I shall hear" how to behave. I.e., when I consider matters carefully, after removing myself from the equation, I shall know what to do.

COMMENT

Indecision seems to be a constant companion in modern Western life. We are constantly bombarded with invitations to buy such and such a product or service, to support this or that cause, or to vote for this or that person. Of course, having the freedom to choose is very important, and few would wish to deny us that freedom, but the essential point is: how do we choose? The nineteenth-century French philosopher and student of the American political system Alexis de Tocqueville taught that the best choice is one based on enlightened self-interest, what he termed "self-interest rightly understood."

The Ba'al Shem Tov, by contrast, wants us to remove ourselves from any thinking about the choices facing us. We can only reach the proper decision if we take out any hint of ego or thought of the pleasure we might derive. For him, self-interest can never be "enlightened" nor "rightly understood," because it will always carry the taint of hidden, ulterior motives.

---

[131] No Two the Same

"And in the wilderness, where thou hast seen that the Eternal
thy God carried thee, as a man carries his child, in all the
way that you walked, until you came to this place."
Deuteronomy 1:31

CONTEXT

In his first speech to the Israelites, Moses speaks metaphorically of God's protection during the period that the people were nomads in the Sinai wilderness. (I have retained the archaic "thou" in order to bring out the contrast between the singular and plural expressions upon which the following comment is based.)

Elazar of Worms was the second great leader of the Hasidei Ashkenaz (German pietists) after Yehudah HeHasid. He is the author of a number of interesting works, including a commentary on the Torah and Five *Megillot*.

[The text begins:] "And in the wilderness, where thou hast seen that the Eternal thy God carried thee"—in the singular, but it continues, "in all the way that you walked, until you came to this place" [in the plural]. For no [two] miracles are the same. Some saw what another did not see. Some carried [God] on the cloud; some higher, some lower; some were as if they had walked. Therefore, [the verse says] "carried thee" [as well as] "that you walked."

Elazar ben Yehudah of Worms (ca. 1160–1237), *Perush HaRokeach al HaTorah* [The Torah commentary of the "pharmacist"] (Bnei Brak, 1986), v. 3, p. 163

COMMENT

Spiritual experience is deeply personal. You and I might both be present at the same moving event, but when we delve into what we experienced, we will discover that we each have our own recollection and interpretation of what happened. The Israelites in the wilderness may have understood their shared experience in their own individual ways; some felt that it had been more miraculous than did others.

For me, this text bears the message that all spiritual experiences must be respected, despite the fact that we will all hold our own views of what may have occurred. These views will be colored by our background, including our religious upbringing and faith, and our personal life story, but our experiences and our views are all part of the great collage, the supreme symphony, that is the human spiritual quest.

---

[132] Concentration and Humility in Prayer

"See, I have put into your hand Sichon, the sovereign
of Cheshbon, the Amorite, and his land."

Deuteronomy 2:24

CONTEXT

Moses recounts how God promised that Israel would overcome Sichon, the king of the Amorites, as they passed through his territory.

Menachem Mendel of Rymanov was an important disciple of Elimelech of Lyzhansk, who brought Hasidism to Poland. Yitzchak Podvah edited an anthology devoted primarily to the Rymanover's teachings.

"Sichon" is connected to conversation [*siach*] and prayer, and the Prayer is "sovereign," that is to say, through it, we make a crown for the Sovereign beyond all sovereigns, through "CHeSHBon the AMorite." For you contemplate [*meCHaSHeV*] the intention of each word you say [*amirah*] and concentrate on your prayer.

It also alludes to the assessment, the self-assessment [*cheshbon hanefesh*], that you do as you arrange your supplications before God.

"And his land"—until you arrive at the stage of humility, which is like the land.

Yitzchak Mordechai ben Yisra'el Aharon Podvah (1884–1942), ed., *Ilana deChayyei* [The tree of life] (Jerusalem, 1986), pt. 1, p. 93

The Prayer. The term "the Prayer," with the definite article, usually designates the *Amidah* (Standing prayer), also known as the *Shemoneh Esrei* (Eighteen benedictions).

Through it, we make a crown for the Sovereign beyond all sovereigns. The reference here is probably to the *Kedushah*, the declaration of God's holiness, which forms the third paragraph of the *Amidah*. There are many versions of this prayer for different occasions, and with variations between Sephardic and Ashkenazi texts. The (Sephardic) version of the *Shabbat Musaf* ("additional" service) used in most Hasidic communities begins with the word *keter* (crown): "A crown do the angels, the supernal host, give You, Eternal our God, with Your people Israel assembled below."

Which is like the land. I.e., low, compared to the sky.

COMMENT

The Rymanover has effectively "translated" the verse as follows: "I put into your hand prayer, which declares God as sovereign. Through the contemplation of each word you say, (or, through self-assessment at each word,) you will arrive at humility." Put more simply, for our author prayer is a gift from God, through which we can meditate and achieve humility.

Prayer is often misunderstood, or thought of in limited ways that demean it by restricting its meaning. The kabbalists and most Hasidic teachers thought of it less as a way of achieving specific aims and more as a method of contemplating divinity in our lives. If Judaism is to thrive and flourish in an increasingly sophisticated cultural milieu, we must adapt more flexible, and more spiritual, models of prayer. The rebbe of Rymanov calls upon us to use the traditional prayer service as a vehicle for our contemplation of God and our role in God's universe.

Va-'ethannan

---

[133] Nothing but God

"You should know this day, and take it to heart, that the Eternal is God in the heavens above and on the earth beneath; there is nothing else."

Deuteronomy 4:39

CONTEXT

Because God has done such amazing things by rescuing Israel from slavery and bringing the Israelites through the wilderness, Moses tells the people that they are obliged to acknowledge and be loyal to God alone.

Yishayah Horowitz was a prominent Polish rabbi in his own time and author of one of the period's most popular books.

> The meaning [of this verse] is not that there is no other God, for that is obvious, and God has already revealed this in the verse, "Hear O Israel, the Eternal is our God, the Eternal is one" [Deuteronomy 6:4]. Rather, the intention is to say that there is no other existence in the world apart from God's and that if God were to be [completely] concealed everything would be destroyed.

Yishayah HaLevi Horowitz (ca. 1570–1626), *Shnei Luchot HaBrit* [The two tablets of the covenant (Deuteronomy 9:9,11)], *Be'Asarah Ma'amarot*, no.1 (Jerusalem: 1975), v. 1, p. 30a.

NOTES

"There is nothing else." Hebrew: *ein od*. JPS: "there is no other." This is a more normal translation, as if to say that there are no other gods. Horowitz explicitly rejects this interpretation, on the principle that the Torah does not repeat itself.

"The Eternal is one." There are many interpretations of these words. Horowitz understands the phrase to mean there is only one God.

Does Horowitz wish to imply further that all matter is an illusion, as the Hindu mystics say, or simply that everything has real existence only through the divine energies within it? My view is that he would have preferred the latter interpretation, on the grounds that belief in the illusory nature of reality would undermine the performance of the commandments.

Many modern Jews are skeptical of a transcendent God, because this notion may entangle them in issues of God's omnipotence versus God's goodness. ("If God is all powerful and all good, how could God allow the Holocaust, for example, to happen?") Divine immanence, the notion of God within each and every individual and within all that exists, may offer a spiritual way forward for them. We are all capable of good deeds and feats of heroism and goodness beyond our normal capacity. Might these things not be aspects of God within us? And if God is within all of us and within all creation, might that not inculcate in us greater respect for others and for the environment?

---

[134] Ego Gets in the Way

"I [was] standing between the Eternal and you at that
time to convey the Eternal's words to you. . . ."

Deuteronomy 5:5

CONTEXT

Moses reminds the people of how they received the Ten Commandments and says that he acted as an intermediary between them and God.

Kalonymus Epstein was a disciple of Elimelech of Lyzhansk and author of a Hasidic commentary on the Torah. Yechiel Michal of Zlotchov (ca. 1731–86) had been a disciple of the Ba'al Shem Tov and later of the Maggid of Mezritch.

I heard in the name of our rabbi and teacher Yechiel Michal of Zlotchov [an interpretation] of the verse "I, standing between the Eternal and you": When Jewish people claim that they are elevated to a [particular] level of Torah or the service of God, they are making a barrier between themselves and the Creator, and this is "I." For those who claim that they are [really] something and think that they are on the level of [actual] existence stand between themselves [and God]. Meaning that those who speak in this way are making a partition and barrier between themselves and God.

Kalonymus Kalman HaLevi Epstein (d. 1823), *Ma'or VaShemesh* [Lamp and sun] (Jerusalem: Levin-Epstein, 1970), on Deuteronomy 5:5

NOTE

"I [was] standing." JPS: "I stood between the Lord and you at that time." The subject of the sentence is Moses, but the verb "to be" is not represented in the Hebrew.

COMMENT

If there is really nothing in the universe but God, then our egos are simply illusions. In order to experience the divine that surrounds and infuses us, we need to take our egos out of the equation. Begin, Yechiel Michal suggests, by not fantasizing about what you imagine you have achieved in spiritual matters, like your knowledge of Torah or your performance of the mitzvot. Whatever your spiritual achievements, you are still nothing before God, and your ego only holds you back.

---

[135] The Meaning of Divine Unity

"Hear O Israel, the Eternal [is] our God, the Eternal [is] one."
Deuteronomy 6:4

CONTEXT

In the course of a speech encouraging loyalty to God and God's commandments, Moses proclaims what has been called "the watchword of our faith." This may be the most important sentence in all Jewish thought. Observant Jews recite it as part of the service every evening and morning.

Moshe Alsheich was one of the important kabbalists who made up the community of Safed in the Galilee in the late sixteenth century.

It would have been fitting had [the text said] "the Eternal our God is one." But it says "Hear O Israel" [meaning] all of you, [even though] the expression is singular, referring to the unity of hearts as one. This is obligatory for us since the Eternal is our God. For even within the Eternal there exists the aspect of judgment, and "our God" that is mentioned here is the Eternal, for within the divine there exists the aspect of mercy. So, these two [divine] names are [in fact] entirely one. And we are obliged to emulate our Creator; hence God is called "our God" [here] rather than "God of the nations," on account of the unity of the Root of our souls, for God is the One who formed everything. And therefore we are obligated to emulate God.

Alternatively, one might say that *Shema* [in the singular implies] "with one heart," that Israel should accept [whatever God sends us,] whether God deals with us through the name "the Eternal" that signifies mercy, or through the name "our God" that signifies judgment, [which] is included in "the Eternal," for are not both aspects [actually indicative of] mercy? Hence [it says]: "the Eternal our God the Eternal." For the sufferings [we experience] are for good and not for punishment. Do not be surprised [at this] for are not these two aspects [really] one name in fact? Hence, it says "one."

Moshe Alsheich (d. after 1593), *Torat Moshe* [The Torah of Moses] (Warsaw, n.d.), pt. 5, pp. 46–47

NOTES

It would have been fitting had [the text said] "the Eternal our God is one." So, why is the four-letter divine name ("the Eternal") repeated?

But it says "Hear O Israel." The imperative *shema* (hear!) is singular, although the term "Israel" clearly refers to every Israelite and could thus be taken as plural.

This is obligatory for us since the Eternal is our God. The unity of God should be mirrored in the unity of the Jewish people.

For even within the Eternal. Even God's unity is a reconciliation of opposing forces, exactly as the unity of the Jewish people is. Thus, the divine name YHVH (the Eternal) stands for the *sefirah* of Hesed (Lovingkindness), while Eloheinu (our God) stands for Din (Judgment), also known as Gevurah (Might), as explained in the following note.

And "our God." *Eloheinu* (our God) is a grammatical combination of *Elohim* (God) and the suffix *nu*, meaning "our." *Elohim* usually denotes divine judgment.

God is called "our God" [here] . . . on account of the unity of the Root of our souls. According to the Kabbalah, all souls have their root in particular *sefirot,* and all Jewish souls (i.e., those born as Jews and converts to Judaism) share the same root.

We are obligated to emulate God. We should also combine mercy and judgment, lovingkindness and strength, Hesed and Gevurah, in our actions and thoughts.

Are not both aspects [actually indicative of] mercy? Even Gevurah derives ultimately from divine mercy. In the kabbalistic scheme, all the *sefirot* emanate from Keter by way of Hochmah and Binah, and Keter is pure mercy.

COMMENT

The unity of God is a frequent subject of Jewish theologians throughout the ages but is actually a very difficult concept to grasp because we experience life in multiplicity, not unity. We encounter each other, and physical and mental objects, as distinct and separate from ourselves. But the unity of God affirmed twice each day by observant Jews implies the unity of all that is, and the unity of our inner and outer lives. Alsheich asserts that divine unity implies the unity of all Jews, and indeed all human beings, as well as the unity of our psyche. But these are ideals, easier to state than to attain. But what wonders could we achieve if we could attain them!

The unity of humanity would usher in an era of peace and prosperity for all. The unity of our souls would unleash creativity within each of us. And these two are intertwined: if we could maintain the proper balance between our Hesed and our Gevurah, between our lovingkindness and our strength, and infuse them both with our Keter, the deep well of our compassion, we could make a more substantial contribution to the well-being of all humanity.

The unity of God, rightly understood, is the key to our wholeness and our individual and collective salvation.

'Ekev

---

[136] The Spirituality of Eating

*"In order to teach you that it is not by bread alone that a
human being lives, but from everything that comes from
the mouth of God does a human being live."*

Deuteronomy 8:3

CONTEXT

In this section Moses recounts the passage of the Israelites through the
wilderness in miraculous terms, including the divine provision of manna. Apart from survival, this had a didactic purpose, as expressed in
this verse.

Rabbi Hayyim Vital, a kabbalist of Italian origin, was a key disciple
of the Ari, Yitzchak Luria, the most inspired teacher of the kabbalistic
community of Safed in the late sixteenth century. Vital is also our most
important source for his master's teachings.

"It is not by bread alone that a human being lives." The meaning is
that the life force of the soul [*neshamah*] does not come from food,
"but from everything that comes from the mouth of the Eternal does
a human being live." This is [the meaning of] the blessing that issues
from the mouth, bringing forth holy sparks from "uncleanness," and
that is purified by the mouth of the Eternal, by the chewing of the
thirty-two teeth, which [symbolize] the thirty-two [occurrences of]
elohim [God], and the thirty-two paths.

Hayyim Vital (1542–1620), *Likkutei Tanach veTa'amei HaMitzvot* [Gleanings
on the Bible and the meanings of the commandments] (Jerusalem: Yeshivat
Kol Yehudah, 1970), p. 247

The soul [*neshamah*]. In the kabbalistic scheme, this represents the intellect or the mind, in contrast to the *nefesh*, which gives us life, and the *ruach*, which represents our emotional drive. According to this view, it would be quite obvious that food sustains the *nefesh*.

Bringing forth holy sparks from "uncleanness." In Lurianic theory, the holy sparks of divine light that came from the original act of divine emanation are trapped in the shards from the "breaking of the vessels" that represent the forces of uncleanness and physicality.

The thirty-two teeth. The average adult has thirty-two teeth, including wisdom teeth—barring extractions, of course.

The thirty-two [occurrences of] *elohim* [God]. In Genesis 1, the story of Creation.

The thirty-two paths. The paths of wisdom with which the world was created, according to *Sefer Yetzirah* 1:1. As delineated there, the paths are the twenty-letters of the Hebrew alphabet, plus the ten *sefirot*. The act of eating that sustains the body parallels and symbolizes how the soul derives from God. Reciting a blessing makes that explicit.

COMMENT

Vital's comments are based on medieval logic: If the spirit is not physical or material, then from where does it draw its sustenance? Its source cannot lie in the physical act of eating, for the spirit has higher origins than the body. According to this view, it cannot be the physical act of eating that keeps us alive (although not eating would ultimately bring about death); it is the soul or spirit that keeps death at bay. If we ate but had lost the will to live, the food would not sustain us.

So how does the soul, the *neshamah*, receive nourishment? Vital's answer is that saying a blessing over food activates the spiritual force latent in the food, and it is this spiritual force that sustains the soul.

I am not sure about latent spiritual forces in food, but I am certain about latent spirituality in ourselves. Saying a blessing over food may serve to activate the latent spirituality within us, and it is this that sustains our souls. For our spirit itself may be said to "issue from the mouth of God."

[137] The Weight of the Law

"The two tablets of the covenant were over my two hands. . . . You
had made a molten calf. . . . I took hold of the two tablets and threw
them down from my two hands, and broke them before your eyes."
Deuteronomy 9:15–17

CONTEXT

Moses reminds the people that God will be with them when they cross
the Jordan into the Promised Land, and he urges them not to imagine
that they have accomplished everything through their own efforts or
innate goodness. Instead he recalls that they have frequently rebelled
against God, not least when they built the Golden Calf. Moses relates
his own reaction to the calf and how he smashed the tablets of the Ten
Commandments in his anger.

Ibn Attar was a Moroccan kabbalist and Bible commentator. His book
was particularly popular in the circles of the Ba'al Shem Tov in Ukraine.

We need to know why it was necessary for [Moses] to take hold of
them; were they not [still] in his hands? But perhaps when Israel had
not yet sinned the tablets hovered just above Moses's hands and his
hands did not have to reach out to take them. And thus the earlier
verse is precise in saying "and the two tablets of the covenant were
over my two hands" [Deuteronomy 9:15], whereas it does not say "in
my two hands" or "in my hands." On the contrary, it seems to inten-
tionally say that they were not actually in his hands, but hovering
over them and that they carried themselves. But after he saw the calf,
the power of their holiness departed and he had to take hold of them.

Hayyim ben Moshe ibn Attar (1696–1743), *Or HaHayyim* [The light of life]
(Jerusalem: A. Blum, 1994), pt. 5, p. 33

NOTE

"Over my two hands." A literal rendering, based on Ibn Attar's comments.
JPS: "in my two hands."
Israel had not yet sinned. By making the Golden Calf.

Hovering over them and that they carried themselves. Based on a legend first recorded in the Jerusalem Talmud (*Ta'anit* 4:5): "Rabbi Yochanan in the name of Rabbi Yose bar Abaye said: The tablets wanted to fly away, so Moses had to take hold of them, as it is written, 'I took hold of the two tablets' [Deuteronomy 9:17]."

COMMENT

Since Paul of Tarsus, opponents of Judaism have argued that the laws of the Torah constitute a burden upon Jews. The facts are often very different. Religious Jews celebrate the Torah not as a burden, but as a liberation from being enslaved to personal whim and desire. The image of the two tablets hovering over Moses's hands, so that he was unaware of their weight, seems an apt symbol for this.

But when we become aware of sin, both our own and the sins of those we love and care about, the weight of the Torah may impinge itself upon our consciousness. We realize that we are not as free as we thought, and it troubles us. But the Torah also gives us a way forward, a way of liberating ourselves once again. It is called *teshuvah*, repentance.

---

[138] Prayer Is Divine

"[God] is your praise and is your God."

Deuteronomy 10:21

CONTEXT

Continuing his second speech through chapter 10, Moses outlines what the people owe God and what God has promised them.

Pinchas of Koretz was a younger contemporary of the Ba'al Shem Tov.

On the verse "[God] is your praise and is your God": The prayer that a person speaks is itself divine, for it unites all the upper attributes. But those who pray before the Holy One as if the prayer were something else are like those who receive something from outside, like servants who make requests and the king commands that their wish be fulfilled. In contrast to them are those for whom the prayer is itself divine— they are like children [of a king] who search in the king's treasury and themselves take what they want, because they are trusted by the Holy One. Then he added: Since the generation of King David no one has prayed like that, except me.

Pinchas of Koretz (1726–91), *Imrei Pinchas* [Pinchas's sayings] (Tel Aviv, 1974), §123, p. 40

NOTES

"[God] is your praise and is your God." JPS: "He is your glory and He is your God." The translation "praise" is required by the Koretzer's interpretation.

It unites all the upper attributes. In kabbalistic symbolism, prayer acts as a bridge between the *sefirah* of Malchut (or, the Shechinah, or the Community of Israel), on the one hand, and Tiferet, where all the energies of the remaining *sefirot* are concentrated.

COMMENT

What is prayer? This question seems to have an obvious answer, until we begin to consider it more closely. If you think of yourself as religious in any way, you probably engage in prayer regularly, but what do you think you are doing? My guess is that most people would define prayer as talking to God, and within that definition, there are at least two different approaches: praying your own prayers from the heart and praying other people's prayers using a prayer book. Either way, we are talking to God . . . or so it would seem.

The Koretzer posits a different, more "Eastern" view of prayer, which he reads into his literal rendering of the text. Your praise is God! So are you, because ultimately everything derives from God and partakes of God's divinity. In this view, the three elements are essentially one. This turns prayer from a conversation into a meditation. This grants enormous power and, by implication, responsibility, to the worshiper, but also reflects a more intimate connection with God. It means that prayer is our opportunity to reflect on our essential unity with the divine. We are not supplicants asking God to intervene to save us; we are full participants in the divine enterprise that is the world and life. If our hearts and minds are pure, we can purify the world.

Re'eh

---

[139] Today

"See, I set before you today blessing and curse."
Deuteronomy 11:26

CONTEXT

Moses concludes his second speech by setting before the People of Israel the stark choice between blessing and curse, life and death. Choosing blessing and life means adhering to Torah. If Moses set these choices before the Israelites "today," that is, thousands of years ago, do they still apply in our time?

Levi Yitzchak of Berditchev, one of the Maggid of Mezritch's most brilliant students, had a reputation for always seeing the good in people.

The word "today" is apparently unintelligible. But it is known that the Holy One "out of divine goodness, continually renews the work of Creation every day"—meaning that God gives new illumination and sends out new kindnesses each day. Hence, a person who serves God receives illumination and new insight each day, something they had not known the day before. Hence it is written, "See, I set before you today," in accordance with what our sages have said: "'Today'—let [words of Torah] seem to you each day as if they were new." That is, each day you will receive a blessing and a new kindness.

Levi Yitzchak of Berditchev (1740–1809), *Kedushat Levi* [The holiness of Levi] (Munkacs, 1829), p. 88d

NOTES

"Today" is apparently unintelligible. It seems to add nothing to the meaning of the verse.

"Out of divine goodness." A quotation from the prayer *Yotzer Or* (Who forms light) in the daily morning service.

"Let [words of Torah] seem to you each day." See the Talmud, *Berachot* 63b: "Was it on that day [when Moses was speaking] that the Torah was given to Israel? Was not that day the end of the forty years [of wandering in the wilderness]? It is, however, to teach you that the Torah is as beloved every day to those who study it as on the day when it was given on Mount Sinai."

COMMENT

For those, like Levi Yitzchak of Berditchev, seeking up-to-date meaning from the Torah rather than dry historical facts, the word "today" is a gift. The blessing referred to was not simply about those far-off historical circumstances of a former slave people grown strong in the wilderness. Divine blessing applies to each of us everyday. Each day those who serve God with awareness are granted gifts from God. Would that we could all become aware of them!

---

[140] Testing Times

"For the Eternal your God is testing you. . . ."
Deuteronomy 13:4

CONTEXT

Deuteronomy 13 is concerned with issues of idolatry and with those who may lead others into idolatry. How can one tell whether a prophet is authentic or not? What is to be done with one who entices others to serve other gods? What should you do if the seducer is a relative? Or if an entire city turns to idolatry? (In some Bibles, the verse numbers in this chapter may be different from the Hebrew Bible. In those editions, this is verse 5.)

The Ba'al Shem Tov's comment is embedded in a discussion in which he attempts to reconcile God's foreknowledge of events with the doctrine of free will.

For this world is a world of testing. The soul is sent here to be tested in this world.

Yisra'el ben Eliezer, Ba'al Shem Tov (1700–1760), *Keter Shem Tov* [The crown of a good name (*Pirkei Avot* 4:13)] (Brooklyn: Kehot Publication Society, 1972), §348, p. 101b

The phrase "for the Eternal your God is testing you" forms part of Moses's warning against listening to false prophets; he suggested that such prophets were a test of the people's loyalty and devotion.

For the Ba'al Shem Tov, the phrase, lifted out of its original context in a discussion about the relationship between divine foreknowledge and divine will, offers a way of understanding life. It is now seen as a series of God-given challenges, obstacles to be overcome. The problems we each face in life now have meaning (even if that meaning is not immediately apparent to us).

The question, though, is what is the goal of all this testing? Some would say it is to assign us a place in the next world, others that it is to determine how we should be reincarnated on our return to this world, and still others that it is to refine and spiritualize our coarse nature so that we may be more worthy creatures of God. My own preference is to see life's challenges as opportunities to refine ourselves, to become better, more caring, more spiritual people, because at each and every moment we are being tested by our Divine Parent.

---

[141] Why Eating Is Like Sleeping

*"Within your gates shall you eat it, the clean and the
unclean together, like the deer and the gazelle."*

Deuteronomy 15:22

CONTEXT

Deuteronomy 15, part of the central, legal unit of the book, is concerned with the laws of the sabbatical year and treatment of the poor. Its last verses deal with the consecration of firstborn cattle and eating meat outside the Temple in Jerusalem, that is, in a nonsacrificial setting.

Ya'akov Yitzchak HaLevi Horowitz is known as the Seer of Lublin, both as a tribute to his reputed gift of second sight and to distinguish him from his favorite student, Ya'akov Yitzchak, the Holy Jew of Pshische.

We have to say that a person should always be attached to the Eternal, so that you should have no other love apart from love for the

Creator, as it is written: "You should love the Eternal your God with all your heart, with all your soul and with all your might" (Deuteronomy 6:5). Whether you want to or not, you must eat, and the same applies to anything else that may be called "eating," as is well known. "Apart from" (Genesis 39:6) [implies] that you must separate yourself a little each moment, in order to recall [your] attachment to the Creator.

Look, on [the verse] "Flee, my beloved, and be like a deer or like a young gazelle" (Song of Songs 8:14), [tradition] says that it is the way of the deer to sleep with one eye [closed and one open] and that when it runs it keeps looking behind. We have to say something similar here: "You shall eat it like the deer and the gazelle," for when you eat, it should be considered like sleep, the opposite of attachment to the Creator and divine love. You should "sleep" with only one eye, and look "behind" yourself to the love of the Creator at every moment. The same applies to the gazelle, but that would only be repetition.

Ya'akov Yitzchak HaLevi Horowitz, the Seer of Lublin (1745–1815), *Zot Zikaron* [This is the memorial (Exodus 17:14)] (Jerusalem, 1992), p. 123

NOTES

Anything else that may be called "eating." The reference is to sex; see Genesis 39:6: "For he [Potiphar] left everything he owned to Joseph, and knew nothing of it, apart from his bread that he ate." On this verse, Rashi says: "'apart from his bread'—[refers to] his wife." See *Shemot Rabbah* 1:32 and *Bereshit Rabbah* 86:6. The expression "apart from" is picked up by the next sentence of our text.

[Tradition] says that it is the way of the deer. This rather strange notion is found in the midrash *Shir HaShirim Rabbah* 8:15 and Zohar II, 14a.

COMMENT

When we are eating, we tend to focus our minds on how hungry we are and on satisfying that hunger. If we have more leisure, we might consider the taste and texture of the food. If we have less, we probably have our minds on what we have to do next. Or perhaps we are enjoying the company of those we are with as we eat. Spiritually, though, we are probably sleeping. And the same may be said of sex. We concentrate on our sensations, on our partner's responses, but not on our spirituality. Once again, we are spiritually asleep.

But what if we could engage in those vital activities while also thinking about our connection with God? Would that enhance our appreciation of eating and drinking, and of sex? If spirituality is important to us, then there can be no areas of life where it is not allowed to enter.

Shofetim

---

[142] Judgment Within

"Judges and officers shall you appoint for yourself in all your gates. . . ."
Deuteronomy 16:18

CONTEXT

Though most of Deuteronomy 16 is concerned with the laws of the festivals, in verse 18 (the opening verse of Shofetim) the subject shifts to the duty to set up a justice system. Impartiality is to be the hallmark of Israelite justice.

Menachem Mendel of Kotzk set very high standards of personal integrity and honesty for his followers.

The meaning is that you should appoint judges and officers precisely "for yourself," that is, for your own character in every aspect of yourself, so that you can assess [*leSHa'eR*] yourself. For according to your assessment [*SHi'uRin*] of yourself should you judge and criticize yourself. Hence, [the text says] "in all your gates [*SHe'aRecha*]."

Menachem Mendel of Kotzk (1787–1859), *Ohel Torah* [The tent of Torah] (Lublin, 1909), p. 62

NOTES

Precisely "for yourself." The word *lecha* (for yourself) is in the singular, and apparently unnecessary. (The JPS leaves it untranslated.)

Hence, . . . "in all your gates." The Kotzker's interpretation is "in all your assessments."

COMMENT

Judging ourselves is crucial if our personal religion is not to become a method of self-justification. We "religious" people sometimes imagine that, by virtue of our religious practices, we are somehow better than others, better than those who are not as practicing as we are. We Jews seem to be prone to this kind of snobbery. It is what one of my colleagues calls "the game of out-*frum* thy neighbor." This game is pointless. It serves only to demean others in our eyes and inflate our own egos. Instead, we should be assessing and criticizing ourselves. The question is how do we measure up to our religious ideals, not how do others measure up.

[143] Raising Love and Fear to God

"Perfect [Tamim] shall you be with the Eternal your God."

Deuteronomy 18:13

CONTEXT

Verses 9–14 of Deuteronomy 18 are aimed at discouraging the acceptance of Canaanite religious practices, in particular, divination, sorcery, and other occult rites. Instead we are to be loyal ("perfect") to God.

Unlike most later Hasidic leaders, the Ba'al Shem Tov was peripatetic, wandering around Ukraine, preaching and encouraging Jews to greater spiritual awareness. His efforts proved to be the start of the modern Hasidic movement.

> The external fear that comes over people [does so] in order to awaken them to the fear of God. A parable: What is this like? Like a warrior sent by the king to summon a certain person. [The one who has been summoned] is very fretful and afraid, solely because the agent may go immediately to the king to do the royal will.
>
> Similarly, the external love that comes over people [does so] in order to awaken them to the love of the Eternal. A parable: What is this like? Sometimes a person is sent by the king to another on a mission of love, but someone who is ignorant enjoys and plays with [the king's] agent, while the wise person says: "What is playing with the agent to me? I will go to the root, the love of the king."
>
> Hence the text: "Perfect [*Tamim*] shall you be with the Eternal your God"—the *Tav* [of *Tamim*, "perfect"] is large. So despite the fact that

the [letter] *tav* is far from [the letter] *alef*, [this] alludes to [the need] to raise everything that is far, whether love or fear or joy or physical pleasure, to the Ruler [*aluf*] of the universe.

Yisra'el ben Eliezer, Ba'al Shem Tov (1700–1760), *Keter Shem Tov* [The crown of a good name (*Pirkei Avot* 4:13)] (Brooklyn: Kehot Publication Society, 1972), pt. 1, §207, p. 26b

NOTES

The *Tav* [of *Tamim*, "perfect"] is large. In some Torah scrolls, the opening letter of *tamim* is larger than the surrounding letters. This is also sometimes the case in printed Bibles.

The [letter] *tav* is far from [the letter] *alef*. *Tav* is the last letter of the Hebrew alphabet; *alef* is the first.

COMMENT

The Ba'al Shem Tov (nicknamed "the Besht") builds his discourse on the premise that the primary inner components of serving God are the love and fear/awe of God. Without these components, our service is purely mechanical; with them, it comes alive.

Both love and fear are emotions that we can experience in "ordinary" life, while God may seem remote and abstract; so what is the relationship between these "ordinary" emotions and those same emotions when applied to our relationship to God? For the Besht, our everyday experience of these emotional states is a pointer to how to love and fear God. We should set aside our "lower" fear and love, which are focused on passing objects, and instead raise our fear and love toward God, who is eternal. We need to see those emotions as somehow calling us toward higher things. If we can love and fear God fully, instead of being distracted by other, transient fears and loves, we shall be perfect in our service of the divine, as the Torah suggests.

[144] Making God Real

"You shall not remove your friend's boundary marker, which
ancient ones set up, in your inheritance that you shall have
in the land that the Eternal your God gives to you."

Deuteronomy 19:14

CONTEXT

Much of this chapter is concerned with the land. The first thirteen verses present the laws of the levitical cities, where those who kill inadvertently may flee to safety. Verse 14 continues the theme of land with the injunction not to move boundary markers.

Moshe Hayyim Efraim of Sudylkov was the more scholarly of the Ba'al Shem Tov's two grandsons.

One may interpret this in an allegorical way, for it is known that the ancient Patriarchs drew the Shechinah [the Presence of God] down, as it were, to earth, because they drew down and exalted [God's] divinity in the world. Afterward, the sins of the [succeeding] generation came and drove the Shechinah upward, along the lines [of the verse]: "Be high over the heavens, O God" (Psalm 57:12). For example, Abraham at the beginning: His quality was that of lovingkindness and the love of God. He publicized [God's] divinity, and the Shechinah, as it were, descended to the earth, for he had opened the eyes of all and revealed that "God's glory fills the universe" (Isaiah 6:3). Later, due to the sins of the generation, the Shechinah was removed to the firmament, that is, a contraction occurred, as it were, in God's greatness, so that [the divine] was neither seen nor revealed to anyone's eyes.

Then Isaac came and dug those wells that the Philistines had stopped up, and [thus] made the light of the Holy One shine. But afterward, the Philistines stopped them up a second time, until Jacob came. This is alluded to here [as a] "moral lesson" (Proverbs 1:3).

The Shechinah is called a "boundary marker," because it is the end of all levels. And "your friend" means the Holy One, blessed be He, as it is said: "Do not forsake your friend or your father's friend" (Proverbs 27:10). Hence it says, "Do not remove your friend's boundary marker," meaning, do not make the Shechinah ascend because of your deeds. The Shechinah is called "your friend's boundary marker," meaning [that She belongs to] the Holy One, blessed be He, along the lines [of the verse]: "Be high over the heavens, O God" (Psalm 57:12).

"Which ancient ones set up in your inheritance that you shall have," that is, the ancient ones made the presence of the glory of God appear in the land. "Inheritance" [*nachalah*] is a word meaning "drawing down," as in *nachal*, a stream. Hence, [an inheritance] is called a "stream" because it lasts from generation to generation, like a flowing, rushing stream. So they [the Patriarchs] also drew down the presence of [God's] glory into the lower [worlds].

"In the land that the Eternal your God gives to you"—that is, along the lines [of the verse] "In every place where I cause My name to dwell" (Exodus 20:21)—which the Targum translates as "In every place where My Shechinah dwells"—"there will I come to you and bless you" (Exodus 20:21). And the enlightened person will understand.

Moshe Hayyim Efraim of Sudylkov (d. 1800), *Degel Machaneh Efraim* [The flag of the camp of Ephraim (Numbers 2:18)] (Jerusalem, 1963), pp. 248–49

NOTES

"You shall not remove your friend's boundary marker." The word *rei'acha* may be translated "your neighbor" or "your friend." Most translations of this verse choose "neighbor," but "friend" is required by the Sudylkover's comments. (JPS: "You shall not move your countryman's landmarks.")

The ancient Patriarchs drew the Shechinah [the Presence of God] down. See the midrash *Bereshit Rabbah* 19:7, where it is said that the Shechinah ascended through the seven heavens when Adam sinned, but that the Patriarchs (and others) succeeded in bringing her back down to earth step by step.

"Be high over the heavens, O God" (Psalm 57:12). Here, "God" *(elohim)* indicates the Shechinah. The verse suggests the banishment of the Presence of God to the heavens. At a kabbalistic level, Malchut (Sovereignty) is banished from contact with the world.

His quality was that of lovingkindness. Abraham represents the *sefirah* of Hesed (Lovingkindness).

A contraction occurred, as it were, in God's greatness. The word translated here as "contraction" is *tzimtzum*, a Lurianic technical term. By saying "as it were," Moshe Hayyim clearly puts himself into the camp, which includes most Hasidic teachers, of those who do not understand the term literally. God's contraction is apparent only from our limited, human perspective.

The Shechinah is called a "boundary marker," because it is the end of all levels. As Malchut, it is the boundary between the lower world of this universe and the upper realm of the *sefirot*.

And "your friend" means the Holy One, blessed be He. A teaching from *Shemot Rabbah* 27:1, discussing Proverbs 27:10. I have retained a masculine translation because the kabbalistic context requires it. See next note.

The Shechinah is called "your friend's boundary marker," meaning [that She belongs to] the Holy One, blessed be He. The Shechinah (Malchut) is the feminine consort of Tiferet (Beauty, but also indicated by the expression "the Holy One, blessed be He").

The ancient ones made the presence of the glory of God appear. The phrase "the ancient ones" indicates the Patriarchs here.

"In the land." In the original biblical context, "land" means "the Land of Israel." In the Sudylkover's interpretation, it means "the earth," that is, any place on earth, as implied by what follows.

The Targum. *Targum* means "translation," but when the word appears in traditional texts without qualification, it refers to the *Targum Onkelos*, the ancient Aramaic rendering of the Torah.

COMMENT

Our behavior has a direct bearing on whether others will perceive God's activity in this world. If we behave well, with due respect for others, people will see that our faith is real, that God's presence is real for us. And the converse is also true: if we are seen to behave in ways that are contrary to our highest ideals, our faith will be brought into disrepute. This is not just a matter of good or bad publicity for Jews and Judaism; our behavior has a direct spiritual impact in the world.

Ki Tetse'

---

[145] The War against Evil

"If you go to war against your enemies, and the Eternal your God has delivered him into your hands, and you shall take him captive. . . ."

Deuteronomy 21:10

CONTEXT

This fifth book of the Torah presents us with what are probably the first attempts in history to set legal limits on warfare. Here the concern is to avoid the rape of any woman who may be captured in war. If a soldier desires a captive woman, he may marry her, but only after she has had a suitable period to mourn her dead, and then, should his ardor cool, he may not divorce her. The opening verse sets the scene for the rule that follows.

Yitzchak Podvah was a Hasidic scholar who perished in the Holocaust. Most of his *Ilana deChayyei* is devoted to transmitting the teachings of Menachem Mendel of Rymanov, but he does include points made by other teachers. Like the Rymanover, Moshe Teitelbaum of Ujhely was a disciple of the Seer of Lublin and one of the first rabbis to bring the Hasidic message to the Jews of Hungary.

Our holy teacher, R. Moshe Teitelbaum, explained this on the basis of the saying of our Rabbis: "People should always engage in Torah even if not for its own sake[, since by doing it not for its own sake, they may come to do it for its own sake]." The commentators have explained that later they may perform a commandment for its own sake, and in this way they would elevate even the commandments that they had not performed for their own sake.

Hence, it says, "If you go to war against your enemies"—meaning, "with your enemies," for he will go with you. Nevertheless, do not refrain from going, for it says next "the Eternal your God has delivered him into your hands." Then "you shall take him captive." You shall take from him what he took from you, "and you shall take out what is precious from what is vile" [Jeremiah 15:19].

Yitzchak Mordechai ben Yisra'el Aharon Podvah (1884–1942), ed., *Ilana deChayyei* [The tree of life] (Jerusalem, 1986), pt. 1, p. 105

NOTES

"If you go to war against your enemies, and the Eternal your God has delivered him." The Hebrew text shifts from the plural ("enemies") to the singular ("him"). Most translations do not bring this out, but recognizing this is required for the interpretation that follows. JPS: "When you take the field against your enemies, and the Lord your God delivers them into your power."

R. Moshe Teitelbaum. Of Ujhely in Hungary (1759–1841).

"People should always engage in Torah even if not for its own sake." Talmud, *Sanhedrin* 105b and *Horayot* 10b.

They would elevate even the commandments. Observing one commandment for no ulterior motive would purify all those that had been observed with other intentions in mind, raising their spiritual level.

For he will go with you. The reference is to your "enemy," meaning, the inclination toward evil, the enemy within that goes wherever we go and is involved in whatever we do.

You shall take from him what he took from you. If we learn to overcome the inclination toward evil within us, we can redeem all the commandments that we have sullied with our ulterior motives and that were therefore in the power of our inclination toward evil. The verse from Jeremiah reinforces the point.

COMMENT

We can be our own worst enemies. The classical Rabbinic teaching about an inclination toward evil that we have within us is another way of helping us realize that our true enemy is within ourselves. We carry him wherever we go, and yet he can be defeated and made into a friend. He must be tackled, held captive, and his energies turned to good. If and when we achieve that, we will have achieved a wonderful transformation of ourselves. We will have become what we were meant to be. We will have become truly ourselves, truly human.

[146] Praying without Desire

"You shall not bring the fee of a prostitute or the price of a dog
into the house of the Eternal your God in payment of any vow,
for both of these are abhorrent to the Eternal your God."

Deuteronomy 23:19

CONTEXT

Deuteronomy 22 and 23 present a wide variety of laws with no apparent connection between them other than the general good of society.
The second of these chapters focuses mainly on sexual morality, as does
verse 19 quoted above.

Mordechai Leiner of Izbica was a student of Menachem Mendel of
Kotzk until a dramatic, if mysterious, event that occurred one Friday
evening in the autumn of 1840.

"The fee of a prostitute" means "desire"; "the price of a dog" means
"anger." Scripture is warning us not to bring them into the "house of
the Eternal your God." For no one should pray for [anything] out of
desire or anger, for you may compromise your actions because "both
of these are abhorrent to the Eternal." . . . Even if you amend them
by saying that you want this for the sake of heaven, it is still forbidden to pray for them, because the desire or the anger is still in your
heart. Therefore, even for the sake of heaven it is forbidden; on the
contrary, you should be purified seven times forty-nine times!

Mordechai Yosef Leiner of Izbica (1814–78), *Mei HaShiloach* [The waters of
the Siloam (Isaiah 8:6)] (Bnei Brak, 1995), v. 2, p. 122

NOTES

Not to bring them into the "house of the Eternal." I.e., into our prayers.
You should be purified seven times forty-nine times! A footnote to this
   text in the original version points out that Ki Tetse' is the forty-ninth parashah of the Torah.

Removing our desires and anger from our prayers may be one of the hardest tasks religious people have to accomplish. Our prayers need to be purified of ego, because the world is full of egos all demanding what they want. And all those wants cannot be compatible. Where would the world be if all our prayers out of anger were answered? So set aside emotion, and pray for what you know in your heart is right. You will feel better, and the world too will be purer.

---

[147] Blotting Out Amalek Within

"Blot out the memory of Amalek. . . ."

Deuteronomy 25:19

CONTEXT

Deuteronomy presents us with a miscellany of social legislation, concluding with the command to remember what the Amalekites did to the Israelites after they emerged from Egyptian slavery. The story of how they attacked defenseless stragglers is told in Exodus 17:8–16. (Deuteronomy 25:17–19 is the *maftir* for Shabbat Zachor, the Sabbath before Purim.)

The Ba'al Shem Tov is the name by which the charismatic founder of the modern Hasidic movement is usually known. This title probably indicates his skill in healing the sick and making protective amulets, but his fame is more firmly based on the quality and depth of his spiritual teachings.

> It says in the holy writings of our master, R. Yisra'el, the Ba'al Shem Tov, that he taught as follows: The essence of the blotting out of Amalek is that first we must blot out the heavenly prince known as Arrogance . . . , and then Amalek will be blotted out below.

Yisra'el ben Eliezer, Ba'al Shem Tov (1700–1760), *Sefer Ba'al Shem Tov* [The book of the good master of the Name], ed. Shimon Menachem Mendel of Govarchov (Jerusalem, n.d.), v. 2, p. 225

The heavenly prince known as Arrogance. Rabbinic literature frequently refers to the heavenly princes that represent the nations of the world in the angelic realm. This text is unusual in referring to a moral attribute in this way.

COMMENT

Nowhere does the Torah itself actually say that the Amalekites were to be killed. But, I am sorry to say, this command was understood in that way in ancient times, and we know this because in 1 Samuel 15, the Israelites under King Saul, their first king, attempt to do just that. Did they succeed? Probably not. Later on, through the story of Purim as told in the biblical book of Esther, Amalek became a symbol for all those who would destroy the Jewish people, a symbol of ultimate wickedness. Has Amalek, the symbol, lost all connection with real people? One might have thought so, because there are no Amalekites around anymore. Sadly though, I am ashamed to say that there are some Jews for whom the term "Amalek" still refers to real, living people, who, they say, have to be killed before they kill us. Thankfully they are a tiny minority, but we, the majority, have to be on our guard against such literalism and potential terrorism.

The Ba'al Shem Tov says that in order to blot out the memory of Amalek, that is, in order to remove the irrational hatred and cowardliness that Amalek displayed in the ancient story, we need to blot out the heavenly prince known as Arrogance. I believe he is using mythical language to describe a psychological truth. Arrogance isn't up there in the heavenly reaches; it's down here on earth. Arrogance isn't out there in Amalek or others who behave like Amalek; Arrogance is alive in our own hearts.

Ki Tavo'

---

[148] How to Rejoice

"Then you shall rejoice in all the good things that the
Eternal your God is giving to you. . . ."

Deuteronomy 26:11

CONTEXT

The first fifteen verses of this chapter of Deuteronomy concern the bringing of the first fruits to the sanctuary. Each person had to bring their first fruits of the Land of Israel in a basket to the Temple and hand them over to the priests, with a declaration that "a wandering Aramaean was my ancestor" (v. 5) and that it is God who grants the land to us. In temple times, this ritual was performed on Shavuot, the Festival of First Fruits (Chag HaBikkurim).

Mordechai of Neschiz was famous in his own day as a miracle worker.

That is to say:

[1] (For) the simple person: You should rejoice with all the good things of this world, with wealth and the like, that the Eternal has given you. And you should know that it was not the work of your hands that achieved this, but it was from the Eternal. You should also appreciate that at each and every moment, [God] "is giving to you," not "has given," for it is in God's power to remove divine influence at any moment. In this way, you should understand that you may not turn away from God with all your great wealth or the rest of the good things of this world.

[2] For the person who is "slightly" perfect: Throughout all your Torah and service—anything that has a good flavor—you should celebrate and rejoice only over what the Eternal gives. You

should know truly that without the life force of the Creator who gives you life, you are only dust.

[3] Regarding the more perfect person, that is to say, in the totality of the good, you should rejoice that you are within the Eternal your God, who bestows the divine life force on you.

Mordechai of Neschiz (d. 1800), *Rishpei Esh* [Coals of fire (Song of Songs 8:6)] (Jerusalem, 1997), p. 27

NOTES

"That the Eternal your God is giving to you." Virtually all English translations render this verb in the past. JPS: "that the Lord your God has bestowed upon you." The present tense is required by the interpretation that follows.

That is to say. The rebbe of Neschiz now presents three approaches to this rejoicing, depending on our spiritual level.

The person who is "slightly" perfect. Apparently he means those who are a bit more dedicated to Jewish observance.

The more perfect person. Those who combine observance with spiritual insight.

COMMENT

To be happy with what God gives us is to go against the grain in the modern capitalist world. Capitalism is based on the premise that we will always want more and better products. It aims to feed our greed, but actually our greed is boundless, and the end result is not happiness but frustration. In contrast, Mordechai of Neschiz sets out three possible ways of being happy with God's gifts of life, sustenance, and companionship. There may be many others ways of reaching the same goal, but reach it we must, if we and our global society are not to end in increasing frustration and conflict.

[149] Timeless Prayer

*"This day the Eternal your God is commanding you
to observe these laws and rules. . . ."*

Deuteronomy 26:16

CONTEXT

In the last four verses of chapter 26, Moses ends his third speech with
a reminder of the covenant, or contract, that now exists between God
and the People of Israel. But this could also be a reference back to the
commandment of bringing the first fruits on Shavuot found earlier in the
chapter (verses 1–11) or the giving of the tithes (verses 12–15).

The Kotzker rebbe placed great emphasis on the inner work of prayer
and on self-criticism.

In Midrash Tanchuma: "This is what Scripture says: 'Come, let us
prostrate ourselves and bow down, let us bend low before the Eternal
our Creator' (Psalm 95[:6]). But isn't 'bowing' within the category
of 'prostration'? Nevertheless, it says: 'Let us prostrate ourselves and
bow down.' Rather, Moses perceived with the holy spirit and saw that
the Holy Temple would be destroyed in the future and that the first
fruits would [therefore] cease [to be offered] in the future. [So] he
arose and ordained that Israel should pray three times a day." Thus
far the midrash.

It seems that the explanation for this is that since he perceived that
the [bringing of] first fruits would cease in the future, he deduced
from this that it was not essential, for essential things do not cease.
Therefore, he arose and ordained prayer, which may be found at any
time without interruption.

Menachem Mendel of Kotzk (1787–1859), *Ohel Torah* [The tent of Torah]
(Lublin, 1909), pp. 63–64

NOTES

In Midrash Tanchuma. *Parashat* Ki Tavo', paragraph 1.

But isn't "bowing" within the category of "prostration"? Don't you have
to bow in the process of prostrating yourself? Prostration means laying

oneself flat on the ground as a sign of submission, much as Muslims do in prayer, and many Jews do on Yom Kippur; and bowing is usually the first step in prostration.

Moses perceived with the holy spirit. God granted Moses knowledge of the future. (Moses is mentioned because the midrash credits him with the authorship of Psalm 95.)

The Holy Temple would be destroyed. In the Temple, prostration was an everyday occurrence, but it ceased after the destruction by the Romans in 70 CE. When the Temple fell, the offering of the first fruits, mentioned in the preceding verses of the Torah, also came to end, as did all sacrifices.

He arose and ordained that Israel should pray three times a day. "Bending low" is a feature of praying the *Amidah* (Standing prayer), during which it is customary to bow at the beginning and end of the first and penultimate blessings.

Thus far the midrash. This is the end of the quotation from Tanchuma.

He perceived. The subject is Moses.

COMMENT

The Kotzker offers a reason why Moses should have ordained prayer. His suggestion is that the sacrificial system must have been less than eternal if it was to come to an end. Prayer, on the other hand, is eternal. It can be practiced virtually anywhere and at any time. It can cover all contingencies. It may be assisted by, but is not bound by, any rituals. The sacrificial system was time bound; prayer may be undertaken "this day."

---

[150] Backward Curses

"Your ox will be slaughtered before your eyes, but you will not eat of it. Your donkey will be stolen from you, and not returned. Your flock shall be taken by your enemies, with no one to save it."

Deuteronomy 28:31

CONTEXT

The opening verses of Deuteronomy 28 paint a lovely picture of all the good things that will accrue if the people keep the Torah. Verses 15–69, however, are known as the "curses" or "reproofs," and comprise a list of terrible consequences that will befall the people if they fail to live up to this challenge.

Pinchas of Koretz was a younger contemporary of the Ba'al Shem Tov and may have been influenced by him.

> On the subject of the Reproof, he said that it is all blessings! And in the name of the author of the *Akedah*, [he said]: Thus it seems to me: When [we] read the verse backward it is a blessing, [for example, reading the final phrase of Deuteronomy 28:31 backward gives you] "and you will not be given over to your enemies [but you will have a savior]." This is [the meaning of the verse]: "And the Eternal changed the curse [to a blessing] for you" [Deuteronomy 23:6]. When we read it backward, it is a blessing.
>
> And in the name of the Rav: Just as a person has 248 limbs, so too the Torah; and the Reproof is the Torah's bile. Just as in the case of a person the vital force depends on the bile, so that if it is lacking or [the liver] is pierced [or] torn one is unable to live, so too [in the case of] the Reproof. . . . As Rashi says on *parashat* Nitsavim, the curses set you up and establish you in the world.

Pinchas of Koretz (1726–91), *Imrei Pinchas* [Pinchas's sayings] (Tel Aviv: Arnberg, 1974), §134, p. 42

NOTES

The Reproof. Deuteronomy 28:15–69.

The author of the *Akedah*. *Akedat Yitzchak* (The binding of Isaac) is a philosophical commentary on the Torah in the form of extended essays by Yitzchak Arama (ca. 1420–94), a Spanish rabbi and philosopher.

"And you will not be given over to your enemies." The Hebrew of the original reads: *netunim le'oy'vecha v'ein lecha moshi'a*—literally, "given to your enemies and not for you a savior." Reading the words in reverse order gives: "a savior for you and not to your enemies given."

The Rav. In the literature of this school, "the Rav" always indicates Pinchas of Koretz.

A person has 248 limbs. This figure is first mentioned in the Talmud, Makkot 23b.

So too the Torah. The notion that the Torah is a body with limbs corresponding to the human body goes back at least as far as *Tikkunei HaZohar*, *Tikkun* 21, page 52b.

The Reproof is the Torah's bile. *Marah* (bile) literally means "bitterness." In medieval medicine, it was believed that the body's health was determined by the balance (or lack of balance) among the four "humors." These four include: blood centered in the heart, black bile in the spleen, phlegm in the brain, and yellow bile in the liver.

Rashi says on *parashat* Nitsavim. On Deuteronomy 29:12, Rashi writes: "Why is the parashah of Nitsavim adjacent to the curses [of the previous chapter]? Because when the Israelites heard the ninety-eight curses on top of the forty-nine in Leviticus (26:14–41), they became pale and said: 'Who can stand up to these?!' Moses began to calm them down[, saying]: 'You are all standing today [before the Eternal your God]' (Deuteronomy 29:9). You have provoked God to anger many times, but God has not put an end to you. On the contrary, you are established before God."

COMMENT

The Koretzer's view may stem from the "magical" element within Hasidism, but I prefer to think of his suggestion that we approach the curses in reverse order in a different way. The crises of life can be viewed as opportunities if we can look at them from a different angle.

This does not mean that we should pretend to be happy no matter what may be happening to us. Just as you have to read the verse forward before you can read it backward, so too we may have to enter into the depths of our troubles fully before we can begin to see the opportunities that lie within them.

In the second part of the teaching, based on the four humors, the point is that tragedy and crisis are a normal part of life, and indeed they are necessary for a normal, healthy life. Without them, people would never learn, grow, or adapt. We have to be grateful to God for life's problems and challenges too.

Nitsavim

---

[151] Standing before God

"You are all standing today before the Eternal your God."

Deuteronomy 29:9

CONTEXT

Here Moses continues his third speech by reminding the Israelites that the covenant they have made with God is not restricted by time. Not only are those present covered by its terms, but also all those who are to come. (In some Bibles, the verse quoted above is verse 10.)

Yisra'el of Ruzhyn was the great-grandson of the Maggid of Mezritch and founder of the Sadgora Hasidic dynasty.

> When will there be a presence and "standing" for you in the world? When you are "before the Eternal your God"; that is, when you are attached to the Holy One, as it says of the Holy One: "[You who are attached (to God)] are all alive this day" [Deuteronomy 4:4].

Yisra'el Friedman of Ruzhyn (1797–1850), *Irin Kadishin* [Holy angels] (n.p., 1885), pt. 1, pp. 71–72

NOTE

When you are attached. Attachment to God *(devekut)* is a central goal of Hasidic thought and practice. It indicates a heightened awareness of God's presence.

COMMENT

We don't always "stand before God," that is, we are by no means always conscious of being in the presence of God. Only when we are can we be truly "standing before God." True existence in the world demands that we be connected with higher things, with God. Anything less is not real life but only a shadow, something unreal, but something that can become real for us when we connect ourselves with the divine.

Being attached to God is something one does internally, within our minds and souls. If our attachment is true, we can purify our lives and bring enlightenment to those around us, but the real transformation takes place within us, not outside. That transformation makes us truly human, turning us into beings who really are in the presence of God.

[152] The Hidden and the Revealed

"The hidden things belong to the Eternal our God, but the revealed things belong to us and to our children."

Deuteronomy 29:28

CONTEXT

Chapter 29 of Deuteronomy presents the first part of Moses's final speech to the Israelites before his death. In it, he reminds them of their responsibility to keep the Torah and of the consequences if they do not.

Hayyim Vital is a central figure in the history of Kabbalah. In addition to some writings of his own, he organized and collated the teachings of his master, Yitzchak Luria, the Ari.

> "The hidden things belong to the Eternal our God"—[these are] awe and love, which are in the heart. "But the revealed things belong to us and to our children"—meaning the Torah and the commandments that are revealed to us.
>
> Hayyim Vital (1542–1620), *Likkutei Tanach veTa'amei HaMitzvot* [Gleanings on the Bible and the meanings of the commandments] (Jerusalem: Yeshivat Kol Yehudah, 1970), p. 280

COMMENT

The modern Jewish landscape is characterized by a wide variety of religious and secular organizations and ideologies, and one way of thinking about this divergence is to view them as placing varying degrees of emphasis on what Rabbi Leo Baeck called "the mystery and the commandment," and what Vital terms "the hidden and the revealed." But actually both are necessary. Total concentration on the revealed, on the commandments, becomes mere conformity. Total devotion to the hidden things, to inwardness, destroys social cohesion; the individual becomes supreme, the community nothing. Somewhere in the middle, we—each of us separately and groups of us together—have to find that happy place where commandments may be observed with inner devotion that gives heart to rituals and allows the soul to express itself in both old and new ways.

---

[153] The Shechinah in Our Mouths

"This command is not too wonderful for you, nor too remote. It is not in heaven that you should say: Who will go up to heaven for us and get it for us and let us hear it so that we can do it? . . . Rather, it is something very near to you, in your mouth and in your heart for you to do."

Deuteronomy 30:11–12,14

CONTEXT

The teaching about repentance expressed in the first ten verses of Deuteronomy 30 is followed in verses 11–15 with an almost mystical passage detailing the idea that repentance is not to be sought outside oneself (in heaven or across the sea) but within.

Baruch of Medzibodz, the less scholarly of the Ba'al Shem Tov's two grandsons, was more famous in his own time for his coach and horses and his sumptuous "palace" than for his teachings. Yet there are some pearls of wisdom recorded in his name.

"It is not in heaven"—[This is God's] mighty Presence, for the Holy One makes the Shechinah [the Presence of God] reside in our midst, in the mouths of [God's] people, the house of Israel, according to the saying of the holy Zohar: "Malchut is a mouth." For the Shechinah dwells within a person's mouth, and when you cleanse yourself in order to speak in holiness and purity by setting aside the "accusers" and the "separating curtains" that prevent you from speaking your words in truth before the Holy One—for these depress the Shechinah that dwells within your mouth—[only then the Shechinah can speak].

Baruch ben Yechiel of Medzibodz (1757–1810) in *Hesed leAvraham* [Lovingkindness to Abraham (Micah 7:20)] (Jerusalem: Levin-Epstein, 1954), p. 104

NOTES

[God's] mighty Presence. In Hebrew, *shechinat uzzo*, a phrase recycled from the first paragraph of the *Aleinu* prayer.

"Malchut is a mouth." The *sefirah* of Malchut (Sovereignty) is also known as the Shechinah (the Presence of God). The quotation is from *Tikkunei HaZohar*, second introduction, p. 17a.

The "accusers." The angels that accuse us when we sin or, alternatively, our guilty thoughts.

The "separating curtains." Our sins and our thoughts of guilt separate us from the God within.

COMMENT

In its original context, this verse may already be a mystic's charter, but there are differences of opinion as to what it refers to. Perhaps it is the commandment of "returning" or repentance alluded to in verses 1–10 of the same chapter. Repentance is something that comes from within us. We do not have to undertake great journeys to heaven or overseas to find it.

Alternatively, it is the Torah itself that is meant. (This is the view taken by the great medieval commentator Nachmanides.) In that case, the message is that the essence of Torah, of God's teaching, is to be found within us, and this in turn suggests a particular purpose of Torah study: to refine further the spiritual essence that we already have within ourselves as our human heritage from God.

Baruch of Medzibodz, however, goes one step further. In his view, the verse is referring to the Shechinah (the Presence of God) that resides within us. This is the source of the repentance that comes from within as well as the spiritual center that we refine when we engage in Torah study. Baruch suggests that we can access this center when we set aside those things that distract us from our spiritual task on earth. Then the Shechinah itself can speak through us.

Va-yelekh

---

[154] Controlling Our Words

"So Moses went and spoke these words to all Israel."

Deuteronomy 31:1

CONTEXT

Moses begins his sixth and final speech to the Israelites, reminding them of how God granted them victory over the nations who opposed their passage through the lands on the eastern bank of the Jordan River.

Elimelech of Grodzhisk was the grandson of two Hasidic masters: Yisra'el, the Maggid of Koznitz, and Elimelech of Lyzhansk.

Look here: it is written "Take with you words and return to the Eternal" [Hosea 14:3]. It is the nature of human beings to speak words mindlessly, without thought or desire. However, the people who give their minds freely to returning to the Eternal must shut mouth and lips and guard the tongue from allowing words to issue from the mouth, until they have considered in their minds whether this thing they intend to say is in accord with the will of the Eternal. This is what is meant by "Take with you words"—that is, you should see if your words are "with you," under your control, so that you do not rush to speak mindlessly, and then [you can] "return to the Eternal."

This is also what is meant by "so Moses went and spoke": *MoSHeH* [Moses], with an extra point for the word as a whole, has a numerical value equal to *RaTZON* [will, desire], that is, that people should lead the will to the word, to join the will and the thought to the word, as described above.

"These words to all Israel"—that is, that everyone of Israel should see that they arrive at this [stage].

Elimelech ben Hayyim Meir Yechiel of Grodzhisk (1824–92), *Imrei Elimelech* [Elimelech's sayings] (n. p., 1876), p. 329

"Take with you words" . . . **[Hosea 14:3]**. This verse forms part of the *haf-tarah* (the reading from the prophets) for Shabbat Shuvah (the Sabbath of Repentance), which falls between Rosh Hashanah and Yom Kippur. Shabbat Shuvah frequently coincides with the reading of Va-yelekh.

MoSHeH [Moses], **with an extra point for the word as a whole, has a numerical value equal to** *RaTZON*. The letters of *MoSHeH* give us a total of 345 (*mem* = 40, *shin* = 300, *heh* = 5). *RaTZON* is 346 (*resh* = 200, *tzadi* = 90, *vav* = 6, *nun* = 50). It is quite common in equations of this kind for an extra "1" to be added for the word as a whole, thus rendering the two words numerically equal.

COMMENT

Much (most?) of what we say is unnecessary and thoughtless. Most of the time that may not matter too much. But occasionally we all get into difficulties for things that we have said without the benefit of fore-thought, and suddenly relationships are broken and trust undermined. Although other animals communicate in often quite sophisticated ways, none has the level of sophistication achieved by our species, even before the advent of modern communication devices. For the religious person, this marvel of human speech, writing, and other forms of conveying facts, emotions, and worldviews is nothing less than a gift from God. It should be used wisely.

[155] Fixing Holiness in Our Minds

"Gather together the people, the men, women, children. . . ."

Deuteronomy 31:12

CONTEXT

In verse 9 of this chapter, Moses writes the Torah down. He then gives instructions for it to be read in its entirety every seven years when all the people are gathered together. This commandment is known by the name of *hakhel* (gather together).

Mordechai of Izbica, a disciple of Menachem Mendel of Kotzk, is considered one of the most original Hasidic thinkers of his age.

On the subject of the commandment of *hakhel* at [the start of] the eighth [year]: the sabbatical year teaches us that it is not human activity [that creates agricultural produce] but that "the earth and its fullness belong to God" [Psalm 24:1]. Now the eighth year was about human activity, and therefore the command to read "this Torah" in the presence of all Israel, in their hearing, was intended to fix the holiness of the sabbatical year in their hearts, so that even while they are engaged in human activity, they would recognize that everything comes from God.

Mordechai Yosef Leiner of Izbica (1800–54), *Mei HaShiloach* [The waters of the Siloam (Isaiah 8:6)] (Bnei Brak, 1995), v. 2, p. 129

NOTES

At [the start of] the eighth [year]. Following Rabbinic interpretation (Mishnah, *Sotah* 7:8), *hakhel* would have been performed, and the entire Torah read, during Sukkot at the start of the year after the sabbatical year.

The sabbatical year. According to Torah law, the land was to lie fallow every seventh year, with no planting or harvesting undertaken (see Exodus 23:10–11; Leviticus 25:1–7,18–22; and Deuteronomy 15:1–11).

The eighth year was about human activity. Once the sabbatical year was concluded, people could resume planting and harvesting as normal.

COMMENT

Human activity is, by definition, what we engage in all the time. Of course, in farming, the actions of human beings (planting, weeding, tending, harvesting, etc.) are very important, even vital, but they are not the whole story. All our farming efforts will come to naught if the weather and climatic conditions are not right. To the religious mind, this means that God is the ultimate source of agricultural success, for even the very fact of plant growth must, from this point of view, derive from the divine.

The same applies, I believe, in all areas of human endeavor, including economic activity. We may plan, prepare, and carry out our schemes, but the results are beyond our control. Although we must be concerned about the consequences of our actions, and try to make decisions that will produce the best for all concerned, in the end the consequences will be what they will be. They lie in the hands of God.

[156] When God Is in Hiding

"I will surely hide My face on that day, because of the evil that they have done by turning to other gods."

Deuteronomy 31:18

CONTEXT

God speaks to Moses once more, as he stands with Joshua before the Tent of Meeting, and God predicts that after Moses has departed this life the people will depart from his teachings. Then God will withdraw divine protection—described in biblical terms as "a hiding of God's face." Simchah Bunam of Otvotzk was the son of Menachem Mendel of Vorki.

I also heard a teaching from him on the verse "I will surely hide My face" in *parashat* Va-yelekh. He said: It is like children playing hide-and-seek. The child who is hiding cries out, "I am hiding!" and the child that possesses understanding follows the sound that has gone forth and looks until he finds [the hidden child]. It is the same here. God cries out "I am hiding!" and, in those of understanding, the voice of God arouses them until they seek and find [God].

Simchah Bunam of Otvotzk (d. 1907), in *Gedulat Mordechai uGdulat HaTzadikim* [The greatness of Mordechai and the greatness of the righteous] (Warsaw, 1934), pt. 2, §49, p. 18

NOTE

I also heard a teaching from him. The anonymous editor is speaking of Simchah Bunam of Otvotzk.

COMMENT

Many people find the notion of God a difficult one to fathom. "Where is God when tragedy or injustice occurs?" they ask. Even religious people may feel the same way in times of deep emotion. Both the biblical prophet Jeremiah and the main protagonist of the book of Job felt this way. One metaphor to help us make sense of God's apparent absence is that of the "hiding of God's face." In Deuteronomy 31:18, it indicates a withdrawal of God's favor, but it frequently has a wider connotation, being used to suggest any sense of the absence of God.

The Otvotzker rebbe suggests a more playful explanation for the hiding of God's face. Perhaps, he opines, this is just God's way of encouraging us humans to seek God. If God were always and instantly accessible, perhaps we would take God for granted. Experiencing the presence of God requires dedication and effort on our part, effort expended in study, prayer, meditation, and good deeds.

Ha'azinu

[157] Without Knowing What We Say

"Give ear, O heavens, that I might speak, and let
the earth hear the words of my mouth."

Deuteronomy 32:1

CONTEXT

This chapter is entirely taken up with the Song of Moses, an enigmatic poem composed and recited by the greatest of the prophets shortly before his demise, and said to predict Israel's future. In this verse, Moses calls upon heaven and earth as if they were witnesses to his words.

Menachem Mendel of Rymanov was a disciple of Elimelech of Lyzhansk. The Ba'al Shem Tov is the founder of the Hasidic movement. Yitzchak Podvah is the editor of an anthology devoted primarily to recording the teachings of the Rymanover rebbe.

You might say, in accordance with what is known from the Ba'al Shem Tov, that, if you [really] want to pay attention, you would hear that every person speaks of the fear of the God, but without knowing what their mouth has said. Hence, "Give ear, O heavens, that I might speak"—that is, if you want to, [you could] hear words of the fear of heaven in what they say.

"And let the earth hear"—you could hear this even from people on a [purely] earthly plane.

Yitzchak Mordechai ben Yisra'el Aharon Podvah (1884–1942), ed., *Ilana deChayyei* [The tree of life] (Jerusalem, 1986), pt. 1, p. 111

NOTE

Hence, "Give ear, O heavens, that I might speak." The Rymanover interprets the verse to mean: "Give ear to the heavenly things that I speak."

Many people say "God bless you" when others sneeze, or "God willing" when others speak of their plans and hopes. My mother always used to say "amen" after anyone else expressed any sentiment or hope with which she agreed. When I was a child, my atheist grandmother used to invoke God whenever I fell over. People speak of God often without realizing what they are saying. Menachem Mendel is right: there is more awe of God around than we might appreciate. We, as religious people, should not be lecturing others on their apparent lack of thought in invoking God's name. Instead, we should be taking their unthinking interjections as reminders for us to deepen our awareness of God's presence in our lives.

---

[158] Forgetting God

*"You are unmindful of the God who bore you; you
forget the God who gave you birth."*

Deuteronomy 32:18

CONTEXT

After several verses depicting God's care for the People of Israel, Moses turns to their ingratitude in verses 15–18.

The Kotzker rebbe was always demanding ever more spirituality and honesty from his followers. He was no believer in easy options.

Meaning: God created you with the quality of forgetfulness in order that you may forget the vanities of this world, but in the end, on the contrary, "you forget the God who gave you birth."

Menachem Mendel of Kotzk (1787–1859), *Ohel Torah* [The tent of Torah] (Lublin, 1909), p. 33b

COMMENT

If everything has a purpose in this world, what is the purpose of forgetfulness? The Kotzker gives us an answer and then criticizes us for using the gift of forgetting in a sinful way. His point is that we were sent into this world by God with the power to be able to forget material things, to rise above them toward the life of the spirit, but instead we forget God who sent us and lose sight of the spirit. Our journey through life is a spiritual journey. We are sent here to learn how to live in God's world. Instead we live in our bodies and in our egos. Menachem Mendel was right to be angry.

---

[159] The Torah as Advice

"For it is not an empty thing from you; it is your life, and through this thing your days will be lengthened in the land that you are crossing the Jordan to inherit."

Deuteronomy 32:47

CONTEXT

In the closing verses of Ha'azinu, before God commands him to ascend Mount Nebo, where he will die, Moses encourages the Israelites once more to be faithful to God and to God's Torah.

Meshullam Feibush was a disciple of the Maggid of Mezritch, and thus a teacher of the third generation of the Hasidic movement.

For our entire Torah, the Written and the Oral, contains nothing, not even a single letter, that does not pertain to the service of the Eternal. It was given for that reason, and is called *torah* [teaching] because it teaches, as if it were saying: "this is the way; walk it!" [This applies] even to the laws of finance and other legislation that seem as if they have no practical significance. "If it is an empty thing, it is from you." But those who serve the Eternal wholeheartedly have secrets of Torah revealed to them. And these are those secrets: how to derive advice for the service of the Creator from all the 613 commandments, even those that are impossible to observe in themselves, like those that are dependent on being in the Land [of Israel] or other commandments. Hence, the Zohar's saying: "The 613 commandments?—The 613 kinds of advice." That is to say, they give human beings advice on how to adhere to the Creator.

Meshullam Feibush HaLevi Heller of Zbarazh (d. 1785), *Yosher Divrei Emet* [Upright words of truth (Ecclesiastes 12:10)] (Bnei Brak, 2004), §24, p. 108

"An empty thing from you." An overly literal translation, as required by the comment that follows. JPS: "For this is not a trifling thing for you."

That seem as if they have no practical significance. Many Torah laws do not apply in modern situations where Jewish courts have no jurisdiction. Our author affirms their spiritual significance.

"If it is an empty thing, it is from you." Jerusalem Talmud, *Pe'ah* 1:1. If it seems pointless, the fault lies not in the text, but in your attitude. The Jerusalem Talmud text reads: "Rabbi Mana said: 'For it is not an empty thing for from you'—if it is an empty thing, it is from you! And why? Because you did not labor in the Torah. 'For it is your life'—When? It is your life when you labor in it."

Hence, the Zohar's saying. Zohar II, 82b.

The 613 kinds of advice. This is not to suggest that the laws of the Torah might not have practical significance. Obviously a great many of them do.

COMMENT

Meshullam Feibush of Zbarazh lived in a community that still had the legal right granted by the state, at least up to a point, to enforce the Torah's laws as interpreted by the rabbis. He is concerned with those Torah laws that cannot be enforced, even in such communities, because they depend on there being a Temple in Jerusalem. Without the Temple and its sacrificial rituals, these laws fall into abeyance for all practical purposes. Yet we read them year after year in synagogues all over the world. According to Meshullam Feibush, even though they have no practical significance, they still contain clues for our personal service of God.

What are some of those clues? The laws of Torah help us appreciate that our tradition has a long and proud heritage, that hundreds of generations have devoted their lives to its preservation and development. Torah teaches respect for all creation and sets up an ideal of personal and communal life devoted to God. If only our devotion could match that of our pious ancestors!

Ve-zo't Ha-berakhah

---

[160] The Never-Recurring Now

"This is the blessing that Moses the man of God bestowed upon the descendants of Israel before his death."

Deuteronomy 33:1

CONTEXT

Shortly before his ascent of Mount Nebo, where he will depart this life, Moses blesses Israel in general and each of the tribes in turn.

Hayyim of Kosov succeeded his father as rabbi of the town, after studying with him and other teachers.

Rashi explains: "[He] was near death, so 'if not now, when.'" It seems to me that Rashi's intention here [was to say] that this was the source of the blessing that our teacher Moses bestowed: that each individual should consider each moment as [belonging] to the service of God, for no moment or hour will ever recur. Hence, "if not now, when."

Hayyim ben Menachem Mendel of Kosov (1795–1844), *Torat Hayyim* [The Torah of life] (Ordea, Rumania: 1927), p. 39b

NOTES

Rashi. The preeminent Bible commentator of the Middle Ages (1040–1105).
"If not now, when." Part of Hillel's saying in *Pirkei Avot* (Ethics of the Fathers) 1:14.

COMMENT

It is clear that the Torah only wishes to indicate that the blessing following this verse was spoken by Moses in his final moments, while Rashi is merely confirming that fact and suggesting Moses's awareness that his time was running out.

However, it is also clear that Rabbi Hayyim of Kosov is concerned with something else. He takes the view that Moses's blessing consisted of not only the words that follow, but also in his teaching that each unique moment should be dedicated to God. If we can live in the full consciousness of this truth, that God is present in every moment and that every moment presents us with new opportunities to serve God, then we will be truly blessed. And after all, isn't every moment we live "before" our death?

---

[161] Business and Study

"And to Zebulun he said: 'Be happy Zebulun when
you go out and Issachar in your tents.'"
Deuteronomy 33:18

CONTEXT

For the most part, Moses blesses the twelve tribes one by one throughout this chapter. Zebulun and Issachar are unique among Jacob's sons in being mentioned together. (In v. 17, Ephraim and Manasseh appear together, but they are both sons of Joseph and grandsons rather than sons of Jacob, and they frequently appear as a pair. See Genesis 48.)

Hayyim ibn Attar was a Moroccan kabbalist and author of a Torah commentary that is popular to this day in traditional communities.

Even though, in general, you should not rejoice over the things of this world, as it is written, "And as for joy, what does it achieve?" (Ecclesiastes 2:2), the prophet [Moses] said that Zebulun would have joy even when he went out of the house of study for business, and the reason is [that he went out to business] in order to sustain Issachar in his [Zebulun's] tents, as it says: "And Issachar in your tents."

Moreover, it means [that] although [normally] when you go out to business you do not know if you will be successful until you have returned, Zebulun is told: "Be happy" because you will certainly be successful. And the reason is that since Issachar is in his tents, you are an agent [doing] a mitzvah by sustaining those who study the Torah.

Hence, Issachar's tent is mentioned in relation to Zebulun because he is the builder of the tent [in which Issachar dwells].

Alternatively, it could be [that] "in your tents" relates to Issachar, and [Scripture] uses the word "tents" for two reasons:

One is that they should not make this world the essential thing, but merely a temporary dwelling, whereas their essential home is in the House of Eternity.

The second is that this refers to the One who makes a "tent" over them, namely the Shechinah [the Presence of God], which is a called a "tent." Even though some may engage in business, of them it is said: "Righteousness shall go before them" (Psalm 85:14).

Hayyim ben Moshe ibn Attar (1696–1743), *Or HaHayyim* [The light of life] (Jerusalem: A. Blum, 1994), pt. 5, pp. 111–12

NOTES

Sustaining those who study the Torah. This view of the relationship between Issachar and Zebulun derives from an ancient midrash (Sifre, Devarim §354; *Bereshit Rabbah* 99:9) that depicts Zebulun as an entrepreneur "going out" to make money to support the scholarly Issachar in the house of study ("tents").

House of Eternity. Meaning "life beyond death."

"Righteousness shall go before them." Righteousness (*tzedek*) is a cipher for Malchut (Sovereignty, but also known as the Shechinah). By devoting himself to study of Torah, Issachar dwells within God's tent, the Shechinah.

COMMENT

We each have our own unique gifts. Some people may be talented in business like Zebulun or scholars like Issachar. Others may possess exceptional craft or artistic skills, conceptual abilities, mechanical ingenuity, or a deep sense of caring. But whatever our gifts, like these two brothers we all have within us the capacity to help each other on our life's journey, to make the world a more civilized place. And whatever our gifts, we have a right to be happy, provided that we are using those gifts for the positive benefit of others, provided that we are "builders" on behalf of others.

And as we do our work and strive to fulfill the potential of our gifts, we may be both comforted and inspired by two thoughts:

First, that this material world is not permanent. We are spiritual beings passing through a physical universe. Whatever we do here, we must take neither our triumphs nor our defeats as final. They are only stepping-stones to further growth before we return to our true home.

Second, watching over all we do is the divine Presence, a Presence of love, strength, and righteousness. We have the obligation to use our precious God-given skills as best we can; the results of our labors rest with God.

---

[162] Returning to the Beginning

"And for all the great might and awesome deeds that Moses did before all Israel."

Deuteronomy 34:12

CONTEXT

As Moses leaves the world and the Torah comes to its conclusion, the text reminds us of the crucial role played in Israel's history by the greatest of the prophets. Ve-zo't Ha-berakhah is the final portion of the Torah, and as such is read only on the festival of Simchat Torah at the close of Sukkot. This reading is followed almost immediately by the opening section of Genesis that describes the act of Creation (Genesis 1:1–2:3). In many communities, it is customary to place the two scrolls from which these portions have been recited side by side on the *bimah* (reading desk) to make the connection between them more ritually explicit.

Moshe Hayyim Efraim of Sudylkov was the scholarly grandson of the Ba'al Shem Tov. Though he had few followers of his own, his book became, and remains, a Hasidic classic.

One might say that by joining the end of the Torah, *Yisra'el* ["Israel"], with the beginning, *B'reishit* ["In the beginning"; Genesis 1:1], [we could learn] how everyone should begin to study the Torah. It follows along the lines of "If there is no awe, there is no wisdom." Look here, *YiSRa'eL* [Israel] contains the letters of *YeRe'* [awe] [and] *SHaL,* where *SHaL* indicates *SHaLem* [perfect], as in *YeRUSHaLaYiM* [Jerusalem]. That is, when you have perfect awe, that is, internal awe, then you will become a vessel for the aspect of Hochmah [Wisdom], and with it, you will enter the aspect of *B'reishit*, that is, Hochmah, which means the entire Torah. Thus, we begin the Torah with *B'reishit*. And the enlightened will understand.

Moshe Hayyim Efraim of Sudylkov (d. 1800), *Degel Machaneh Efraim* [The flag of the camp of Ephraim (Numbers 2:18)] (Jerusalem, 1963), p. 270

NOTES

"If there is no awe, there is no wisdom." *Pirkei Avot* 3:17.

SHaL **indicates** *SHaLem*. The Sudylkover takes *SHaL* as an abbreviation for *SHaLem*. Hence, *Yisra'el* means "perfect awe."

YeRUSHaLaYiM **[Jerusalem]**. Our author suggests we divide the word into *YeRU* (as if it came from the root meaning "to fear, be in awe") and *SHaLaYiM*, as if from *shalem* (perfect), so that *Yerushalayim* also comes to mean "perfect awe."

The aspect of *B'reishit*, **that is, Hochmah**. The term *reishit* (beginning) represents the *sefirah* of Hochmah (Wisdom), based on the phrase "the beginning [is] wisdom" (Psalm 111:19; Proverbs 4:7). The Targum Yerushalmi (a free ancient Aramaic "translation" of the Torah incorporating many midrashim) renders the opening verse of Genesis: "With wisdom did the Eternal create the heavens and the earth."

Hochmah, which means the entire Torah. The midrash *Bereshit Rabbah* 44:17 states: "Torah is the unripe fruit of the supernal wisdom"; and supernal wisdom is identified with the *sefirah* of Hochmah in the kabbalistic tradition.

COMMENT

Torah study requires humility if it is to lead to wisdom. If you are not humble, you will not acknowledge that you have anything to learn; therefore, you will not learn. But humility is also a requirement for teachers: the humble teacher acknowledges that he or she does not know everything, that even students may teach their teachers. There is no end to Torah because there is no end to wisdom. Ultimately, wisdom is divine, and the divine is infinite.

פרשת בראשית

[1]   כשחזר רבי לייבלי אייגר מקוצק שאלו אביו רבי שלמה: מה למדת בקוצק.

השיב למדתי שלשה דברים: א) שאדם הוא אדם ומלאך הוא מלאך. ב) אם ירצה

האדם יוכל להיות יותר ממלאך. ג) "בראשית ברא אלקים" הקב״ה ברא רק את

הראשית ואת השאר השאיר בשביל האדם.

ר׳ מנחם מענדל מקאצק, ס׳ עמוד האמת, דף י״א.

[2]   ע״כ יעזב איש את אר״א ודבק באשתו והי׳ לבשר אחד. יתבאר ע״ד אומרם ז״ל

ג׳ שותפין באדם הקב״ה ואביו ואמו לזה אה״כ ע״כ יעזב איש את אר״א יעזוב הנאת

הגופניות ודבק באשתו רק ידבק בהשכינה ואשתו הוא ר״ת א׳ שפתי תפתח שהוא קאי

על השכינה...

ר׳ מנחם מענדל מרימנאוו, ס׳ אילנא דחיי, חלק א׳ דף 10.

[3]   ויתהלך חנוך את האלהים וגו׳, אמרו רבותינו ז״ל (הובא בילקוט ראובני בשם

עשרה מאמרות) חנוך תופר מנעלים היה ועל כל תפירה ותפירה היה מייחד קודשא

בריך הוא ושכינתיה ע״ש. שמעתי בשם מורי פירוש הפסוק (קהלת ט׳) כל אשר תמצא

ידך לעשות בכחך עשה כי אין בשאול דעת וחשבון כו׳. כי ענין מט״ט שהיה מייחד

קודשא בריך הוא ושכינתיה אל כל תפירה וכו׳. הוא כך. דמחשבה נקרא אין סוף

הוי״ה, והמעשה הוא אדנ״י. וכאשר מחבר המעשה עם המחשבה, בעת עשיית המעשה,

נקרא יחוד קודשא בריך הוא ושכינתיה, וזהו שאמר כל אשר תמצא ידך לעשות

בכח״ך עשה. רצונו לומר כי המחשבה נקרא חכמה כח מה, ותעשה המעשה בכחך

שהוא המחשבה לחבר שניהם שהוא יחוד קודשא בריך הוא ושכינתיה...

ס׳ הבעש״ט, כרך א׳ דפ׳ ק״ז-ק״ט.

פרשת נח

[4]   אמר בלשונו הקדוש לשעבר הי׳ ר״ת של ׳חכמה׳ חילו מלפניו כל הארץ.

ועכשיו בעוה״ר הר״ת של חכמה כי מלאה הארץ חמס.

ר׳ חיים מקראסנע, בס׳ בית פנחס, דף 19.

[5]   מה השיב הקב״ה לנח כשיצא מן התיבה וראה את העולם חרב והתחיל לבכות

לפניו ואמר רבונו של עולם נקראת רחום היה לך לרחם על בריותיך וכו׳ השיבו

הקב״ה ואמר רעיא שטיא השתא אמרת דא. למה לא אמרת בשעתא דאמרית לך כי

אותך ראיתי צדיק לפני וגו׳ ואח״כ הנני מביא את המבול מים ואח״כ עשה לך תיבת

עצי גופר כל האי אתעכבית ואמרית לך בגין דתבעי רחמין על עלמא. ומכדין שמעתא

דתשתזיב בתיבותא לא עאל בלבך למבעי רחמין על ישובא דעלמא ועבדת תיבותא

ואשתזיבת וכען דאתאביד עלמא פתחת פומך למללא קדמי בעיין ותחנונים. כיון דחזא

נח כך אקריב קרבנין ועלוון דכתיב (בראשית ח) ויקח מכל הבהמה הטהורה ומכל

העוף הטהור וגו׳.

ס׳ הזהר, סתרי תורה, חלק א׳ דף רנ״ד עמוד ב׳ (השמטות סימן י״ב).

[6]   ונטיעת כרם לנח ואמרם בו ביום שנטעו. בו ביום שתה מיינו. ובו ביום גלה

ערותו. הוא שהיין הוא יינו של תורה וביום שאדם נוטע שרשו מיד שותה ומתגלת

ערותו בחכמתו והיא ערות מציאות וערות מהותו. שאז ידע שאמתת מהותו משגל והוא

ראשית מציאותו והוא בעצמו טפה סרוחה שכבת זרע מינים. והוא איש הוה בשעתו

ונפסד לשעתו ואילו חיה אלף שנים פעמים הנה מאין בא עם היותו יש מיש ולאין הולך

עם היות כל חלק מחלקיו יש אבל לא לעצמו בסוף.

ר׳ אברהם אבולעפיה, ס׳ מפתח החכמות, דף נ״ט.

פרשת לך-לך

[7]   אח״כ אמר. לך לך. לעצמך. פירוש צריך כ״א לנסות את עצמו להטיב את

דרכיו. עוד יש כונה אחרת בפסוק זה כנודע למבין. פי׳ דצריך אדם לרגוש בעצמו

באיזה מדריגה הוא עומד. ואין (אצ״ל ושאין) עושה כלום.

ר׳ שמחה בונם מפשיסחא בס׳ שיח שרפי קודש מאת ר׳ יועץ קים קדיש ראקאץ.

חלק א׳ דף 20.

[8]   קום התהלך בארץ. ע״ד הפשט רצה הקב״ה שיהיה אברהם מחזיק בארץ

הקדושה אשר יתן לו ולזרעו מעתה ואמר שיתהלך בה לארכה ולרחבה כאדם הנותן

לחברו קרקע במתנה ומראה לו מצריו ואומר לו שיחזיק בה.

וע״ד השכל מלת התהלכות נזכרת אצל החכמה. כענין שכתוב (משלי ו)

בהתהלכך תנחה אותך... היא צורת הנפש השכלית ולא נזכרה כי אם ביחידי הצדיקים

מחפשי החכמה, כנח וחנוך ואברהם וכיוצא בהם.

ולפי שאברהם העתיק שכלו בחפוש החכמות ממדרנה למדרנה, ומסיע נפש

השכלית הלוך ונסוע בהשגת העניין הכולל הנגבה, א״ל הש״י קום התהלך בארץ.

כלומר נענע צורת שכלך בדרישת הנמצאים שבארץ. כי לא מצינו שהלך אברהם את

הארץ לארכה ולרחבה כמו שא״ל השי״ת. אבל מצינו בו שישב ולא הלך. הוא שכתוב

ויאהל אברם ויבא וישב. ועל כל פנים ההלוך הזה הוא תנועת הנפש השכלית והשקט

הגוף. וזהו ויאהל מלשון יושב אוהלים. כי דרישת החכמות צריך תנועת הנפש השכלית

והשקט הגוף. בהפך מצרכי הגוף שהם צריכים נענוע הגוף והשקט הנפש. ואמר כי לך

אתננה אתן לך דעת וחכמה לדעת מהות הנמצאים. כענין שכתוב (מלכים א ה) וה׳ נתן

חכמה לשלמה.

רבנו בחיי, פירוש על התורה, חלק א׳ דף ע״ח.

[9]   התהלך לפני והיה תמים (בראשית יז א). להבין הענין לפני. הנה לפי פשוטו

היינו בחינת מקיף. שיאמין באמונה שלימה שאור אין סוף ברוך הוא מקיפו ומסבבו

מכל צד. בחינת ממלא כל עלמין וסובב כל עלמין (זח״ב רכה.) וכמאמר הכתוב

(תהלים לב י) והבוטח בה׳ חסד יסובבנו. ובהיות כן כביכול הוא הולך לפני ה׳. ואז

על ידי כן והיה תמים. אף שלפעמים נופך ונשבר. אף על פי כן כשמתמיד באמונה זו

חוזר ונעשה תמים ושלם.

ר׳ מרדכי מטשערנאביל. ס׳ ליקוטי תורה. דף נ״א.

פרשת וירא

[10]   המכסה אני מאברהם וגו׳. אין שום פעולה משמים בעולם שלא יהיה בה מדת

החסד. ואפילו בימי עברה ודין ר״ל. וכן בהיפכת סדום היה חסד מה שהציל את לוט.

וזהו שכתוב המכסה אני מאברהם, היינו מדת אברהם שהיא מדת חסד, אשר אני עושה,

כי לא תתכן שום עשיה מבלי שתהיה בה ממדת החסד.

ר׳ יצחק מוואָרקה, ס׳ בית יצחק, דף י״א.

[11]   ... וכן אמר הרב לאדם אחד שהי׳ ירא מפריץ אמר אל תירא ממנו ואני מזהירך

שלא תירא. כמ״ש בירמיהו אל תחת, כי כשהאדם אינו ירא מהדבר אז הוא למעלה

מהדבר משא״כ כשהוא ירא מהדבר אז הדבר גבוה ממנו ואז באמת יש לו לירא. ע״כ.

וזה שאומרים העולם. יש לי מורא מהמורא, והבן, וזה [שאמר לאבימלך] כי אמרתי רק

אין יראת וגו׳ דכיון שבא בלבו יראה רעה, מזו מוכרח שאין יראת ה׳ במקום זה,

והמקום גורם שמתבלבל המוח במחשבות זרות.

ר׳ פנחס מקאריץ, ס׳ אמרי פנחס. סימן י׳ דף כ׳.

[12]   גם שמעתי על פסוק ״וישמע אלקים אל קול הנער״ (כי לא נמצא בתורה

שישמעאל הי׳ צועק ואמר איזה דיבור כלל) ואמר בזה״ל א שטיל שווייגענדיג נישרייַ

(ובאמת הוא בעצמו הי׳ במדרגה זאת שעשה תמיד בשתיקה קולי קולות להשי״ת בלי

הפסק).

ר׳ מנחם מענדל מוואָרקה, בס׳ גדולת מרדכי וגדולת הצדיקים, חלק ב׳ דף 18

סימן מ״ה.

פרשת חיי שרה

[13]   ... וה׳ ברך את אברהם בכל כי יש צדיק אשר כל מבוקשו בשביל הכלל ויש

צדיק אשר מבוקשו על עצמו ואברהם היה מבוקשו על הכלל וזהו וה׳ ברך את

אברהם כלומר עם אברהם בכל כי את הוא כמו עם ברך ה' אותו בכל כאשר היה

מבוקשתו וזהו שרמזו רז"ל בת הי' לאברהם אבינו ובכל שמה כי בת הוא לשון מדה

כנאמר אלפים בת יכיל כלומר מדתו הי' בכל שמה שהשפיע על הכל.

ר' לוי יצחק מברדיטשוב. ס' קדושת לוי. דף י"ב עמוד ג'.

[14] ...דהנה יש חילוק בין מדת חסד לרחמים. דרחמים הוא כאשר מבקש אחד

מחבירו על איזה דבר החסר לו והוא מרחם עליו ונותן לו מבוקשו. מה שאין כן מדת

החסד הוא לחסד עם חבירו גם בדבר שלא לא ביקש ממנו... בעניין העבד עם רבקה

שעשה לעצמו סימן כשהנערה תתן לו מה שלא ביקש ממנה, דהיינו באומרה (בראשית

כד מד) גם לגמליך אשאב היא האשה אשר הוכיח ה' לבן אדוני ראויה ליכנס בביתו

של אברהם איש החסד...

ר' צבי אלימלך מדינוב. ס' בני יששכר, כרך א' דף נ"א עמוד ב'.

[15] ויצחק בא מבוא באר לחי רואי. י"ל בדרך רמז ע"ד דאיתא בריש ש"ע או"ח

שויתי ה' לנגדי תמיד זה כלל גדול בתורה וכו' ויחשוב האדם כאילו יושב לפני המלך

כי מלא כל הארץ כבודו והש"י רואה במעשיו וכו' ומזה ימלה יראה ע"ש וי"ל שזה

מרומז כאן בפסוק ויצחק היינו בחינת יראה שהוא בחינת יצחק בא לאדם מבאר היינו

מאותו נביעו לחי רואי שהוא מסתכל תמיד שלפני חי עולמים הוא עומד ורואה ומשגיח

עליו על כל תנועותיו ומעשיו ועסקיו מזה הנביעו נובע לו יראה והכנעה כנ"ל והבן.

ר' משה חיים אפרים מסדילקוב. ס' דגל מחנה אפרים, דף ל"ג.

פרשת תולדות

[16] ויקראו שמו עשו וכו' יש להבין זה השינוי שאצל עשו נאמר ויקראו ואצל יעקב

נאמר ויקרא שמו יעקב לשון יחיד ודרשת חז"ל ידוע [ב"ר סג. יב] וי"ל דרך רמז ע"ד

המדרש הנ"ל שעשו הוא שוא ושקר והוא מרמז הפסוק ויקראו לשון המשכה ואסיפה

היינו שרוב המון נמשכים אחר השקר והשוא אבל אצל יעקב שהוא מדת אמת ע"ד תתן

אמת ליעקב [מיכה ז, כ] כתב ויקרא לשון יחיד והיינו מחמת שזה המעט מן המעט והוא

אחד בעיר שמקרב עצמו אל האמת.

עוד י"ל מחמת שהשקר הוא הפרידה ע"ד ונרגן מפריד אלוף היינו אחד לכך

נכתב ויקראו שהוא בפירוד שקר הנקרא עשו כנ"ל שהוא גורם פירוד ח"ו ואמת הוא

להיפוך שמקשר ומייחד באחדות גמור לכך נכתב אצל יעקב שהוא אמת ויקרא לשון

יחיד.

או י"ל ויקרא שמו יעקב שהוא מרמז ויקרא שמו של הקב"ה היינו מי הוא

שיכול לקרוא הש"י ב"ה. יעקב היינו מי שהוא ממדריגת אמת כמ"ש [תהלים קמה, יח]

קרוב ה' וכו' לכל אשר יקראוהו באמת והבן.

ר' משה חיים אפרים מסדילקוב. ס' דגל מחנה אפרים. דף ל"ו.

[17] וכל הבארות אשר חפרו וגו' סתמום פלשתים וגו' נראה [פירושו] דהנה כל דרך

שעושין להשם צריך להיות בו חיות פנימי. ואם אין בו חיות פנימי אינו עושה למעלה.

והנה פלשתים רצו ללכת בדרכי אברהם אבינו ע"ה והיו עושים כמו שהיה א"א עושה

רק שלא היה בו חיות פנימי וזה היה סתימת הדרך הזה והבן. ויצחק אבינו רצה

לחפור הבאר הזה אף שהיה לו דרכים לה' מצד עצמו אעפ"כ לא נמנע מלחפור באר

אביו כמ״ש. ואח״כ חפר הוא עצמו בארות דהנה כל איש הישראלי הנגש לעבודת השם

ב״ה צריך שיחפור בעצמותו באר אשר על [ידו] יוכל להתדבק בבוראו יתברך

ויתעלה. ומתחלה הבאר הזה אינו בשלימות מצד עצמו כי עדיין מעורב בטוב וברע

מצד עצמו וזה נקרא עשק כי התעסקו עמו. ואח״כ כשהולך מזה המדריגה שאין לו

[מניעה] מצד עצמו אזי הוא במדריגת שטנה שהשטן עומד לנגדו ומבלבלו. ואח״כ הוא

במדריגת רחבה ונקרא רחובות כמאמר הכתוב (משלי טז) ברצות ה׳ דרכי [איש] גם

אויביו ישלים אותו. וזה סוד הבארות.

ר׳ שמחה בונם מפשיסחא, ס׳ מדרש שמחה, כרך א׳ דף ל׳.

[18]   וילך עשו אל ישמעאל ויקח את מחלת וכו׳. איתא במדרש [בראשית רבה פרשה

ס״ז,י״ג] מחלת מכאן שמחל לו הקב״ה על כל עונותיו. הענין בזה כי עשו היה אופיו

רציחה ואופיו של ישמעאל הוא ניאוף, והנה כל החסרונות הנמצאות בעולם יש בהם

צד טוב. כגון שורש הכעס אף שהוא רע מ״מ נמצא בו צד טוב כי יכעוס גם על עוברי

רצון השי״ת. ושורש הניאוף שהוא רע מ״מ נמצא בו צד טוב. כי חסרון הניאוף הוא

שמטיב במקום שאין רצון השי״ת ונמצא בו צד טוב כי לטובים מותר להיטיב...

ר׳ מרדכי ליינר מאיזביצ׳א, ס׳ מי השלוח, כרך א׳ דפ׳ ל״ז-ל״ח.

פרשת ויצא

[19]   והנה האדם הוא סולם מצב ארצה וראשו מגיע השמימה, רצה לומר גוף האדם

לקח הקב״ה האדמה ממקום מזבח האדמה כדי שיתקדש. וראשו דהיינו הנשמה היא

מרום המעלות...

ר׳ ישעיה הורוויץ, ס׳ שני לוחות הברית, בית הגדול, כרך א׳ דף כ״ז עמוד ב׳.

[20]   ...והוא סוד הפסוק ועיני לאה רכות ורחל היתה יפת תאר ויפת מראה ולא נזכר
עיינין לכן היא נקראת עולמתא שפרתא דלית לה עיינין וצריכים אנחנו עבדיה לעשות
לה עינים בכוונותינו והחידה הזאת נזכרת בריש סבא פ׳ משפטים ורבי יוסי ע״ה תמה
מאוד על החידה הזאת וחשב שאין זה אלא מילי דעלמא ח״ו וכמעט שלא נענש וממש
זה הסוד...

נפתלי הירץ בן יעקב אלחנן בכרך, ס׳ עמק המלך, דף קנ״ד עמוד א׳.

[21]   אמר, האדם צריך להיות בכל עת בבחינת רצוא ושוב. וסיפר: פעם אחת הלך
בעל צבא אחד על משמרתו לפני פתח שר הצבא בליל החורף, כמנהג מלכים ושרים
נכבדים שהולכים לפני פתחיהם תמיד. ואמר הבעל צבא לעצמו אני איני בר מזל כלל
כי ביום אכלני חורב וקרח בלילה ותדד שנתי מעיני (בראשית ל׳א מ׳), הלא אם אהיה
בהתמנות יותר גדולה קצת מנוחה יהיה לי על כל פנים במקצת ענינים.

ואחר כך חזר וניחם מדבריו, כי ראה והבין שיש עוד יותר חסרונות בהתמנות זו
אשר הוא יותר גדולה קצת, וכן הלך בכל שעה ממדריגה למדריגה יותר גדולה ולא
מצא מנוחה לנפשו רק אם יהיה בעצמו מלך אז יהיה לו מנוחה שלימה. ואחר כך חזר
גם מדבר זה ומצא עוד יותר ויותר חסרונות ודאגות, ועל ידי זה בחר לעצמו היותר
טוב לפניו להיות אחד מבעלי הצבא הפשוטים שבפשוטים ובבחינה זו ממש צריך
האיש ישראל להיות רצוא ושוב בכל עת ובכל רגע ורגע.

ר׳ אורי השרף מסרעליסק, ס׳ אמרי קדוש, דפ׳ נ״ט-ס׳.

[22]   וישלח יעקב מלאכים לפניו אל עשו אחיו ארצה שעיר שדה אדום וכו׳. הנה ע״פ

דאיתא שאחשורוש נקרא הקב״ה ופשיטא שנוכל לומר עש״ו נקרא הקב״ה. כי הוא לבדו

עשה ועושה ויעשה לכל המעשים. וז״ש וישלח יעקב מלאכים אל עשו אחיו. כי בכל יום

צריך אדם להתפלל לפני הקב״ה. ואל יאמר כבר התפללתי אתמול. רק שבכל יום

יהיו בעיניך כחדשים. והתפלות נקראים מלאכים כי מכל דיבור ודיבור שיוצא מפי

צדיק, נברא מלאך. ושולח אותם להקב״ה.

ר׳ אהרן (השני) מקארלין, ס׳ בית אהרן, דף 21.

[23]   ויבן לו בית ולמקנהו עשה סוכות. עבודתו של האדם היא לתקן א״ע בחלק

הנפש שבו. הגם שצרכי עוה״ז נצרכים לאדם שבלא זה א״א לקיים את חלק הנפש. מ״מ

עיקר עבודתו הוא לראות לתקן את הנפש. וע״י מצוות ומעש״ט בונה הוא לנפש בתים

ובנינים נאים. וזהו הנרמז בפסוק ויבן לו בית, היינו שעשה לעצמו בית שהוא העיקר.

ולמקנהו, היינו עניני עוה״ז שהם טפלים, עשה סוכות.

ר׳ שלום רוקח (שר שלום) מבעלזא, ס׳ מהר״ש מבעלזא, חלק א׳ דף רי״ט.

[24]   כי חפץ בבת יעקב איתא במד״ר שחשב הקב״ה את ישראל בדביקה וחשוקה

וחפיצה, דביקה כ״ש ואתם דבקים בה׳ חשיקה רק בה׳ חשק ה׳ באבותיך חפיצה מארץ

חפץ. מפרשה של אותו רשע נלמוד כמה צריך לעבוד השם ית׳ בחשיקה וחפיצה

ודביקות ולמסור נפשו להשם יתברך כמו שמסר אותו רשע נפשו על תאותו...

ר׳ חיים מקאסוב, ס׳ תורת חיים, דפ׳ 9-10.

[25]   והוא נער. כי הוא בכל פעם בבחי׳ נע״ר. נער הייתי גם זקנתי. וצריך להתחדש

בכל פעם כמו שכתוב תתחדש כנשר נעוריכי. ולכך נמשלו ישראל כלבנה שהיא

מתחדשת בכל פעם כמו שאנו אומרים שתתחדש עטרת תפארת לעמוסי בטן. ומהו ענין

החידוש שנתמעט אורה בכדי שתתחדש אח״כ ביתר שאת. ועבודת האדם הוא ג״כ על

דרך זה. כי לאחר שעבר היום והוא חושב מה הוא ומה בעובדות חדשות ומלחמת

היצר מחדש כאלו לא עשה עד הנה כלום. ובתוך הדברים סיפר המעשה מר׳ סעדי׳

גאון ז״ל שמתאחרה אצל בעל הבית אחד כו׳. ומאז עשה בכל יום תשובה על יום שלפניו

וזאת תורת האדם בכל יום עד עת קץ. וזהו והוא נע״ר. וסיים בשם אביו זצוק״ל.

ר׳ אהרן (השני) מקארלין, ס׳ בית אהרן, דף 76.

[26]   וישלחו את כתונת הפסים ויביאו אל אביהם. א״ר יהודה בנין ההיא חרדה

דחרד יעקב ליצחק אתעניש יעקב במעשה דיוסף דחרד בההוא שעתא חרדה גדולה.

ואמרו זאת מצאנו. יצחק מי אפוא נתענש יעקב דכתיב איפה הם רעים. ותמן

יוסף מעניש. (זוהר פ׳ תולדות ע׳ תי״ז).

ר׳ ראובן האשקי, ס׳ ילקוט ראובני, חלק א׳ דפ׳ 310-311.

[27]   ויהי ה׳ את יוסף ויהי איש מצליח ויהי בבית אדניו המצרי (לט. ב). רצה לומר.

שעמד בשני הנסיונות שהיה ה׳ עמו כלומר בקרב לבו. בין בעת שהיה בבחינת איש

מצליח ברום המעלה. בין בעת שהיה בבית אדניו המצרי בשפל המדרגה.

ר׳ שמחה בונם מפשיסחא. ס׳ מדרש שמחה, כרך א׳ דף ס״ו.

[28]   ויהי מקץ שנתים ימים ופרעה חולם והנה עומד על היאור על זה אמר כ״ק מהר׳

 וש״ב הגה״ק מפרשיסחא זצ״ל זכותו יגן עלינו בזהל״ק יעדערער יוד זאל מאכען א

ענדע צו די פערשלאפענע יאהרען נאר צו טוהען אלעס בהתגלות וואכענדיג דאס

הייסט תשובה און זיך אבשטעלען ביי דעם ליכטיגקייט עומד על היאור נר מצוה

ותורה אור עכל״ק ודפח״ח והמב״י.

יועץ קים קדיש ראקאץ. ס׳ שיח שרפי קודש. חלק ג׳ דף 128.

[29]   בראשית באורייתא שנקראת (משלי ח׳ כ״ב) ראשית דרכו ברא קוב״ה עלמא.

נמצא כל העולמות נבראו ע״י התורה. וכח הפועל בנפעל. א״כ בכל העולמות ובכל

דבר ודבר כח התורה בהם. שהיא כח הפועל. וכדכתיב (במדבר י״ז י״ד) זאת

התורה אדם. שהאדם הוא התורה כאשר ית׳ למטה. ואורייתא וקוב״ה חד. נמצא חיות

הקב״ה בכל דבר. כדכתיב (נחמי׳ ט׳ ו) ואתה מחי׳ את כולם. וצמצם כביכול עד

מדרגה התחתונה. והושם חלק אלוה ממעל תוך משכן החומר. כי כל עיקר תענוג הוא

כביכול שיתעלו מדרגות תחתונות למעלה, כי יתרון האור מן החושך וגו׳ (קהלת ב׳

י״ג):

והוא ענין ירידת יוסף במצריי״ם. במצ״ר י״ם המדרגה התחתונה. והענין שכבר

אמרנו שהכל נברא ע״י התורה. וכח הפועל בנפעל. ובכ״ד יש בו אותיות התורה

המהווים ומחיים. ובלתי זה היו אפס ותוהו. ובאמת אמרו (ב״ר פ׳ מ״ד) נובלות

החכמה שלמעלה תורה. שיש תורה שהיא נובלות:

וזהו (בראשית מ״ב א׳ ב׳) וירא יעקב כי יש שבר במצרים. שראה ששם

במצרים יש תורה שבורה שהיא נובלות כאמור. ויאמר גו׳ רדו שמה, שירדו שם לתקן

ולהעלות ולהביא אל החיות העצמי. וזהו ונחי׳ גו׳...

ר׳ מנחם מענדל מוויטעפסק, ס׳ לקוטי אמרים. דף מ׳ עמוד ב׳.

[30]   ואתם עלו לשלום אל אביכם. ואתם הוא אותיות אמת ע״י אמת יעלה ויגיע

לעשות רצון אביו שבשמים וכמ״ש רבינו הק׳ זצ״ל מלובלין שחביב עליו הרשע שיודע

שהוא רשע מהצדיק שיודע שהוא צדיק כי הרשע שיודע שהוא רשע דבוק באמת וע״כ

דבוק עם השי״ת שחותמו אמת אבל הצדיק שיודע שהוא צדיק אינו דבוק באמת כי כ׳

אין צדיק בארץ וע״כ הוא דבוק בשקר ששנואי להקב״ה כמ״ש דובר שקרים לא יכון

לנגד עיני יען שהוא נגדו ית׳ שחותמו אמת ואמת הוא סמא דכולא בי׳ שאין לך מדה

טובה הימנה. (בשם הק׳ משפאלע זי״ע).

יצחק מרדכי פאדוואה. ס׳ אילנא דחיי, חלק א׳ דף 29-30.

פרשת ויגש

[31]   במדרש ויגש אליו יהודה אין הגשה אלא למלחמה אין הגשה אלא [לפיוס] ואין

הגשה אלא לתפלה ע״ש. מפרשי התורה הקשו הא יהודה היה עומד עם יוסף ומדבר

עמו [ויוסף] אמר לו ואתם וגו׳ ומה זה הלשון ויגש. אכן נראה דהתפלה היא מקובלת

דווקא אם היא מעומק הלב ועצמות הנפש הוא מתפלל אז התפלה הזאת רצויה וגם

לענין מלחמה צריך לעורר עצמו עם פנימיותיו ללחום עם שכנגדו וכן לפיוס וד״ל.

וזה ויגש אליו יהודה שיהודה נגש אל עצמותיו ועפ״ז נתבאר המדרש עי״ש ודו״ק.

ר׳ שמחה בונם מפשיסחא, ס׳ מדרש שמחה, כרך א׳ דף נ״א.

[32] והקל נשמע בית פרעה... מאן דצלי צלותיה קמי מאריה. אצטריך ליה דלא
למשמע קליה בצלותיה. ומאן דאשמע קליה בצלותיה. צלותיה לא אשתמע. מאי
טעמא. בנין דצלותא לאו איהי ההיא קלא דאשתמע. דההוא קול דאשתמע לאו היא
צלותא. ומאן איהי צלותא דא קלא אחרא דתליא בקלא דאשתמע. ומאן הוא קלא
דאשתמע. דא ההוא קול דהוא בוא״ו. קלא דתליא ביה דא ההוא קל בלא וא״ו. ובנין
כך לא אצטריך ליה לבר נש למשמע קליה בצלותיה. אלא לצלאה בלחש בההוא
קלא דלא אשתמע. ודא היא צלותא דאתקבלת תדיר. וסימנך והקל נשמע. קל בלא
וא״ו נשמע. דא היא צלותא דהיא בחשאי. דכתיב בחנה (ש״א א יג) וקולה לא ישמע.
דא היא צלותא דקב״ה קביל. כד אתעביד גו רעותא וכוונה ותקונא כדקא יאות.
וליחדא יחודא דמריה כדקא יאות בכל יומא.

ס׳ הזהר, כרך א׳ ר״ט עמוד ב׳ - ר״י עמוד א׳.

[33] ויאמר אלקים לישראל במראות הלילה ויאמר יעקב כו׳. וקשה למה פתח
בישראל וסיים אח״כ ביעקב. אך נוכל לומר שכך הוא פי׳ הפסוק. ויאמר אלקים
לישראל היינו אם תעלה למעלת בחינת ישראל שהוא גבוה מאד אל יבא לך גדלות
מזה, רק תזכור שאתה יעקב בחינה קטנה. וזהו ויאמר יעקב. וגם מסיפא לרישא מדרש.
בעת שאתה בבחינת יעקב היינו בקטנות אל תהי׳ מזה בעצבות, רק אדרבה תזכור
שתוכל להעלות לבחי׳ ישראל בתשובה ומעש״ט ותתחזק יותר ויותר וד״ל. וזה ענין
הכרחי לעבודת השי״ת במעלות החסידות.

ר׳ אהרן מקארלין (השני). ס׳ בית אהרן, דף 110.

פרשת ויחי

[34]   ויקרבו ימי ישראל למות... וע״ד הפשט מה שהזכיר ישראל ולא אמר ימי יעקב

כמו שאמר בתחלה ויחי ויהי ימי יעקב. מעת שקראו הקב״ה בשם ישראל ואמר

לו (בראשית לב) לא יעקב יאמר עוד שמך כי אם ישראל. הפרשיות נוהגות כמנהג הזה

לקרותו פעם ישראל פעם יעקב. כי מה שאמר לא יעקב יאמר עוד שמך כי אם ישראל.

אין זה מניעה אלא שיהיה שם ישראל עיקר ושם יעקב טפל לו...

וע״ד השכל מה שהזכירו הכתובים בפרשה זו פעם יעקב פעם ישראל הכל

בהשגחה ובכונה ידועה. כי שם יעקב נאמר על מדות הגוף בעניני הגוף בעוה״ז, כי מה

שנקרא יעקב על שם (בראשית כה) וידו אחזת בעקב עשו. ושם ישראל נאמר על מדות

הנפש הוא שכתוב (בראשית לב) כי שרית עם אלהים.

וידוע כי עיקר הכונה במדות הנפש ולא במדות הגוף. מ״מ א״א לו לאדם

לעקור לגמרי מדות הגוף ושלא ישתמש בהם כי לא יוכל לחיות זולתם. אבל הכונה

להיות הנפש עיקר ומדות הגוף טפל. וכל מי שעושה מדות הגוף עיקר ומדות הנפש

טפל שהיא עבודת ה׳ יתברך הנה הוא ממית את נפשו...

רבנו בחיי, פירוש על התורה, חלק א׳ דף רי״ח.

[35]   יהודה אתה וכו׳ י״ל ע״ד ששמעתי בשם אא״ז זללה״ה כל הכופר בע״ז נקרא

יהודי וע״ז נקרא גאוה וכל הכופר בע״ז היינו במדת הגאוה ואוחז במדת הענוה

והשפלות נקרא יהודי ולי נראה שעצבות ומרה שחורה נקרא ג״כ ע״ז כי היא גרועה

מכל המדות הרעות וידוע שאפילו יש ביד אדם תורה ומעש״ט אם אין בו יראת שמים

אין כלום. וויו״ד היא קטנה שבאותיות ומ״מ יכולים לעזות ממנה כל הכ״ב אותיות

שבתורה כי כשמתחילין לכתוב עושים מתחלה נקודה קטנה ואח״כ מושך ממנה איזה

אות שירצה ונמצא כמו שמיו״ד קטנה נעשה כ״ב אותיות וה׳ חומשי תורה כך כל

הכופר בע״ז נקרא יהודי וזוכה לכל כ״ב אותיות וה׳ חומשי תורה וזהו יהודה היינו

כשנקרא בשם יהודי אתה מזה נמשך ונעשה א״ת ה׳ היינו כ״ב אותיות מא׳ ת׳ וה׳

חומשי תורה... והבן.

ר׳ משה חיים אפרים מסדילקוב. ס׳ דגל מחנה אפרים. דף ע״ו.

[36]   וזאת אשר דבר להם אביהם ויברך אותם איש אשר כברכתו ברך אותם. כי

שרש העבודה נקודה אחת והיא נקראת זאת אעפ״כ יתחלפו צורת העבודות כפי

מחצבת הנשמות אשר משם חצובות. וזה וזאת כללא דכל דרגין דיבר להם אביהם.

[דיבר] הוא מלשון הנהגה והוא בכלל. אולם בפרט איש כברכתו מלשון בריכה אשר

נברך משם בירך אותם.

ר׳ שמחה בונם מפשיסחא. ס׳ קול שמחה. דף נ״ב.

פרשת שמות

[37]   הנה יש לשית לב ארבע כנוים הללו פרו וישרצו וירבו ויעצמו ועוד אומרו

ותמלא הארץ אותם דמשמע שהארץ מלא אותם היל״ל ותמלא הארץ מהם או וימלאו

את הארץ... ארבע כנויים הללא לרמוז שמארבע עולמות שהיו נשמות בקליפה באו

וזהו פרו וישרצו כו׳ ותמלא הארץ אותם פי׳ והשלים הארץ דהיינו מלכות אותם ר״ל

שהשלים אותם שבנה להם גופים מהקדוש׳ וזהו השלימות של הנשמות משום הכי לא
את׳ ותמלא הארץ מהם דלא קאי לארץ מצרים שנתמלא מהם אלא הכונה שנשלמו
הנשמות שנבנה להם גופים מהקדושה כנזכר ודוק.

ר׳ מאיר בן חליפה בקיאם. ס׳ מאורי אור. דף מ״א עמוד ב׳.

[38] אל תקרב הלום של נעליך מעל רגליך כי המקום אשר אתה עומד עליו אדמת
קודש הוא (שמות ג׳) ואמר ז״ל אל תקרב הלום שלא תאמר אם הי׳ לי כך וכך בוודאי
הי׳ טוב לי לעבודת השי״ת אבל כעת קשה מאוד העבדות אל תאמר כן רק של נעליך
מעל רגליך היינו הסר השטותים מהרגילות שלך ואז תראה אשר המקום שאתה עומד
עליו אדמת קודש הוא שמאותו מקום תוכל לעבוד את השי״ת כמאמר הבעש״ט זי״ע
ובקשתם משם את ד׳ אלקיך ומצאת (דברים ד׳) היינו משם דווקא במקום שהוא שם
ובאיזה מדריגה שהוא עומד שם אף שאינו במקום גבוה אעפ״כ משם תמצא את ד׳
אלקיך ותוכל להתדבק בו ית׳.

ר׳ יוסף מיאמפאלי בס׳ צרור החיים. דף 25.

[39] וישב משה אל ה׳ ומאז באתי [אל פרעה] לדבר בשמך הרע לעם הזה והצל לא
הצלת׳ [שמות ה כב-כג בדילוגים]. לכאורה ׳הצל לא הצלת׳ הוא כפל לשון כיון
שאמר: ׳הרע לעם הזה׳ ממילא לא הציל אותם. ונראה כך פירושו: דהנה אנחנו בגלות
המר הזה אשר בצרותינו לו צר וגלה השכינה עמנו אין לנו לדאוג ולהתאונן אלא על
גלות השכינה ולא לחשוב כלל על צרותינו כי אם על צער וגלות השכינה, ואלו היה
מגמותינו וצערנו רק על צער השכינה ולא על צערינו בודאי היינו נגאלים מיד. אך כי

בשר אנחנו ובלתי אפשר לסבול לנו צרותינו ומכאובינו, לכן ארכו לנו הימים בעונינו

הרבים בגלות המר מחמת שאנו משתתפים צערינו עם צער השכינה ואנו חוששים על

צערינו ואלו הי׳ צדיק א׳... הי׳ מציל את כל העולם כולו מן הגלות.

וזה שאמר משה רבינו עליו השלום: ׳ומאז באתי [אל פרעה] לדבר בשמך.

[שם]. פירוש: כל דבורי לא היה רק בעבור שמך הגדול והקדוש שהוא בגלות ולא

בשביל גלותינו...

ר׳ אלימלך מליזנסק. ס׳ נועם אלימלך. כרך א׳ דף קע״ה.

פרשת וארא

[40]   שמעתי את נאקת בני ישראל אשר מצרים מעבידים אותם. כל נאקתם של

ישראל הי׳ אשר לעבודת השי״ת צריך כל אחד מישראל לעבוד אותו בשמחה רבה

ובבהירות הלב. לסוף זאלין די מצרים צוא ברייננען אונז דער עבודה זה הי׳ עיקר

נאקתם של ישראל.

ר׳ משה מקאברין, ס׳ אמרות טהורות, דף ח׳.

[41]   כי ידבר אליכם פרעה לאמר תנו לכם מופת. ולכאורה היה צ״ל תנו לי מופת.

והענין, כי באמת אין חפץ לכסיל בתבונה, וכמו שמצינו באחז שאמר (ישעיה ז, יב) לא

אשאל ולא אנסה את ה׳, ולכן מצדו לא ביקש כלל מופת. רק בגודל רשעתו היה אומר

להם שאתם בעצמכם אינכם מאמינים באמונה שלימה ואמיתית. ולכן תנו לכם מופת.

ויש להוסיף, דאי׳ בספרים ביאור הענין דיש צדיקים אשר אין פועלים ישועות,

ויש צדיקים שכמעט קטנים מהם והם ממשיכים ישועות. וההסבר הוא, שמפני שפלות

רוחם אינם במדת אמונה ובטחון שיהיה כח בידם להמשיך טובות וישועות. ועל כן באמת אינם יכולים לפעול זאת. וזהו שאמר פרעה: 'תנו לכם מופת', כי אתם בעצמכם אינכם מאמינים שהיכולת בידכם לעשות מופת.

ר' שלום רוקח (שר שלום) מבעלזא. ס' מהר"ש מבעלזא, חלק ב', דף ד'.

[42] ויאמר משה לא נכון לעשות כן וגו' הן נזבח את תועבת מצרים לעיניהם ולא יסקלונו (ח כב). רוצה לומר. הן אמת הדבר שבודאי לא יסקלונו כי בטח בה' ברוך הוא. רק לא נכון בעיני לעשות כן דבר המתנגד לעיניהם מצד טבעי הרך. אין זה לשונו ממש.

ר' מרדכי מנעשכיז, ס' רשפי אש. דף' ט-י.

פרשת בא

[43] ויהי חשך אפלה וגו', לא ראו איש את אחיו וגו'. לא ראו איש את אחיו, אין לך חשכות ואפלה גדולה בעולם מזו, שאין רואים ולא רוצים לראות איש את אחיו, רק כל אחד ואחד דואג לעצמו, לגופו.

לא ראו איש את אחיו ולא קמו איש מתחתיו וגו'. כשאין איש רואה את אחיו ודואג רק לעצמו, כי אז, ולא קמו איש מתחתיו, שאין תקוה לתקומה ולהתקדמות.

ר' יצחק ור' מנחם מענדל מווארקה, ס' בית יצחק, דף מ"ד.

[44] ...אמרו רז"ל שנים אכלו את הפסח אחד אכלו לשם פסח והשני אכלו לשם אכילה גסה על הא' נאמר צדיק אוכל לשובע נפשו ועל השני נאמר ובטן רשעים תחסר הורו בזה כי אחד האכילת בשר הפסח היא פעולה גשמית היא נמשכת הכל אחר

הכוונה אם ימשיך האדם בכוונתו הטוב׳ רוחניות ממקום הקודש באומרו שאוכל אותה

לשם פסח. לפי מה שצווה מבוראו הרי הפעול׳ ההיא ע״י המשכה העליונ׳ נעשית

שלימות לנפש...

ר׳ משה קורדווורו. סידור תפלה למשה. שער א׳ סימן ד׳ דף ד׳ עמוד א׳.

[45]   קדש לי בכור וגו׳. בכור הוא המחשבה הראשונה בקומו בבקר לקדש אותה

לה׳. הן של אהבה לאהבת ה׳ והן של שאר מדות. וזה לעומת זה כשנפל המחשבה עם

המדות של סט״א נקרא בכור מצרים. והעצה לקשר המחשבה לשורשו שיהיה בלתי

לה׳ לבדו היא בעטיפת ציצית. כי ציצית עולין ל״ב חוטין והוא השם אשר הכה בכור

מצרים כמש״ה (שמות יב) וה׳ הכה כל בכור דהיינו שם ל״ב. כשמבטל לבכור

דקליפה מקשר עצמו בכור דקדושה. ולכן תיכף אחר הנחת ציצית אפשר להניח

תפילין שהוא פרשת קדש והבן.

ר׳ ישראל מרייזין, ס׳ עירין קדישין, חלק א׳ דף 23.

פרשת בשלח

[46]   וחמשים עלו בני ישראל ועל זה אמר כ״ק אדמו״ר מחו׳ וש״ב הרבי מפרשיסחא

זצ״ל יודען ברויכען צו גיין למעלה מעלה ״עלו״ גיין ארויף עכל״ק ודפח״ח

והמב״י.

ר׳ שמחה בונם מפשיסחא בס׳ שיח שרפי קודש מאת ר׳ יועץ קים קדיש ראקאץ,

חלק ב׳ דף 130.

[47]   מה תצעק אלי דבר אל בני ישראל (יד טו). אחד מתלמידי הרה״ק מלענטשנא

היה פעם אצל רבינו. שאלו לשלום רבו. והוסיף: אני אוהבו מאד אבל מה זה שהוא

צועק לקב״ה לשלוח את המשיח. למה אינו צועק לבני ישראל שישובו בתשובה. וזה

פירוש "מה תצעק אלי דבר אל בני ישראל."

ר׳ מנחם מענדל מקאצק, ס׳ עמוד האמת, דף מ״ה.

[48]   מלחמת עמלק שהוא מלחמת היצר היא מלחמה ארוכה מאד. ועיקר הכנעתו

הוא ע״י התחזקות שבכל מה העובר על האדם כל ימי חייו יהי׳ חזק מאד לבלי להניח

להפיל א״ע בשום אופן בבחי׳ ואציעה שאול הנך. וגם משם יקרא ויצעק אל ה׳ בכלות

הנפש בבחי׳ מבטן שאול שועתי וכו׳. וזה עיקר דרך התשובה שאנו עוסקים להמשיך

בימים הנוראים הק׳ ר״ה ועשי״ת ויו״כ. וזה עיקר ניצחון המלחמה שאנו עוסקים בימים

הללו. כי כל זמן שהאדם אינו מייאש א״ע ומחזק א״ע להתחיל בכל פעם מחדש איך

שהוא הוא נקרא נוצח את המלחמה. כי באמת לה׳ המלחמה כי א״א להאדם בעצמו

לנצחו כמארז״ל אלמלא הקב״ה עוזרו וכו׳ כמ״ש מלחמה לה׳ בעמלק וכו׳ רק שהאדם

מחוייב לחזק א״ע בכל פעם מחדש לבלי להיות נסוג אחור ממלחמה הזאת ולבלי

לייאש א״ע בשום אופן. וזה מרומז בדברי הזה״ק שאמר מאן נצח מאן דאחיד מאני

קרבא בידוהי. כי וודאי במלחמה הזאת אין רואין עדיין בחוש מאן נצח כי עדיין

המלחמה ארוכה מאד והגלות מתגבר ועל כ״א עובר מה שעובר. אעפי״כ כל זמן

שאוחזין עדיין הכלי זיין בידינו ועיקר הכלי זיין שלנו הוא תפלה כמבואר במ״א. וכל

זמן שאין אנו מייאשין עצמינו ממלחמה הזאת ח״ו ואוחזין עדיין הכלי מלחמה בודאי

אנחנו מנצחים. כי כל זמן שהאדם מחזק א״ע בתפלה וצעקה להשי״ת הוא מכלל מנצח את המלחמה כי זה עיקר מניצחון כנ״ל.

ר׳ נתן מנמירוב (מברסלב). ס׳ משיבת נפש. דפ׳ נ״ו-נ״ז.

פרשת יתרו

[49] במדרש תנחומא. וישמע יתרו. יש שמע והפסיד ויש שמע ונשכר וכו׳ וכן שמעו עמים ירגזון אבל יתרו שמע ונשכר שהי׳ כומר לע״ז ובא ונדבק במשה וכו׳. עכלה״מ. להבין מאי משמיענו המדרש בזה נראה הפי׳ שבשמיעה אחת יש שמע ונשכר וזה שמע ונפסד יתרו שמע נסים של קריאת[1] ים סוף והי׳ פחד מהשי״ת ע״כ בא ונתקרב. והעמים שהי׳ להם נ״כ פחד ברחו מהשי״ת שרצו לפטור את הפחד.

ר׳ מנחם מענדל מקאצק. ס׳ אהל תורה מהרבי מקאצק. דף 26.

[1] צ״ל קריעת.

[50] והייתם לי סגולה. פירוש והייתם לי זהו הסגולה מכל הסגולות.

ר׳ משה בן ישראל מקאברין. ס׳ אמרות טהורות. דף י׳.

[51] תחילה צריך האדם לידע ולהאמין באמונה שלימה וחזקה. שיש אלוה מצוי אחד יחיד ומיוחד. שהמציא כל הנמצאים כולם יש מאין. הן מצד אמונת האבות. והן מצד אמונת הידיעה. כמאמר הכתוב (דה״א כח ט) דע את אלקי אביך ועבדהו. ויש בפסוק זה משמעות ב׳ האמונות.

ועל אמונתו ית״ש צריך האדם הנלבב לעבודתו. למסור נפשו על זה. כי זה אנכי ולא יהיה לך מפי הגבורה שמענום (מכות כד.). כי צריך איש ישראלי להגביר את

עצמו על החומר להכניעו ולזככך אותו. ואז מאיר קומתו הרוחני בקומתו הגשמי ונעשה

מרכבה אליו ית״ש. ואנכי ולא יהיה לך הם כלל כל התורה כולה, וקיומה.

ר׳ מרדכי מטשערנאביל. ס׳ ליקוטי תורה, דף י״ב.

פרשת משפטים

[52] עין תחת עין וגו׳ (שמות כ״א כ״ד) כבר ידעת כי זה הפסוק אמרו רבותינו ז״ל

שאינו כפשוטו אלא לממון כמו פסוק כאשר יתן מום באדם כן ינתן בו (ויקרא כ״ד כ׳).

הכוונה בו לממון דבר הניתן מיד ליד... ואולי תשאל אחרי שאין הכוונה בו ככתבו

למה נכתב כך לתת מקום למינים לרדות והתשובה היא מה שאמרו רז״ל שבעים פנים

לתורה. ופירוש המצוה כפי פשוטה ניתן בתורה שבעל פה ואחריה נלך. אמנם בא

לשון הפסוק בענין אחר שיובנו בו הפנים האחרים שלא היו מובנים בלתי הלשון ההוא.

דוגמא לדבר באומרו עין תחת עין האמת הוא כפי הקבלה כי החובל בחברו חייב

בחמשה דברים. אמנם נכתב כך לסוד גדול מאוד ... כי צורת האדם כולה באיבריו

ותבניתו נעשית על צורת האדם העליון והנה בהיות איברי האדם על כוונת הבריאה

יהיו איבריו דוגמת כסא לאיברים העליונים ומוסיף בהם כח והמשכה מאפיסת האין

ובהפך זהו סוד כאשר יתן מום באדם הידוע כן ינתן. והבן זה מאוד...

מנחם בן בנימין רקנאטי. פירוש על התורה, חלק ב׳ דפ׳ צ״ח-צ״ט.

[53] וכי ישאלו איש מעם רעהו וגו׳. אם בעליו עמו לא ישלם (כב. ינ-יד). כל אדם

קיבל את נשמתו ואת חייו בהשאלה מן השמים על מנת שישתמש בהם לטובה, והרי

הוא שואל וחייב אפילו באונסין. ואם כן כיצד יכול אדם לפטור עצמו מן העבירות

שהוא עושה באונס או בשוגג. אך כאשר "בעליו עמו", שהוא זוכר תמיד את השם

יתברך ומקבל על עצמו עול מלכות שמים, אזי "לא ישלם". כי הדין כן, ששאלה

בבעלים פטור. והוא שאמר דוד המלך (תהלים כז), אחת שאלתי מאת ה׳, הרי נשמה

אחת ויחידה זו רק שאלתי אותה מאת הבורא, אם כן קיים פן החשש מן אתחייב אפילו

באונסין, אך מכיון שאותה אבקש שבתי בבית ה׳ כל ימי חיי, ששאיפתי תמיד להתקרב

אל השם יתברך ולהיות עמו, הרי זה איפוא שאילה בבעלים.

ר׳ שמחה בונם מפשיסחא, ס׳ מדרש שמחה, כרך א׳ דף קי״ג.

[54]   בשעה שהקדימו ישראל נעשה לנשמע יצאת בת קול ואמרה מי גילה רז זה לבני

לשון שמלאכי השרת משתמשין בו כו׳...

וצריך להבין איך אפשר לעשות קודם שישמע מה לעשות גם היה ענין

התפארות הש״י בזה כל כך במה שהקדימו נעשה לנשמע.

אך האמת שהאדם הוא אינו יכול לעמוד תמיד על מדריגה אחת כי החיות רצוא

ושוב שבא ומסתלק דהיינו כשהוא דבוק בהש״י הוא מרגיש חיות ותענוג ואח״כ מסתלק

ונופל מדריגתו ויש בזה רזין דאורייתא בטעם הדבר למה צריך ליפול ממדריגתו

וטעם אחד הוא כדי שיבא אח״כ למדריגה יותר גדולה שבכל דבר צריך להיות העדר

קודם להיוה וכשרוצי׳ להגביה ולמדריגה יותר גדולה צריך להיות העדר קודם לכן

צריך ליפול ממדריגה שהוא עכשיו.

והנה צריך האדם שגם בנפלו ממדריגתו יתאמץ לעלות אל ה׳ באותו מדריגה

שהוא עכשיו כי צריך להאמין שמלא כל הארץ כבודו ולית אתר פנוי מיניה ואפי׳

במדריגה שהוא עכשיו יש ג״כ השי״ת כי לית אתר פנוי מיניה רק שהוא מצומצם מאוד...

וזהו נקרא נעשה קודם לנשמע אף בנפילתינו ממדריגתינו להדבק בהשי״ת במותה מדריגה כנ״ל ואח״כ נשמע שעיקר השמיעה הוא לשון הבנה דהיינו שבא למדריגה יותר גדולה כנ״ל וזה הוא עיקר קבלת התורה שקבלו ישראל ולכן התפאר הקב״ה בזה מאוד שקבלו התורה בגודל האמת והשיגו האמת שלעולם יהיו דבוקים בהש״י ולא יפרדו ממנו אף בנפלם ממדריגת׳ וזהו עיקר ההילוך הנהגת הישראלית ובזה צריך להילוך ובמה יבא להשי״ת כשנפל ממנו המוחין והדעת אך שהש״י הוא מלא כה״כ דהיינו אפילו במקום שהוא כל הארץ כולו ארציות שהוא רק חומר עב אעפ״כ מלא כבודו ית׳ והנה הש״י נקרא חיי החיים דהיינו שכל החיים שבעולם בהמות חיות ועופות ועין האדם החיות שלהם הוא הש״י וזהו חי החיים שהוא ית׳ החיים של כל החיים ויחשוב כשנפל ממדריגתו הלא חי אני ומי הוא החיות שלי הלא הבורא ית׳ ונמצא יש כאן ג״כ הוא ית׳ אך שהוא מצומצם מאוד.

וזהו אמר הקב״ה מי גלה רז זה לבני ר״ל מי דהיינו כשהם חושבים מי הוא החיות שלה׳ זה גילה להם רז זה להקדים נעשה לנשמע כנ״ל...

ר׳ מנחם נחום מטשארנאביל. ס׳ מאור עינים. חלק א׳ דפ׳ 68-69.

פרשת תרומה

[55]   וידבר ה׳ אל משה לאמר. דבר אל בנ״י ויקחו לי תרומה מאת כל איש אשר ידבנו לבו תקחו את תרומתו... וזה הוא כלל גדול בתורה ועבודה את האלהים אשר

בכל דבר בעולם יש רמיזא דחכמתא שיכול המשכיל לעורר לבו בקרבו לעבודת

בוראו אפילו באכילה ושתיה ומשא ומתן וזהו שנרמז בכתוב הקודם מאת כל איש אשר

ידבנו לבו תקחו את תרומתי כלומר לאו דוקא עתה בעת הצווי על הפרשת התרומה

ומלאכת המשכן כי באמת התורה היא תמידיות וישנה בכל זמן וזהו מאת כל איש אשר

ידבנו לבו לעבודת בוראו מעתה ועד עולם עד ביאת המשיח ב״ב תקחו את תרומתי

תוכלו ליקח את בחינת תרומתי כי עניני עבודת בני ישראל נוקב והולך...

ר׳ זאב וואלף זוטאמיר, ס׳ אור המאיר, חלק ב׳ דף 34.

[56]   ועשית מנורת זהב טהור מקשה תיעשה המנורה (כה לא). פירוש. עבודה הקשה

ביותר הוא זהב טהור, שיהיה הכסף והזהב של האדם טהור מבלי שום איסור ח״ו,

ומשום מחשבה פסולה ח״ו. ואיש כזה המטהר כספו וזהבו ביותר, תיעשה המנורה,

נעשה במדריגה אשר יוכל להאיר ברוב קדושתו בעולם.

ר׳ מרדכי מנעשכיז, ס׳ רשפי אש, דף ט״ו.

[57]   מזבח. [רמז שיעשה הכנה בגופו מזבח גדול להיות] זובח יצרו. ומחשבות הבל

ישרוף באש של גבוה תורה. [ומצוה להביא] מן ההדיוט סיגופים ותעניות, [ותיכף

משמיא מיהב יהבי אש של גבוה רבוצה כארי בלבו בל טהור וזבח עליו כל יצר

הרהורים רעים והיו לבער] מקריב קרבנות אוהב את הבריות ומקרבן [לתורה]

צדקות, ג״ח. מדות המזבח שלמות ה׳ ארך, וה׳ רחב, וג׳ קומתו גימטר׳ י״ג אחד. [שיהיה

כל כוונתו ליחד הדודים]. כל יום מצוה בהרמת הדשן [להסיר] שירי מחשבות רעות.

ר׳ חיים יוסף דוד אזולאי (החיד״א), ס׳ חדרי בטן, דף קמ״ז, עמוד א׳ סימן ח׳:

[58]   ואלה הבגדים אשר יעשו חשן ואפוד ומעיל. באלו הבגדים מראה הקב״ה

לישראל באיזה נפש הוא בוחר. כי מהבגדים יוכר ומובן היקרות הנמצא בתוך נפש

אהרן הכהן. הציץ מרמז עליו כי הוא דבוק בהש״י כמצווה עליו שיהיה תמיד על

מצחו. על הציץ היה נחקק קודש לה׳ היינו בעומק מחשבתו היה תמיד [דברי הימים א׳

כ״ח ט׳] דע את אלקי אביך. והחושן מרמז עליו כי לא נמצא בלבו שנאה לשום נפש

מישראל. כי היו שבטי ישראל חקוקים על לבו. ואפוד שהיה חגור בו ומרמז על בטחונו

בהש״י שהוא תומכו תמיד. ומעיל מורה על גודל יראתו כי היה כלו מתכלת שמרומז

על יראה....

ר׳ מרדכי ליינר מאיזביצא. ס׳ מי השלוח, כרך א׳ דף פ״ח.

[59]   שלא לקרוע המעיל. כתב הרב הנ״ל: טעם המצוה הזו, שישים הכהן עוז חומה

חזקה לפיו סביב שלא יקרע. אחר שהוא המעתיר על עם קודש לא יצא מפיו דבר

מגונה. אחר שהוא הקושר והתופר לא יעשה פירוד וקריעה, דכתיב (משלי כג, כא)

וקרעים תלביש נומה השכל. ואחר שהגוף לבוש הנפש. והמעיל לבוש הגוף. וקשורים

זה בזה. ראוי שלבוש הנפש הנקרא חלוקא דרבנן שלא יקרע. עד כאן לשונו. וכל אדם

שהוא עבד ה׳ הוא ככהן. וזכותו עומד לרבים. על כן יקדש את פיו בקדושה יתירה.

ר׳ ישעיה הורוויץ. ס׳ שני לוחות הברית, כרך ב׳ דף נ׳ עמוד ב׳.

[60]   אני ה׳ אלהיהם. טעם שכפל לומר כן ב׳ פעמים. אולי שנתכוון לרבות אפילו

בזמן שאין שכינתו בתוכנו הוא ה׳ אלהינו לו ואנחנו: או ירצה על זה הדרך בידיעתם

ובהכרתם הדבר כאומרו בתחלה וידעו וגו׳ בזה יהיו ראוים ליקרות שמי עליהם. לומר

ה׳ אלהיהם. אבל זולת זה יפרקו עול ויהיו לאלהים אחרים ב״מ.

ר׳ חיים ן׳ עטר. ס׳ אור החיים. חלק ב׳ דף קנ״ח.

פרשת כי תשא

[61]   ונתנו איש כופר נפשו וגו׳ כשיתנו כ״א את נפשו לכופר אז לא יהיה בהם נגף.

ר׳ פנחס מקאריץ. ס׳ אמרי פנחס. סימן ס״ז דף ל׳.

[62]   עיקר להאמין באמונה שלמה שהבורא ברוך הוא מלא כל הארץ כבודו ולית

אתר פנוי מיניה, וכשאתה מסתכל על העולם אתה מסתכל על הבורא ברוך הוא, וכמו

שאתה מדבר עם האדם אתה מדבר עם הנשמה שבו, כי כשהנשמה יוצאת מן הגוף אין

אתה יכול לדבר עמו כי הוא כאבן דומם. וכשהוא חי אתה מדבר עם הנשמה שבו,...,

ואין אתה יכול לראות את הנשמה, כל שכן שאין אתה יכול לראות את הבורא ברוך

הוא, כי הוא נשמה לנשמות... לכן תאמין שהוא ית׳ בכאן ואין אתה יכול לראותו.

כמאמר הכתוב (שמות ל״ג כ) כי לא יראני האדם וחי.

ר׳ מרדכי מטשערנאביל, ס׳ ליקוטי תורה, דף י״ד.

[63]   אלהי מסכה לא תעשה לך. מסכה היינו כללים וע״ז אמר הכתוב בעת שיהיה

לך בינת הלב מפורשת אז לא תביט על הכללים להתנהג על פיהם רק בבינת לבך

תדע בכל פרט דבר איך להתנהג. כמו שמצינו באליהו בהר כרמל...

ר׳ מרדכי ליינר מאיזביצ׳א. ס׳ מי השלוח, כרך א׳ דף צ״ו.

פרשת ויקהל

[64] זכאה איהו מאן דנטיר דירה לשבת דאיהו לבא דלא אתקריב תמן עציבו

דטחול וכעס דמרה דאיהו נורא דגיהנם. דעלה אתמר לא תבערו אש בכל מושבותיכם

ביום השבת. והכי הוא ודאי. דכל מאן דכעיס כאלו אוקיד נורא דגיהנם.

ס׳ תיקוני הזהר, תקונא מ״ח דף פ״ה עמוד א׳.

[65] ובחרשת אבן למלאות ובחרשת עץ לעשות בכל מלאכת מחשבת. י״ל בדרך

רמז. אבן היינו היצה״ר הנקרא אבן כידוע. ועץ היינו התורה עץ חיים כידוע. ואומנות

היצה״ר למלאות היינו להתדמות לאדם שכבר הוא מלא ונדוש ומושלם בכל המעלות.

ז״ש ובחרשת אבן היינו אומנות היצה״ר למלאות כאמור. ואומנות התורה הוא בהיפך.

אחר כל מה שעשה תר״מ ומעש״ט נדמה תמיד לו שעדיין לא עשה כלום וצריך לעשות

מחדש. ז״ש ובחרשת עץ היינו אומנות התורה עץ חיים לעשות בכל יום מחדש. בכל

מלאכת מחשבת היינו כראוי ובשלימות:

ר׳ ישראל ממאדזיץ. ס׳ דברי ישראל,חלק ב׳ דף 91.

[66] ... שמעתי בשם מורי זלה״ה ביאור משנה איזהו חכם הלומד מכל אדם (אבות

פ״ד) ע״פ משל המסתכל במראה יודע חסרונו וכו׳ כך ברואה חסרון זולתו יודע שיש

בו שמץ מנהו וכו׳ ודפח״ח.

ובזה יובן הפסוק ויעש כיור נחושת דהיינו לרחצה וקשה שמא יאמר שאין

צריך לרחצה ומשני דלכך נעש׳ כיור במראות הצובאות שיסתכל במראה שרואה

חסרון זולתו אז ירגיש שחסרון זולתו יש בו בעצמו ג״כ ואז ידע שצריך לרחצה והבן...

אמנם דוק׳ חכם הוא הלומד מכל אדם כמו המסתכל במראה יודע חסרונו ע״י שרואה

חסרון זולתו משא״כ מי שאינו בגדר חכם אינו רואה חסרונו ע״י חסרון זולתו.

ר׳ יעקב יוסף מפולנאי. ס׳ תולדות יעקב יוסף. כרך א׳ דף רנ״ט.

פרשת פקודי

[67]   אלה פקודי המשכן (שמות לח כא). הקב״ה פוק״ד את האדם מיום אל יום.

מיום שברא הקב״ה את עולמו. כך האדם צריך לפקוד ולעשות חשבון עם עצמו קודם

שמדבר דיבורים לפני הקב״ה. השוכן בתוכם אלקותו.

ר׳ מרדכי מטשערנאביל. ס׳ ליקוטי תורה, דפ׳ ק״נ-ק״ד.

[68]   כן עשו בני ישראל את כל העבודה. היה לומר את כל המלאכה. אבל הכתוב

קרא למלאכת המשכן עבודה שעשו אותה לעבודת הש״י. כענין שכתוב (שמות כג)

ועבדתם את ה׳ אלהיכם וכתיב (דברים יג) ואותו תעבודו.

רבנו בחיי. פירוש על התורה, חלק ב׳ דף רל״ג.

[69]   ובהעלות הענן מעל המשכן יסעו בני ישראל בכל מסעיהם. נראה לרמז בזה

דהנה האדם צריך לראות שלא יהי׳ דבר חוץ בינו לבין הקיר בעת התפלה היינו בינו

לבין השכינה הקדושה שתוכל לשרות עליו וזה בהעלות הענן מעל המשכן. היינו

המסך המבדיל אזי יסעו בני ישראל בכל מסעיהם היינו שיוכלו ללכת בדרכי עבדות

השי״ת ודו״ק.

ר׳ אברהם יששכר בער הכהן מרדאמסק, ס׳ חסד לאברהם. דף 258.

פרשת ויקרא

[70] ויקרא אל משה (א, א). ויקרא אלף זעירא. משל לציפור קטנה שהעמידוה על גג היותר גבוה. הגג אמנם גבוה אך הציפור נשארת בדמותה כמות שהיא, כמו כן משה רבינו ע״ה. אף שהקב״ה קרא אותו. בכל זאת היה בעינו עצמו אותו דבר כמקודם.

ר׳ שמחה בונם מפשיסחא, ס׳ מדרש שמחה, כרך א׳ דף קכ״ד.

[71] וכל קרבן מנחתך במלח תמלח. כדי להמליך את הקב״ה על כל ההפכים הנראין בעולם וגרמו לרבים לצאת לאפיקורסי׳ לומר מהתחלה אחת לא יצאו ב׳ הפכים והנה מלח יש בטעמי דבר והפכו כי יש בו כח האש וחמימות ותולדות המים עד שאמרו חכמי הקבלה שהוא כנגד מדה״ד ומדת הרחמים ע״כ נקרא ברית אלהיך כי בהקרבה זו כורתים ברית עם ה׳ להשליטו על כל ההפכים. וכל המנחות חוץ משל כהן היו נאכלים לכהנים וזה הוא כמו צדקה שנמשלה למלח המעמיד ומקיים את הבשר כך מלח ממון חסר והצדקה שבקרבן גדולה מן הקרבן עצמו כמ״ש עשות משפט וצדקה נבחר לה׳ מזבח עז״א על כל קרבנך תקריב מלח שהמלח הוא העולה על כל הקרבנות ונבחר לה׳ מזבח ופשוטו על כל קרבנך קאי גם על הבשר.

ר׳ אפרים שלמה בן אהרן מלונשיץ, ס׳ כלי יקר. על ויקרא ב׳ י״ג.

[72] ונפש כי תחטא ועשה אחת מכל מצות ה׳ אשר לא תעשינה ואשם כי הנה ידוע יותר מה שהאדם עובד את הקדוש ברוך הוא יותר הוא בעיני עצמו כלא נחשב נגד גדולת הבורא יתברך אבל כשהאדם עושה מצוה והוא סובר שהוא עובד את ה׳ זה המצוה אינו נחשב לכלום וזהו פירוש הפסוק ונפש כי תחטא כלומר מה החטא ועשה

אחת מכל מצות ה׳ אשר לא תעשינה ואשם כלומר שהמצוה הזאת יעשה לו כלא והוא

סובר שעובד ה׳ כראוי ואשם.

ר׳ לוי יצחק מברדיטשוב, ס׳ קדושת לוי, דף ס׳ עמוד ב׳.

פרשת צו

[73]   צו את אהרן הנה צו לשון ע״ז כמו צו לצו. דהנה פירשנו ובחטא יחמתני אמי כי

תשובה נקרא (אם) כי ע״י נעשה האדם כמו שנולד אתה בריה חדשה וידוע שצריך

חשק גדול לעבודת שמים והחשק בא מצד היצה״ר וזה ובחטא יחמתני אמי נותן לו

חמום לה׳ ית׳ לעובדו בהתלהבות וזה צו את אהרן ואת בניו כו׳ לשון זריזות וחשק

שבא מיצה״ר נקרא צו...

ר׳ יעקב יצחק, החוזה מלובלין, ס׳ דברי אמת, דף פ״א עמוד ב׳.

[74]   זאת התורה לעולה ולמנחה ולחטאת ולאשם ולשלמים כי האמת היא שהתורה

בעצמה הלומדה באמת לשמה ולקיים מצותיה נאמר עליו צדיקים ילכו בם וח״ו

להיפך נאמר ופושעים יכשלו בם וזה הפי׳ זאת התורה לפעמים לעולה ולמנחה

ולפעמים ולחטאת ולאשם וד״ל.

ר׳ ישראל מריזין, ס׳ עירין קדישין, חלק ב׳ דף ח׳ עמוד א׳.

[75]   ויקח משה את החזה וגו׳ לשון ראי׳ וחוזה כמו ואשר חזה (ישעי׳ א׳). ר״ל ויקח

את החזה הוא הראי׳. ויניפהו תנופה לפני ה׳. הוא התקדשות ראית העינים.

ר׳ ישראל ממאדזין, ס׳ דברי ישראל, חלק ב׳ דף 45.

פרשת שמיני

[76] זה הדבר אשר צוה ה׳ תעשו וירא אליכם כבוד ה׳. י״ל הפסוק הזה בפני עצמו

ואינו מובן. עפ״י מה שא׳ בר״מ אלשיך ז״ל על ועשו לי מקדש ושכנתי בתוכם. כי

הקב״ה מתאוה לשכון בתוכנו ממש ולא במשכן דוקא. והנה ישראל התאוו במשכן וצפו

וייחלו ע״ד המשכן שתשרה השכינה וירא אלינו כבוד ה׳. אמר להם אל תבטחו בזה

כ״א העיקר הוא זה הדבר אשר צוה ה׳ תעשו קאי על התורה. וירא עליכם כבוד ה׳.

שלא תצטרכו לשום משכן ופשוט שלא תלוי במשכן כ״א במה שתעשו אשר צוה ה׳.

ר׳ יעקב יצחק. החוזה מלובלין, ס׳ זכרון זאת. דף צ׳ עמוד א׳.

[77] ויקחו בני אהרן נדב ואביהוא איש מחתתו וגו׳ ותצא אש מלפני ה׳ ותאכל אותם.

הנה כל חטאי ישראל הכתובים בתורה הם להורות דברי תורה לכלל ישראל

כדאיתה בגמ׳ (ע״ז ד׳:) לא עשו ישראל את העגל אלא ליתן פתחון פה לבעלי תשובה

וכו׳ לא דוד ראוי לאותו מעשה וכו׳ שאם חטא יחיד אומרים לו כלך אצל יחיד ואם

חטאו צבור אומרים להן כלך אצל צבור. וכן ענין נדב ואביהוא הכתוב בתורה הוא

להורות יראה ליחיד. שאף שהם היו נקיים אנם אמם כי היתה אחות נחשון בן עמינדב

שממנו יצא מלכות בית דוד. ומלך פורץ גדר. יען שהוא בטוח שרצונו הוא רצון

השי״ת, לכן היה לכם תקופות לסמוך על רצונם שבטח הוא מהשי״ת, אכן בזה הראה

השי״ת שלא יעשה האדם שום דבר בלתי כשמבררו שבעתים.

ר׳ מרדכי ליינר מאיזביצא. ס׳ מי השלוח. כרך ב׳ דף ע״ו.

[78] להיות לכם לאלהים. בשם הריב״ש ז״ל. הפירוש. שצריך האדם להסתכל שגם

הלכם היינו תאוות ההיתר יהיו לאלהים בלתי לה׳ לבדו. ודל״ל.

ר׳ ישראל בן אליעזר, הבעל שם טוב. ס׳ בעל שם טוב. כרך ב׳ דף צ״ג.

פרשת תזריע

[79] אשה כי תזריע וילדה זכר כתיב מי הקדימני ואשלם א״א כי האדם צריך לידע

שכל עשיותיו הכל הוא מהש״י היינו כל מצוה שעושה הקב״ה מזמין לידו כי הוא נותן

לו בית והוא עושה מזוזה נותן לו טלית והוא מטיל בו ציצית וכמו במעשה המצות

הקב״ה הוא העיקר כמ״כ פנימיות כל ענין ידע באמת שהכל מאתו י״ת ד״מ אם

נתעורר אתערותא דלתתא צריך להיות בשברון לב ולידע שאמת שהוא אינו עושה

כלל רק מה שהקב״ה משפיע לו אבל אם בדעתו שהוא העושה הכל הוא וגרוע מאד גם

תורתו ותפלתו הוא מהש״י וזהו א״ר שמלאי כשם שיצירתו של אדם כך תורתו כי

באמת האדם הוא הגרוע מכל הברואים כי הוא צריך לכל הנבראים גם לכמה לבושים

עד שיוכל להתפרנס אבל כל הברואים מתפרנסים שלא בצער וזהו כשם שיצירתו כך

כך תורתו כי בתורה יש איסור והיתר טמא וטהור והאדם מטמא בחייו מטמא במותו

אבל שאר הברואים אינם מטמאים בחייהם אמנם אעפ״י שבגוף האדם גרוע מכל

הברואים עכ״ז כתיב ויהי האדם לנפש חיה ומתרגמינן לרוח ממללא שבזה הוא

למעלה מכל הברואים כדי שיוכל להחזיר את הכל להש״י וזהו אשה כי תזריע פי׳

אפילו כשיש לו איזה הרהור תשובה ולמד או מתפלל ויכול לעשות אתערותא דלתתא

אעפ״י כן צריך להיות בבחי׳ אשה בחי׳ מקבל וידע שהכל מאתו י״ת ואז וילדה זכר

יוכל להיות משפיע בחי׳ זכר.

ר׳ ישראל מריזין, ס׳ עירין קדישין, חלק ב׳ דף 30.

[80] ואם תחתיה תעמוד הבהרת לא פשתה צרבת השחין היא. הענין שיש שני מיני

צדיקים. אחד שנקרא הולך שהולך בכל יום ויום למדרגה יותר גדולה. ומין הב׳ הוא

שעומד תמיד במדרגה אחת ובכל יום ויום מתפללים ולומדים תורה וכאתמול כן היום

ומחר. ואם באמת שגם המין הב׳ הוא טוב מאוד אך עכ״ז יש בהם עוד אחיזה וקצת

רושם מהס״א כי אם היה מטוהר מכל וכל היה מוסיף בכל יום ויום בהירות נפלא

כדרך הצדיקים וכמ״ש מזה במ״א וזהו אם תחתיה תעמוד ר״ל הבהירות

תעמוד תמיד במקום א׳ לא פשתה שאינו הולך ממדרגה למדרגה ומוסיף תורה

ומעש״ט בכל יום אז צרבת השחין היא ר״ל ידוע כי יש עוד קצת רושם מהס״א ות״א

רושם שיחנא היא שנראה שיש בו קצת רושם מהס״א הנקר׳ שחין.

ר׳ יעקב צבי יאליש. ס׳ אמת ליעקב. דף י׳ עמוד א׳.

[81] זאת תורת נגע הצרעת בגד צמר וגו׳ ... כי השכינה נקראת זאת. ואמה״כ כי

צרעת היינו הרע של בני ישראל היא פגם בשכינה הקדושה גם בתורת היינו בשתי

תורות שבכתב ושבע״פ כי אורייתא וקוב״ה וישראל חד.

ר׳ אברהם יששכר בער הכהן מרדאמסק. ס׳ חסד לאברהם. דפ׳ 283-284.

פרשת מצורע

[82] בשם ההה״ק הרי״ם זצל״ה מגור... בטהרת המצורע הי׳ עץ ארז ואזוב. פירש״י

אם הי׳ מגבי׳ עצמו כארז. ישפיל עצמו באזוב. ואמר די״ל להיפך ג״כ מי שמכניע עצמו

כאזוב יגבי׳ עצמו כארז. כי לפעמים צריכין כפרה על העניוות. למשל אם בא עני

לאחד ומבקשו שיעשה לו טובה. משיבו מי אנכי שאוכל לעשות לו טובה. הלא שפל

אני. ואינני מכובד כלל בעיני הבריות ואע״פ שאם אחד יפגע בכבודו ירד עמו עד

לחייו. אבל לעשות טובה לחבירו שפל הוא בעיניו ואל עניוות כזה צריכין כפרה.

ודפח״ח.

ר׳ יועץ קים קדיש ראקאץ. ס׳ שיח שרפי קודש. חלק ג׳ דף 128.

[83]   ובא אשר לו הבית וגו׳ בר״ת שלהם שם החסד ... והוא סוד אור ... וזה סוד

מארז״ל כנגע נראה לי ולא לאורי ובית אפל ואין פותחין לו חלונות לראות את נגעו

והרז״ל לעולם הוי קבל וקיים וכו׳ וסמכוהו לכאן והנה שם זה חסד לאברהם ומדתו

עין טובה ולהיפך נגעי בתים באים על צרות עין כמארז״ל.

ר׳ צבי הירש בן שמואל זנוויל מסעמייאטיטש. ס׳ מרגוליות התורה. דף צ״ו

עמוד א׳.

[84]   והזהרתם את בנ״י מטומאתם והזהרתם מלשון נזר ועטרה ור״ל שיתקנו א״ע עד

שיעלו את החטאים לבחי׳ נזר ועטרה וכמאחז״ל שמחשיבה מאהבה נעשה הזדונות

כזכיות ולא ימותו בטומאתם מיתה היא ענין הכנעה והשפלה היינו שלא ישארו בעונותם

בטמאם את משכני ר״ל כי ע״י העונות הוא עושה פגם וכחם בנשמתו אשר הוא חלק

אלקי ממעל וע״כ יעשו תשובה כזה שיתכפרו העונות ולהביאם בתוך הקדושה אכי״ר.

ר׳ מנחם מענדל מרימנאוו. ס׳ אילנא דחיי. חלק א׳ דף 64.

פרשת אחרי מות

[85]   ויאמר ה׳ אל משה דבר אל אהרן אחיך ואל יבוא בכל עת אל הקודש (ט״ז ב׳).

אמר בדרך הלצה על פי דברי רבותינו ז״ל (כתובות נ׳ ע״א) איזהו עושה צדקה בכל

עת, זה הזן בניו ובנותיו כשהן קטנים. וזה ואל יבוא בכל עת. פירש בזו הצדקה של

בכל עת לא יגיע להקדושה.

ר׳ אורי השרף מסרעליסק, ס׳ אמרי קדוש, דף י״א.

[86] כי ביום הזה יכפר עליכם לטהר אתכם וגו׳. היינו שהחיוב מוטל עליכם לטהר

עצמכם מכל חטאתיכם.

ר׳ מנחם מענדל מקאצק, ס׳ אהל תורה, דף 42.

[87] וחי בהם (יח ה). יעשה המצוות עם חיות ולא כמצוות אנשים מלומדה.

ר׳ מנחם מענדל מקאצק, ס׳ עמוד האמת, דף ע״א.

פרשת קדושים

[88] ...קדושים תהיו, לשון עתיד. פירוש אין הפסק למצוה זו, כי כל שער מהקדושה

אשר יכנס עדיין ישנו בגדר הכנסת שער אחר למעלה ממנו, כי אין שיעור להדרגות

הקדושה המזומנת לכל הרוצה ליטול את השם: וצא ולמד ממדרגות הנביאים זו

למעלה מזו, ומשה עולה על גביהן. ואולי שיכול להיות הדרגה גדולה ממשה, והוא

מדרגת מלכנו משיחנו המעוטר בעטרי עטרות, כמובן מפסוק ונחה עליו רוח ה׳ וגו׳

(ישעיה יא ב). ולדברי רבותינו ז״ל כי משה שהיה הוא הגואל העתיד. וכמו שהארכנו

בפירושין של דברים במקומן. אם כן אין שיעור וגבול להדרגות הקדושה. לזה אמר

תהיו כי מצוה זו אין לה הפסק, ותמיד ישנה בגדר מצוה זו להיות קדושים. ונתן טעם

לדבריו כי קדוש אני ה׳ אלהיכם. שאין שיעור אל קדושתו יתברך, וחפץ ה׳ בבניו

ידידיו להדמות לקונם בהפלגת הקדושה. ומעתה דון בדעתך ההדרגות אשר תבא בהם:

ר׳ חיים ן׳ עטר. ס׳ אור החיים. חלק ג׳ דף צ״ט-ק׳.

[89]   והין צדק יהיה לכם (ויקרא י״ט ל״ו) אפי׳ הן שלך ולאו שלך יהיה צדק ומנין שאף רמיזות שלך צדק שנאמר (משלי ו׳ י״ג) קורץ בעיניו מולל ברגליו מורה באצבעותיו וכתיב (ישעי׳ נ״ח ט׳) שלח אצבע ודבר און ואף נענוע שלך בראש יהיה אמת כשאדם רוצה לומר הן כופף ראשו וכשרוצה לומר לאו מנענע ראשו לצדדין ואף האיברים כולם יהיו אמתיים שנאמר (שה״ש א׳ ד׳) מישרים אהבוך.

ר׳ יהודה בן שמואל החסיד. ס׳ חסידים. סימן תתרנ״ח, דף תקמ״ו.

[90]   והייתם קדושים וגו׳ (כ. ז.). שמעתי מאת כבוד אדמו״ר הרב הק׳ מהרמ״מ זצוק״ל: ״קדושה״ מלשון הזמנה כמ״ש וקדשתם היום ומחר (שמות י״ט, י) שתהיו תמיד מוכנים ומזומנים להשראת הקדושה, כמו אשה לבעלה המכינה את עצמה בטהרה, פן בפתע יבוא בעלה וימצאנה טהורה, והבן מאד.

ר׳ מנחם מענדל מרימנאוו. ס׳ ילקוט מנחם. דף ק״ע.

פרשת אמור

[91]   ויאמר ה׳ אל משה אמור אל הכהנים בני אהרן ואמרת עליהם לנפש לא יטמא בעמיו ולכאורה יש לדקדק מהראוי לומר לנפש לא יטמאו כיון שמדבר על הכלל בני אהרן ופתח בכלל וסיים בפרט אמור אל הכהנים לשון רבים בני אהרן ג״כ לשון רבים ואמרת עליהם הכל מדבר מכלל הכהנים וגמר אומר בלשון יחיד לנפש לא

יטמא בעמיו... שאנו כללות עם ישראל עיקר קדושתינו וטהרת נפשינו תולה רק

בפנימיות מחשבות אדם לאן שפונה במחשבתו ככה משרה בקרבו השראת אלהות

ונעשה מרכבה לסטרא דקדושה... ובכלל זה תורת עבודת אדם לטהר מחשבותיו

ופרטי חושיו לעבודת בוראו ואזי ראוי לכנותו ולקרותו בשם כהן כינוי לעובד את

עבודת הקודש...

ר׳ זאב וואלף זוטאמיר, ס׳ אור המאיר, חלק ב׳ דף 59.

[92]   מועדי ה׳ אשר תקראו אותם מקראי קודש אלה הם מועדי (ויקרא כ. ב) .

כלומר שאתם מקדשים את המועדים לשמוח בהם לשם יהו״ה. ולהיות הסעודה

כמטעמי יצחק. לעורר הרוחניות לדביקות הש״י ולהשגת תורתו הקדושה. ואז הם

מקראי קדש. אומר הש״י אלה הם מועדי. אמנם העושים חגים וששים ושמחים למלאות

בטנם קיא צואה בלי מקום. עליהם נאמר (ישעיה א. יד): מועדיכם שנאה נפשי. וכבר

הארכתי בזה בהלכות מועדים שלי. וזה טעם איסור מלאכה במועדים. כדי שלא יהיה

טרוד במלאכתו וישכח הדביקות בהש״י. כי המועדים מקודשים. ובהם יוסיף הדביקות

בהשם יתברך. ואז הם מועדי ה׳.

ר׳ ישעיה הורוויץ, ס׳ שני לוחות הברית, כרך ב׳ דף ס״א עמוד ד׳.

[93]   ואיש כי יתן מום בעמיתו כאשר עשה כן יעשה לו פי׳ ואיש כי יתן מום בעמיתו

שמגנה את חבירו ומבזה אותו. את עצמו הוא מבזה כאשר עשה כן יעשה לו. ע״ד

ומכבדי אכבד (ש״א ב׳) גם הוא הסימן שהמום הזה בעצמו בו הוא. כאן נמצא וכאן

הי׳. ע״ד (ב״מ נ״ט:) מום שבך אל תאמר לחברך...

ר׳ ישראל ממאדזין, ס׳ דברי ישראל.חלק ג׳ דף 123.

פרשת בהר

[94]   דבר אל בני ישראל וכו׳ ושבתה הארץ שבת לה׳. ענין שלש פרשיות הנאמרין

כאן פרשת שמיטה ופרשת דרור עבדים ביובל ופרשת ריבית, והוא שהש״י מזהיר

לישראל שלא ישימו בטחונם בשום דבר הנראה לעיני האדם שיוכל לבטוח בו. ואלו

השלשה דברים שמיטה ויובל וריבית הם בעולם ושנה ונפש כי קנין שדות וכרמים הוא

קנין שיש לאדם בעולם אשר יוכל לבטוח בו. וצוה הש״י נגד זה מצות שמיטה היינו

שלא ישים האדם בטחונו בהם ויראה כי לה׳ הם. כי בשנת השמיטה אין לאדם שום

הכרת קנין בקנינו. ויראה כי לה׳ הארץ. ונגד הבטחה שיש לאדם בזמן, היינו שיש לו

מבטח שיאסף הון מחיר הזמן היינו שיקח ריבית. אמרה תורה אל תקח מאתו נשך כי

עיקר ריבית הוא שלוקח מחיר הזמן כמאמר הגמ׳ [בבא מציעא ס״ג:] כללא דרביתא

כל אגר נטר ליה אסור. ונגד קנין שיש בנפשות עבדים ויכול לבטוח בהם שישתמש

בהם לכל צרכיו. נגד זה צוה הש״י מצות דרור עבדים בגופם וצריך לשלחם לחפשי

וגם בעת היותם עבדים צוה הש״י שלא ירדה בו בפרך. היינו שיבין שאין גופו שייך לו.

וצוה הש״י אלו שלשה המצות היינו שנראה שהעולם והשנה והנפש אין שום מבטח

להאדם בהם. רק ה׳ הוא מבטח האדם...

ר׳ מרדכי ליינר מאיזביצא, ס׳ מי השלוח, כרך א׳ דף קל״א.

[95]   כי גרים ותושבים אתם עמדי. י״ל בזה בדרך רמז להבין זה ע״פ ששמעתי

מחכם אחד על פסוק [תהלים קי״ט] גר אנכי בארץ אל תסתר ממני מצותיך כי ידוע מן

איכות טבע העולם כי מי שהוא גר אין לו עם מי לדבק ולקרב עצמו ולספר לו כל

מאורעותיו וכל לבו שאין לו חבר לא ישראל ולא גוים אך כשרואה חבירו הגר אזי

מספר כל אחד בפני חבירו כל מאורעותיו וידוע שהקב״ה הוא כמו גר בעוה״ז שאין לו

על מי להשרות שכינת כבודו יתברך כי זעירין אינון וכו׳ והוא שהתפלל דוד המע״ה

גר אנכי בארץ היינו אני ג״כ רוצה להיות תושב בעוה״ז ואני רק כגר בעוה״ז ולכך אל

תסתר ממני מצותיך כמו גר אחד בפני חבירו שמספר לו כל לבו י״ל הרמז בפסוק

כי גרים ותושבים כשתהיו בבחינת גר בעולם הזה ותושב בעוה״ב אז אתם עמדי כי אני

ג״כ גר בעוה״ז כנ״ל וממילא אל תסתיר מכם מצותי כנ״ל והבן.

ר׳ משה חיים אפרים מסדילקוב, ס׳ דגל מחנה אפרים. דפ׳ קפ״ג-קפ״ד.

[96] 'אל תקח מאתו נשך ותרבית [ויקרא כה לו]. פירוש: כשתעשה איזה דבר טוב

לא תרצה אצל השם יתברך. ברוך הוא, ליקח ממנו רווחים עבור מעשיך הטובים.

שיבא לך איזה פניה או גאות חלילה, ובזה תחשב כאלו אתה נושך. כביכול, להבורא

שיש לו צער גדול מזה, ו'תועבת ה' כל גבה לב' [משלי טז ה]. אלא אדרבא יהיו כל

כוונתך לשם שמים. ובזה יקובל לרצון לפני בוראינו. ועל ידי זה נזכה לגאולה

במהרה בימינו, וזו היא: 'אני ה' אלקיכם' כו'. 'לתת לכם ארץ כנען להיות לכם

לאלהים' [ויקרא כה לח].

ר׳ אלימלך מליזנסק, ס׳ נועם אלימלך. כרך ב׳ דפ׳ שנ״ה-שנ״ו.

פרשת בחקותי

[97]   ועשיתם אותם. מאי ועשיתם אותם. כיון דאמר תלכו ותשמרו אמאי ועשיתם אלא

מאן דעביד פקודי אורייתא ואזיל באורחוי כביכול כאילו עביד ליה לעילא אמר קב״ה

כאלו עשאני...

ס׳ הזהר. כרך ג׳ דף קי״ג עמוד א׳.

[98]   ואולך אתכם קוממיות (ויקרא כו יג). פירוש שתי קומות (ע׳ ב״ב עה.). הענין

הוא. כי יש קומת הקדושה וקומת הקליפה. וכאשר נבנה קומת הקדושה על ידי התורה

והמצות אזי נתבטל כח קומת הקליפה. וזהו ואולך אתכם קוממיות, שתי קומות, וכאשר

זה קם זה נופל כנ״ל.

ועוד שתי קומות. קומה שלמטה באדם התחתון וקומת אדם העליון. פירוש

כאשר האדם הוא בכל בחינת קומה, שאין בו פגם בשום אחד מאבריו מדבר עבירה

והרהור. ובפרט בכלי המעשה, והוא סוד סור מרע ועשה טוב (תהלים לד טו) מפני

שבינה יתירה נודעת לו ממקום גבוה. אזי מתקן הוא בחינת קומת העליון בכלל. וגורם

יחודים בעולמות העליונים. ומתייחד גם הוא עמהם בכללם. וזהו קוממיות, שתי קומות

וד״ל.

ר׳ מרדכי מטשערנאביל. ס׳ ליקוטי תורה, דף קי״ט.

[99]   ואם המר ימירנו והיה הוא והיה תמורתו יהיה קודש היינו אהבת הגרועים שנפלו

למטה בסוד שבירת הכלים ועלו אותו למעלה. ויקח אותה אהבה לעבוד את ה׳. וזהו

והי״ה לשון שמחה הוא ותמורתו יהיה קודש.

ר׳ דוב בער, המגיד ממיזעריטש. ס׳ אור תורה, דף 88.

[100] ...במדבר סיני באוהל מועד וגו' זה מורה לנו על קדושת התורה, שהולכת

ממקום גבוה למקום נמוך. כי אפילו השפל בשפלים יוכל לבוא לעבודת ה' ע"י

התוה"ק. ולזה בא לנו הכתוב לומר שדיבורו ית' הי' במדבר שהוא מקום פחות מאוד

ומקום תוקף הקליפות כמ"ש [דברים ח', ט"ו] נחש שרף ועקרב וצימאון אשר אין מים

[במדבר כ. ה'] לא מקום זרע ותאינה וגפן ועכ"ז במקום הפחות הגרוע הזה שם הי'

דיבורו ית' ושם הי' משכן השכינה הקדושה ואוהל מועד. כי זאת הוא השלימות התורה

הקדושה שתוכל להתפשט לכל מיני שפלים ועומקים ולהעלות כל הבחי' אפילו

הפחותים מתעלים ע"י התוה"ק.

ר' נפתלי צבי הורוויץ מראפשיץ, ס' זרע קודש. כרך א' דף ק"ז עמוד א'.

[101] איש על דגלו באותות לבית אבותם. דגלו הוא אותיות גדול הרמז על הגדלות

ואמר הכתוב כי אם אדם רוצה להיות בחי' איש היינו להתגבר על ענין הגדלות

העצה לזה באותות לבית אבותם היינו להביא את אות וראי' נכונה להסתכל לבית אבותם

היינו שיסתכל לאבות הקדושים אשר רוח ה' הי' בהם ואין אדם יוכל להשיג קדושתם

אעפ"כ הי' בעיניהם בבחי' עפר ושפלות וא"כ היאך האדם אשר מלא בתאוות ירצה

להתגדל.

א"י כי העצה נגד גדלות שיסתכל לבית אבותם היינו בהמחשבה וברצון שלו

אם הוא בלתי לה' לבדו כי הגם כי יוכל אדם לחשוב כי במעשה המצות ובעסק

התורה עושה כפי יכלתו אבל מידי מחשבה לא יצאה כי אין אדם יאמר שהוא זכאי

במחשבה שהתורה והמצות יהי׳ במחשבה נכונה בלתי שום פניה.

ר׳ אברהם יששכר בער הכהן מראדאמסק, ס׳ חסד לאברהם. דף 315.

[102] ולא יבואו לראות כבלע את הקודש ומתו. י״ל הרמז בזה ע״ד ששמעתי מן אא״ז

זללה״ה שיש לפעמים שבא א׳ אצל הצדיק כדי ללמוד ממעשיו והצדיק הוא אז

בבחינת קטנות והוא מקבל ממנו כן ולא ידע לאזדהורי בי׳ וכמו שאירע שבא אחד אל

הרב המפורסם מוהר״ן זללה״ה וראה ששתה אז קאווע בטלית ותפילין ונסע לביתו

והתחיל לנהוג נ״כ כך וזהו אזהרה ולא יבואו לראות היינו בשביל לראות את מעשיו

ולקבלם תיכף כבלע את הקודש היינו שיש לפעמים שהוא ביומי הקטנות ונבלע אז

הקדושה בו ולכך מתו היינו שנפלו ממדריגתן לא יבואו לקבל זה כ״א שיראה זמן

הגדלות ויקבל ממנו והבן זה כי קצרה דעת השומעים ולא הבינו ויש בזה דברים

טובים ואי״ה כשיזכה ה׳ אותי ואהיה בריא עדיף אפרש.

ר׳ משה חיים אפרים מסדילקוב, ס׳ דגל מחנה אפרים. דף ק״צ.

פרשת נשא

[103] שמחה לצדיק עשות משפט ומחתה לפעלי און... והנה שלמה ע״ה כוון בזה

להודיענו שיתחייב האדם להיותו שמח במצות כשיעשה אותן או יראה אחרים עושין

וזהו שאמר עשות משפט ולא אמר עשותו משפט. וידוע כי השמחה במעשה המצות

מצוה בפני עצמה. וכשם שהמצוה עבודה לשי״ת כך השמחה על המצוה נקראת

עבודה. וכן כתיב (דברים כח) תחת אשר לא עבדת את ה׳ אלהיך בשמחה. באר כי

השמחה שלמות העבודה. ועל כן היה ענין השיר במקדש ובמשכן בשיר הפה והכלי

שהוא מביא נפש האדם לדרך השמחה. ומכאן אמר הכתוב בלוים לעבוד עבודת

עבודה, ודרשו רז״ל אי זו עבודה לעבודה הוי אומר זה השיר. כי היו הלוים מוזהרין

ומצווים לשורר ולעורר השמחה על מצות קרבן כדי להיות מעשה המצוה בשמחה....

רבנו בחיי, פירוש על התורה, חלק ד׳ דף י״א.

[104] במדרש רבה ד״א ישא ה׳ פניו וכי הקב״ה נושא פנים והלא כבר נאמר (דברים

י, יז) אשר לא ישא פנים אמר הקב״ה כשם שהם נושאים לי פנים כך אני נושא להם

פנים כיצד כתבתי בתורתי ואכלת ושבעת וברכת (שם) ואדם מישראל יושב הוא ובניו

ובני ביתו ואין לפניהם כדי שביעה ונושאין לי פנים ומברכין ודקדקו על עצמן עד כזית

עד כביצה לפיכך ישא ה׳ פניו ע״כ. המאמר הזה הוא פלאי למבין. אכן נ״פ דהנה אם

אדם הדיוט נותן לחבירו מתנה מועטת אינה נחשבת בעיני המקבל כלל משא״כ אם

המלך נותן לו מתנה אף שהיא מועטת אעפ״כ היא חשיבות גדול מצד הנותן שהוא מלך

ומגיע לקבל הנאה גדולה יותר ממה שלקח מתנה מרובה מהדיוט. כן הוא הדמיון ג״כ

בענין ברכת המזון שאע״פ שכתוב בתורה שצריך לאכול כדי שביעה זו מצד

המקבלים אבל כיון שאנו יודעים שהמלך מלכי המלכים הוא הנותן לחם לכל בשר

והוא המכין לכן ברי׳ה הצטרכותו וקיומו ונמצא אף שאינו אוכל רק כזית הוא נחשב

בעיניו מאוד ויגיע לו הנאה ממנו עד מאוד כיון שהוא בא מיד ה׳ כמשל [הנ״ל]. וז״פ

המדרש כיצד אדם וכו׳ ואין לפניהם כדי שביעה והם נושאים לי פנים ומברכין כלומר

שהם מסתכלים ממי בא להם המאכל ההוא ומגודל חשיבות הנותן הם נהנין במאכל

מועט ומזה בא להם שביעה ומברכין וזו ענין שהם נושאין לו פנים והבן. כן ג״כ הוא

המדה שהקב״ה נושא להם פנים ומשתעשע בעבודתן המועטת שעובדין לפניו כיון

שהוא מסתכל ממי בא העבודה ההיא כיון שאנחנו ב״א וקצרי השכל ואף על פי כן אנו

עובדין אותו. וזה פירוש ישא ה׳ פניו אליך. והבין כי עמוק הוא.

ר׳ שמחה בונם מפשיסחא, ס׳ קול שמחה, דף פ״ז.

[105] כי עבודת הקדש עליהם בכתף ישאו (ז ט). בעבודת קודש צריך לעמל רב.

בכתף ישאו, כי מי שיאמר לא יגעתי ומצאתי אל תאמין לו.

ר׳ מנחם מענדל מקאצק, ס׳ עמוד האמת, דף ע״ו.

פרשת בהעלתך

[106] ויעש כן אהרן. פירש״י להגיד שבחו של אהרן שלא שינה. שינה פירש שלא היה

אצלו כדבר ושונה בה, שעשה כדעת האדם בהרגל. רק תמיד היה עושה את המצוה

כדבר חדש שאדם עושה בשמחה וזריזות, וזה שאמר בגמ׳ [ר״ה ט״ז:] חייב אדם לטהר

את עצמו ברגל שנאמר ובנבלתם לא תגעו, כי נבלה מורה על דבר שיצא מאתה החיים

וכן הוא העושה מצוה בלא שמחה וזריזות. רק כמצוה אנשים מלומדה דומה שאין בו

חיים. ולכן ברגל לפי שהש״י משפיע חיים לישראל צריך האדם לקבל החיים במשחה.

ר׳ מרדכי ליינר מאיזביצא, ס׳ מי השלוח, כרך א׳ דף קמ״ז.

[107] על פי ה׳ יסעו ועל פי ה׳ יחנו (במדבר ט, יח) , ואח״כ כתיב (ט, כ) : על פי ה׳

יחנו ועל פי ה׳ יסעו. יש רמז מוסר בכאן על כל פעולה או תנועה שהאדם עושה יאמר,

אם ירצה השם או בעזרת השם. למשל, בלכתו בדרך יאמר הנני נוסע בעזרת השם

יתברך. ובדעתי לחנות במקום פלוני בעזרתו יתברך יתברך אם ירצה. וכשבא למקום החניה

אז יחזור ויתן שבח. ויאמר הנה בעזרת הש״י באתי הנה. ובדעתי ליסע לזמן פלוני

בעזרתו יתברך אם ירצה. נמצא שם שמים שגור בפיו בשעה שעולה במחשבתו, ובשעת

מעשה. ככה בכל פעולותיו.

ר׳ ישעיה הורוויץ, ס׳ שני לוחות הברית, כרך ב׳ דף ס״ז עמוד ג׳.

[108] והאיש משה עניו מאד וגו׳ (י״ב, ג׳). פירש רש״י ז״ל, עניו, שפל וסבלן, רבינו

הקדוש היה אומר על שני אנשים: האחד, אם היה חושב שאינו כראוי ממש ח״ו לא היה

יכול לחיות, והשני יודע שפלותו ועם כל זאת סובל עצמו, דזה האחרון עבודתו מעולה

יותר, שהוא שפל וסובל השפלות.

והאיש משה עניו מאד וגו׳ (י״ב, ג׳). ופירש רש״י ז״ל, עניו, שפל וסבלן, פירוש,

אף על פי שהיה משה רבינו ע״ה שפל בעיניו, היינו שידע שפלות מצבו, עם כל זאת

היה סובל את עצמו, בבחינת (דברי הימים ב. י״ז). ויגבה לבו בדרכי ה׳.

ר׳ שמחה בונם מפשיסחא, ס׳ מדרש שמחה, כרך א׳ דפ׳ קל״ה-קל״ו.

פרשת שלח-לך

[109] שמעתי מהמגיד זללה״ה שביאר פ״ה ארץ אוכלת יושביה ירצה מדריגות

התחתונים המכונים בשם ארציות אוכלת ומכלת את היושבים ושוהים שם כי אין האדם

רשאי לשהות עצמו בבחי׳ ארציות אפילו כמעט רגע...

ר׳ זאב וואלף זוטאמיר, ס׳ אור המאיר, חלק ב׳ דף 33 עמוד א׳.

[110] ...מבלתי יכולת במדרש אמר משה רבון העולמים כי עין בעין נראה אתה מהו כי עין בעין אמר ריש לקיש הרי מאזנים מעוין אתה אומר אכנו בדבר ואני אומר סלח נא נראה של מי יקום שנאמר ויאמר ה' סלחתי כדבריך עכ״ל המדרש ולהבין הענין נראה ע״ד משל למלך בשר ודם צריך לעשות הנהגת נימוסי המדינה בשביל שלא יהיה איש את רעהו חיים בלעו ע״ד המשנה באבות הוי מתפלל בשלומה של מלכות שאלמלא מוראה מוראה איש את רעהו חיים בלעו ולכאורה מאי איכפת לי' להתעבר על ריב לא לו אך מורא עולה על ראשו פן יגיע הדבר לעצמותו לאפוקי מלך מלכי המלכים הקב״ה אשר כל היכולת בידו אין צריך לעשות נימוסי המדינה בשביל מורא רק בשביל טובת האדם עשה הנימוסים ונתן להם את התורה וזה פירוש המדרש מאזניים מעוין כך אמר מרע״ה לפני הקב״ה מפני מה אתה רוצה לענוש את ישראל אם חטאו מה יפעיל לך ואם בשביל שיהיו מנוקים מעון אני אומר סלח נא ונ״כ יהיו מנוקים מעון ונראה מי יעמוד מיד אמר הקב״ה סלחתי כדבריך שנאמר סלחתי כדבריך.

ר' משה ליב מסאסוב. ס' ליקוטי רמ״ל. דף כ״ה.

[111] ולא תתורו אחרי לבבכם ואחרי עיניכם (טו לט). ולמה לא נאמר אחרי לבבכם הרע, כלום מי שיש לו לב טוב אף הוא אסור ללכת אחרי לבו. אלא ללמדנו כי אפילו טוב אין צריכים לעשות מתוך נטיית הלב, אלא מתוך דעת ויגיעה, כי טוב שעושים מתוך נטיית הלב הרי הוא בבחינת כי בשרירות לבי אלך (דברים כט) ואינו הטוב האמתי. וזהו שאמר שלמה המלך (קהלת יא) והלך בדרכי לבך ובמראה עיניך ״ודע״ היינו שתלך בדרכי לבך מתוך דעת ובקשת עצות מיגיעת עצמך.

ר׳ מנחם מענדל מקאצק. ס׳ עמוד האמת. דף פ״א.

פרשת קרח

[112] קרח הוא גלגול קין ומשה הוא גלגול הבל וע״כ חלק קרח על משה וקנא בו

ועורר קנאה הישינה שהי׳ לקין על הבל והנה האדמה נתאררה אז על אשר פצתה פה

לקחת דמי אחיך וכאן תיקן אותה משה במה שפצתה את פיה לבלוע את קרח פצה

תחת פצה ...

ר׳ יעקב צבי יאליש. ס׳ קהלת יעקב. חלק ד׳ דף ז׳ עמוד ד׳.

[113] ויאמרו אל אלהי הרוחת וגו׳. אמר שם אל. לצד שראה התעוררות תגבורת

הדינים. הזכיר חסד אל למתק הדינים:

ואומר אלהי הרוחות לכל בשר. טען טענה הנשמעת לפני הבורא. כי ה׳ חפץ

שכל הרוחות יקבלו אלהותו עליהם. בעודם בבשר בעולם הזה, ...: ולזה נתחכם משה

וריצה ה׳ בדבר שהוא חפץ בו. ואמר אלהי הרוחות לכל בשר. שאתה חפץ שאלהותך

תהיה לרוחות בזמן שהם בבשר. ואם אתה ממיתם. אתה חסר רצון זה. ואין נכון

להגביר הדינים. שיסובבו הפסד קבלת אלהותך לרוחות שבבשר. שהוא רום תכלית

חשקך ...

ר׳ חיים ן׳ עטר. פירוש על התורה, חלק ד׳ דף ס״ה.

[114] ויצא פרח ויצץ ציץ ויגמל שקדים (י״ז, כג). וקשה מאי קמ״ל בזה דכתיב פרח

ויצץ ציץ. דכל העיקר הוא להשמיענו ויגמל שקדים כמובן. ויש לפרש. שהפסוק

משמיענו ומרמז לנו דרך לעבודת הבורא יתברך שמו. שאף על גב שנראה לאדם שהוא

בגדר השלמות דהיינו לעת זקנתו. כמו ויגמל שקדים. צריך עוד להיות וייצא פרח ויצץ

ציץ. להתנהג עוד בזריזות ובשפלות המדריגה כמו בעת נעורים.

ר׳ שמחה בונם מפשיסחא, ס׳ מדרש שמחה, כרך א׳ דף קמ״ג.

פרשת חקת

[115] ויקחו אליך פרה אדומה וגו׳. סוד פרה אדומה הוא. ואהבת לרעך כמוך.

(הסביר נכדו, רבי מנדל בן בנו רבי שמחה בונם מאוטבוצק זצוק״ל: שהרי פרה

אדומה מטהרת טמאים ומטמאת טהורים, היינו שהכהן מטמא את עצמו כדי לטהר את

זולתו).

ר׳ יצחק מוואָרקה. ס׳ בית יצחק, דף פ׳.

[116] ...וישלח משה מלאכים מקדש כי משכן הנשמה הוא במוח הנק׳ קדש ושלחה

הנשמה שלוחים אל החומר שהוא הגוף הרודף אחר תאוות המותרות כמ״ש הלעיטני נא

(בראשית כה) לזה נקרא אדום והוא מלך אדום המולך על כל אברי הגוף מבלי היותו

נכנע אל הצורה עד שרצה לעורר לבו במחשבות קדושות שהם הרהורי תשובה הבא

מקדש כה אמר אחיך ישראל שיתן לב על תכלית בריאתו בחומר ובצורה בעה״ז כדי

שיכניע חומרו אל הצורה שיהיה להם אחווה ושלום ולא נגדיים באופן שיהיה אחיך

ישראל...

ר׳ יעקב יוסף מפולנאי. ס׳ תולדות יעקב יוסף, כרך ב׳ דף תקנ״ח.

[117] ע״ד הקבלה אז ישיר ישראל את השירה הזאת. השירה כמו התפלה ממשיך

הכוונה במחשבתו ממעלה למטה. כך היחיד או הרבים האומרים שירה ממשיכין

הברכה ממעלה למטה.

ודע כי שיר״ה בגימטריא תפל״ה... ואמר את השירה הזאת כבר ידעת מהו

זאת... עלי באר ענו לה, יתחיל ממטה למעלה כדי להעלות המדה העשירית אל מקום

מוצאה ואח״כ ממשיך הברכות משם וממשיך והולך ממעלה למטה. וזהו שאמר עלי

באר ענו לה כלומר עלינו לשבח המדה הזאת ולומר לה עלי באר. וקרא המדה הזאת

באר לפי שהיא מקבלת כח מכלן ונאצלת מהם. כי כן הבאר בית קבול למים ... וענין

עלי באר התעלי אל המקום אשר נחצבת ממנו. חפרוה שרים. החכמה והבינה. נדיבי

העם. הגדולה והגבורה והתפארת. הם אברהם יצחק ויעקב... במחוקק זה צדיק יסוד

עולם. במשענותם. הנצח וההוד. הרי כל הבנין נרמז בלשון השירה הזאת כמו שנרמז

בשירת הים...

רבנו בחיי. פירוש על התורה, חלק ד׳ דף צ״ז.

פרשת בלק

[118] ותרא האתון את מלאך ה׳ נצב בדרך וכו׳ (כ״ב כ״ג). עוד שמעתי משמו זלה״ה

שדיבר עמו איש אחד על אודות פרנסתו והצלחתו. והשיב לו בזה הלשון. הנה מצינו

באתונו של בלעם כתוב ותרא האתון וגו׳ ובלעם לא ראה, והדבר תמוה לפי גודל

מעלתו שהיה נופל וגלוי עיניים לא ראה את המלאך והאתון ראה.

אבל האמת כי הנפש יכול לראות הכל ומה שהאדם אינו רואה. הטעם כי

החומר של האדם הוא מסך המבדיל ומניע ומכסה אל הנפש לבלתי לראות. לכך אל

יכול לראות בעצמו. לבד בעת אשר ה׳ היה רוצה לגלות עיניו היה נופל ונתבטלו

חושיו והתפשטות הגשמיות ואז היה גלוי עיניים. אבל החומר של בהמה אינו מסך

המבדיל בעד הנפש ואינו מונע ומכסה עליה והנפש מונח בתוכה כמו שמונח בכד על

כן רואה הכל ולכן ראתה האתון את המלאך.

ר׳ אורי השרף מסטרעליסק. ס׳ אמרי קדוש. דפ׳ ט״ז-י״ז.

[119] הן עם לבדד ישכון ובגוים לא יתחשב אמרו חז״ל מברכותיו של אותו רשע אנו

למדים מה ה׳ בלבו לקללם אלא שנתעקם פיו ונתהפך עד שהי׳ מוכרח לברכם מעין

אותן קללות ולכאו׳ תמוה הלא באמת היו ברכותיו רק מהשפה ולחוץ ולבו בל עמו

וא״כ איך יכולים ברכות כאלה לשרות ולחול על המתברך כשאין בהם שום חיות

דאנן קיי״ל שהמברך את חבירו צריך ליתן חיות ושכל טוב לתוך הדיבורי׳ היינו שיתן

את דעתו ורצונו וכל חפצו באהב׳ עזה ועי״ז יכולה הברכה לאתקיים ולחול על

המתברך משא״כ מי שמברך בפיו ולבו בל עמו בודאי שתיקתו יפה מדיבורו אך התי׳

הנכון הוא שבשעה שאנו קוראים בתורה אותן הברכות או כשאנו לומדי׳ ועוסקי׳ בהם

צריכי׳ אנו להמתיק את כל הדיבורים האלה וליתן בהם שכל טוב וחיו׳ של שפע

ברכות וטובות וחסדים ועי״ז החיות הם יכולים לשרות על ישראל והנה גם בפסוק זה

הי׳ בלבו של אותו רשע לקלל אותם שישבו בבדידות ח״ו כל אחד לבדו בלא

התחברות ולא יהיו חשובים וספונים אצל האומות כמ״ש ובגוים יתחשב. אבל אנחנו

צריכים להפך ולכון בזה ברכה גדולה ולפרש תיבת בדד על אחדות הנפלא והיינו

שיהיו כולם יחד כדודים בלי שום פירוד וזה כונה פשוטה לטובה ויש עוד רמז כי

בדד בנ׳ עשר׳ שהוא אות יו״ד נקודה אחת בלי שום שיתוף והוא האחדות האמיתי

ועוד ירמז לטובה שאם תחלק תיבת בדד על אותיות הוא מרמז על המשכות כל

השפעות טובות בני חיי ומזוני וזהו בא דד ר״ל רומז על יניקת השפעות טוב׳ מצינורות

הקדושי׳ העליוני׳...

ר׳ מנחם מענדל מרימנאוו, ס׳ דברי מנחם, דף י״א.

[120] מה טובו אהליך יעקב משכנותיך ישראל. כי תכלית היראה היא להיות

בפנימיות ולא בגלוי רק דווקא בסתר, ולא כנוסח דלעולם יהא אדם ירא שמים בסתר

כבגלוי. וזהו פירוש מה טובו אוהליך. פירוש כי היריעות היו לאוהל כל המשכן

מלמעלה. וטוב הוא להיות אוהל שלך כלומר מלמעלה בגלוי יהיה יעקב. דהוא

מדרגה פשוטה. אבל משכנותיך פירוש הפנימיות יהיה ישראל דווקא. דהוא מדרגה

גדולה וק״ל. אחר כתבתי זאת שמעתי ממש דברים אלו אומרים החסיד ר״י בעש״ט

ושמחתי על זה.

ר׳ אברהם נח העליר, ס׳ זריזותא דאברהם, דף ה׳ עמוד א׳.

פרשת פנחס

[121] ונודע מ״ש בזוהר (פ׳ ויצא בס״ת קמ״ח ע״ב ...) ... כי נדב ואביהו אינון תרי

פלגי גופא דלכך נטל פנחס נשמת שניה׳ שהם נחשב לאחד כמ״ש בזוהר יער״ש וז״ש

הנני נותן לו בריתי שלום וכו׳ (במדבר כה) כי נודע עפ״י ששמעתי מרבותי כי

המחבר ב׳ דברים יחד נקרא שלום ולכך נקרא היסוד שלום לסיבה זו ומבשרי אחזה אלדי וג״כ כשיש פירוד בין אנשים ואדם המחברן נקרא רודף שלום וסבת חטא נדב ואביהו שלא נטלו עצה זה מזה (פסיקתא ובילקו״ש ח״א רמז תקכד) שנא׳ ויקחו איש מחתתו והי׳ פירוד ביניהם ופנחס שתיקן זה וניתקן ע״י שניתן לו ברית שלום וחברן בחי׳ נשמת נדב ואביהו לחד גופא וא״ש.

ר׳ יעקב יוסף מפולנאי, ס׳ תולדות יעקב יוסף, כרך א׳ דף שכ״ה.

[122] ...כתבתי בשם מורי זלה״ה יפקוד ה׳ איש אשר יוציאם ואשר יביאם (במדבר כ״ז) כי ראש הדור יוכל להעלות כל הדיבורים והסיפורים של אנשי דורו לקשר הגשמי ברוחני כמו (תענית כ״ב.) תרי בדחי וכו׳ ... ודפח״ח...

ר׳ יעקב יוסף מפולנאי, ס׳ בן פורת יוסף, דף פ״ב עמוד א׳.

[123] אין אדם יכול לעבוד את הקב״ה כ״א שיקשור א״ע להקב״ה כי ישראל זנין ומפרנסין להקב״ה וזהו את קרבני דהיינו שמקרבין אצלו הוא לחמי לאשי הם המלאכים ריח נחוח הוא משיח.

ר׳ פנחס מקאריץ, ס׳ מדרש פנחס.סימן רל״ג דף כ״ד עמוד א׳.

פרשת מטות

[124] נקום נקמת בני ישראל וכו׳. כי הצדיק אינו נפטר מעולם הזה עד שעושה מצוה גדולה ובזה ידבוק בשכינה. והרשע בהיפך אינו מת עד שעושה עבירה גדולה ונתמלא סאתו וכו׳, וב׳ הרב ע״פ הנ״ל דאיתא בזוהר דאתפשטותא דמש״ר בכל דרא ודרא

ובכל חכם ע״ש. ואין חכם יכול לחדש דבר עד שנתחדש בו בחי׳ משה שיש בעולם

בתוך ישראל וזה תאסף אל עמך דייקא. שתהיה לעולם בתוך עם ישראל.

ר׳ פנחס מקאריץ. ס׳ אמרי פנחס. סימן קי״ב דף ל״ח.

[125] ויאמר אלעזר הכהן אל אנשי הצבא הבאים למלחמה (לא כא). והרי צריך

לומר הבאים מהמלחמה, אלא שבאו כעת למלחמה חדשה, נאמרה להם עתה פרשת

גיעולי מדין ומוכח דהרהור הוי כמעשה, התחילו לחשוש גם על הרהורי עבירה וע״כ

באו למלחמה חדשה, וזה הבאים למלחמה.

ר׳ מנחם מענדל מקאצק, ס׳ עמוד האמת, דף׳ פ״ח-פ״ט.

[126] ונכבשה הארץ. פי׳ במה יכולים לכבוש התאוות והארציות לפני ד׳ ע״י שתזכירו

שאתם עומדים לפני השי״ת ע״ד שויתי ד׳ לנגדי תמיד (וכמבואר באו״ח ס״א) ואחר

נקרא היצה״ר ע״ש אלהים אחרים תשובו ר״ל תשובו ותסירו מכם והייתם נקיים מד׳

ומישראל כי ע״ז שאתם תהי׳ זכאין לא תגרמו שום צער ופגם לד׳ ולישראל והיתה

הארץ הזאת ארץ נקרא רצון כמ״ש חז״ל למה נקרא שמה ארץ שרצתה לעשות רצון

קונה לכם לאחוזה לפני ד׳ ר״ל אף שלא תוכלו להגיע לבחי׳ זו אם יהי׳ לכם תשוקה

ורצון לזה ג״כ הוא יקר בעיני השי״ת וכמ״ש קדוש א׳ על ישמח לב מבקשי ד׳ דהנה

בעניני עוה״ז כשמחפש איזה דבר שאבד אזי בשעה שמחפש אינו שמח עד שמוציאו

אבל בעיני עבדות השי״ת הוא תיכף שמח על שזכה לחפש בגנזי דמלכא קדישא וז״ש

ואם לא תעשון כן הנה חטאתם לד׳ שתגרמו בחטאתכם פגם בנשמה הוא חלק אלקי

וגורם צער לשכינתו ית׳ וע״ד קדושתי למעלה הוא מקדושתכם ואם האדם חוטא ח״ו

גורם צער לשכינה. וע״ז ידוו הדוים.

ר׳ מנחם מענדל מרימנאוו. ס׳ אילנא דחיי. חלק א׳ דף 90.

פרשת מסעי

[127] והנה אדומ״ו הגאון מהד״ב זלה״ה אמר כי כל המסעות שנסעו ישראל העיקר

היה לתקן כל המקומות ולהגביה הניצוצין קדישין מהם. ולכן נכתבו בתורה שמות

המסעות והמקומות אשר תקנום בתקנה. וזה ויכתוב משה את מוצאיהם למסעיהם על פי

ה׳. שמשה כתב כל מה שהוציאו ניצוצין קדושין במסעיהם שנסעו. ושנסעו אל פי ה׳.

ולא נסעו במקום אחד זולת שהוצרכו לתקן. וזהו ואלה מסעיהם למוצאיהם ודפח״ח.

ר׳ ישראל בן שבתי. המגיד מקאזיץ. ס׳ עבודת ישראל. דפ׳ ר״ו-ר״ז.

[128] ...׳צו את בני ישראל׳ כו׳. ׳כי אתם באים אל ארץ כנען׳ [במדבר לד ב]. פירוש:

כשתבואו להכניע ולשבר כח החיצונים וסטרא אחרא נקרא ארץ כנען, ׳זאת הארץ אשר

תפול לכם׳ [שם]. כפירוש רש״י: על ידי שהפיל הקדוש ברוך הוא שרי האומות

לפניהם. ולפי דרכנו פירושו: אתם תפילו הסטרא אחרא בנחלה, רצה לומר: על ידי

התורה הקדושה הנקרא נחלה.

׳ארץ כנען לגבולותיה׳ [שם]. רצה לומר: שתראו לשבר הגבולים של הסטרא

אחרא...

והשם יזכנו לעבדו בתמים שלא ישלוט בנו יצר הרע ונזכה במהרה לביאת

משיחנו שיתוקן חטא הנחש ומלאה הארץ דעה. אמן כן יהי רצון.

ר׳ אלימלך מליזנסק, ס׳ נועם אלימלך. כרך ב׳ דפ׳ ת״ס-תס״א.

[129] ואת הערים אשר תתנו ללוים את שש ערי המקלט ועליהם תתנו ארבעים ושתים עיר גו׳. בהעיר לב להבין ולדעת יש לרמז בזה כי מצוה זו נוהגת בכל זמן כי התורה נצחית וע״כ אפילו בזה״ז יש לה שייכות והוא תקון למכה איש בשגגה. ר״ל מי ששגג בחטאים ועונות ומשחית את נפשו הוא יעשנה. ר״ל שיעשה תיקון זה. בקבלת עמ״ש באהבה שלימה ובמס״נ גדול באמת בכל לבבו להש״י בהששה תיבות שמע ישראל כו׳. והמה בחי׳ שש ערי מקלט. ועליהם תתנו מ״ב עיר. הוא בחי׳ פ׳ א׳ של ק״ש שהוא ואהבת. שיש בה מ״ב תיבות. והיינו קבלת אהבתו ית׳ ותורתו בכל לב ונפש. וע״י המס״נ באמת בכל לבבו לקבל עליו עמ״ש. וע״י קבלתו באמת אהבת הש״י בכל לבבו בזה נתכפר לו על שהכה את נפשו בשגגה... והש״י יזכנו לעבדו ולאהבה אותו ית׳ באמת ובתמים ובדעת. וכיה״ר אמן. והבן כ״ז היטב.

ר׳ אברהם יהושע העשיל מאפטא. ס׳ אוהב ישראל. דף 158.

פרשת דברים

[130] ... והוא דשמעתי ממורי בשם הרמב״ן שצוה לבנו אם יסתפק לך באיזה דבר מצוה איך לעשותו כשיש בו דרכים לצדד לכאן ולכאן או שיש לך ספק אם הוא מצוה או לאו ואם יש לעשותו או למנוע ממנו אז תראה קודם כל לסלק מעסק דבר זה הנאת עצמך או כבודך, ואחר כך תראה לצדד לכאן ולכאן. אז השם יתברך יודיעך האמת ותלך לבטח ודפח״ח... ובזה יובן והדבר אשר יקשה מכם ר״ל הדבר אשר יקשה שאינכם יודעים איך לעשותו או למנוע כלל אם הוא מצוה או לאו הספק נולד מכ״ם

שיש בו הנאתכם כמו ל״ך לכ״ם להנאתכם מה שאין כן אם תסלקו מהדבר הנאתכם

וכבודכם ותקרבון אלי״י שהוא יותר פנימי מן לי. והכוונה שיהיה רק לשם שמים בלי

שום פניה והנאה אז ושמעתיו איך יתנהג וק״ל.

ר׳ יעקב יוסף מפולנאי. ס׳ בן פורת יוסף. דף נ״ו עמ׳ א׳-ב׳.

[131] ובמדבר אשר ראית אשר נשאך לשון יחיד. ושוב בכל הדרך אשר הלכתם עד

באכם. כי לא היה נסים שוה. יש ראה מה שלא ראה חבירו. יש אשר נשאך על הענן יש

בגובה יש בנמוך ויש כאילו הולכים לכך אשר נשאך אשר הלכתם.

ר׳ אלעזר מגרמייזא, פירוש הרוקח על התורה, כרך ג׳ דף קס״ג.

[132] ראה נתתי בידך את סיחון מלך חשבון האמורי. סיחון הוא מלשון שיח ותפלה

והתפלה הוא מלך ר״ל שנעשה ע״י כתר למלך מלכי המלכים ע״י חשבון האמורי

שמחשב הכוונה של כל אמירה ומכוון בתפלתו גם ירמוז חשבון שעושה חשבון הנפש

בשעה שעורך תחינתו לפניו ית׳ ואת ארצו עד שמגיע לבחי׳ הכנעה שהוא כארץ.

ר׳ מנחם מענדל מרימנאוו. ס׳ אילנא דחיי, חלק א׳ דף 93.

פרשת ואתחנן

[133] וידעת היום והשבות אל לבבך כי ה׳ הוא האלהים בשמים ממעל ועל הארץ

מתחת אין עוד. אין הפירוש שאין אלוה זולתו, שזהו פשיטא. ומבואר בפסוק שמע

ישראל וגו׳. אלא רצה לומר שאין עוד מציאות בעולם זולת מציאותו יתברך. כי

בהסתרו יאבד הכל.

ר׳ ישעיה הורוויץ. ס׳ שני לוחות הברית. בעשר מאמרות. כרך א׳ דף ל׳ עמוד
א׳.

[134]   והנה שמעתי בשם הרב המגיד איש אלקי׳ מו״ה יחיאל מיכל מזלאטשוב
זצוק״ל על פסוק אנכי עומד בין ה׳ וביניכם פי׳ כשאיש מישראל מחזיק בעצמו שהוא
מעולה באיזה מעלה בתורה או בעבודת ה׳ אזי הוא עושה מסך מבדיל בינו לבין קונו
וזה אנכי שמי שמחזיק עצמו ליש וסובר שהוא במדריגה ישיות אז עומד בין גו׳ פי׳
שדבר זה הוא חוצץ ומסך מבדיל בין האדם להשי״ת.

קלונימוס קאלמן בן אהרן הלוי עפשטיין. ס׳ מאור ושמש על דברים ה׳ ה׳.

[135]   שמע ישראל ה׳ אלהינו כו׳. הראוי יאמר ה׳ אלהינו א׳. אך יאמר שמע ישראל
כולכם לשון יחיד שהוא באחדות הלבבות כא׳ וזה יחוייב לנו יען כי ה׳ הוא אלהינו כי
גם בה׳ בחינת דין ואלהינו הנזכר הוא ה׳ כי בו גם בחינת רחמים ושני השמות כלם
אחד וחייבים אנחנו להדמות לקוננו יתברך כי על כן נקרא אלהינו ולא אלהי האומות
כל שורש אחדות נפשותנו עם שיוצר הכל הוא ועל כן נתחייב להדמות אליו. או יאמר
שמע בלב אחד וקבל ישראל בין יתנהג עמך בשם ה׳ שהוא רחמים בין בשם אלהינו
שהוא דין נכלל בה׳ כי הלא ב׳ הבחינות הם רחמים וזהו ה׳ אלהינו ה׳ כי הם ייסורין
לטובה ולא להנקם ואל תתמה כי הלא ב׳ בחינות א׳ שם בעצם. וזה אומר א׳.

ר׳ משה אלשייך. ס׳ תורת משה. חלק ה׳ דפ׳ 46-47.

פרשת עקב

[136] כי לא על הלחם לבדו יחיה האדם. פי׳: כי חיות הנשמה, הוא לא ע״י מאכל. כי על כל מוצא פי ה׳ יחיה האדם. וזה הברכה המוציאה בפה, מוציא ניצוצי קדושה מן הטומאה, ונבררת ע״י פי ה׳, בלעיסה ל״ב שנים, שהם ל״ב אלהים, ל״ב נתיבות.

ר׳ חיים וויטל, ס׳ לקוטי תנ״ך וטעמי המצות, דף רמ״ז.

[137] ואתפש בשני וגו׳. צריך לדעת למה הוצרך לתופשם, והלא בידו היו. ואולי כשלא חטאו ישראל היו הלוחות גבוהות על יד משה, ולא היתה ידו משגת לקחת אותם, וכמו שדקדק לומר בפסוק שלפני זה, ושני הלוחות על שתי ידי. ולא אמר בשתי ידי או בידי. אלא נתכוון לומר שלא היו בידיו ממש אלא גבוהות למעלה מידיו והיו נושאות עצמן, ואחר שראה העגל הוסר כח קדושתם והוצרך לתופשם בידו:

ר׳ חיים ן׳ עטר, ס׳ אור החיים, חלק ה׳ דף ל״ג.

[138] בפסוק הוא תהלתך והוא אלקיך. כי התפלה שאדם מתפלל היא בעצמה אלקות שמייחד המדות העליונים, ואותם המתפללין לפני הקב״ה שהתפלה דבר אחר הוא מבחי׳ יהבין ליה מלבר כעבד שבא לבקש וצוה המלך שיתנו לו שאלתו, ולאותם שהתפלה בעצמה אלקות הוא מבחי׳ בן שמחפש בגנזי דמלכא ונוטל הוא בעצמו שאלתו שהוא נאמן להקב״ה. ואמר כי מדוד המלך ע״ה ואילך לא היה אדם מתפלל כן אלא אני.

ר׳ פנחס מקאריץ, ס׳ אמרי פנחס, סימן קכ״ג דף מ׳.

פרשת ראה

[139] ראה אנכי נותן לפניכם היום ברכה לכאורה תיבת היום אינו מובן אך דידוע

שהקב״ה מחדש בכל יום תמיד מעשה בראשית דהוא ית׳ נותן בכל יום בהירות חדש

ומשפיע חסדים חדשים ואדם העובד שמו יתברך מקבל עליו בכל יום בהירות ושכל

חדש מה שלא היה יודע אתמול וזהו שכתוב ראה אנכי נותן לפניכם היום ע״ד שאמרו

חכמינו ז״ל היום בכל יום יהיו בעיניך כחדשים רצה לומר בכל יום תקבל ברכה

וחסד חדש.

ר׳ לוי יצחק מברדיטשוב. ס׳ קדושת לוי. דף פ״ח עמוד ד׳.

[140] ... כי מנסה ה׳ אלקיכם אתכם כי העה״ז הוא עולם הנסיון שהנשמה נשלחת שם

להיותה בנסיון בעה״ז...

ר׳ ישראל בן אליעזר. בעל שם טוב. ס׳ כתר שם טוב. דף 101. עמוד ב׳.

[141] ...(דברים טו. כב.) בשעריך תאכלנו כו׳ כצבי וכאיל. יש לומר דהנה צריך

האדם להיות דבק בה׳ יתברך. שלא תהיה לו אהבה אחרת כי אם אהבת הבורא ב״ה.

כמו שכתוב (דברים ו. ה). ואהבת את ה׳ אלקיך. בכל לבבך. ובכל נפשך. ובכל

מאודך. על כרחך צריך לאכול. וכן שאר דבר שנקרא גם כן אכילה. כידוע (בראשית

ל״ט ו). כי־אם. צריך לפרוש עצמו בכל רגע כמעט. לזכור מהדביקות הבורא ב״ה.

והנה איתא (שה״ש ח. יד). על ברח דודי ודמה לצבי. או לעופר האילים. כי

דרך הצבי שישן בעין אחת. וכן שהוא רץ מביט לאחוריו (שה״ר פ״ח טו. זהר ח״ב

יד.) כן יש לומר גם כאן. תאכלנו כצבי ואיל. כי בשעת אכילה נחשב לשינה. נגד

דביקות הבורא ב״ה ואהבתו. יהיה ישן רק בעין אחת. וכן יביט לאחור לאהבת הבורא

ב״ה בכל עת וזמן. וכן נמי כאיל. אלא שהוא לשון כפול.

ר׳ יעקב יצחק, החוזה מלובלין, ס׳ זאת זכרון, דף קכ״ג.

פרשת שופטים

[142]   שופטים ושוטרים תתן לך בכל שעריך וגו׳. פי׳ שתתן שופטים ושוטרים לך

דייקא והיינו לעצמותך בכל ערך בחינתך שאתה תוכל לשער עצמך דלפום שיעורין

דילך תשפוט ותדין את עצמך. וזהו בכל שעריך.

ר׳ מנחם מענדל מקאצק, ס׳ אהל תורה מהרבי מקאצק, דף 62.

[143]   יראה חיצונית הבאה לאדם הוא כדי לעוררו ליראת אלקים מלה״ד לאיש חיל

שלוח מהמלך לקרוא לאדם והוא בכעס גדול ופחד אין לירא מהשליח כ״א תיכף ילך

להמלך לרצונו וכן אהבה חיצונית הבאה הוא כדי לעוררו לאהבת ה׳ מלה״ד

לפעמים בא איש מהמלך שלוח לאדם בתנועת אהבה ומי שהוא טפש הוא מתענג

ומשתעשע עם השליח והחכם אומר מה לי להשתעשע אם השליך אלך לשורש האהבה

של מלך וזהו שכתוב תמים תהי׳ עם ה׳ אלקיך והתי״ו גדולה דלכאורה התי״ו רחוקה

מן האלף לרמוז להעלות כל דבר רחוק הן אהבה הן יראה או שמחה ותענוג נשמי אל

האלוף הרומז לאלופו של עולם...

ר׳ ישראל בן אליעזר, בעל שם טוב, ס׳ כתר שם טוב, דף 52, עמוד ב׳.

[144]   לא תשיג גבול רעך אשר גבלו ראשונים בנחלתך אשר תנחל בארץ אשר ה׳

אלקיך נותן לך. י״ל בזה בדרך רמז כי ידוע האבות הראשונים הם המשיכו השכינה

כביכול ממעל לארץ שהם המשיכו והגדילו אלהותו בעולם ואח״כ באו חייבי דרא

וסילקו השכינה למעלה ע״ד רומה על השמים אלקים (תהלים נז. יב) כמו בתחלה

אברהם זה היה מדתו מדת חסד ואהבת השם ב״ה והיה מפרסם אלהותו וירדה

השכינה כביכול לארץ שהוא האיר עיני כל וגילה שמלא כל הארץ כבודו ואחר כך

ע״י חייבי דרא נסתלק השכינה לרקיע היינו שנעשה צמצום כביכול בגדלותו יתב׳

שלא היה נראה ונגלה לעין כל כבודו יתב׳ ואח״כ בא יצחק וחפר אותן בארות אשר

סתמו פלשתים והאיר אור הקב״ה ואח״כ סתמו פלשתים עד שבא יעקב וזהו רמז בכאן

מוסר השכל כי השכינה נקרא גבול ע״ש שהוא סוף כל המדריגות וריעך היינו הקב״ה

כמ״ש ריעך וריע אביך אל תעזוב וזהו שאמר לא תסיג גבול רעך היינו לא תגרום

במעשיך שתסתלק ח״ו השכינה הנקרא גבול של רעך הוא הקב״ה למעלה ע״ד רומה

על השמים אלקים (תהלים נז. יב) אשר גבלו ראשונים בנחלתך אשר תנחל היינו מה

שהראשונים הופיעו שכינת כבוד אל בארץ ונחלה הוא לשון המשכה כמו נחל וע״כ

נקרא נחל ע״ש שהוא קיים מדור לדור כנחל הנמשך והולך כך הם המשיכו שכינת

כבודו בתחתונים. בארץ אשר ה׳ אלקיך נותן לך היינו ע״ד בכל מקום אשר אזכיר את

שמי וכו׳ ותרגומו בכל אתר דתשרי שכינתי תמן אבא אליך וברכתיך והמש״ב.

ר׳ משה חיים אפרים מסדילקוב. ס׳ דגל מחנה אפרים. דפ׳ רמ״ח-רמ״ט.

פרשת כי תצא

[145] והק׳ מהר״ם ט״ב זצ״ל פי׳ ע״ד שאחז״ל לעולם יעסוק אדם בתורה אפילו שלא

לשמה כו׳ ופי׳ המפורשים דהיינו שיעשה אח״כ איזה מצוה לשמה וע״ז יעלה ב״כ

המצוות שלא לשמה וז״ש כי תצא למלחמה על אויביך דהיינו אפילו עם אויביך שגם

הוא ילך אתך אעפ״כ אל נא תמנע מהלוך כי אח״כ ונתנו ד׳ אלקיך בידיך ואז שבית

שביו תקח ממנו מה שלקח ממך ותוציא יקר מזולל.

יצחק מרדכי פאדוואה. ס׳ אילנא דחיי. חלק א׳ דף 105.

[146] לא תביא אתנן זונה ומחיר כלב בית ה׳ אלהיך. אתנן זונה הוא תאוה ומחיר כלב

הוא כעס. והזהיר הכתוב שלא יביא אותם בית ה׳ אלהיך שלא יתפלל האדם על דבר

תאוה או דבר כעס שיוכל לבצע מעשהו, כי תועבת ה׳ גם שניהם ... שאפילו אם ישנה

אותם שיאמר שרוצה בזה לשם שמים גם אסור להפלל עליהם. כיון שנמצא עוד התאוה

או הכעס בלבו לכן אפילו לש״ש אסור. רק יהיה מזוקק שבעתים מ״ט פעמים...

ר׳ מרדכי ליינר מאיזביצא. ס׳ מי השלוח. כרך ב׳ דף קכ״ב.

[147] תמחה את זכר עמלק וגו׳. איתא בכתבי קודש של מרן ר״י בעש״ט זצוקללה״ה

זי״ע וז״ל. עיקר מחיית עמלק הוא כי מתחלה צריכין למחות שר של מעלה שנקרא נס

רוח... ואחר כך נמחה עמלק מלמטה.

ר׳ ישראל בן אליעזר. הבעל שם טוב. ס׳ הבעש״ט. כרך ב׳ דף רכ״ה.

פרשת כי תבוא

[148] ושמחת בכל הטוב אשר נתן לך ה׳ אלקיך (כו יא). רצה לומר. [לפני] האיש

הפשוט ישמח בכל טוב העולם הזה בעושר וכדומה במה שה׳ נותן לו, וידע כי לא

פועל ידיו הוא לו רק מאת ה׳ היתה זאת. וגם יבחין כי בכל עת ובכל רגע ׳נותן לך

ולא נתן. כי בידו יתברך לסלק שפעו ח״ו תמיד בכל רגע, ובזה ישכיל שלא לסור

מאחרי השם יתברך ח״ו ברוב עשרו ושאר טובות עולם הזה.

ולפני איש השלם קצת. בכל תורה ועבודה אשר יש לו בו טעם הטוב יגל

וישמח רק במה שה׳ ברוך הוא וב״ש נותן לו. וידע נאמנה כי הוא בעצמו רק הוא עפר זולת

חיות הבורא ב״ה המחיה אותו.

ולפני איש השלם יותר. רצה לומר. בכללות הטוב ישמח שהוא בה׳ אלקיו

אשר משפיע בו חיות האלקות.

ר׳ מרדכי מנעשכיז, ס׳ רשפי אש, דפ׳ כ״ז.

[149] היום הזה ה׳ אלהיך מצוך לעשות וגו׳. במדרש תנחומא, זשה״כ (תהלים צה)

בואו נשתחוה ונכרעה נברכה לפני ה׳ עושינו והלא כריעה בכלל השתחוי׳ וכו׳ ומה

תלמוד לומר נשתחוה ונכרעה אלא צפה משה ברוה״ק וראה שביהמ״ק עתיד לחרב

והביכורים עתידין ליפסק עמד והתקין להם לישראל שיהיו מתפללין שלשה פעמים

בכל יום עכלה״מ. נראה הביאור שכיון שראה כי הביכורים עתידין ליפסק התבונן

מזה שאינו עיקר דבר עיקרי לא הי׳ נפסק ע״כ עמד והתקין תפלה שהוא מצוי

בכל עת בלתי הפסק.

ר׳ מנחם מענדל מקאצק. ס׳ אהל תורה מהרבי מקאצק, דפ׳ 63-64.

[150] בענין התוכחה אמר דכולה ברכות. וב׳ הרב בעל עקידה כך דומה לי שהפסוק

כשקורין בהיפך הוא ברכה, לך ואין לאויביך נתונים וכו׳ וזה ויהפך ה׳ לך הקללה

וכו׳ כשקורין בהיפך הוא ברכה. וב׳ הרב כמו שיש באדם רמ״ח אברים כך יש

בתורה, והתוכחה הוא המרה של התורה וכמו באדם תלוי החיות במרה, שאם נחסרה

או ניקבה טריפה ואינו יכול לחיות, כך התוכחה וכו׳. וכמ״ש רש״י פ׳ נצבים שהקללות

מציבין ומקיימין אתכם בעולם.

ר׳ פנחס מקאריץ, ס׳ אמרי פנחס, סימן קל״ד דף מ״ב.

פרשת נצבים

[151] אתם נצבים היום כלכם לפני ה׳ אלהיכם. אימתי יהיה לכם מעמד ומצב בעולם

כשתהיו לפני ה׳ אלהיכם. היינו כשתהיו דביקים בהקב״ה כמו שנאמר בהקב״ה חיים

כולכם היום. יהיה לכם החיות האמיתי.

ר׳ ישראל מריזין, ס׳ עירין קדישין, חלק א׳ דפ׳ 72-71.

[152] הנסתרות לה׳ אלהינו (דברים כ״ט כ״ח) יראה ואהבה. שהם בלב. והנגלות לנו

ולבנינו. הם תורה ומצות הנגלים לנו...

ר׳ חיים וויטל, ס׳ לקוטי תנ״ך וטעמי המצות, דף ר״פ.

[153] לא בשמים היא לאמר מי יעלה לנו השמימה ויקחה לנו וישמיענו אותה ונעשנה

וגו׳ כי קרוב אליך הדבר מאוד בפיך ובלבבך לעשותו... כי לא בשמים היא שכינת

עוזו שהקדוש ברוך הוא השרה שכינתו בתוכינו בפיפיות עמו בית ישראל כמאמר

הזוהר הקדוש מלכות פה שהשכינה שורה בתוך פיו של אדם וכשמטהר עצמו לדבר

בקדושה ובטהרה להסיר המקטריגים והמסכים המבדילין שמונעין את האדם מלדבר

דיבורו באמת לפני הקדוש ברוך הוא שהם מעיקין לשכינה השורה בתוך פיו.

ר׳ ברוך ממזבאז, בס׳ חסד לאברהם, דף 104.

[154] ...דהנה כתיב קחו עמכם דברים ושובו אל ה׳ והיינו כי בטבע האדם לדבר

דבורים בלא לב ובלא מחשב׳ ורצון. אמנם האדם אשר התנדב לבו לשוב אל ה׳

צריך לבלום פיו ושפתיו ולשמור לשונו מלהוציא דיבור מפיו, עד שיתבונן במחשבתו

אם דבר זה יהי׳ לרצון לפני ה׳. וזהו קחו עמכם דברים היינו שתראו שהדבורים

שלכם יהי׳ עמכם ברשותכם לבל ימהר להוציא דבר בלא לב ואז שובו אל ה׳. וזהו

וילך משה וידבר משה עה״כ בגימ׳ רצו״ן היינו שתוליכו הרצון להדיבור לחבר

הרצון והמחשב׳ עם הדבור כנ״ל את הדברים האלה אל כל ישראל. היינו שכל איש

ישראלי יראה לבוא לזה.

ר׳ אלימלך מגראדזיסק, ס׳ אמרי אלימלך, דף 329.

[155] הקהל את העם האנשים והנשים והטף וגו׳. ענין מצות הקהל בשמינית כי שנת

השמיטה מורה שאין שום פעולת אדם רק לה׳ הארץ ומלואה, ושנה השמינית הוא

התחלת פעולת אדם. ועל זה היה המצוה לקרות את התורה הזאת נגד כל ישראל

באזניהם לקבוע בלבם קדושה משנת השמיטה, שגם בעסקם בפעולות אדם יכירו

שהכל מהשי״ת...

ר׳ מרדכי ליינר מאיזביצא. ס׳ מי השלוח. כרך ב׳ דף קכ״ט.

[156] שמעתי עוד תורה ממנו אל הפסוק ואנכי הסתר אסתיר פני בפ׳ וילך אמר

בזה״ל אזוי ווי קינדער שפילען זיך אין באהעלטענישין און דאס קינד וואס באהאלט

זיך שרייט איך האבע מיך בעהאלטען זוך מיך און דאס קינד וואס האט דעת, לויט

דעם קול וואס עס איז ארויס גיגאנגען זוכט עהר נאך ביז עהר געפונט אזוי איז דא אויך

השי״ת שרייט איך האב מיך בעהאלטין זוך מיך לכן דער וואס איז א בר דעת הקול

של השי״ת הנ״ל מתעורר אצלו עד שיחפש וימצא.

ר׳ שמחה בונים מאטוואצק. בס׳ גדולת מרדכי וגדולת צדיקים. חלק ב׳. דף 18.

סימן מ״ט.

פרשת האזינו

[157] או יאמר ע״פ הידוע מהבעש״ט זצ״ל שאם ירצה לשים לב. ישמע שכ״א מדבר

מענין יראת השי״ת והאדם בעצמו לא ידע מה שפיו יאמר וז״ש האזינו השמים ואדברה

שבאם אתה רוצה להאזין דברי יראת שמים מהדיבורים ותשמע הארץ תוכל לשמוע

אם מהאנשים שהם בבחי׳ ארציות...

ר׳ מנחם מענדל מרימנאוו. ס׳ אילנא דחיי. חלק א׳ דף 111.

[158] צור ילדך תשי ותשכח אל מחולליך. פי׳ השי״ת בראך במדת השכחה כדי

שתשכח מהבלי עוה״ז ולבסוף ותשכח אל מחולליך בתמי׳.

ר׳ מנחם מענדל מקאצק. ס׳ אהל תורה מהרבי מקאצק, דף 66.

[159] כי כל תורתנו כולה, שבכתב ושבעל פה. אין דבר אחד אפילו אות אחת יוצא

לדבר אחר זולת לעבוד ה׳ יתברך. כי לזה נתנה. ונקרא תורה על שם שמורה לאמר

זה הדרך לכו בה. ואפילו בדיני ממונות ושאר דינים. הדומים שאין נפקותא ועובדא

מהם. אם רק הוא מכם הוא (ע״פ דברים לב. מז. ראה ילקוט בראשית ג). אבל מי

שעובד ה׳ יתברך בשלמות. מגלין לו רזי תורה. וזהו הרזין. איך ליקח עצה מכל תרי״ג

מצות לעבוד בהם הבורא יתברך. אף על פי שאינם באפשר לקיימם בעצמם. כמו

מצות התלויין בארץ ושאר מצות. וזה שקרא הזהר (יתרו פב. ב) את התרי״ג מצות -

תרי״ג עיטין. רצה לומר. שנותנים לאדם איך להתדבק ביוצרו...

ר' משולם פייבוש הלוי העליר. ס' יושר דברי אמת. סימן כ״ד דף ק״ח.

וזאת הברכה

[160] וזאת הברכה אשר ברך משה וכו' לפני מותו פרש״י סמוך למיתתו שאם לא

עכשיו אימתי. נ״ל שכוונ' רש״י בזה שזה הי' מעין הברכה שבירך מרע״ה שיהי' אצל

כל א' וא' כל רגע ורגע נחשב לעבודת הש״י כי הרגע והשעה לא יהיה עוד וזה אם לא

עכשיו אימתי.

ר' חיים מקאסוב. ס' תורת חיים. דף 39.

[161] שמח זבולן וגו'. הגם שבעניני עולם הזה בכללות אין לשמוח בהם. דכתיב

(קהלת ב ב) ולשמחה מה זה עושה. אמר הנביא שזבולון ישנו בשמחה. הגם ביציאתו

מבית המדרש לסחורה. והטעם כדי שיתקיים יששכר באהלו כאומרו ויששכר באהליך:

עוד ירצה. לפי שאין אדם יודע ביציאתו לסחורה אם יצליח אם לא עד שיחזור מוצלח.

לזה אמר לזבולון שמח מעת יציאתך. כי בודאי שתצליח. והטעם כיון שיששכר

באהליך שליח מצוה אתה לזון לומדי תורה. וכינה אהל יששכר לזבולון, כי הוא

הבונה אהלו: או ירצה באהליך. כינוי ליששכר. ואמר לשון אוהל. לשתי סיבות. אחד

שאין עושין עיקר בעולם אלא ישיבת עראי. ועיקר דירתם הוא בית עולמים ב'. כינוי

למאהיל עליהם. שהיא השכינה שנקראת אהל. הגם שעוסקים בסחורה. עליהם נאמר

(תהלים פה יד) צדק לפניו יהלך וגו׳:

ר׳ חיים ן׳ עטר. ס׳ אור החיים. חלק ה׳ דפ׳ קי״א-קי״ב.

[162] עוד י״ל לחבר סוף התורה בתחלתה ישראל בראשית האיך כל אחד יתחיל

ללמוד התורה והוא ע״ד אם אין יראה אין חכמה. והנה ישראל אותיות ירא של לשון

שלם כמו ירושלים היינו כשיהיה לו יראה שלם דהיינו יראה פנימית אזי הוא נעשה כלי

לבחי׳ חכמה ויכנס בו בחינת בראשית היינו חכמה שהיא כל התורה כולה ומתחיל

התורה מבראשית והמש״י.

ר׳ משה חיים אפרים מסדילקוב. ס׳ דגל מחנה אפרים. ד. ע״ר.

Most Sephardi and Italian teachers are usually cited under their family names. Hasidic teachers are cited under their first names; their surnames are not usually given, unless they are in common use. Numbers listed after entries refer to specific texts, not pages.

Abulafia, Avraham ben Shmuel (1240–after 1291), was a self-proclaimed prophet and founder of the school of prophetic Kabbalah, based on Maimonides's *Guide for the Perplexed* and the mystical *Sefer Yetzirah* (Book of formation). He was born in Saragossa, grew up in Toledo, and spent many years traveling and teaching around the Mediterranean. A prolific writer, he composed five books of commentary on the Torah, of which four are extant.
[6]

Aharon (II) ben Asher of Karlin/Stolin (1802–72) was the fourth leader of the Karliner Hasidim in Lithuania, founded by his grandfather Aharon the Great, and led them for almost fifty years. He was a great proponent of the importance of joyfulness in worship and in life, but incurred the wrath of the *mitnagdim* ("opponents" of Hasidism), who forced his departure to Stolin before 1864. Yet in his day the Karliner Hasidic community grew to its greatest numbers. He is said to have had a confident and imposing appearance.
[22], [25], [33]

Alsheich, Moshe (d. after 1593), was a kabbalist of Safed and Torah commentator, author of *Torat Moshe* ("The Torah of Moshe," but usually known as "Alsheich on the Torah"), based on his sermons. Born in Adrianople, he studied in Salonika with Yosef Karo and was Hayyim Vital's teacher in Jewish law. He served as a communal rabbi and traveled extensively raising funds for the community of Safed.
[135]

Ari. *See* Luria, Yitzchak.

Aryeh Leib, the Zayde (Grandfather) of Shpole (1725–1812), known as a miracle worker and healer, had been a disciple of Pinchas of Koretz. He was renowned (and criticized) for his close connections with the common people.
[30]

Attar, Hayyim ben Moshe (ibn) (1696–1743), was a kabbalist and author of the popular Torah commentary *Or HaHayyim* (The light of life). He was born in Morocco, but decided to move to the Land of Israel. On the way, he stopped in Leghorn (Livorno), Italy, where he soon gained renown in the community for his erudition and saintly qualities. He traveled extensively throughout Italy, encouraging emigration to Israel, and eventually settled in the Holy Land, establishing a yeshivah in Jerusalem.

[60], [88], [113], [137], [161]

Avraham Noach HaLevi Heller of Dolina (d. 1786) was the brother of Meshullam Feibush HaLevi Heller of Zbarazh and, like him, a disciple of the Maggid of Mezritch. He was head of the rabbinic court in Dolina, in western Ukraine.

[120]

Avraham Yehoshua Heschel of Apt/Apta (Opatow) (1755–1825) was a disciple of Elimelech of Lyzhansk and known as the Ohev Yisra'el (Lover of Yisra'el, or Israel) after the title of his collection of sermons. He was a key figure in the spread of Hasidism in Poland and Rumania. One of his descendants was the great American Jewish thinker Abraham Joshua Heschel (1907–72).

[129]

Avraham Yissachar Ber HaCohen of Radomsk (Radomsko) (1843–92) was the second leader of the Hasidic dynasty of Radomsk, a town in south-central Poland, near Lodz. He succeeded his father Shlomo after the latter's death in 1866. He was renowned for his pursuit of peace and modesty as well as for the melodies he composed.

[69], [81], [101]

Azulai, Hayyim Yosef David (1724–1806), was a renowned mystic and kabbalist, bibliographer and writer, and outstanding rabbi of the Ottoman Empire and Italy. He studied with Hayyim ibn Attar, among others. He traveled widely, collecting funds for his yeshivah in Jerusalem and making extensive notes of the Hebrew books and manuscripts he found. He was born in Jerusalem and died in Leghorn, Italy. Also known as the CHIDa, an acronym of his name.

[57]

Ba'al Shem Tov. *See* Yisra'el ben Eliezer, the Ba'al Shem Tov.

Bachya ben Asher ben Chlava (thirteenth century), known as Rabbenu (Our rabbi) Bachya, is author of the Torah commentary that bears his name, in which he offers four levels of interpretation, including the kabbalistic. He was a renowned preacher in his own day, and tradition says that he lived in Saragossa, Spain, though little else is known of his life.

[8], [34], [68], [103], [117]

Baruch ben Yechiel of Medzibodz (Medzibedzh) (1757–1810) was a grandson of the Ba'al Shem Tov and a disciple of Pinchas of Koretz. He is perhaps best known for his sumptuous court, which led to attacks by other Hasidic leaders. His sayings are recorded in a variety of sources.

[153]

Bikayam, Meir ben Chalifa (d. 1769), was a kabbalist, rabbinic scholar, and secret follower of the failed messiah Shabbetai Zevi (1626–76). He lived in Smyrna, where he was respected and supported by the community. He is the author of several books, including two Torah commentaries based on the principles of the Lurianic Kabbalah.

[37]

Cordovero, Moshe (1522–70), was one of the great kabbalists of Safed, author of *Pardes Rimmonim* (Orchard of pomegranates [Song of Songs 4:13]) and other influential kabbalistic works. He was a student of Yosef Karo, author of the Shulchan Aruch, and of Shlomo Alkabetz, the author of the Friday night hymn *Lechah Dodi*, and teacher of Yitzchak Luria, the Ari.

[44]

Dov Ber, the Maggid (Preacher) of Mezritch (Mezhirech) (d. 1772), might be considered the second "founder" of the Hasidic movement. He was a learned scholar of Talmud, keen student of Lurianic Kabbalah, and renowned for his ascetic way of life. He was the teacher and mentor of a whole generation of Hasidic masters, and all his teachings were recorded by others.

[99]

Efraim Shlomo ben Aharon of Luntshits (Leczyca) (1550–1619) was a Polish preacher and commentator, author of *Keli Yakar* (A precious vessel), which is often published in standard collections of Torah commentaries in Hebrew. He makes occasional use of kabbalistic concepts in his works. He headed a yeshivah in Lvov, Poland, before taking up a position as head of the rabbinic court in Prague.

[71]

Elazar ben Yehudah of Worms (ca. 1160–1237) was a leader of the Hasidei Ashkenaz (German pietists), author of *Sefer HaRokeach* (The book of the pharmacist), a law code, and a host of esoteric and mystical works. His Torah commentary, *Perush HaRokeach*, places great emphasis on *gematria* (numerology) and other techniques for manipulating the text. His wife and two of their children were murdered, and he himself injured, in anti-Jewish riots during the Crusades.

[131]

Elimelech ben Hayyim Meir Yechiel of Grodzhisk (Grodzisk Mazowiecki) (1824–92), grandson of two Hasidic masters: Yisra'el, the Maggid of Koznitz; and Elimelech of Lyzhansk. He founded a Hasidic dynasty centered in his town in Poland. His thousands of followers are said to have included many great Torah scholars.

[154]

Elimelech of Lyzhansk (Lezajsk) (1717–87) was a key disciple of the Maggid of Mezritch, and his book *No'am Elimelech* (The pleasantness of Elimelech) is a Hasidic classic. He wandered extensively with his brother Zusya of Hanipol, imitating the exile of the Shechinah, before settling in Lyzhansk in southeast Poland, where he became a popular Hasidic teacher. He was a keen proponent of the theory and practice of the wonder-working abilities of the tzadik.

[39], [96], [128]

Epstein, Kalonymus Kalman Halevy, of Cracow (d. 1823), disciple of Elimelech of Lyzhansk and Ya'akov Yitzchak, the Seer of Lublin; author of the Hasidic Torah commentary *Ma'or VaShemesh* (Lamp and sun).

[134]

Hayyim ben Menachem Mendel of Kosov (Kosów) (1795–1844) was a Hasidic teacher who studied with his father, Menachem Mendel of Kosov, and his father-in-law, Ya'akov Meir of Shepetovka, and visited the Seer of Lublin. He succeeded his father as leader of the Hasidim of Kosov.

[24], [160]

Hayyim of Krasna (eighteenth century) was a disciple of R. Yisra'el ben Eliezer, the Ba'al Shem Tov. He is mentioned very rarely in Hasidic texts, and virtually nothing is known of his life.

[4]

Levi Yitzchak ben Meir of Berditchev (Berdichev) (1740–1810) was a disciple of Dov Ber, the Maggid of Mezritch, and one of the best-loved Hasidic rebbes, author of *Kedushat Levi* (The holiness of Levi). His outspoken Hasidic views led to the loss of two rabbinic positions. He placed great emphasis on joy in all aspects of life, attachment to God, and fervent prayer. He is reputed to have shown great love and concern for the common people.

[13], [72], [139]

Luria, Yitzchak ben Shlomo (the Ari, meaning "Lion") (1534–72), was the greatest kabbalist of Safed. He wrote almost nothing himself, so his ideas and interpretations are transmitted in the works of his disciples, notably Hayyim Vital. His ideas changed the language and imagery of Kabbalah forever, adding a greater emphasis on the historical drama of the conflict between the forces of good and evil. He came to be known as the Ari from the initial letters of the Hebrew words of *HaElohi* Rabbi Yitzchak, "the divine Rabbi Yitzchak." Before coming to Safed, where he lived only a few years, he is said to have spent seven years in seclusion on an island in the Nile in Egypt studying Kabbalah. *See* Vital, Hayyim.

Menachem ben Moshe Bavli (d. 1571) was a kabbalist in the community of Safed. Although called "Babylonian," he may have hailed from Rome. He lived for a time in Greece, and wrote a book called *Peri Chevron/Ta'amei HaMitzvot* (The fruit of Hebron/The meanings of the commandments). He is mentioned twenty-four times in Yishayah Horowitz's *Shnei Luchot HaBrit.*

[59]

Menachem Mendel of Kotzk (Kock) (1787–1859), a disciple of Ya'akov Yitzchak, the "Holy Jew" of Pshische (1765–1814), and Simchah Bunam of Pshische, he was known for his stern, challenging approach. This provoked much criticism, but also drew many followers to him. A troubled soul, he locked himself away from his Hasidim for twenty years, seeing only a select few. He also burned the books he had written and opposed the collecting of his teachings for publication. Fortunately, this was done after his death.

[1], [47], [49], [86], [87], [111], [125], [142], [149], [158]

Menachem Mendel of Rymanov (Rymanow) (d. 1815) was one of the closest disciples of Elimelech of Lyzhansk and a key figure in the next generation of Polish Hasidim. He was known in his own day for his asceticism.

[2], [84], [90], [105], [119], [126], [132], [157]

Menachem Mendel of Vitebsk (1730–88) was a disciple of Dov Ber, the Maggid of Mezritch, and was sent by his teacher to Eliyahu ben Shlomo, the Vilna Ga'on, to seek reconciliation between the Hasidim and their opponents. The mission was unsuccessful. He was a crucial figure in bringing Hasidism to Belarus and Lithuania, but in 1777 he was one of three Hasidic rebbes who led some three hundred people to live in the Land of Israel.

[29]

Menachem Mendel of Vorki (Warka) (d. 1868) was the second son of Yitzchak of Vorki, and was known as the "Silent Tzadik" because he rarely spoke. He believed that one should speak only when one could no longer contain it and that the real work of prayer takes place in silence. Out of humility, he succeeded his father only reluctantly.

[12], [43], [115]

Menachem Nachum of Chernobyl (1730–97) once visited the Ba'al Shem Tov and later became a disciple of the Maggid of Mezritch. He was an itinerant preacher, spreading the Hasidic message and incurring the wrath of the movement's opponents. He was a great believer in the value of moral purification.

[54]

Meshullam Feibush HaLevi Heller of Zbarazh (d. 1785) was a disciple of Yechiel Michal of Zlotchov, having also served the Maggid of Mezritch. He placed great emphasis on attachment to God, and the infallibility of the tzadik. His brother was Avraham Noach of Dolina.

[159]

Mordechai of Neschiz (Neskhiz, Nesukhoyshe) (d. 1800) was the founder of his dynasty, having been a disciple of Yechiel Michal, the Maggid of Zlotchov. He was famous in his own day as a miracle worker. He also served as a communal rabbi in several towns.

[42], [56], [148]

Mordechai of Chernobyl (d. 1837) succeeded his father Menachem Nachum as *maggid* (preacher) of Chernobyl and is considered the real founder of the Twersky dynasty of rebbes. Unlike his father, who was poor throughout his life, Mordechai of Chernobyl had a sumptuous court, sustained by his large following.

[9], [51], [62], [67], [98]

Mordechai Yosef Leiner of Izbica (1800–54) was originally a disciple of Simchah Bunam of Pshische, but switched his allegiance to Menachem Mendel of Kotzk when Simchah Bunam died. Gradually he came to oppose Menachem Mendel's teachings and leadership style, and broke away amid a great deal of strife. An original and controversial thinker, his book was burned upon publication for its "heretical" views, often contradicting talmudic and other traditional Jewish teachings.

[18], [58], [63], [77], [94], [106], [146], [155]

Moshe Hayyim Efraim of Sudylkov (Sudylkow) (d. 1800) was the grandson of the Ba'al Shem Tov and famous as the author of the Hasidic classic *Degel Machaneh Efraim* (Flag of the camp of Ephraim). He served as a preacher in Sudylkov, but remained in poverty throughout his life. His book played an important role in popularizing Hasidism.

[15], [16], [35], [95], [102], [144], [162]

Moshe ben Yisra'el Polier of Kobrin (1784–1858) was the founder of the Kobrin Hasidic dynasty. He was known for his short, pithy sayings and his concern for his followers. In his teachings, he stressed humility, truth, and patience in suffering.

[40], [50]

Moshe Leib of Sasov (d. 1807) was a disciple of the Maggid of Mezritch and Elimelech of Lyzhansk, among others. He was renowned for his love for all Jews and his charitable giving as well as for the melodies he composed.

[110]

Moshe Teitelbaum of Ujhely (1759–1841) was a disciple of the Seer of Lublin and a key figure in bringing Hasidism to large regions of Hungary. He was known as a scholar and a wonder-worker. Members of his family still lead the Satmar Hasidic community.

[145]

Naftali Hertz ben Ya'akov Elchanan Bacharach (first half of seventeenth century) was born in Frankfurt, but the dates of his birth and death are unknown. He also spent some years in Poland. His book, *Emek HaMelech* (The valley of the sovereign), presents the Lurianic Kabbalah, but in ways that emphasize its magical, demonic, and messianic aspects. It had a strong influence on later Kabbalah, including some Hasidic schools and Eliyahu ben Shlomo, the Vilna Ga'on.

[20]

Naftali Zevi Horowitz of Ropshitz (Ropczyce) (1760–1827) was a student of Elimelech of Lyzhansk, Yisra'el the Maggid of Koznitz, and Menachem Mendel of Rymanov. He ultimately became one of the main Hasidic leaders in Galicia, Poland, after the death of Ya'akov Yitzchak, the Seer of Lublin. Details of his life are found only in legends.

[100]

Natan of Breslov/Nemirov (1780–1844) was Nachman of Bratzlav's primary disciple and amanuensis as well as an outstanding Hasidic teacher in his own right. He maintained the unity among R. Nachman's followers after the death of the latter, without appointing a successor. This ultimately earned the group the nickname of *die tote hasidim*, "the dead Hasidim," because their rebbe was dead.

[48]

Pinchas of Koretz (Korzec) (1726–91) was an independent Hasidic teacher. Although he met the Ba'al Shem Tov several times, he is not to be considered his disciple. He came into conflict with the Maggid of Mezritch, offering a more enthusiastic, and less intellectual, type of Hasidism.

[11], [61], [123], [124], [138], [150]

Recanati, Menachem ben Binyamin (late thirteenth to early fourteenth centuries), was an Italian kabbalist, author of three kabbalistic books, one of which is referred to here: his *Perush al HaTorah* (Commentary on the Torah). These works brought the teachings of the Spanish Kabbalah to the Italian Jewish community. Little is known of his life, although there is a family tradition that his knowledge and wisdom came to him in a miraculous fashion.

[52]

Reuven Hoeschke (d. 1673) was a rabbi and kabbalist who lived in Prague. He was the grandson of Efraim of Luntshits, but there are few biographical details.

[26]

Shalom Rokeach of Belz (d. 1855) was a disciple of Yisra'el ben Shabbetai Hapstein, the Maggid of Koznitz, and Ya'akov Yitzchak HaLevi, "the Seer" of Lublin, and was also known as Sar Shalom ("Prince of Peace," Isaiah 9:6). As a descendant of Elazar of Worms, the Belzer rebbe also came to be called "Rokeach" (the pharmacist) after his ancestor's most famous work. He founded the Belz Hasidic dynasty, one of the most important in Galicia. He was known as a miracle worker, but also as an outstanding talmudist.

[23], [41]

Simchah Bunam of Otvotzk (Otwock) (d. 1907) was the son of Menachem Mendel of Vorki. Otvotzk is a town near Warsaw. Simchah Bunam emigrated to Israel in 1887, but was imprisoned by the Turkish authorities. He eventually returned home, but came back to the Holy Land in 1906 and died in Tiberias.

[156]

Simchah Bunam of Pshische (Przysucha) (1765–1827) was a disciple of Ya'akov Yitzchak, the "Holy Jew" of Pshische, and succeeded him upon his death. Simchah Bunam is an extraordinary figure in the Hasidic movement: he was trained and worked as a pharmacist; wore modern Western European clothing; spoke German, French, and Latin; and was friendly with "enlightened" (nonreligious, Westernized) Jews.

[7], [17], [27], [28], [31], [36], [46], [53], [70], [104], [108], [114]

Sitrei Torah is one of the twenty-two (mostly) independent literary units that make up the Zohar, the most important text of Kabbalah. In the main, *Sitrei Torah* is concerned with issues of the soul, commenting primarily on verses in the book of Genesis.

[5]

Tikkunei HaZohar (Repairs to the Zohar) is an anonymous work that appeared in Spain perhaps a decade or two after the publication of the Zohar in the late thirteenth century. It offers more than seventy commentaries on the opening verse of Genesis.

[64]

Uri of Strelisk (d. 1826), a Hasidic rabbi, was known as the Seraph because of his "fiery," enthusiastic prayer style. He had been a disciple of Shlomo of Karlin, the second rebbe of that dynasty.

[21], [85], [118]

Vital, Hayyim ben Yosef (1542–1620), was the primary disciple of Yitzchak Luria (the Ari), having previously studied with Alsheich and Cordovero. He was a prolific writer, not only producing extensive versions of the Ari's teachings, but also a number of independent works, including a mystical diary. He proved to be one of the most influential kabbalists in history.

[136], [152]

Ya'akov Yitzchak HaLevi Horowitz, the Seer of Lublin (1745–1815), was a descendant of Yishayah Horowitz. He was a disciple of Elimelech of Lyzhansk, but caused a rift with his teacher when he set up his own "court" without the latter's permission. He was a key figure in the spread of Hasidism in Poland and Galicia and taught many of the next generation of Hasidic masters. Known as a wonder-worker, mystic, and prophet, he was given the epithet of "Seer" after his death.

[73], [76], [141]

Ya'akov Yosef of Polonnoye (d. ca. 1782) was the chief disciple of the Ba'al Shem Tov and author the first Hasidic books, notably *Toledot Ya'akov Yosef* (The generations of Jacob Joseph), *Ben Porat Yosef* (Joseph is a fruitful bough), and *Tzafnat Paneach* (the biblical Joseph's Egyptian name, cf. Genesis 41:45). His books reveal him to have been a penetrating scholar and keen critic of the social order. His propagation of Hasidism led him into communal difficulties, particularly in the first community he served, where he was expelled from his post.

[66], [116], [121], [122], [130]

Ya'akov Zevi Yolles (Jolles, ca. 1778–1825) was a disciple of Ya'akov Yitzchak, the Seer of Lublin, and author of the kabbalistic encyclopedia titled *Kehillat Ya'akov* (The congregation of Jacob). There is a small book of sayings attributed to him. He was also a keen talmudic scholar.

[80], [112]

Yechiel Michal of Zlotchov (Zloczow) (ca. 1731–86) was one of the few disciples of the Ba'al Shem Tov to switch his allegiance to the Maggid of Mezritch after his teacher's death. There are many miracle stories about him, but his popular teaching incurred the anger of the opponents of the Hasidim.

[134]

Yehudah ben Shmuel HeHasid of Regensburg (d. 1217) was the first leader of the Hasidei Ashkenaz movement and the reputed author of *Sefer Hasidim* (The book of the pious). He came from a long line of scholars and mystics stretching back to the ninth century. Little is known of his life apart from legends that describe his great humility and the miracles he performed on behalf of others. The *Sefer Hasidim* is one of the most important works of medieval Jewish ethics and folklore.

[89]

Yishayah HaLevi Horowitz (ca. 1570–1626), rabbi, kabbalist, and preacher, is the author of *Shnei Luchot HaBrit* (The two tablets of the covenant), one of the most popular and comprehensive books of its day, and the kabbalistic prayer-book commentary *Sha'ar HaShamayim* (The gate of heaven). He served as communal rabbi in Frankfurt, Prague, and for the Ashkenazim in

Jerusalem. He was independently wealthy and refused payment for his rabbinic work.

[19], [59], [92], [107], [133]

Yisra'el ben Eliezer, the Ba'al Shem Tov (Good master of the Name [of God]) (1700–1760), founder of the Hasidic movement. His recorded sayings and the events of his life come down to us through his disciples and folk stories; he offered a new approach to mysticism, making aspects of it accessible to nonscholars. Legend says that he traveled the region extensively, but modern research has revealed that he had a salaried position in the community of Medzhibodzh in Ukraine.

[3], [78], [140], [143], [147]

Yisra'el ben Shabbetai Hapstein, the Maggid of Koznitz (Kozienice) (1733–1814), was a halachic scholar, a popular preacher, and one of the first Hasidic rebbes in Poland. His sermons and his style of prayer were said to have had a great impact on his followers. His teachers included Dov Ber, the Maggid of Mezritch; Levi Yitzchak of Berditchev; and Elimelech of Lyzhansk.

[127]

Yisra'el Friedman of Ruzhyn (Ruzhin) (1797–1850) was the great-grandson of Dov Ber, the Maggid of Mezritch. He was a great organizer and "held court" in opulent surroundings. In 1838, he was accused of ordering the execution of two Jewish informers and spent time in a Czarist jail. To avoid surveillance, he fled to the Austrian Empire, settling eventually in the town of Sadgora, where he reestablished his court. He is said to have been able to go to the heart of any issue with his penetrating intellect.

[45], [74], [79], [151]

Yisra'el ben Shmuel of Modzhitz (1849–1921) was a Hasidic master and founder of the Modzhitz dynasty. He is famous for the melodies he composed and his emphasis on music as a spiritual technique. His most renowned melody (titled "*Ezkerah*," "I will remember") was orally composed by him as he lay on a surgeon's operating table.

[65], [75], [93]

Yitzchak of Vorki (Warka) (1779–1848) was a disciple of Simchah Bunam of Pshische and a friend of Menachem Mendel of Kotzk and Mordechai of Izbica. He was well known for his love and support of the Jewish people against persecution, notably against the Czarist policy of forcibly conscripting Jewish young men into the Russian Army. This attitude earned him the nickname "Ohev Yisra'el" (Lover of Israel).

[10], [43]

Yitzchak Meir of Gur/Ger (Gora Kalwaria) (1789–1866) was a student of the Maggid of Koznitz and a disciple of Simchah Bunam of Pshische and Menachem Mendel of Kotzk. He established the Gerer dynasty and was acknowledged as leader by the majority of the Kotzker's followers after the latter's death. He was active in campaigning against the imposition of Western styles of dress on the Jews of the Russian Empire.

Yosef ben Yechiel Michal of Yampole (Yampol) (d. 1812), one of the five sons of the Maggid of Zlotchov. There seems to be little information available about his life.

[38]

Ze'ev Wolf of Zhitomir (d. 1800) was a disciple of Dov Ber, the Maggid of Mezritch. There is no more information available on his life.

[55], [91], [109]

Zevi Elimelech of Dinov (Dynow) (1785–1841) was a disciple of, among others, Ya'akov Yitzchak, the Seer of Lublin, and Yisra'el, the Maggid of Koznitz. He served as communal rabbi in four towns and opposed rationalism. He is most famous for his book *Benei Yissachar* (The children of Issachar), a compendium of Hasidic and kabbalistic essays on the fasts and festivals of the year.

[14]

Zevi Hirsh ben Shmuel Zanvil Minkovitz of Semyatitch (Semiatycze) (d. 1819) was a student of Eliyahu ben Shlomo, the Vilna Ga'on. No other biographical details are extant.

[83]

Zohar (Book of splendor) is the classic text of the Kabbalah. It was published in Spain in the late thirteenth century, but is traditionally ascribed to the second-century teacher R. Shimon bar Yochai and his school. It is made up of twenty-two largely independent units, and recent scholarship suggests that it may have been the work of a group of kabbalists building on, and reshaping, earlier material. For some three hundred years it stood, and still stands in some quarters, on a par with the Bible and the Talmud in sanctity.

[5], [26], [32], [97]